HOW DO
THEY DO ALL THAT?

HOW DO
THEY DO ALL THAT?

Wonders of the
Modern World Explained

Caroline Sutton
and
Kevin Markey

with

Duncan M. Anderson

Illustrated By Lilly Langotsky

BARNES
&NOBLE
BOOKS
NEW YORK

2003 Barnes & Noble Books

Designed by Michael Mauceri

The vending machine illustration is based on an illustration from *The Way Things Work* by C. Van Amerongen. Copyright © 1967 by George Allen & Unwin Ltd. Printed by permission of Simon & Schuster, a Division of Gulf and Western Corp., and by permission of George Allen & Unwin (Publishers) Ltd.

The magnetc-anomaly pattern is reprinted with permission from *Deep-Sea Research*, vol. 13 J.R. Hertzler, X. Le Pichon, and J.G. Baron, 1966, Pergamon press, Ltd.
The magnetec-anomaly pattern (after Heirtzler, Le Pichon, and Baron, *Deep-Sea Research*) is from *Principals of Physical Geology* by Arthur N. Strahler, Copyright © 1977 by Arthur N. Strahler. Reprinted by permission of Harper & Row, Publishers, Inc.

The Labanotation symbols are reprinted by permission of the Dance Notation Bureau, Inc. All rights reserved.

The Choreology notes and drawings are from *Readings Dance: The Birth of Choreology* by Rudolf and Joan Benesh. Copyright © 1977 by Rodolf and Joan Benesh. Reprinted by permission of Souvenir Press (Educational & Academic) Ltd.

The stages-in-cutting-a-diamond illustrations is from an illustration by Herbert Tillander, Helsinki, Finland. Reproduced from *Diamonds: Myth, Magic, and Reality* edited by Jacques LeGrand. Original text and illustrations copyright ©1980 by Smeets Offset, Weert, the Netherlands. English translation copyright © 1980 in all countries of the International Copyright Union by Crown Publishers, Inc.

ISBN 0-7607-4308-8

03040506FF987654321

Contents

HOW DO
THEY DO THAT?

Wonders
of the
Modern World Explained

Caroline Sutton
with
Duncan M. Anderson

Illustrated by Lilly Langotsky
A Hilltown Book

First Quill edition published 1982

Reprinted in Perennial 2002.

Designed by Michael Mauceri

Library of Congress Cataloging-in-Publication Data

Sutton, Caroline.
  How do they do that?

  Originally published: New York: Morrow, 1981

  Includes index.
  1. Technology—Popular works. 2. Science—Popular works. I. Anderson, Duncan M.
II. Title.
T47.S84   1982   031'.02   82-478
ISBN 0-688-00486-5   AACR2
ISBN 0-688-01111-X (pbk.)

02 03 04 05 06 QW 60 59 58 57 56 55 54

Acknowledgments

I would like to thank Duncan Anderson, who contributed numerous articles to the book, particularly in the areas of astronomy, biology, and technology. His thorough research and lucid presentation of complex material make accessible a wealth of information, for which I am most grateful. He, in turn, would like to thank Dr. Robert Jastrow, Director and Founder, NASA's Goddard Institute for Space Studies, and Dr. Thomas von Foerster of *Physics Today* for their help.

I wish to acknowledge and thank Bruce McCall, Anna Monardo, and Eugene Stone for contributing articles, and Meredith Davis, my editor at Morrow, for her careful editing and enthusiasm. I am grateful to Barbara Wood for her superb copy editing and editorial skills.

Because the very essence of this book lies in revealing how *they* do that, the writing process required the cooperation and help of a great many people and organizations. Their knowledge, expertise, and interest in the project have been invaluable. While I am grateful to all, I would especially like to mention Dana Cranmer of the Guggenheim Museum; Leo B. Gittings, National Geodetic Survey, U.S. Department of Commerce; Alvin F. Goldfarb, M.D.; John A. Gorman, Bureau of Economic Analysis, U.S. Department of Commerce; Arnold Hansen-Sturm, President, Romanoff Caviar Company; Richard D. Heffner, Chairman of the Board, Classification and Rating Administration of the Motion Picture Association of America; Paul K. Kaplan, Lazare Kaplan & Sons, Inc.; Roger L. Larson, Ph.D., Graduate School of

Oceanography, University of Rhode Island; Charles H. Thornton, Ph.D., P.E., President, Lev Zetlin Associates, Inc., and Thornton-Tomasetti, P.C.; Sheila Traut, National Genetics Foundation, Inc.; and Helene Wilson, NASA's Goddard Institute for Space Studies.

With imagination and good humor, many friends have contributed their time and knowledge to help me in writing this book. I extend my warmest appreciation to Henry Pemberton, Steven Welch, Lucy Kinsolving, and Hugh McKellar; to James and Eloise Sutton; and to Brian Dumaine, for his patience, insight, and editorial advice.

Contents

?

How do they sort mail so that a letter you drop into a box in New York arrives at an apartment in Los Angeles a few days later?

When you hastily drop a letter into a mailbox, you might pause to check the collection times posted on the box, but beyond that you may never contemplate the massive operation of sorting and distributing mail which goes on around the clock—and largely behind the scenes.

The mail is picked up and taken either to a local branch office, or straight to a processing center, of which there are four in New York City. Different fates await the various classes of mail—registered, special delivery, and so on—but a first-class letter of standard size travels the following route.

The mail is dumped helter-skelter onto a wide conveyor belt. En route to the first machine, an automatic culler removes oversized letters and packages that can't go through the Mark II facer canceler. This machine (which is about waist high and is overseen by one or several workers) does just what the name implies: it faces the letters in one direction to facilitate later handling, and it cancels the stamp. The letters go in upside down, backward and forward. The machine sends those with stamps in the upper corners (or somewhere in the upper portion) through a canceler and into the first trays; those with stamps on the bottom corners are flipped by two overlapping rubber coils that rotate continuously. After being flipped, these letters shoot through a

17

canceler and into other trays. The canceler, which thus finds the stamp wherever it is, contains an ultraviolet light that picks up a phosphorescent dye in the stamps, so letters with fake stamps or none at all will be caught and separated for return. The letters whiz through at a rate of 20,000 per hour.

If an oversized or bent letter gets into the machine by mistake and jams it, the operator must retrieve it immediately or he'll have a dozen rumpled letters backed up in an instant like a chain-reaction highway accident. Should this occur, wrinkled letters and torn envelopes are handled manually during the remainder of the sorting process.

If all is running smoothly, neat stacks of canceled letters are collected by hand and taken to a huge letter-sorting machine, usually referred to as an LSM. At the Morgan processing center in Manhattan, the largest such installation in the world, there are seventeen LSMs, each consisting of twelve consoles attached to a large wall with 277 different bins. Two loaders place the letters upright in containers beside each console operator. A suction arm picks up one letter at a time and whisks it in front of the operator, who punches its zip code on two rows of keys on the console. The arm puts *a letter per second* in front of the operator, who must in that time find the zip (which is often scrawled and nearly illegible), press the right keys, and get ready for the next letter. If the mail is local, the operator looks only at the last two digits of the code, which represent the local branch; but if it's headed for California, he may have to punch the first three or all five, depending on the breakdown of areas. The first three digits indicate the zone, of which there are nine in the United States, and an area sectional center. (Omission of the zip code automatically causes a delay in service, as these letters are routed to manual handlers.) The numerals that are punched direct each letter into a slot on a large conveyor belt, which takes it to the appropriate bin, along with other letters designated for the same area. Five workers stand by the wall of bins and empty each bin when it's full into a cardboard tray, covered with a sleeve, to be sent to the proper destination.

First-class mail travels by air, so if your letter is not going to a local address or nearby state to which surface delivery is most expedient, it will be taken by truck to an airport. John F. Kennedy, LaGuardia, and Newark airports are all equipped with postal facilities where mail is loaded onto the planes of whatever commercial airlines are available. It's possible that your letter could arrive at the airport only twelve hours after you mailed it, for the processing centers work continuously, handling 17 million pieces per day in New York City alone, with the greatest volume of mail at night. (The earlier you mail your letter the better, for the volume increases as the day goes on.) Most local mail can be delivered the following day; letters to nearby states (such as Pennsylvania, New Jersey, Connecticut, and Massachusetts) may take two days; service from New York to California generally takes three days.

In Los Angeles, a postal facility at the airport sends the boxes of mail to the appropriate area processing center. There the letters again run through an LSM to be sorted for a specific local branch. Local post offices receive mail at night, sort it manually by street and block, and place it in the case of the carrier for that area. A letter carrier arrives early in the morning, picks up his batch of mail, sorts it by building, and makes his rounds. Once the nine-numbered zip system introduced by the Postal Service in February 1981 is fully operative, sorters aided by new technology will be able to sort the mail by precise block and house. The centerpiece of this new technology is the advanced optical character reader (AOCR), which is being used now to a limited degree. This extremely efficient, fully automatic machine faces, cancels stamps, and sorts—all at a rate of 40,000 pieces per hour. The only drawback is that the AOCRs can only handle envelopes of standard business size with typed or printed addresses and zips. Although useful for large mailings by corporations, they can't cope with the glut of multisized envelopes at Christmas and Valentine's Day. By 1986, however, when the new system will be fully deployed, half of the LSMs will have been replaced by optical character readers, which scan the zip code and pass the letter on to another machine that prints the code in bar form on the envelope. This bar code—used on most grocery products—will facilitate handling by machine all the way down the line.

?

How do homing pigeons find their way home?

Scientists have long been baffled by the uncanny ability of these small one-pound birds to make precise point-to-point flights over great distances and to hold their course whether the skies be overcast or clear. The answer to how pigeons home would undoubtedly provide a clue to the related mystery of how birds migrate—how, for example, some small songbirds fly 2,000 miles nonstop without going astray.

Ornithologists today are becoming increasingly convinced that pigeons use multiple clues, some of which overlap, to navigate. Pigeons, like many migratory birds, apparently read the positions of the sun and stars in order to orient themselves. Furthermore, it is possible that pigeons have tiny magnetic substances in their brain which enable them to detect variations in the earth's magnetic field and determine their course accordingly.

This general orientation does not, however, account entirely for the pigeon's point-to-point navigation, which would seem to require another faculty. The pigeons do not locate their home by keen eyesight, as evidenced by experiments in which the birds wear frosted contact lenses and still come home. Researchers in Italy believe olfactory cues play an important part, that the pigeons smell their way home. Biologist Mel Kreither at Cornell University, where extensive research on homing pigeons is being carried out, has several intriguing new theories. Pigeons can see and sense polarized light, says Kreither, and their ability to detect its direction, and changes in its direction, may help the birds to orient themselves. They are also sensitive to ultraviolet light, which perhaps provides a cue. Pigeons can sense an altitude change of as little as 10 feet, because they can detect extremely small changes in barometric pressure, a drop of .07 millimeters of mercury, for example. This sensitivity helps to hold them on a steady course and also to detect advancing, though perhaps distant, weather fronts. Still another clue to the pigeons' navigational skill stems from their ability to hear very low sounds—down to .05 hertz. These infrasounds, which are inaudible to us without assistance, are generated by a variety of sources, including mountain ranges, ocean waves, and thunderstorms. The long waves, which sometimes travel hundreds of miles unbroken, may provide a pattern by which the pigeon miraculously finds its way home.

?

How do they determine a baby's sex before birth?

Cells present in the amniotic fluid within the fetal sac are largely of fetal origin—and they contain the secret of a baby's sex. In the procedure called amniocentesis, a sample of this fluid is examined and the baby's sex revealed. Because of a minimal but nevertheless real risk to the health of the fetus and the mother, however, and because of controversial moral questions about abortion for sex choice, few doctors will perform amniocentesis for the purpose of sex identification alone. There are numerous instances, though, when taking a sample of amniotic fluid for sex determination is justifiable. These include cases of mothers who are carriers of an X-chromosome-linked disorder such as hemophilia, or Duchenne's dystrophy, which can be transmitted only to a male child.

Amniocentesis for genetic purposes—including sex determination—is usually conducted during the sixteenth to eighteenth weeks of pregnancy, calculated from the first day of the mother's last menstrual period. At this time there is enough fetal development to obtain accurate results by chromosome analysis, yet the pregnancy could still legally and safely be terminated should that be desired. First sonography is performed: sound waves are sent through the woman's abdominal wall, reflected back by the intrauterine structures, and translated into shapes on a screen. Those shapes reveal the position of the placenta and of the baby's head and body, thus providing information about the baby's health. Next a 4-inch needle is inserted through the mother's skin and uterine wall, into the amniotic cavity. (At some centers a local anesthetic is administered.) Every effort is made to insert the needle into the best pocket of fluid, as far away from fetal structures as possible; sonography is sometimes used to guide the physician here as well. A sample of fluid is then withdrawn for analysis. Sonography and the fluid collection procedure take about an hour.

Fetal cells obtained by amniocentesis (which derive mostly from the skin but may come from the respiratory or gastrointestinal tract, umbilical cord, and so on) are separated from the surrounding fluid. In order to obtain a substantial number on which to base an analysis, laboratories culture the fetal cells in a medium containing vitamins, minerals, and antibiotics. There, the cells multiply by dividing in half for a period of about three weeks, at which point a chemical is added to the culture to stop the process at a time in cell division when the chromosomes are visible. Then a sample of the cells is stained and examined under powerful magnification; twenty to twenty-five cells are analyzed in detail, and several are photographed. The structure of the chromosomes, made visible by the stain, indicates their type, which in turn reveals the baby's sex.

Chromosomes are elongated structures in the cell nucleus, which contain DNA, the genes that determine hereditary factors. The number of chromosomes is constant for each species; humans have forty-six, for example, but fruit flies have only eight. Chromosomes appear in each cell in pairs, one member of the pair deriving from the egg, or ovum, the other from the sperm. Among our chromosomes are two that determine sex. Females have a pair of equivalent chromosomes—XX—and males have a pair unequal in size—XY, the Y being smaller. Before fertilization, egg and sperm cells both undergo nuclear division, which reduces the number of chromosomes in each cell by half, thus opening the way for linkage with each other. After this "reduction division," each egg cell contains one X chromosome, and each sperm carries either an X or a Y chromosome. If the egg is fertilized by a sperm carrying an X chromosome, the offspring will be female (XX); if a sperm bearing a Y chromosome fertilizes the egg, it will develop into a male (XY).

Chromosome analysis through amniocentesis is therefore a

reliable—99 percent accurate—means of discovering a baby's sex before birth, two identical chromosomes indicating the presence of a female fetus, two different chromosomes indicating that a male is on the way.

?

How do magicians saw a woman in half?

Even when you know it can't *really* be taking place, it's hard not to gasp when the magician begins to saw through the box and edges toward the trapped woman's abdomen. One of the most sensational and popular of illusions, it was first performed in 1921 by P. T. Selbit, an English magician and inventor, and then by the outstanding illusionist Horace Goldin.

The stunt is designed so that a woman appears to be lying full length in a box that rests on a table. Her hands, feet, and head protrude through holes in the ends of the box, and in some versions of the trick, her wrists and ankles are tied with ropes, which come through the sides. The magician (perhaps with a helper) then proceeds to saw the box in half, using either a two-man crosscut saw or a rotary power saw. The two halves are then separated, but you can't see inside because metal sheets have slid down over the cut ends of the box. Finally, the two halves are pushed together again, the sheets of metal removed, and miraculously the woman is whole and very much alive.

If it weren't for skeptical audiences, magicians might consider using fake limbs or a fake head, but members of the audience are frequently invited to come up on stage and hold the woman's hands and feet. The fact is, the illusion involves *two* women. When the props are brought onto the stage, one woman is already hidden in the table. The tabletop appears to be thin, but the underside angles downward sufficiently to make space for one person. As the woman on stage climbs into the box, the one who is hidden climbs up into the box through a trap in the table and pokes her feet out the end. She curls up, with her head bent

23

forward between her knees; the other woman draws her knees up to her chin. Only an empty space then lies in the pathway of the descending saw.

?

How do they measure the speed at which a hurricane is traveling?

Hurricanes are a breed of tropical cyclone. These savage storms are called typhoons in the Pacific, where they occur most frequently; hurricanes in the Atlantic; and cyclones in the Indian Ocean and Australia. They arise near (but not on) the equator, at points at which the surface temperature of the water has been warmed to at least 78 degrees Fahrenheit. As the earth spins, the sloping of the earth to the north and south of the equator may grip and organize potential cloud clusters into an eddy. Suction from winds in the upper air creates an updraft in the center of a wall of clouds, some 35,000 to 40,000 feet high. Moist air spirals in toward this vortex, rises within the wall, and escapes over the top. The storm is driven primarily by heat released by condensing water vapor, a major source being the warm sea surface. The initial speed of the whole storm is about 15 miles per hour, but it may increase to 60 or more miles per hour as the hurricane moves farther from the equator. Most hurricanes rage for five to ten days, covering about 50 to 125 miles with gusting winds that may fluctuate rapidly from 20 or 30 to 100 miles per hour within minutes. The strongest winds surround the eye of the storm, spiraling inward in a clockwise direction in the Southern Hemisphere, counterclockwise in the Northern Hemisphere.

Although winds of hurricane force (65 miles per hour) can be found at nearly any time somewhere in the world, it is the whirling shape of the storm with its distinctive central eye that constitutes a hurricane or cyclone. It is by tracking the eye that forecasters can determine the speed at which the hurricane is moving. Satellites take pictures of the storm every half hour and

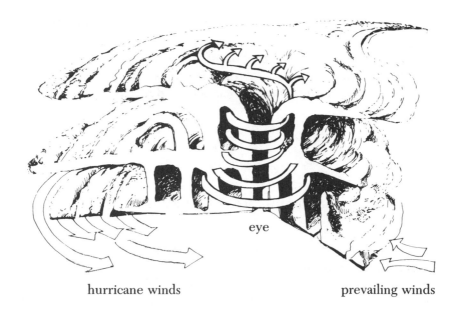

eye

hurricane winds   prevailing winds

plot the clearly identifiable eye on a map over a period of hours or days. (Viewed from the height of a satellite, the hurricane resembles a majestic spiral galaxy.)

If the storm is near a coastline, radar is used to trace the center of the storm, take pictures, and plot the positions on a map. The National Weather Service has a buffer line of overlapping weather radar installations from Texas to New England which can continuously track a hurricane's movement.

During World War II, when a U.S. Navy fleet was battered by a hurricane, the government decided to use reconnaissance aircraft as an early warning system. Today the U.S. Air Force and the National Oceanic and Atmospheric Administration use planes equipped with radar to estimate the position of a storm. For more detailed information, they actually send planes right into the eye of a hurricane to chart its path and measure winds and pressure fields—a task for daredevils, it would seem, but the National Hurricane Center in Miami says this is no more hazardous than driving on the expressway at rush hour.

None of these methods is totally accurate, however. The eye of a storm might be 10 or more miles across, making it difficult to plot

25

precisely. Other errors may arise from navigational difficulties in the plane, for the measurements are accurate only to the extent the pilot knows where he is. Sophisticated navigational systems, including Doppler radar, are used to guide the plane, but the farther from shore the aircraft flies, the harder it is to track it.

?

How do they predict the path of a hurricane?

In order to safeguard against unforeseen destruction by hurricane winds and floods, the National Weather Service, after detecting a storm, tries to predict its course. Forecasting, in actual practice, is very technical, but it rests on several methods that may be described broadly.

According to a theory of persistence, forecasters assume a storm will persist along its present course. This information can supplement findings based on climatology, a study in which the current storm is compared with historical ones that resemble it. There are "families" of storm tracks, and the current storm may behave like one a hundred years earlier that traveled along approximately the same latitude at a similar speed. Another factor to consider is surrounding weather, or large-scale wind patterns, such as the Bermuda high in the Atlantic. Prediction along these lines is called a steering forecast. A numerical weather prediction can be made by modeling the winds around a storm in a computer, which can predict where the vortex of the hurricane will shift. The drawback to this method is that a substantial amount of meteorological data, which may be very difficult to obtain is required—particularly if the storm is mid-oceanic. Finally, a statistical forecast may be drawn up by collating information from the other four methods and actually formulating an equation that can indicate the future behavior of the storm.

?

How do they get a whole pear into a bottle of pear brandy?

If you're driving through France and gazing serenely at the lush valleys and vineyards, you may suddenly feel you've lost your senses. You squint, wonder what was in the wine you've been drinking, and look again; bottles appear to be growing on trees.

Although on TV they might squeeze a whole tomato undamaged into a thin bottle of Heinz tomato ketchup, in the real world there's no way to get a ripe, fragile pear (or a tomato for that matter) into a bottle in one piece. So, the French pear growers tie the bottle onto a tree branch over a blossom or a tiny, developing fruit, which proceeds to grow and ripen inside the bottle. Bottle and pear are shipped to Alsace, where distillation and bottling of the finished brandy take place.

Connoisseurs of brandy and spirits find an *eau-de-vie* containing a whole pear a conversation piece more than anything else—the pear doesn't guarantee high quality.

?

How does a steel ship float?

Archimedes' principle states that a body immersed or partially immersed in water loses an amount of weight that is equal to the weight of the fluid it displaces. Whether or not an object can float depends on the density (weight ÷ volume) of both the object and the water. If the density of the object is less than that of water, the object will sink into the water only to the point where the weight of displaced water equals the weight of the object. A one-foot wooden cube, for example, might weigh 50 pounds. In water, the submerged part of the cube will displace a volume of water weighing 50 pounds. Because the cube is less dense than water, it needs an equal weight *but* a smaller volume of water to support it. The force of the displaced water pressing in on all sides is called buoyancy.

If this principle holds, how can a steel ship possibly float, when steel has a density approximately 8 times that of water? In fact, the hull of the ship is filled with air, and air's density is 816 times less than that of water. If the overall size and weight of the ship are considered, then, its density is actually less than that of water— and the ship will float.

?

How does an artificial pacemaker help a weak or damaged heart?

Artificial pacemakers are able to correct low cardiac output primarily because of the remarkable qualities of the heart itself. Ever since the experiments of the prominent Italian physician Luigi Galvani in the eighteenth century, men have known about the ability of muscle to respond to electrical stimulation. The fibers of the myocardium (the middle muscular layer of the heart wall) are excitable and able to conduct impulses from one fiber to another. The speed of the impulses received—hence the rhythm of the heart—depends to some extent on the autonomic (involuntary) nervous system. A healthy heart is able to produce a sufficient stimulus because cardiac muscle has an inherent rhythm that causes it to contract. Even if severed from the nerves, fresh cardiac muscle (unlike skeletal muscles) is not paralyzed, but continues to contract rhythmically. Both the atrial and the ventricular myocardia have this quality, but the rate of the former's contractions is actually somewhat faster than the rate of the latter's. To initiate and maintain one steady rhythm, the heart has its own natural pacemaker; the sinoatrial node. Lying in the right atrium at the recess of the vena cava superior, this node beats the fastest of all myocardial muscles. If the sinoatrial node fails, the atrioventricular node takes over, causing the heart to

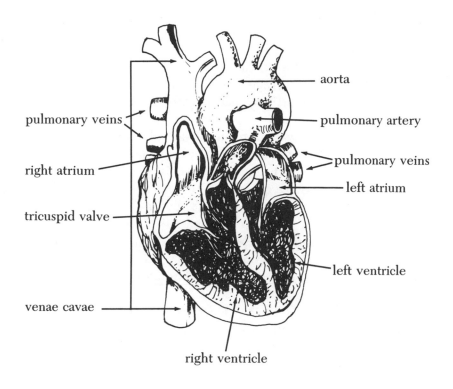

aorta

pulmonary veins

pulmonary artery

pulmonary veins

right atrium

left atrium

tricuspid valve

left ventricle

venae cavae

right ventricle

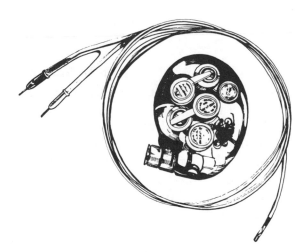

Implantable cardiac pacemaker.

beat about 50 to 60 times per minute rather than 70 to 80.

Any number of problems, including sinus or ventricular arrest, atrioventricular (AV) block, and Stokes-Adams syndrome, may cause an insufficient or irregular heartbeat, which physicians are able to correct with an artificial pacemaker. A pacemaker can start a ventricular contraction by transmitting repetitive, evenly spaced current pulses to the heart from an outside electrical source.

Various types of pacemakers are available to correct different problems, but basically the machine consists of electrodes, conducting wires, and a pulse generator. The electrodes, made of gold or platinum, are good conductors. They may be unipolar or bipolar, but the latter are more efficient. If the electrodes are in direct contact with the heart, less voltage is required than if they do not actually touch the cardiac tissue. The conducting wires are made up of stainless-steel coils. The generator controls the rate and amplitude of impulses, which may be fixed or may change according to the needs of the heart. If the heart is weak, for example, but needs stimulus only from time to time, the pacemaker shuts off when the heart is working well so as not to compete or interfere with it.

An artificial pacemaker can be implanted by thoracotomy or introduced transvenously. In the transthoracic method the chest is opened between the fifth and sixth ribs. The electrodes are put on the outer left ventricular wall and sewn in place. Either an external or an implanted generator may be connected to the electrodes. The latter is usually placed in the right anterior chest, below the clavicle.

The transvenous method of installing a pacemaker doesn't require major surgery. After a local anesthetic is administered, a catheter is put into the jugular, subclavian, or antecubital vein. With the help of fluoroscopic visualization, physicians thread the catheter through the vein, all the way through the right atrium to the right ventricle. There the electrodes are wedged into the ventricular wall. Again the generator may be implanted or external. Most have an amplitude of 1 to 10 volts and provide a stimulus of 1 to 2 seconds.

?

How do they write the *Encyclopaedia Britannica?*

The accumulation of knowledge that went into the making of the fifteenth edition of the *Encyclopaedia Britannica* is astounding, for the ambitious publishers and editors of this edition actually started from scratch—a feat to give even the most knowledgeable scholar reason for misgivings. The first *Encyclopaedia Britannica,* published in 1771 and comprising only 2,659 pages in three volumes, had been updated and expanded over two centuries, the fourteenth edition having been published in 1929. This edition was revised forty-one times in an effort to keep abreast of rapid scientific and technological advances in the twentieth century, but editorial advisers, scholars, and particularly the determined publisher, William Benton, realized the need for a totally new encyclopedia to meet the demands of this century and the next. Planning for the fifteenth *Britannica,* which appeared in 1974, began in 1960, and the task involved some 300 editors, 200 advisers, and more than 4,000 contributors.

Before any writing could begin, however, what to include and how to organize the full scope of human knowledge had to be determined. Director of Planning Mortimer J. Adler, founder and president of the Institute for Philosophical Research, undertook the intellectual design. For two years he and 162 other scholars formulated an "outline of knowledge," the backbone of the encyclopedia, which they then decided to publish as a guide to understanding the entire work. The outline, published in one volume called the Propaedia, is, says Adler, a "circle of learning," divided into ten categories: Matter and Energy, Earth, Life on Earth, Human Life, Human Society, Art, Technology, Religion, History of Mankind, and Branches of Knowledge. This revolutionary idea in encyclopedia design provides a topical mode of access to the alphabetically organized general encyclopedia. An essay by a distinguished expert in each field introduces each of the ten parts, describing the general scope and showing how various parts are related to one another. Each part is then broken down into divisions, sections, and subsections—15,000 in all. For example, Art is separated into "Division I: Art in General" and "Division II: Particular Arts." "Art in General" includes (1) "Theory and classification of the arts," (2) "Experience and criticism of works of art," and (3) "Nonaesthetic contexts of art." Each of these topics is further broken down into several pages of meticulous subheadings. Opposite the outline is a key that refers the reader to articles, article sections, or other references in the encyclopedia. The eighteenth-century French encyclopedist Denis Diderot actually had been attracted to this method of systematizing knowledge by topic, but he became frustrated by it—understandably so.

After Adler and his colleagues completed the exhaustive outline, they had to make sure that the scholars who undertook each article stayed within their strictly defined boundaries—a demand that thoroughly discouraged some 200 writers. Candidates for writing long articles for the so-called Macropaedia ("big learning") were nominated by the senior editor of each subject area. These twelve editors (one from each of the ten major categories, plus the editors responsible for two other areas, geography and biography) frequently consulted academic advisers on who was considered preeminent in their particular field. The senior editor then made an informed nomination to the editor in chief, Warren E. Preece, whose final approval was necessary in every case. A great deal of discussion usually took place, which included recommendations from Adler and from Robert M. Hutchins, chairman of the Board of Editors. If Preece and the editor, after much debate, reached an impasse, they turned for advice to the faculties of the University of Chicago. Whenever necessary they went farther afield, contacting individual scholars and/or special committees of faculty members at the universities of Oxford, Cambridge, London, Edinburgh, Toronto, Tokyo, and the Australian National University. In an attempt to keep the encyclopedia international, one out of three candidates for each article was non-English and non-American. Milton Friedman, Arthur Koestler, Arnold J. Toynbee, and Anthony Burgess are among those who contributed major articles. Although the entire editorial staff assisted in the editing process, Preece and Executive Editor Philip W. Goetz carried the heaviest load, sometimes wading through 200,000 words of text a week. In all, the nineteen-volume Macropaedia contains 4,207 authoritative articles, each running somewhere between 750 and 250,000 words.

For those who want a quicker reference guide of short, concise entries, the fifteenth edition of the *Encyclopaedia Britannica* also includes a Micropaedia ("little learning"). This is a ten-volume set with 102,000 entries that provide basic facts on noted people, nations, politics, agriculture, education, plants, animals, and so on. The Micropaedia also acts as an index to the Macropaedia.

All told, development and publication of the fifteenth edition of the *Encyclopaedia Britannica* was a $32 million venture resulting in 43 million words which—as far as its publishers, at least, are concerned—contain the entirety of human knowledge.

?

How do they decide who is pictured on United States paper currency?

An act of Congress in 1962 designated the Secretary of the Treasury as the one responsible for choosing who will have the honor of appearing on our money. In most cases the secretary consults other Treasury officials, the Director of the Bureau of Engraving and Printing, and sometimes the President before making a final decision.

The portraits on our notes today were decided upon by a special committee appointed in 1925 by Secretary of the Treasury Andrew W. Mellon. They altered the size of the notes, revised printing methods, and in 1928 decided that portraits of Presidents should go on the notes because they have "a more permanent familiarity in the minds of the public than any other." This decision was overruled by Mellon, who thought the first Secretary of the Treasury, Alexander Hamilton, and Benjamin Franklin were also sufficiently well known by Americans. The most familiar face was George Washington, so the committee decided to put his likeness on the note people have the most of: $1. Previously, currencies worth $1 had carried a variety of images: legal tender notes issued from 1861 to 1864 bore the likeness of Secretary of the Treasury Salmon P. Chase; silver certificates carried a likeness of Martha Washington in 1886; and in 1896 an educational series was printed with such historical images as the Washington Monument and the names of great Americans in wreaths.

According to the *History of the Bureau of Engraving and Printing 1862–1962*, the committee in 1928 suggested James A. Garfield for the $2 note "because of the sentiment attached to our martyred Presidents and because his flowing beard would offer a marked contrast to the clean-shaven features of Washington. . . ." Mellon turned down the recommendation, though, and decided on an image of Thomas Jefferson for the $2 bill.

The precise selection process remains a mystery, for the Bureau of Engraving and Printing admits that "records do not reveal the reason that portraits of certain statesmen were chosen in preference to those of other persons of equal importance and prominence."

?

How do they decide what goes on American coins?

The Director of the Mint, with the approval of the Secretary of the Treasury, has the prerogative of choosing new coin designs, though changes cannot be made on any coin more than once every twenty-five years, according to an act of Congress, Title 31, Section 276, enacted in 1890. It wasn't until the one hundredth anniversary of Abraham Lincoln's birth that public sentiment was sufficient to override one long-standing prejudice, now rather hard to imagine: until the Lincoln cent, there had never been a portrait on a United States coin. There is a stipulation, commanded by act of Congress, that every American coin bear a symbol of liberty. The advent of the Lincoln penny marked the Mint's acknowledgment that certain prominent people in the

34

history of the country who were no longer living could represent liberty.

In some instances Congress has prescribed new designs for coins. At the bicentennial of Washington's birth, for example, Congress decided to put his portrait on the quarter. An act of Congress in 1963 placed the likeness of John F. Kennedy on the half dollar, and legislation in 1970 placed a portrait of Dwight D. Eisenhower on the obverse of the dollar coin.

The Director of the Mint also responds to public sentiment, which was the motivating factor in placing the likeness of Franklin D. Roosevelt on the dime in 1946, one year after his death.

Inscriptions on the coins are required by law, as stated in Title 31, Section 324, U.S. Code, whose derivation dates as far back as 1873; it was last amended in 1970:

> Upon one side of all coins of the United States there shall be an impression emblematic of liberty, with an inscription of the word "Liberty," and upon the reverse side shall be the figure or representation of an eagle, with the inscriptions "United States of America" and "E Pluribus Unum" and a designation of the value of the coin; but on the dime, 5-, and 1-cent piece, the figure of the eagle shall be omitted. The motto "In God we trust" shall be inscribed on all coins. Any coins minted after July 23, 1965, from 900 fine coin silver shall be inscribed with the year 1964. All other coins shall be inscribed with the year of the coinage or issuance unless the Secretary of the Treasury, in order to prevent or alleviate a shortage of coins of any denomination, directs that coins of the denomination continue to be inscribed with the last preceding year inscribed on coins of that denomination.

?

How do they get the lead into a pencil?

You might think that lead gets into a pencil by being inserted into a hole drilled the length of a cylindrical piece of wood, for if you look closely at a pencil, it certainly appears that the wood is all one piece. "That's the sign of a good pencil," says a salesman for the Joseph Dixon Crucible Company, producer of the famous yellow Dixon Ticonderoga pencil. Even if you inspect an unpainted Dixon pencil, you can't see that it is actually made of two pieces of wood glued together. The seams are invisible.

Dixon starts with cedar wood cut into slats, measuring roughly 7¼ by 2¾ inches and less than ¼ inch thick. The slats are sent through a machine with saws that cut thin grooves, usually four to nine per slat, depending on the size of the pencil to be made. Next, fine strips of hardened lead are placed in the grooves. This "lead," actually composed of graphite, clay, and a little water, has been dipped in wax for extra strength, baked, pushed into a mold, and cut to the proper 7-inch length. A second slat, also cut with grooves, is fitted over the one that now holds the lead, and the two are glued together with a high-strength industrial glue. There is now a slim rectangular box with strips of lead concealed inside. This is run through two similar machines. One cuts the top slat into a series of faceted semicircular shapes, the number corresponding to the number of strips of lead. When the next machine performs the same operation on the bottom slat, the facets meet and the slat is divided into four to nine individual pencils.

Then the finishing touches are added, such as paint, a green and gold ferrule at one end, and an eraser, which is glued in. The Joseph Dixon Crucible Company, employing one hundred workers in this operation, produces 576,000 pencils in a single eight-hour day.

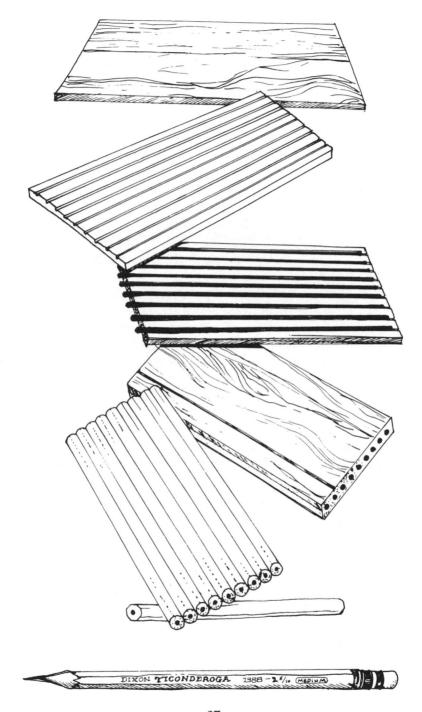

?

How do they remove tar from cigarettes?

Cigarette companies keep talking about reducing the "tar" in their latest brands, as though it were a single ingredient, easily removed for better health, easily replaced for more taste. Actually, "tar" is not tar at all but a combination of some 2,000 to 10,000 elements—including alkaloids, ammonia, carbon dioxide, carbon monoxide, and hydrogen cyanide—known in the tobacco industry as "total particular matter." TPM is formed by the burning of organic matter; in a cigarette this includes both tobacco leaves and paper.

The Federal Trade Commission (FTC) measures the amount of TPM in a cigarette by drawing smoke through a special filter on a mechanical smoking machine. Each cigarette, previously conditioned for twenty-four hours at 75 degrees Fahrenheit and 60 percent relative humidity, is smoked to a predetermined butt length. The TPM "wet collection" is the net weight gain in the filter after the cigarette has been smoked. TPM "dry" is then calculated by subtracting the weight of nicotine and water. This figure is what shows up on some cigarette packages for the interested consumer. In 1979 the FTC published a list of the "tar" and nicotine contents of 176 varieties of domestic cigarettes. Marlboro, for example, has 17 milligrams of "tar" per cigarette, and Merit has 8. The difference is, of course, intentional, and the cigarette manufacturers use a variety of techniques to accomplish it.

One method involves, simply enough, decreasing the amount of tobacco in the cigarette, by reducing slightly the circumference of the cigarette or by using "fluff" tobacco—tobacco that has been dried by a special process so that it retains its original dimensions even after the moisture has been removed. Smaller circumference or smaller volume means less burning time, which means less "tar." Another method of reducing tar is to pack the tobacco so that it burns more quickly, even during the idle periods between puffs.

Porous paper, too, aids in increasing the rate of burning and dilutes the smoke so that the smoker gets less TPM in his lungs. The paper is perforated mechanically with tiny holes that cannot be seen. Additives are also used to make the tobacco burn more quickly, but tobacco companies can go only so far before totally frustrating their market.

The filter is also an effective device for reducing "tar." Perforated filters dilute the smoke with air; large, long filters that are difficult to draw through are yet more efficient.

?

How do they measure the speed of a fastball?

The game is tied, the crowd hushed with anticipation, as "Goose" Gossage winds up for one of his famous fastballs. The batter swings, misses—strike three—the inning is over and Howard Cosell tells us Gossage's deadly pitch went 98 miles an hour. How does he know?

Just as the police use radar to trap speeders on a highway, baseball teams use radar guns to measure the speed of a fastball. The person who operates the gun stands behind home plate, behind the backstop. He activates the gun, which may then work continuously throughout the game if so desired. The gun registers a measurement of speed each time the ball whizzes toward home plate.

A radar gun emits microwave beams of a known frequency. These beams have a conical shape and a width of 16 degrees. A baseball moving within this radar field toward the gun reflects the waves back toward the gun. The difference in frequency between the reflected waves and the original waves is then calculated, and that information is translated into miles per hour.

?

How does a high-speed elevator take you 60 floors in 30 seconds?

When an elevator lifts you almost instantaneously to the 60th floor, you feel you must be traveling at a tremendous speed. Actually, the elevator rises 800 feet in 30 seconds, or only 18 miles an hour. Compared with the slow hydraulic elevators used in buildings of five stories and less, however, this speed is indeed fast. Tall office and apartment buildings use electric elevators, and one of the fastest in the country is located in the John Hancock Building in Chicago. That elevator can travel 900 feet in 30 seconds.

A modern electric elevator is operated by a gearless traction machine, which is based on a system of hoists first developed by the Egyptians to build the Pyramids. Six to eight steel cables, or hoisting ropes, are attached to the top of the elevator car. They extend to the top of the hoistway, where they are wrapped around a grooved wheel, or drive sheave, measuring 30 to 48 inches in diameter. The ends of the cables then drop back down the hoistway, holding a counterweight that slides up and down on its own guide rails. The weight of the elevator car on one end of the ropes and the total mass of the counterweight on the other end press the cables down into the grooves of the drive sheave. A large, slow-speed electric motor turns the drive sheave at a rate of 50 to 200 revolutions per minute, thereby moving the cables and lifting the elevator. The electric hoisting motor does not have to lift the full weight of the elevator car and its passengers, for the weight of the car and about half its passenger load is balanced by the counterweight, which slides down as the car goes up. Any elevator that travels more than 250 feet in 30 seconds requires additional traction, which is achieved by wrapping the hoisting ropes around a secondary gearlike sheave located just below the main drive sheave.

41

?

How does an archaeologist or anthropologist know where to dig?

Finding a spot where prehistoric man camped, worked, played, or died usually comes about by accident. Most sites are found by construction crews, say, or by amateur bone collectors who might notify a local newspaper or university that they have found something out of the ordinary. Usually the object is an elephant or buffalo bone—too huge to have come from a cow—or an ancient-looking stone arrowhead. Professionals may then find a prehistoric site when they excavate the area. Since most of the evidence of early man has been covered over by 10,000 to 2 million years of dust and civilization, the clues to finding such a doorway into the past are hard to come by.

"It's very hit-or-miss," says anthropologist Dennis Stanford of the Smithsonian Institution in Washington, D.C. "If it's under a parking lot, you're not going to find it."

There are a few ways of looking for sites besides relying on blind chance, however. Aerial photographs of a region can lead to important discoveries. The thing to watch for, according to Stanford, is water. People and animals must drink to stay alive, and early man had to camp and live near a water source. Tools, bones, and artifacts of all kinds turn up along the ancient banks of rivers and lakes. In the Olduvai Gorge in eastern Africa, for example, the late Dr. Louis B. Leakey found several skulls and jawbones that proved that man as a species had been on the earth for more than a million years; the australopithecines, as he called them, had apelike faces, but walked upright in manlike fashion and had large brains.

Dennis Stanford's main interest is early North American peoples, who were much more recent than australopithecines and physically indistinguishable from modern man. Near a Texas riverbed Stanford found tiny shards of flint that he thinks were ground off by a prehistoric tool maker while sharpening a stone blade. There were no natural sources of flint in the area, so the stone must have been brought to the site and ground by someone for a specific purpose. Stanford believes the geologic layer in which the shards were lying is 12,000 years old.

Passes through mountains are also likely spots to dig for evidence of early man, since any people who lived in the region probably traveled that way frequently and may have left behind some sign of their presence.

?

How do they predict future crop yields by satellite?

Global crop forecasting, still very much in the experimental stage, is a massive undertaking that calls on the research facilities and technologies of such organizations as the National Aeronautics and Space Administration (NASA), the United States Department of Agriculture (USDA), and the National Oceanic and Atmospheric Administration (NOAA). There is no magical system by which satellites can report a simple and infallible prediction, as crop yields are subject to vagaries of policy, unforeseen weather changes, and other variables. Nevertheless, the study of data from weather satellites, of multispectral and return beam vidicon (television) images from Landsat satellites, combined with analysis of regression models—historical records of particular crops, yield models, and crop calendars—allows scientists to assess current crop status and to estimate harvest yields with a reasonable degree of accuracy.

The *Apollo* 9 flight in March 1969 provided the first significant test of acquiring data about the earth's resources by remote sensing from space. Today, a Landsat satellite *(Landsat 3)*, launched on March 5, 1978, orbits the earth at an altitude of about 570 miles in a circular, near-polar, sun-synchronous orbit. This means that the same point on the earth's surface is viewed every 18 days. The satellite collects data by means of multispectral scanners (optical-mechanical scanners), vidicon TV cameras, and radio systems.

43

Landsat Earth Resources Technology Satellite.

The ability to photograph in each part of the electromagnetic spectrum has proved particularly helpful in studying vegetation and its condition. Color infrared photography (which was developed for detection of camouflaged installations during World War II) records information that the human eye cannot detect. A multispectral scanner is an instrument, which may be mounted on a satellite or aircraft, that senses reflected and/or emitted radiation in any number of bands of the electromagnetic spectrum, depending on the design of the scanner. *Landsat 3*'s multispectral scanner senses radiation in five bands: green, red, thermal infrared, and two in near-infrared. Multispectral scanners contain a device that splits a beam of light into spectral components. The various wavelengths are, in turn, converted to electrical signals, which can be transmitted to the earth by telemetry and then recorded on magnetic tape.

An examination of images taken in, say, three different portions of the spectrum can show that corn, alfalfa, stubble, and bare soil stimulate different responses and thus can be distinguished from one another. Each substance has its own unique "signature," or tone—ranging from black to numerous shades of gray to white—produced by its reflectance within a particular band. The "signature" of each substance over time thus depends on which band is examined, what stage the crop is in, soil moisture conditions, and so on. Within the green band, for instance, mature green alfalfa produces a "medium" amount of reflectance. Bare soil also produces an image of medium brightness. In the near-infrared band, however, alfalfa's reflectance is high, but that of bare soil is medium. It is thus necessary to compare and contrast multiple images, in different bands, in order to differentiate types of crops and soil.

Once various crops are identified, multispectral analysis is used to detect crop disease as well. Infrared photographs show that vigorous plants have very high reflectance, and unhealthy ones reflect less. (It is fortunate that the human eye cannot see infrared light, for we might be blinded by the reflectance of these healthy plants! When translated into color images, the reflectance shows healthy plants as reddish, sickly ones as blue or green.) Other uses for multispectral imagery that relate to crop yields include determining the mineral and moisture content of different soils and recording stages of growth and the area covered by a particular crop.

There is, however, much disagreement among scientists about just how much can be gleaned from such data and to what extent the findings in one area can be applied to another. There is also considerable debate about which factors are the most significant in forecasting crop yields. Everyone has a bias; the National Environmental Satellite Service (NESS), for example, endorses the usefulness of meteorological measurements. NESS has a geostationary operational environmental satellite (GOES) system made up of two spacecraft located on the 75-degree and 135-degree west meridians. (The satellites orbit the earth at the same speed as its rotation, thus retaining constant positions in relation to the planet, 22,000 miles above the surface.) They provide early warning of climatic conditions affecting crops, such as drought, freezing temperatures, precipitation and snow cover estimates, and measurements of solar radiation at the earth's surface. Polar orbiting satellites, circling the earth twelve to fourteen times a day at altitudes of 500 to 900 miles, also gather meteorological data.

Still, whether one studies Landsat images or meteorological data, or both, the information is essentially useless for crop prediction without a corresponding study of yield models and crop calendars. A yield model is a statistical model based on a long history of crop yield and weather conditions in a particular area. (It is also necessary to take into account a trend-line yield, which assumes that yield increases with time because of technological advances.) A crop calendar is the normal schedule of crop development, from seedbed preparation and planting to flowering, maturity, and eventual harvesting. A crop calendar varies not only from crop to crop (and from one crop subclass to another), but also from one geographical area to another. Permanent conditions in an area may determine, to some extent, the impact of weather variations. For example, in Indiana, soil moisture is always high, so a dry year might not seriously affect crop growth; whereas in Iowa, where the soil contains less moisture, a dry year could be harmful.

Using all known technology, NASA, USDA, and NOAA in the mid-1970's collaborated on one of the most successful experimental harvest forecast projects to date. The Large Area Crop

46

Inventory Experiment (LACIE) had three phases, beginning in November 1974 with the study of the nine-state Central Plains region of the United States. Phase II brought the Soviet Union and Canada into the picture. Information collected in those two phases was used in Phase III, which led to a forecast of the size of the 1977 Soviet wheat crop that was accurate within 6 percent of official Soviet figures released six months later.

?

How do they pick Nobel Prize winners?

Alfred Bernhard Nobel was a shy, reclusive man with a fondness for English poetry—and a passion for explosives. Even after killing his youngest brother and four other men in his experiments with nitroglycerin, he persisted: he invented dynamite, the detonating cap, and later blasting gelatin, an even more powerful explosive. Not a very peaceful enterprise, one might say; but Nobel apparently hoped his weapons would bring an end to wars.

Nobel didn't believe in inherited wealth, so rather than leave to relatives the millions from his inventions and his oil fields in Russia, he established the Nobel Prizes. His intent, upon signing his will in 1895, was to reward "those persons who shall have contributed most materially to the benefit of mankind during the year immediately preceding."

Today the Nobel Foundation in Stockholm, run by six members and a chairman appointed by the Swedish government, oversees the investment of Nobel's money, the interest from which is awarded as prizes. Each year, from October 1 to November 15, four prize-awarding Institutions meet to decide upon the foremost persons in the areas of physics, chemistry, medicine, literature, and peace; an annual prize in economics was initiated in 1968. The Royal Swedish Academy of Science awards the prizes in physics, chemistry, and economics; the physicians and teachers at Sweden's foremost hospital, the Caroline Institute, decide upon the prize in medicine; the literature prize is awarded by eighteen

writers of the Swedish Academy; and the neighboring Nor-
wegians—five prominent men appointed by the *Storting*
(Parliament) in Oslo—award the peace prize. (This last arrangement arose because Nobel wished to have closer ties with his
neighbors.) Five Nobel Committees, each having three to five
members, solicit experts to advise in the decision-making process.
There are also four Nobel Institutes, chosen by the prize-awarding
Institutions, which research areas pertinent to the prizes.

Although the prizes frequently do go to the most worthy
persons in each field, prejudices and politics inevitably enter the
picture. The Swedes tend to support Germany in the sciences,
look down their noses at American literature, and shy away from
awarding science or literature prizes to the Russians.

"Behind the Award," a feature in the *Nobelshiftelsens Kalender*,
published each year by the Foundation, allows a glimpse at the
makeup of the Academies and their not always objective methods.

The first literature prize awarded in 1901 went to René F. A.
Sully Prudhomme, chosen over Leo Tolstoi. The question of who
was the superior writer was not the issue; an old conservative, Dr.
Carl David Wirsen, opposed Tolstoi's religious beliefs, and
reported that Tolstoi supported anarchism and didn't believe in
cash prizes for artists anyway. The anti-Russian Academy happily
went along.

The prize for Ernest Hemingway in 1954 arose out of esteem
not for the writer (who was thought to be too modern) but for one
of the Academy's own members. Ninety-year-old Per Hallstrom
was faced with retirement, and because the honorable dean
adored *The Old Man and the Sea*, the members deemed it a
courteous gesture to vote according to his views.

The startling award to Patrick White in 1973 over Graham
Greene and Vladimir Nabokov stemmed largely from an attempt
at geographical distribution. This was the first literature prize for
Australia.

In 1965 Richard P. Feynman, together with Julian S. Schwinger
and Sin-itiro Tomonaga, won the physics prize for their research in
quantum electrodynamics. When he heard that the Nobel Committee actually investigates the private lives of winners before
giving an award, Feynman replied, "Well, that finally explains
something that's puzzled me. I made my prize-winning discovery

in 1949, but I was not honored for it until 1965. Now I can see it was my personal life that kept me from getting the award those many years—until the Nobel Committee finally saw I had settled down with my third wife and I now had a child, and that I had become the model of a family man."

The five Norwegian judges designated to award the peace prize in 1935 were a brave and steadfast group. They insisted (despite protests from pro-Nazi novelist Knut Hamsun and from Hermann Goering) on selecting Carl von Ossietzky, who had exposed Hitler's secret rearmament. Not only was the outspoken pacifist and newspaper editor thrown into a concentration camp, where he died of tuberculosis, but the judges themselves were arrested when the Nazis invaded Norway.

The peace prize awarded to Willy Brandt in 1971 for his work in East-West détente was a unanimous choice. But two years later an uproar resulted from the selection of Henry Kissinger for the peace prize—which *The New York Times* called a "war prize." Two members of the committee resigned.

Despite varying opinions and controversy, however, many of the prizes over the years have gone to outstanding and deserving men, as Nobel originally intended.

?

How do they decide whether a fine painting is a forgery?

In 1947 Hans Van Meegeren, Dutch artist and master forger, was brought to trial for having sold a national treasure—a Vermeer painting—to Nazi chief Hermann Goering. Van Meegeren was thrown into jail, protesting that in fact he had fooled Goering. His work was so precise, so convincing, however, that no one believed him—the exquisite picture in Nazi hands could have been painted only by Vermeer. Van Meegeren's only means of salvation was to paint still another Vermeer while in prison to prove himself to the skeptical authorities. The extent of his activities as a forger in the thirties and early forties became fully known a bit later. This insignificant artist, whose own work was scorned by the critics, was the most successful forger ever; his profits amounted to $1,680,000.

Although some methods of scientific analysis of forgery were in practice by the thirties, the war provided Van Meegeren with some cover. For the painting he sold to Goering had a fatal flaw that Dr. Paul Coremans of Belgium detected only when Van Meegeren stood trial: the cobalt blue found in the forgery was a color unknown during Vermeer's lifetime.

Van Meegeren's forgeries, which required intimate familiarity with Vermeer's technique, were evocations of what Vermeer *might* have done early in his career. Other common types of forgery include the direct copy, taken from one original; a pastiche, which draws on elements from various works to form a new one; and a palimpsest, which is an authentic piece embellished or restored so as to falsify the original image or signature.

The various methods of detecting a forgery draw on the expertise of historians and art historians on the one hand, and of scientists trained in mineralogy, metallurgy, organic and inorganic chemistry, crystallography, and wood and fiber identification on the other. No specific procedure is applied in every case. An expert who is extremely sensitive to works of art and their history, iconography, design, and style may know that a particular painting is a fake in a matter of seconds. One story tells of an art collector who came to such an expert with a painting purported to be the work of Duccio. The expert gazed at it and then replied, "Ah, but it is impossible that it is a Duccio, for whenever I behold a Duccio, I swoon!" Before the development of scientific examination techniques, recognition by an art historian—although rather more studied than that of the Duccio expert—was the major test of a painting's validity. Such historians might notice that the brushwork in the fake is calculated and flat, whereas in the original it is direct and spontaneous. They may cite in a forgery a piece of furniture or a style of dress that wouldn't have been used at the time the putative artist lived.

Modern technical examination involves study of the chemical or physical properties of the materials found in the object and of changes wrought by the passage of time. (Many of the tests are in fact useful only on forgeries of paintings of the Old Masters and have little application to forgeries of modern works.)

X rays are used to record the density relationship of the materials in a painting. They may reveal another painting beneath the surface, or a crackle pattern beneath that is different from the one visible on top, indicating that the top layer is more recent. Some forgers scrape away a small section of paint in order to add a false signature. Set down below the surface in this way, it appears to be an integral part of the painting. But infrared rays and X rays can expose the scrape marks surrounding the letters. Other forgers, hoping to make a work of art look old, drill worm holes into the wood. But radiographs (pictures produced by a form of radiation other than light) can reveal that the direction is not the same as that of a hole made by the animal. Radiographs can also determine the date of manufacture of nails used in some panel pictures.

Ultraviolet rays are useful in detecting repainting, added signatures, and restorations, for different materials absorb and reflect those rays differently. Experts must be able to read and interpret various degrees of absorption, reflection, and fluorescence.

Infrared photographs can show how a painter has built up a picture, the stages of development, and mannerisms; this information can help a critic or historian who is familiar with the authentic painter's methods determine whether the work is an original. This technique is also used to track down copies of contemporary works. Infrared rays can reveal a hidden signature or detect that one has been erased.

Chemical identification of metals, fibers, dyes, pigments, and so on is made by spectroscopy and microchemistry. Intense magnification is also used to study the crystalline form, fiber structure, and relationships of paint layers. Forgers frequently use a needle to draw fake cracks, but close examination shows that such cracks are only as deep as the paint layers, whereas real cracks would be deeper. (Another method used by forgers involves putting the painting in an oven, so that it dries and hardens two centuries' worth in a day.) An expert looking through a binocular magnifier can pinpoint artificial crackle and signatures that "float" between layers.

However, if a pastiche, for example, is executed by a master forger using the same ingredients, style, and structure as the original artist, and effectively incorporating technical problems of

51

deterioration, the work may have to go back to the art historian—for a decision based on certain knowledge, a well-informed guess, or an intuition of the moment.

?

How do they turn coffee into instant coffee?

Whether you agree with the ads that freeze-dried instant coffee packs in more flavor, or stand by the powdered brand you've been using for years, the manufacturing process for both is similar—at least until the final step.

When coffee arrives at a factory that will turn it into instant, it already looks like the ground coffee available in your supermarket. The green beans have been roasted to the appropriate color required by each brand, blended for that particular Maxwell House or Yuban flavor, and ground. The factory staff then actually percolates huge amounts of coffee. Whereas you might put 4 tablespoons into your percolator, one factory may brew 1,800 to 2,000 pounds at a time. The coffee then passes through tubes in which high pressure and temperature cause some water to evaporate, leaving behind coffee with a very high concentration of solids. This liquid, known as coffee liquor, is then ready to be dried by one of two methods.

Powdered instant coffee is dried by heat, which some people feel is detrimental to the flavor. The liquor is poured through a large cylindrical drier, roughly 100 feet high and 60 feet across, and is heated to 500 degrees Fahrenheit; by the time the liquor reaches the bottom, the water has evaporated, leaving powdered instant coffee, ready to be collected and packed into jars.

By the freeze-drying method, the coffee liquor is frozen into blocks, which then are broken into granules of the desired size. The granules are then put into a vacuum drier, a box kept in a continuous vacuum, which dries the coffee through sublimation—that is, the frozen water changes directly into vapor, which is in turn removed through valves. High temperatures that might damage the flavor are not required, since the granules are in a vacuum (the thinner the atmosphere, the lower the temperature at which water boils). What remains after vacuum drying are coffee solids that dissolve instantly in hot water for a quick cup of coffee.

?

How do bees know how to build honeycombs?

By accident—that's the biological answer to the question. The dazzling geometric perfection of the honeycomb—with its perfectly flat surfaces made of straight rows of elegant hexagons, compact, yet capacious enough inside to support a population of 80,000—is the product of blind instinct, the artistry of an intricate genetic program. Every action the bees perform in building their metropolis, such as poking the cell walls in a honeycomb with their mandibles (jaws) as they form them to make sure the thickness is right, is dictated by instructions in the genes of their body cells. The instructions were "written" by a series of rare genetic accidents occurring over millions of generations; certain accidents were preserved and passed along to the next generation because they helped the animal survive and reproduce.

Each cell of the bee's body contains a complete set of genes, the "blueprint" in cell language for making an entire bee. The bee gets its genes from its parents, as it is conceived. If something happens to change the molecular structure of those donated genes, either before or shortly after conception, the instructions change, and the creature will develop or behave differently; such genetic accidents or mutations happen at random every so often. Most mutations are so catastrophic that the animal doesn't even hatch.

A few, however, are beneficial, giving the organism a new quality that helps it survive. When it reproduces, it passes on the "good" mutation in its genes to its offspring.

A series of genes for testing the thickness of cell walls would make worker bees much more efficient, since they would not waste wax making walls too thick, or lose hatching young when a section of thin wall collapsed. Greater efficiency in construction would let the "mutant" bees move on to other work, producing more young, while nonmutants were repairing broken walls or making extra wax to replace what was squandered on thick-walled cells. Because of their greater efficiency, the generations of wall testers would soon outproduce all others so dramatically that they would snatch up all the good food and nesting sites. After thousands or millions of generations, *only* wall testers would remain. A beehive is a select combination of the most successful genetic accidents in the history of bees.

But how do they build the hives so exactly once they have their genetic instructions? For example, how do the bees build the comb flat, along a single plane? The tools a worker bee uses are her own body (workers are sexually undeveloped females), raw materials from the environment, and the unseen forces of the planet Earth itself. Experiments have shown that bees can all somehow sense the earth's magnetic field and innately know how to make a structure turned at a certain angle to it. Thus they can all agree on which way the comb should face, with no foreman bee to tell them. Bees can line up the hexagonal cell openings in perfect horizontal and vertical rows because every bee carries her own plumb line wherever she goes: her head. The head is attached to the neck by two pivot points, which are surrounded by bristlelike sensory hairs. When the heavy head is pulled in any given direction by the force of gravity, the hairs on that side of the bee's neck are tickled, so she always knows which way is "down," and can get her bearings accordingly. Each cell is a hexagonal prism—a tube with six sides—because this is the best possible shape to hold a given volume of anything while using as little building material as possible. Furthermore, the cells are tilted back at a grade of 13 degrees, to keep the honey from running out.

No one knows for certain how the bees manage to construct six perfect 120-degree angles in each cell, but it seems that they

measure distances and angles with the span between their two
front legs, as they spread the wax with their mandibles. Since all
the workers in the hive are the same size, it is easy to see why the
results are uniform. Beeswax itself is a fatty secretion from glands
lining the underside of the creature's abdomen; it comes out in
flakes, which the bee passes forward to her mandibles with her
hind legs. Then she chews it awhile, mixing it with her saliva until
it is the right temperature and consistency. She spreads the wax to
a uniform thickness of .003 inch, scraping and adding until the
layer is perfect; she tests it by butting it with her mandibles with
the antennae resting on its surface—the way the layer vibrates in
response to her pokes tells her how thick it is.

Bees start building a section of comb at the top, from two or
three different spots. A crowd of bees huddles together at each
spot like a football team before the hike, keeping the wax warm
with their bodies as they shape it together. They make the cells
three or four at a time, proceeding from common walls. They
"spell" each other so that each bee works at the exhausting process
for about 30 seconds at a stretch before being relieved by a
substitute. Each huddle of bees spreads out as work progresses,

and the sections of the comb are joined—they fit together so perfectly that it's impossible to tell they were begun separately. The cells are not literally all the same size, but come in three carefully delineated varieties: the smallest are for hatching new workers and storing pollen and honey; the next largest are for rearing drones (males); and the largest are for raising new queens.

Bees' reputation for efficiency is well founded: aside from being well organized, they conserve resources by recycling their building materials. When a contingent leaves a hive to found a new one (called "swarming"), they pack supplies of wax taken from abandoned cells in the mother hive into their special leg baskets to use in building their new honeycomb.

?

How does a honeybee find food?

Nothing seems more random than the haphazard-looking zigs and zags of a bee as it buzzes along on a summer afternoon. Yet nothing is more deliberate in all of nature. That bee has been flying a distance of up to 6 miles in a literal "beeline" from its hive to the place where it has been told there is precious food. An amazing inborn system of bee radar guides the insect closer and closer to its destination.

How is a bee told where to find food? Bees use a primitive but truly symbolic language—the only such means of communication known to exist in nonhumans—to guide each other to food. When a worker bee returns to the hive from a foray, it performs a kind of dance. From those simple steps the observing workers collect all the information they need—not only how far to fly, but in what direction. The dance is executed on the vertical face of a comb; the pull of gravity tells the bee which way is "down," so that it can orient the dance steps in space. The direction in which each maneuver points is very important if the other workers are to find the food.

If the food source is closer than about 10 yards, the scout

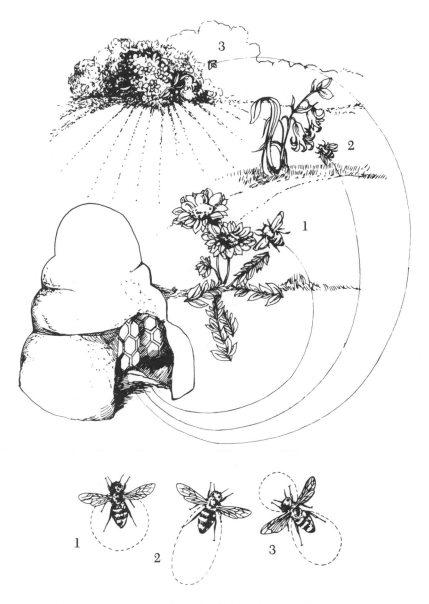

The configuration of the "dance" that a bee performs on returning from the field communicates to bees in the hive the location of a food source. If the source lies within 10 yards of the hive, the dance is small and circular (1). As the distance to the food increases, the figure flattens to an oval (2). For food beyond 100 yards, the scout promenades slowly in a figure eight (3), whose shape indicates the location of the food in relation to the sun.

promenades in a circle about 1 inch in diameter. As the distance increases to 100 yards, the circle flattens to a sickle shape. Beyond 100 yards the sickle becomes a figure eight, and the pace of the dance slows. The greater the flying time, the slower this pace—presumably matching the scout's own fatigue.

To communicate the direction of the food, the dancer uses its figure eight as a pointer. If the "waist" of the eight is vertical, the food lies directly toward the sun. If the waist tilts 20 degrees to the right of vertical, the food is 20 degrees to the right of the sun's position and so on.

But not even clouds can deter the bees. Their eyes are sensitive to ultraviolet light, which penetrates the clouds even when "visible" sunlight is stopped; so the bees can locate the position of the sun when mere humans cannot.

In any weather, the first trip to a new and distant food source may require several minutes' searching after the worker reaches the general area. The bee uses both vision and smell to find the right flower; it remembers the scent of the nectar that the original scout brought back to the hive. For subsequent trips the worker memorizes visual landmarks and is able to make a beeline to its target.

?

How do mountain climbers scale sheer rock walls?

Tools help, as do various specific techniques, but rock climbers depend mostly on sound judgment, careful analysis, and astonishing nerve.

The physical mechanics of rock climbing involve not only the feet, knees, hands, arms, and body. Pressure of the body against the rock, for example, lends support. If a very steep rock affords no hand- or footholds, the climber may secure a grasp on a vertical rock edge and pull on it horizontally as he, in a sense, walks up, his body leaning at a right angle to the rock. This move is called a layback. Other steep faces may require a *courte-echelle*, in which the lead climber uses his companions to reach a hold: he stands on their shoulders or simply receives a boost.

An experienced climber keeps his body as vertical as possible and at a sufficient distance from the rock to be able to move freely. Novices suffering pangs of fear tend to hug the rock, which hinders their progress.

The most astonishing feat of the truly great climbers is known as balance or rhythm climbing. By some uncanny law of nature, a master cragsman can move quickly up a rock, using terrifyingly narrow ledges and tiny fingerholds if he maintains his motion, which creates friction with the rock, and if he is on his way to a counterbalancing position.

A more conventional technique, of course, is climbing in groups, wherein two or more climbers are linked by a rope. The strongest climber is first on the way up and last during the descent. Nylon rope, ½ inch in diameter, has replaced the older manila or hemp ropes, which lacked elasticity. That elasticity proved to be a saving grace for twenty-four-year-old David Harrah of the 1950 Harvard Andean Expedition that climbed Yerupaja in western Peru. After weeks of climbing over snow and ice, Harrah and a companion reached the 21,770-foot summit. When they started down, the snow gave way, and Harrah fell the entire 120-foot length of the rope that bound him to his partner. The time it took for Harrah to fall allowed the other climber a split second in which to lie down and slam his ax into a ridge for support. Harrah bounced at the end of the nylon rope, which fortunately had enough give that it didn't break his ribs. Four thousand feet above a glacier, Harrah dangled in space. It took 45 minutes for him to get back up the rope to his friend—and just how he had the strength to do *that*, no one knows.

Under moderate conditions, rock climbers move all at once. If the way is precarious, an anchor man secures a stance, wrapping a rope around himself or a rock while the others proceed; this is called a belay. The top man may gain additional protection by hammering pitons (spikes, wedges, or pegs) into rock cracks, and by running ropes through carabiners (rings) snapped to the pitons. Prussiking is an elaborate process for extremely difficult climbs: pitons are hammered in at every step, more ropes added between climbers, and a sling-and-pulley system using prussik knots arranged whereby a climber may hoist himself up. During a descent extra ropes may be wrapped around a rock point to allow for a rappel: two lengths of rope are wound under the climber's thigh and over the opposite shoulder, the rest of their length hanging down the mountain. Facing the mountain, the climber walks backward, the ropes slipping slowly through his sure and careful hands.

?

How do car tires grip a wet road?

If roads were always dry, tire manufacture would be a simple operation: all tires would be completely smooth, like racing tires; for the greater the amount of tire in contact with the road, the greater the amount of traction. Our changeable climate creates another set of problems, however, for smooth tires (especially wide ones) speeding along a wet road actually begin to float. With traction drastically reduced, a car may hydroplane at speeds of 45 or 50 miles per hour.

Since no one wants to change tires each morning according to fallible weather reports, tire companies try to produce the best all-weather tire, with rubber soft enough for good traction but sufficiently hard to last. While wide treads provide contact with the road surface, an intricate design of tread grooves and/or slots that are cut into the tire channel water out from between the tread and the road as the tire rotates. Tires used to have five to seven straight, continuous ribs, but today slots are cut across the tread pattern, which shoot water out to either side. These slots and grooves are deeper than those on older tires: ⅜ inch is standard, with ¹⁄₁₆ inch being the legal limit to which a tire may be worn down.

It is essential during a heavy rainstorm that a tire's grooves remain open, and methods of assuring this vary from one type and brand to another. A bias belted tire, for example, made of crisscrossed plies, has two or more circumferential belts of fiberglass or steel wire. These belts, added to the body beneath the tread, are an improvement on the standard bias tire. Perhaps the most efficient tire—in terms of both traction and tread wear— is the radial tire. The name describes the body cords that run radially from side to side, at an angle of 90 degrees to the direction of travel. Two or four belts made of polyester, steel, fiberglass, or aramid (which is lighter than steel but more costly) encircle the tire to stabilize it and hold the treads open.

?

How do they sort eggs into jumbo, large, and medium sizes?

It would be nice if hens were systematically grouped into jumbo, large, and medium sizes, just as their eggs are classified. But even though tall people often have tall children, big hens don't necessarily lay big eggs. In a standard coop all the hens— large side by side with small—are kept in cages of 4 square feet, three or four birds to the cage. While one conveyor belt brings them their meals, another carries away the eggs that roll from their tilted cages.

Placed by either hand or machine in flats (containers holding 2½ to 3 dozen), which are brought to a processing room, the eggs are then picked up by a suction gun, a machine with 2½ to 3 dozen rubber suction cups that fit over the tops of the eggs. The suction gun transfers the eggs to a conveyor belt studded with spindles; each egg is supported by two spindles, separating the eggs and thus preventing them from rattling against each other and cracking. A washing machine cleans away any debris, the pores that allow an egg to breathe are sealed with oil, and the eggs go into a candling booth. Here mirrors on the wall and very bright lights beneath the eggs allow an inspector to check for cracks or blood spots.

Finally, the eggs that pass inspection advance to a scale, which consists of a rocker arm with a weight on the back of it. If the egg is heavy enough to tip the rocker arm, it passes from the conveyor belt into one of two lines of cups, which then lower the eggs into a waiting carton. A carton of jumbo eggs must weigh 30 ounces, so each jumbo egg must weigh 2.5 ounces; the first scale is set accordingly. If the egg isn't heavy enough, it automatically moves on to the next rocker arm with a slightly lighter weight behind it. There are usually five scales that separate the eggs into the various categories: jumbo, 2.5 ounces; extra large, 2.25 ounces; large, 2 ounces; medium, 1.75 ounces; and small, 1.5 ounces. If the egg is too light to tip the last rocker arm, it won't ever reach your local supermarket.

?

How does a submarine dive and resurface?

Submarines dive and resurface simply as a result of changes in the amount of weight on board. It's essential, then, that the captain keep careful track of the number of crew members and the amount of food, batteries, torpedoes, and so on. When the submarine's weight is equal to the weight of water it displaces, the vessel floats. In the case of a standard 273-foot British "T" submarine developed in World War II, this weight is 1,300 tons. When the captain gives the order "Prepare to dive," valves and vents are opened, allowing masses of seawater to rush into tanks aboard the craft, the precise amount being carefully controlled so that the sub will not sink beneath the desired depth. At a weight of 1,575 tons, the British "T" sub is submerged and in a state of neutral buoyancy; that is, the submarine can remain submerged and can move at varying levels with only minor changes in water ballast.

The ballast tanks that fill with water, along with the fuel tanks, are built within the double steel hull of the vessel. The inner hull is extremely strong to withstand water pressure at great depths, and the outer hull is supported by the water in the tanks. When a submarine dives, power-operated vents admit water into a ballast tank in the front a few seconds before allowing water into the tanks farther back. This causes the bow to dip first and the sub to glide gracefully below the surface. Hydroplanes—small horizontal fins on the hull of the sub—aid in directing and controlling the submarine while it is underwater. At the order to resurface, compressed air is forced into the ballast tanks, thereby propelling water out of the vessel and allowing it to rise.

Older submarines ran on large diesel engines that were connected to generators. The electricity produced by these generators drove the propellers. Since the engines required oxygen, a snorkel or breathing tube was developed during World War II so that the submarine could have access to air while traveling just under the surface of the water. At greater depths, storage batteries connected to the generator supplied the necessary power. In 1955 the first nuclear-powered sub, the U.S.S. *Nautilus*, employed a nuclear reactor to generate steam to drive propulsion turbines and turbogenerators. Since these subs don't have to surface to recharge batteries, they may remain submerged for weeks at a time.

?

How does a Xerox machine make copies instantly?

A Xerox machine seems a miraculous thing: it makes a clear, permanent copy of a document on ordinary paper in about 5 seconds and the copy is sometimes easier to read than the original. Like many modern inventions, the Xerox copier should not be possible under the classical laws of physics laid down by Isaac Newton. The machine depends for its miracle on the manipulation of particles smaller than an atom and an understanding of light that did not exist until physicists Max Planck and Albert Einstein explained it at the turn of the century. They proved that light behaves like a stream of particles, called photons.

Since then, technology has discovered the semiconductor, a substance that ordinarily does not conduct electricity but can do so under certain conditions. Electricity is a flow of electrons; in the atoms of a semiconductor, electrons are usually too tightly bound to their nuclei to flow when a current is applied to the material. But when struck by photons vibrating at a certain frequency, the substance becomes a good conductor. This happens because each photon "kicks" an electron away from its nucleus, and the electrons are then free to flow. Compounds containing silicon, selenium, arsenic, germanium, or sulfide have this property. In a Xerox machine, a cylinder coated with semiconductor material receives light, forms a pattern of conducting and nonconducting atoms, and transfers the pattern to a piece of paper to make an image.

When you place a document facedown on the glass top of a Xerox copier and press the "print" button, an aluminum cylinder beneath, coated with layers of the semiconductors selenium and arsenic selenide, begins to turn. An electrode sprays the cylinder with a temporary layer of positively charged particles that are pulled from molecules of air around the machine. Charged particles are called ions; the Xerox image is formed from a pattern of positive ions and neutral particles on the surface of the cylinder.

A light beams up through the glass and across the surface of your document, and the image reflects off the page and back down at the cylinder. The white parts of the original bounce most of the light photons striking it onto the rolling cylinder, whereas the black areas of the page *absorb* light instead and reflect no photons onto the corresponding areas of the cylinder. It is at this stage that the semiconductor coating works its magic. Wherever a vibrating photon reflects off the page and strikes a semiconductor atom on the cylinder, that atom conducts electricity by "kicking" an electron in the atom away from its nucleus. (Electrons have a negative charge; bear in mind that opposite electrical charges attract each other, and like charges repel.) Once away from its nucleus, each negatively charged electron is attracted to the layer of sprayed-on positive ions outside the semiconductor layer of the cylinder; the electron combines with one ion and neutralizes it. (An electric current applied to the aluminum inside the cylinder replaces the electrons "kicked" from the semiconductor atoms.) Where the original page is white, the photons thus create an electrically neutral zone on the cylinder; the black areas of the page leave their corresponding unexposed regions positively

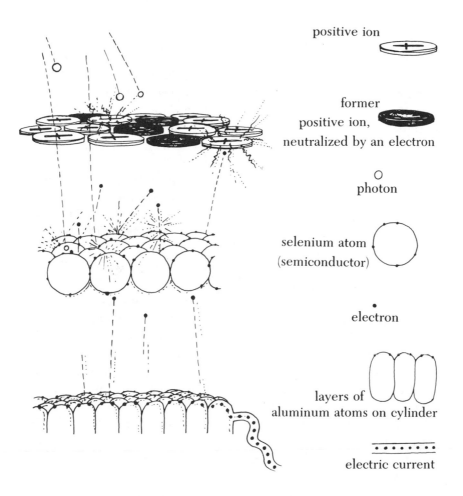

positive ion

former
positive ion,
neutralized by an electron

photon

selenium atom
(semiconductor)

electron

layers of
aluminum atoms on cylinder

electric current

*In a Xerox machine, photons (light particles) strike the cylinder
(whose surface is represented here in cross section) and "kick" electrons away from the layer of semiconducting selenium atoms (center
layer). Those electrons, which are negatively charged, are attracted to
the layer of positive ions above. Each electron combines with one ion,
creating a neutral—uncharged—particle (black disks). The aluminum
layer below feeds new electrons to the selenium atoms to stabilize
them wherever electrons have been kicked away. The positive ions
that remain on the cylinder after exposure (white disks) will attract
negatively charged black toner and transfer it to the paper in the printing process. The neutral zones (black disks) will attract no toner and
leave white areas on the copy.*

charged, where no electrons flowed from the semiconductor to neutralize the positive ions.

The black pigment or toner in a Xerox copy—it's not ink—is made of tiny black spheres less than a millionth of an inch in diameter, called BBs by Xerox scientists. These BBs have a strong negative charge; while they are stored waiting to be used, they adhere to larger "carrier" BBs, which are positively charged. The purpose of the carrier BBs is simply to transfer toner from the reservoir to the image. After the image is flashed onto the surface of the cylinder, the cylinder turns until it pushes against the supply of toner. The positive charge of the unexposed areas of the cylinder is much stronger than the charge of the large BBs, so the small negative BBs are more strongly attracted and hop off onto the positive regions of the cylinder.

Now the image formed in tiny BBs of toner, which adhere wherever the original document was black, is ready to print. Another quarter-turn of the cylinder brings it to a sheet of paper that has been given an even more powerful positive charge than the cylinder's. The BBs hop off as they touch the paper. Then the paper is heated and pressed to melt the toner into its surface, and a finished copy finally emerges from the machine—still hot and full of static electricity, but hard to distinguish from the original within a few minutes.

Meanwhile, the cylinder moves past a cleaning brush, which takes any remaining toner off its surface, and then is blasted with light to erase the old image and make the surface ready for the next copy.

?

How do they effect artificial insemination?

Artificial insemination has been popular among cattle breeders for more than fifty years, for it enables a champion bull to sire 50,000 prize offspring in one year. Although this is not exactly the goal among human beings, artificial insemination has been used with increasing frequency since 1953 for a variety of reasons. The ability to freeze sperm almost indefinitely has allowed men to store sperm before undergoing a vasectomy, for example, or to preserve it in the case of possible radiation hazard. For oligospermic men—men with a low sperm count, less than 20 million per cubic centimeter—multiple ejaculates may be collected and stored. Through artificial insemination a woman can become pregnant by her husband when he is very old, or even after his death. And, of course, women with sterile mates can bear children through artificial insemination with another man's sperm.

Some doctors believe fresh sperm to be more effective than frozen, which inevitably lose some motility in the freezing process. Artificial insemination with fresh sperm may be done by an obstetrician or gynecologist in his office, for the process (which should be as painless as a Pap smear) consists simply of inserting semen into the cervix two or three times during one ovulation cycle. One way to do this is to "cap" the cervix with a cervical cap (resembling a diaphragm) that is filled with sperm. In another method the doctor uses a pipette, or little tube, to suck sperm up, then blow it into the uterine canal. Some gynecologists prefer to attach a syringe to the pipette in order to propel the sperm; the effect, however, is the same. By another method, known as high insemination, a plastic tube is placed high up in the canal, near the entrance to the uterus. A syringe attached to the other end of the tubing pushes sperm into the womb. In rare instances, such as when a woman has prolonged difficulties in becoming pregnant, the gynecologist fills the entire vagina with a Fertilopak. This is a tampon, or sort of plug, filled with sperm, which presses against the vaginal wall. Although conception may occur after only one or two inseminations, it is usually necessary to continue them through at least three menstrual cycles.

Using frozen sperm requires triumphing over hazards such as ice crystal formation, dehydration, and increased salt concentration. The key factor is finding the proper protective solution that will support and preserve the sperm. Glycerol is mixed with semen and suspended in liquid nitrogen at a temperature of -196.5 degrees Centigrade. Recently, a seemingly obvious natural material has proved to be another excellent protective agent: egg yolks. Semen mixed with an egg yolk–glycerol citrate solution is sealed in glass ampuls or plastic straws and frozen in liquid nitrogen. Whenever sperm is needed, the solution is allowed to thaw simply by letting it stand at room temperature for about 30 minutes—whereupon the physician uses the same technique he would employ when using fresh sperm. One advantage to frozen sperm derives from the ability to use sperm from the same donor if a woman with an infertile husband wishes to have children several years apart.

?

How do they select donors at a sperm bank?

In the late 1950's and throughout the 1960's, new knowledge was acquired and new methods developed for the storage and preservation of human sperm. (See "How do they effect artificial insemination?" page 66.) The 1970's saw the natural consequence: the advent of sperm banks and sperm as a salable commodity. Today there are nearly a dozen sperm banks scattered across the country, and the market for sperm is expanding.

Donating semen at a sperm bank might seem like a quick, even pleasant, way to pick up some extra cash, however, most men are not eligible to do so. At the Idant Clinic in New York, initial screening consists of examination of a sperm specimen, and about 80 percent of the candidates are immediately eliminated on that basis alone, as their sperm count is simply not high enough to justify storage. When sperm is stored in a bank, it is chilled rapidly to -196.5 degrees Centigrade and maintained in cylinders of liquid nitrogen until required for use. Since a certain percentage of sperm inevitably dies from the trauma of this freezing process, it is essential to start with an exceptionally healthy specimen. The average American male has a sperm count of 50 to 60 million per cubic centimeter, but Idant accepts no one with a count below 100 to 110 million per cubic centimeter. The clinic counts sperm three times on a modified electronic Coulter counter, a sophisticated machine (also used in hospitals to count red and white blood cells) that counts sperm automatically. Less than a drop of semen is required for the count, thereby preventing needless waste. Technicians then magnify and televise the sperm on a monitor to check for normal or abnormal shapes. Another reason for rejection is insufficient motility: anything less than 65 to 70 percent is inadequate, for motility, too, is reduced somewhat by freezing. If a candidate's specimen does meet the initial requirements, it is frozen and quickly thawed to make sure that 75 percent of the spermatozoa survive the process unchanged.

Next the candidate is required to fill out lengthy questionnaires about his medical and genetic history and undergoes a complete physical examination. He is interviewed and a complete profile is drawn up, including his vocation, hobbies, religion, ethnic background, height, blood type, and so on. While denying that their views are in any way racist, the Idant Clinic holds that many of the elements of the profile are actually hereditary factors. Great care is taken to establish similarities between the donor and the husband, because 99.9 percent of the couples who have children by artificial insemination never tell the child that the husband is not in fact the biological father. (It is interesting to note that about 10 percent of women now pregnant by artificial insemination are not married and live alone.)

Because of touchy emotional and legal questions, a contract is drawn up between each donor and the sperm bank which ensures absolute anonymity. A donor may never know whether his sperm has been used successfully, and he will certainly never learn the identity of the mother, where she lives, or how many children she has had by him. Conversely, the mother can never discover the identity of the donor.

Once accepted by the sperm bank, a donor may submit sperm quite frequently. He must, however, abstain from sex for three days between specimen donations, because after ejaculation sperm count decreases. Each specimen is analyzed on culture plates for traces of contamination or venereal disease, and the donor is paid ($20 per specimen) if the ejaculate proves acceptable.

?

How do they know what the speed of light is?

The velocity of light and how to go about measuring it evaded Galileo in the early part of the seventeenth century when, after experimenting with lanterns, all he could deduce was that light goes *fast*. The problem with his efforts was that light travels far too rapidly for its speed to be detected over the small distances with which he was experimenting. It took a study of light coming all the way from Jupiter for astronomers to solve the mystery.

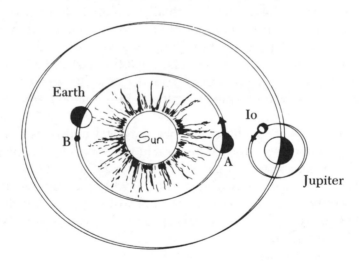

Seventeenth-century astronomers observed that Jupiter's moon Io emerged from the planet's shadow progressively later than predicted. As Earth moved in its orbit from Point A to Point B, it was farther and farther from Io, whose light therefore took longer to reach Earth. From calculations of the difference between predicted and actual times of Io's eclipse, and knowledge of the movements and distances of the planets, astronomers were able to determine the speed of light.

In the mid-seventeenth century, astronomers at the Paris Observatory were studying the revolution periods of the moons by Jupiter. By observing when the innermost satellite, Io, disappeared behind Jupiter, was eclipsed, reappeared on the other side, and passed across Jupiter to disappear again, they calculated that it took Io 1.75 days (1 day and 18 hours) to complete a revolution. Thereafter, they should have been able to predict precisely when Io would be eclipsed. But a perplexing problem arose. The first observations were made when Earth was between Jupiter and the sun—that is, when Jupiter and the sun were in opposition. As Earth moved around the sun and thus farther away from Jupiter, the eclipses of Io occurred minutes later than the predicted times. When Earth had revolved to the opposite side of the sun from which observations were first made—that is, when the sun lay between Earth and Jupiter—the eclipses of Io were 16⅔ minutes late.

In 1675 Ole Römer, a Danish astronomer, came to the rescue of the baffled French. He realized that the delay in eclipses was not a result of any inherent change in either Jupiter or Io, but rather in the amount of time it was taking Io's reflected light to travel to Earth. He knew that the delay in the eclipses was 16 minutes 40 seconds, or 1,000 seconds, and he knew (from the findings of astronomers at Paris and at the French colony of Cayenne in French Guiana in 1672) the distance from Earth to the sun to be 93 million miles. Since Earth was now 186 million miles (the diameter of Earth's orbit around the sun) farther away from Io than when the first observations were made, Römer arrived at the momentous conclusion that light travels at 186,000 miles per second.

?

How do they know how hot the sun is?

Although the sun is 93 million miles away, we can tell what the temperature is on its surface because we can measure the

71

frequencies of the light waves it sends us. Things at high temperatures generate a lot of light of very high frequency (or short wavelength); the frequencies sent out by the sun are the "signature" of an object at about 11,000 degrees Fahrenheit.

Light consists of the regular motion of magnetic fields caused by the vibration of the negatively charged electrons in a substance such as the sun—or, for that matter, a light bulb or a chair. The electrons vibrate because they are being excited by heat; to say that something is hot means that its molecules are colliding very frequently. The hotter the object, the faster its electrons are forced to vibrate by the collisions of the molecules containing them. The magnetic fields made by the electrons move back and forth very frequently, producing a large number of wave fluctuations in each second (cycles per second or cps). The hotter the object, the higher the peak frequency of the energy it emits. Since light always travels at the same speed of 186,000 miles per second, the higher the frequency, the shorter the wave.

You can see the relation between heat and light frequency in everyday life: a poker left in a fire turns from black to dull red to bright orange as it heats up; the fire itself is even hotter and makes a higher-frequency "yellow" light. Burning stove gas is hotter still, giving off a peak of "blue" light from the high-frequency end of the visible spectrum.

The solar temperature is estimated by comparing the light given off by flames on Earth with the light of the sun. Sending light through a glass prism makes a long band or spectrum of light that looks different depending on the elements in the sample and their temperature: hydrogen, helium, and traces of other elements at a man-made 11,000 degrees Fahrenheit make the same spectral pattern as sunlight. Thus have we concluded that that is the composition and temperature of the sun.

The latest and best estimates of the sun's surface temperature have come from spectral readings taken by satellites and spacecraft, which can measure the sun's energy output from above the atmosphere, avoiding any confusion caused by the atmosphere's filtering effect. Gases in the atmosphere absorb many of the lower and higher frequencies before they reach us on Earth; this is fortunate for us, since life probably could not have developed if it were constantly subjected to a deadly fusillade of cosmic, X, and gamma rays.

It is no coincidence that the sun's peak frequency—the frequency at which something sends out the *most* energy—is the span of wavelengths we call visible light. Human eyes evolved under the light of the sun, and the most efficient way to collect the most information about the world is to "see" as much energy as possible bounding off it. The most direct way for an evolving organism to do this is to develop a sensitivity to the most abundant frequency.

?

How do they generate electricity?

A simple combination of motion and magnetism underlies the creation of electricity by turbine generators. In the mid-nineteenth century scientists found that an electric conductor passed near a magnet and through its magnetic field picks up an electric current. In generators today, the magnet is a huge electromagnet bolted to the shaft of a turbine. As the turbine rotates, the electromagnet and its magnetic field also spin, sending an electrical current into several miles of copper wire wound inside a shell surrounding the magnetic field. The current is then conducted from the wires by cables.

A variety of fuels and methods may be used to turn the fanlike metal blades, or vanes, of the turbine. Some plants burn oil, gas, or coal to boil water into steam, which is heated to 1,000 degrees Fahrenheit and to pressures of 2,400 pounds per square inch. This extremely hot steam pushes against the turbine vanes, causing them to turn rapidly. In gas turbines a distillate fuel, similar to diesel oil, or occasionally natural gas is used. The fuel is burned and thrust out of a combustion engine as a hot, expanded gas, which turns the turbine and then passes out through exhaust stacks into the air. If the generator is near a river, falling water can spin the turbine. Other natural sources of power include wind, tides, and rays from the sun.

In nuclear plants, steam pushes the turbine vanes, but the source of heat for the steam is entirely different from that in a conventional plant. A nuclear reactor vessel is composed of thousands of tubes that contain uranium, or some other fissionable material. Control rods, which can regulate the amount of fission, are inserted into this fuel core to start up the operation: neutrons from uranium atoms are set in motion, the uranium atoms split, and in the resulting chain reaction the uranium neutrons split other atoms, releasing neutrons that split millions of other atoms, and so on. The amount of heat produced in this fashion to fuel the generator is, of course, tremendous.

?

How does a Contac time-release capsule know when to release?

In the late 1940's Don MacDonnell of Smith Kline & French, a pharmaceutical company, went into his local grocery store and lighted upon a jar of "petites"—tiny candy beads used for decorating pastry. Scientists at the time were searching for a form of medication that would release slowly, and the candy provided MacDonnell with a clue.

Several years of research and testing resulted in the manufacture of "the capsules that think"—capsules containing some 300 to 900 "tiny time pills" which dissolve in the system gradually, freeing the user from having to take additional doses every 3 or 4 hours. The "Spansule" capsule of Smith Kline & French, used for a variety of medicines including Contac, is designed to dissolve evenly and slowly with no "peaks," "valleys," or "fade-outs." But how do the tiny pills or pellets inside "know" when to go to work?

Each pellet consists of a central core of sugar and starch, known as a starting core. Millions of the cores are placed in a large drum that resembles a cement mixer. As the drum rotates, medication is added as a powder or solution and distributed evenly over the cores. They are then coated with digestible dyes for identification—not of the individual pellets, but of the product as a whole. Finally, an outer waxy coating is applied in the same manner as the medication. Pellets in different pans receive different amounts of coating, so that some will release almost immediately, others more slowly, as the digestive system wears off the waxy coating.

Of the 600 tiny pellets in one Contac Spansule, some go to work about 30 minutes after ingestion. The pellets are not designed to release, say, all the antihistamines first, then all the decongestants, and so on, but rather to distribute medications evenly over a 12-hour period.

?

How do they tell whose shirt is whose at a laundry?

When you drop off two or three shirts at a laundry, they generally go into a machine with at least a dozen others. To keep track of whose shirt belongs to whom, laundry workers actually write on each shirt—sometimes you can see it, sometimes you can't.

One method of differentiating shirts involves writing a series of numbers or letters in indelible ink on the inside of the collar. A customer may retain the same number from one laundry service to the next.

The other widely used method of keeping track of a shirt's identity is known in the business as "phantom marking." Three or four numbers or letters are written on the inside of the collar in a special ink that can be seen only under ultraviolet light. Before each shirt is washed, the number (which also appears on the ticket with which you retrieve the clean clothes) is marked on the collar. Although some laundries then wash the shirts in net bags, this is generally done to protect the garment rather than to separate it from others. After the laundry is dry, a worker passes the shirts under ultraviolet light, sorts, and packages them—the entire process often occurring in plants outside the laundry where you leave the shirts.

?

How do they build a subway under a city?

The first step is to chart the subway precisely, taking note of all underground utilities, existing subways, foundations, and soil and rock conditions. If the route happens to coincide with the path of a street, or if it lies beneath clear areas above ground, a "cut-and-cover" method of digging trenches at the surface several blocks at a time may be used. If, on the other hand, the surface is occupied by buildings, plowing through them for the sake of constructing an underground tunnel may not be the wisest approach. When the streets and buildings of a bustling city cannot be disturbed, subways are made by digging very deep shafts from which the tunnels are bored.

If the cut-and-cover method is possible, the construction crew marks out on the street the exact dimensions of the trench and inserts heavy vertical members on each side of the street. Steel beams are placed to span the vertical members. The crew then proceeds to dig along the designated path of the tunnel. Twelve-inch-thick wooden beams or steel plates are placed across the street to provide a temporary road and a platform from which to lower material into the trench. It is essential to divert all utilities with temporary pipes and ducts, or to support them as the digging progresses with horizontal beams, or shoring. Any water seeping into the trench is channeled into sewers. The floor of the tunnel is constructed first, then the sides, with the aid of supporting rods. Electrical cables for power, signals, and emergency systems are pulled through ducts in the wall to vaults sited every few hundred feet along the tunnel. When the formwork for floor and walls has been erected, the crew pours concrete through long funnels and constructs the ceiling. The tunnel structure thus complete, tracks and lighting are installed and the outside of the tunnel coated with waterproofing. The crew then fills the trench to street level with compacted gravel and soil.

If a deeper tunnel is required, or if the route of the tunnel passes under city buildings, the second method of construction is

76

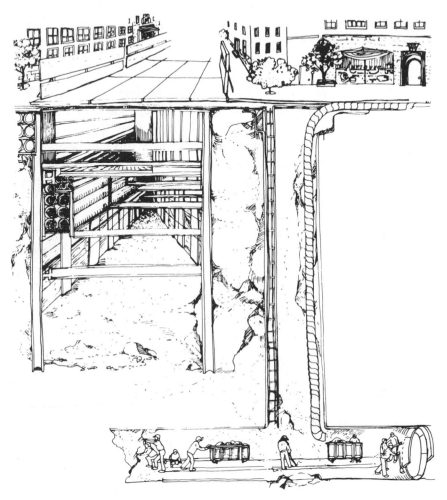

On the left, a subway is being built by the cut-and-cover method. As the route of the subway coincides with the path of the street, trenches have been dug along the street several blocks at a time and then covered while construction continues. On the right, men dig a deeper subway by the tunnel method of boring through the earth and hoisting rock and soil up the shaft.

used. Deep vertical shafts are dug at regular intervals along the charted path of the subway. Steel lining supports the shafts to prevent mud slides and collapse. It is through these shafts that the "muck" (soil and rock) from digging is removed and fresh air pumped in through ventilator pipes.

Deep down in the earth, workers bore away with high-powered drills and boring machines. When they face hard clay or solid rock, they drill small holes into which they insert explosives. The ensuing rubble is carried away in carts. The sides of the hole (slightly larger than the size of the finished tunnel) are covered with a steel tube called a shield. (In solid rock this shield may not be necessary.) Segments of the shield are lowered down the shaft and erected a piece at a time; jacks are used to advance the pieces through the earth. The segment at the top and front of the advancing tunnel always protrudes somewhat to obstruct any rock and soil that might fall. An inner face for the shield is then constructed out of cast iron or precast concrete. Crews can work simultaneously in different shafts, since precise measurements have of course been made in advance so that the tunnels will meet.

Ground containing a great deal of water presents another set of problems. The air pressure at the face of the tunnel must be increased considerably to prevent water from rushing in. This involves construction of two parallel concrete walls within the tunnel; high pressure is maintained between one wall and the face of the tunnel. Between the two walls is a compression chamber, where the workers must remain for a while to adjust when passing back and forth between the normal and high-pressure areas. Steel doors with air locks are constructed in the walls to permit passage without loss of pressure.

After completing the tunnel, the workers construct tracks and string cables along its cylindrical sides. The original construction shafts may be left in place to be used for stairways and elevator shafts, and through which to install ventilating fans to propel fresh air into the tunnel.

?

How does the IRS decide which taxpayers to audit?

Visions of auditors and interminable interrogations may rattle your nerves as you mail in your tax return each year, wondering whether an inscrutable Big Brother will select you as the lucky host to an IRS agent. There is no surefire answer to the question of who will be audited, but you can be aware of some factors that are likely to increase your "audit potential." For when a return comes in and is keypunched and checked for mathematical accuracy, if all is correct and a refund is due, a check is mailed out to you. But, though you may sigh with relief and proceed to spend the money, you remain liable for an audit for a full three years.

The IRS feeds all returns into a computer, which assigns them a score based on a scientifically measured system known as discriminant function (DIF). Your return is compared with a complicated set of standards, arrived at partially by deductions claimed by others in your income bracket. An average profile is established, and if your return varies drastically, it is flagged by the computer. The higher the DIF score, the higher the potential for audit. Furthermore, the higher your income and deductions, the greater your chances of a high DIF score—because there are fewer taxpayers at progressively higher income levels, the likelihood of varying from the standard is greater. Of the 85.6 million returns filed in 1976, 1.7 million were examined, and among those only 3.45 percent were in the $10,000-and-under adjusted gross income bracket (total income minus deductions), whereas 11.35 percent were drawn from the $50,000-and-over bracket—and only .7 percent of all taxpayers that year reported a gross adjusted income of more than $50,000.

The IRS wishes to find those returns with the greatest probability of "change" in tax liability, for if no change occurs there is little purpose to the audit. Over the past several years 70 percent of all those audited had to pay additional tax, 7 percent received a refund, and 23 percent of the audits resulted in no change.

If your return comes out of the computer with a high DIF score, an agent reviews the return to determine whether or not it has "audit potential" and is worth pursuing. Does the refund seem high in relation to your income and exemptions? Are your deductions appropriate? Most audits of individual taxpayers result from the need to verify high deductions, such as for charitable contributions, travel expenses, and medical bills. In scanning your return, an agent considers whether or not you might be moonlighting and failing to report a certain income, or receiving money in interest and dividends that fails to correspond to what you are claiming, and whether or not it seems feasible for you to support yourself (and a family if you have one) on the reported income. If you own a business, the agent investigates the gross profit ratio and also checks whether a standard deduction was taken with a large gross income and low net. Frequently, a letter is simply mailed to you requesting verification, but if further information is necessary, an agent pursues the audit, examining the relevant parts of your tax return—not necessarily the entire return.

Even if you are scrupulous about your deductions and careful to report all income—honest from start to finish—the IRS may not leave you in peace. There is another system by which you may be selected *at random* for thorough examination. The Taxpayers' Compliance Measurement Program (TCMP) is a relatively new services enforcement and research program which measures taxpayers' compliance with tax law. Returns are chosen at random, all of which are examined. But because these audits are extremely intense and take a considerable amount of time, samples are taken only about every three years. Of the 85.6 million individuals who filed returns in 1976, 50,000 were selected for audit by TCMP, and only 22,500 passed—that is, got away with "no change." Individuals and corporations alike are measured by TCMP, and pertinent information is used to update and improve the DIF system.

?

How do they teach dogs to sniff out drugs at borders, bombs at airports?

Hiding your marijuana in an unlikely cranny of your car or wrapping it in clothes doused with perfume won't fool a dog properly trained in narcotics detection. Although training begins as a simple exercise in retrieving, an intelligent, hardworking dog can learn to uncover up to three different kinds of drugs—even when the scent it smells is 90 percent detractor and only 10 percent narcotics.

The Army and the Air Force actually maintain schools for training dogs to sniff out drugs or bombs. More than olfactory acuity is required in a dog trained for such purposes—it must be willing to retrieve repeatedly without losing interest. German shepherds and, occasionally, Labrador retrievers are used. The dog must be taught to discern a particular scent and to alter its behavior when it does so. In the presence of bombs, for example, the dog may be instructed to sit or lie down upon discovering the scent; it could of course be disastrous if the dog tried to ferret out explosives.

If all runs smoothly, initial training in marijuana detection takes approximately ten weeks. Necessary equipment includes about a half kilo of marijuana, a harness, and a 25-foot line. (Early attempts at teaching dogs to find heroin failed utterly, for during the training process the dogs became addicted by sniffing the stuff and eventually died. More recently laboratories have been able to divide heroin into individual components and manufacture a material bearing the scent of heroin whose formula is highly classified.) The first step is to get the dog interested in an ounce of marijuana, placed in a small plastic bag and wrapped sufficiently to protect it from the dog's teeth. At one point the Army used gauze around the marijuana to soak up saliva—but suddenly discovered that the dogs were being trained to sniff out bandages rather than dope! If the dog naturally likes to retrieve, the training process is easier. Much as in training a dog to retrieve, say, a stick, the handler tosses the bag about 10 feet and encourages the dog to bring it back, with praise and rewards for successful completion of the retrieve.

Later, the handler asks the dog to stay while he hides the bag at a particular distance, so that the dog must depend on its nose—not its eyes—to find the bag. After about a month of such work, the dog may be ready to find the bag in luggage and packages. At first there may be only two from which to choose; later, more may be added. Then the handler hides the bag in a car or a building, the complexity of places increasing only as long as the dog succeeds. After two months the handler begins to disguise the marijuana with nearby articles smelling of perfume, formaldehyde, or some other scent frequently used by dope smugglers. The percentage of scent of the detractor in relation to that of the marijuana may be increased gradually. The handler can then cross-train the dog to find other types of narcotics or to discern black powder, sulfur, and other materials used in making bombs.

?

How does truth serum work?

The plain fact is it doesn't—at least not well or consistently enough to be accepted by our legal system as a reliable means of extracting the truth from unwilling subjects. Most courts of law do not admit information produced by drug analysis as legal evidence.

The catchy phrase *truth serum* appears to have lodged in the public imagination many years ago; and, like *lie detector*, it seems to have been taken at face value. It was coined in the early 1920's, when an American anesthesiologist named T. S. House popularized a new anesthetic called scopolamine with the graphic term *truth serum*. House claimed that his drug could induce patients to tell the truth, whether they wanted to or not, as they emerged from unconsciousness, and in those less sophisticated times— abetted by a sensational Alabama murder trial, in which a gang of men confessed to an ax killing under the influence of scopolamine—the legend of "truth serum" was fixed.

That legend was never medically justified. Neither scopolamine nor its successor "truth drugs," most psychiatrists agree, are any more reliable or effective than alcohol in drawing out the truth. A Yale University study concluded that "suspects who would not ordinarily confess under skillful interrogation without drugs are just as likely to continue the deception while under the influence of drugs." The authors added that moral masochists—persons with strong self-punitive tendencies—may confess to crimes never committed. And character neurotics may invent elaborate lies or continue earlier patterns of lies.

Today, most drugs used as "truth serums" are the barbiturates sodium amytal and sodium pentothal, administered by intravenous injection. Both depress higher brain functions such as counting and reasoning. By mechanisms still not understood, a patient may become more talkative and more open and less afraid while under the influence of these drugs. Psychiatrists have found that this tendency may relieve some symptoms of mental "blockage," such as muteness or hysterical amnesia.

But much the same effect can be gained by a potion known since the time of Pliny the Elder: *in vino veritas*—"in wine lies truth." The multisyllable truth drugs of today, ballyhoo notwithstanding, produce no better results than a simple dose of booze.

?

How do they get the stripes onto Stripe toothpaste?

Although it's intriguing to imagine the peppermint stripes neatly wound inside the tube, actually the stripes don't go onto the paste until it's on its way out. A small hollow tube, with slots running lengthwise, extends from the neck of the toothpaste tube back into the interior a short distance. When the toothpaste tube is filled, red paste—the striping material—is inserted first, thus filling the conical area around the hollow tube at the front. (It must

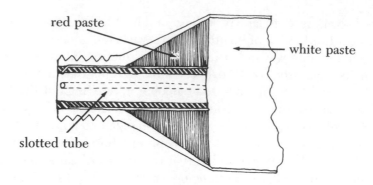

red paste

white paste

slotted tube

not, however, reach beyond the point to which the hollow tube extends into the toothpaste tube.) The remainder of the dispenser is filled with the familiar old white stuff. When you squeeze the toothpaste tube, pressure is applied to the white paste, which in turn presses on the red paste at the head of the tube. The red then passes through the slots and onto the white, which is moving through the inserted tube—and which emerges with five red stripes.

Stripe
TOOTHPASTE
FIGHTS CAVITIES
WITH FLOURIDE

?

How do they predict solar eclipses?

"The day was turned to night" reads an inscription on a Babylonian tablet, describing the total eclipse of the sun of July

31, 1062 B.C. Eclipses were momentous and terrifying events in ancient times; the Babylonians took them to be signs from the gods. They are less mysterious to us in the twentieth century, now that we understand our solar system better and can even predict when an eclipse will occur. Nevertheless, a total solar eclipse is still a startling event: the black circle of the moon slides in front of the sun and seems to swallow up its light, although the fiery corona of the sun still burns around its edges like a halo. The earth becomes unnaturally dark and quiet for several minutes as people, birds, and animals look up in puzzlement or fear at this strange interruption of their light and warmth.

When the moon, as it orbits Earth, passes between Earth and the sun, it totally obstructs some region's view of the sun, somewhere in the world. This phenomenon doesn't happen every time the moon orbits Earth (every month) as one might expect, because the moon's orbit of Earth is tilted in a different plane from Earth's orbit of the sun. The orbits cross only once every six months in what are called the eclipse seasons. Each eclipse season is a month long, during which time an eclipse occurs somewhere on the earth when the moon lines up between an observer and the sun. For an eclipse to be total, with the sun completely blocked, two more conditions must be fulfilled:

1. The moon must be in that part of its elliptical orbit where it passes close enough to Earth that it appears to obscure the sun completely—even though the sun is really much larger. When the moon is not sufficiently close, an annular eclipse results (*annulus* is Latin for "ring"), with the yellow perimeter of the sun showing clearly around the shadow, instead of just the thin, ghostly corona of the total eclipse.

2. The other criterion for a total eclipse is that the moon's shadow pass across the center of the sun; partial eclipses result in geographical regions where all of the sun is not covered and the moon seems only to be taking a bite out of it. Since the moon is so much smaller than the sun, eclipses affect only certain areas of the world at a time. A total eclipse happens somewhere on the earth only every 2 or 3 years. A given spot can experience a total eclipse only once every 360 years.

How can anyone tell this? Stargazing is probably the oldest scientific pursuit. In the process of observing the points of light in the heavens—how they seemed to move in relation to one another—man has come up with many different explanations for the system that would produce what he sees. Four thousand years ago the people of Stonehenge used their boulders as an immense astronomical timer, telling the seasons by the positions of stars sighted along different rocks; some scientists think the stones were used to predict eclipses. Ancient Chinese civilizations were certainly able to predict them, without necessarily understanding them.

From the earth, the stars seem fixed relative to each other, whereas the planets are independent, moving at different speeds, seeming to double back on themselves as they traverse the sky, forming looped trajectories over the course of a few months. (*Planets* is from the Greek word *planetes,* or "wanderers.") Until the sixteenth century, mankind assumed that Earth was the center of the universe; then the Polish churchman Nicolaus Copernicus came up with the simplest explanation for what he saw. Since Copernicus's model fits in with other knowledge we have acquired since his time, we accept it as fact: the moon indeed orbits Earth, and the planets all orbit the sun. (We have refined his model over the centuries, so that it better suits our purpose of understanding and predicting astronomical events.)

Now, the calculation of eclipses for American scientists is carried on with computers in the U.S. Naval Observatory in Washington, D.C. Into those computers is fed the latest information gleaned from instruments planted on the surface of the moon by the Apollo astronauts; we know better than anyone in history the shape of the moon and its distance from us at different times. Identifying which lunar mountains and valleys will lie along the perimeter of the moon at the time of an eclipse tells us the shape of the shadow it will cast—and therefore who will see the eclipse and when. The technology of prediction is still being refined; we are even now as much as 5 miles off at predicting the "edge of totality"—the borderlines of the areas on the earth where the eclipse is total—but our timing of the period of totality is now correct to within a second or two. Considering the sizes of the bodies involved, such accuracy is impressive.

The last total eclipse in the United States was on February 26, 1979, along an arc-shaped swath of territory in the Northwest extending into Canada. The next will be in Alaska in 1990, and in Hawaii in 1991. An annular eclipse will take place in the southeastern United States in 1984.

Why, finally, do scientists bother to keep such careful track of eclipses? It would probably make us nervous if they didn't, but there are also many practical reasons: to find out more about the sun, the stars, the climate on the earth, and even energy production. During total eclipses, and only then, we can observe and photograph the solar corona. The corona is the faint outer region of the sun. Its light is too weak to be seen during the day, since the blue of the sky itself is much brighter; and at night, obviously, the sun is obscured from us by the earth. But during a total eclipse, the lunar shadow covers the main light-generating area of the sun, so its rays do not scatter off the air molecules in front of us to make a bright blue sky. Instead, the sky is dark, and the glowing gases of the corona appear around the edge of the moon. Sunspots—"weather" on the surface of the sun—seem to have an effect on weather on the earth, and we can watch those tempests raging in the corona better when the full blaze of the sun does not overload our instruments. Our observation of the gases of the sun's corona is helping our efforts to make energy from a new source, which does not begin in Arabian oil wells or leave vast quantities of deadly radioactive waste behind: atomic fusion. In fusion, energy is released when two atoms are joined. It is cleaner and more powerful than conventional nuclear power, which is based on fission or the splitting of atoms.

Fusion occurs only under incredibly high temperatures such as those on the sun (11,000 degrees Fahrenheit and hotter), where gases are compressed by the attraction of the sun's powerful magnetic field. Scientists in the United States and the Soviet Union are trying to make fusion occur by compressing gases in a man-made magnetic field inside a huge, doughnut-shaped reactor called a tokamak. During total eclipses, energy researchers analyze the corona to understand better how gases behave under extreme pressure, to improve the design of fusion reactors.

?

How do they time stoplights to keep traffic moving?

Although one sometimes wonders whether downtown traffic moves at all, the traffic lights are timed to help clear congestion and keep the arteries moving at a regular pace. When plotting the timing of lights in a certain area, a traffic control department has to consider how fast the traffic should move, the length of the blocks, whether the street is one- or two-way, and also the volume of traffic. The stoplights in New York City are generally gauged for traffic moving at 23 to 30 miles per hour. If a light on a main avenue turns green at 40th Street, the one at 41st Street will change 6 seconds later, and that at 42nd Street 6 seconds after that. This progressive system works quite effectively on one-way streets, but would obviously cause complications if traffic were coming the other way. On two-way streets a group of signals—say, four at a time—all change at once. This number naturally depends on the distribution of stoplights and the length of the blocks.

The signals in New York are based on a 90-second cycle, staying green for 60 seconds on main streets, 30 seconds on side streets. Many communities also vary the cycle according to the time of day and the preponderant direction of travel.

?

How do they turn on street lights automatically?

The magic lies in a little metal box with a glass top perched high up on the pole of one light in a given area. Inside is a highly sensitive photoelectric cell which reacts to the absence of light. When it gets dark, the cell automatically closes the circuits, allowing electricity to run through and turn on the particular series of lights. With the first light of dawn, the "eye" opens the circuits, causing the lights to go off. The amount of light or absence of light necessary to stimulate the cell can be varied from one device to another in order to accommodate varying conditions in different areas; some streets receive direct light from the sun, for example, whereas others are shrouded by the tall buildings or trees.

?

How do they count populations of animals?

Humans are the only beasts who use telephones or permanent addresses, or fill out census forms. How are the other animals counted? How can anyone tell that the timber wolf and the California condor are rare and "endangered"? How do we know how many robins chirp every spring? The task of taking a census of wild animals is one of the most difficult in biology.

The methods of enumeration scientists use vary with the species; its size, behavior, and habitat make certain ways more practical than others. The best way to count ducks, whistling swans, elephants, antelope, caribou, and timber wolves is to fly over them in a helicopter or bush plane and count them one by one, taking photographs to verify the number. This is obviously not a good method for counting field mice; they are too small to be seen from the air, are too well camouflaged by the color of their fur, and spend too much time in their burrows. The only way to determine the number of mice living in a field is by "saturation trapping"—catching every single mouse until no more are left and counting them.

Lizards are counted by the "capture, recapture" method. To find the population in a certain area, a herpetologist (one who studies reptiles and amphibians) might catch 50 lizards, mark them all with a harmless paint or metal tag, and set them free again. After a few weeks, the marked lizards have dispersed back into the general population. The scientist then captures another 50 lizards and finds that some of this batch are creatures he marked in his first catch, and some are unmarked—meaning they were *not* in the first batch. The herpetologist's next step is to make assumptions for the purpose of his census. He assumes that the new batch of 50 marked and unmarked lizards is a representative sample—a microcosm—of the population as a whole. He assumes that after he marked the first 50 lizards and released them, they distributed themselves at random throughout the population. Thus, when he catches the second 50 and finds that he earlier marked, say, 10 of them—or 20 percent—he assumes that 20 percent of the *entire lizard population* is marked. He knows that he originally marked 50 lizards; concluding from the second sample that 20 percent were marked, he assumes that 50 is 20 percent of the total population. Since $5 \times 20\% = 100\%$, 5 times 50 lizards is the whole population: 250 lizards.

Fish are counted a similar way. Experimenters put a knockout solution in the water, which does the fish no permanent harm but makes them float to the surface belly-up. They then collect the fish, count them, mark them with dye or tags, and revive and release them. The same number are later recaptured, the marked ones counted, and the total figured as for lizards.

How about animals that are harder to grab, such as songbirds? Ornithologists often use a grid system in a wooded area to get an approximate number. They mark evenly spaced, parallel straight trails through the region that interests them. People carrying pads and pens walk down the trails in a phalanx, each member keeping another in sight to the left and right, counting every bird they see or hear. Each member only counts birds observed a certain distance to either side of him, so that two people don't count the same bird. This ritual is performed several times and the results averaged.

How does one count things as small as the microscopic plankton that live in the ocean? A sample of ocean water is whipped around in a centrifuge, so that all the solids collect at one end, including the tiny plankton. This residue is slid under a microscope bit by bit and the plankton counted. That gives the plankton per unit volume of ocean water.

As you can see, different methods are needed to keep track of animals living in different niches or habitats. To get an idea of the total number of a species in an entire region or country (or planet), scientists determine the size of the habitat available to the species, instead of counting individuals, and multiply by the number of individuals that usually live in a given area of habitat. It is in the nature of living things that they fill any habitat with as many individuals as the food and space in the area will allow.

Knowing the number of acres of woodland, mountain, prairie, and city in the United States, we can arrive at a ballpark estimate of 6 billion land birds of all kinds in the country. By contrast, some water birds such as the whooping crane are not nearly so adaptable; whoopers can live only in certain areas of Texas marshland, where about 100 nest each year.

Other forms of life build on a minuscule scale and fit vast numbers of individuals into their ecological niches. Insects have adapted through evolution to live in an incredible variety of conditions. The world population of insects in their many habitats is estimated to total a *billion billion,* or 10 to the 18th power (10^{18})—the number 1 followed by 18 zeroes. That's roughly a billion times the world's human population; if the world insect population were represented by a bucketful of sand, the human population would be a single grain of sand in that bucket. More amazing still, if we look closely at the bodies of those insects, we find as many as a hundred thousand one-celled animals called protozoa living in the digestive tract of *each insect,* eating what the insect is unable to digest. There are therefore about 10^{23} of these digestive protozoa living in the world's insects. That number is greater than the number of stars in the universe.

As Jonathan Swift wrote after the invention of the microscope, which revealed for the first time the existence of protozoa, animals smaller than the naked eye could see:

> *Big fleas have little fleas*
> *Upon their backs to bite'em;*
> *And little fleas have lesser fleas,*
> *And so* ad infinitum.

?

How do they determine whether a species is endangered or extinct?

A very small mammal or insect endemic to a particular area might be considered endangered while several million are still known to be alive, but a lesser number of another species, spread out over a broad area, would not give rise to concern. Determining whether or not a species is endangered is a complex task for which no fixed criteria exist to be applied across the board. Just as the species and subspecies of animals and plants are multitudinous, so are the variables that enter into an evaluation of their status. In the small-scale example, the nature of the habitat is significant, for if the specific area were destroyed by pollution, or a natural disaster, all existing members of the species would go with it.

Just such a situation surrounds a particular subspecies of wren endemic to San Clemente Island off the coast of California. Just prior to World War II, farmers and ranchers brought goats and pigs to raise on the small island, which stretches 13 miles and is only 1 to 3 miles wide. During the war, the Navy used the island as a bombardment range to test artillery, which naturally destroyed some vegetation. In addition, the goats and pigs multiplied so rapidly and devoured so much of the grass and lower vegetation that by 1955 the wrens and several other species of birds were in desperate need of shelter. With the plants that used to provide a cover gone, the wrens became endangered—and finally extinct, for no one has seen one since 1960. Five or six species of plants are also severely threatened.

The fecundity of a species is another factor weighed in determining whether or not it is endangered: how frequently its members reproduce, what percentage of newborn members generally survive, how many offspring are produced at a time, and so on. Average life span and rate of reproduction are especially important considerations when authorities decide how long to wait after an animal's or plant's last sighting before calling it extinct.

Although a decision might be arrived at after only a year in the case of, say, fruit flies, a 50- to 60-year wait might be justified in the case of a species of condor with an average life span of 30 years.

In the United States the director of the Fish and Wildlife Service in the Department of the Interior determines which animal species to call endangered, based on the most up-to-date and thorough scientific and commercial data available. Those data come from specialized biologists, botanists, and naturalists working in the field, who submit their findings to Washington. According to the Endangered Species Act of 1973, a species can be listed if it is threatened by any of the following:

1. The present or threatened destruction, modification, or curtailment of its habitat or range;
2. Utilization for commercial, sporting, scientific, or educational purposes at levels that detrimentally affect it;
3. Disease or predation;
4. Absence of regulatory mechanisms adequate to prevent the decline of a species or degradation of its habitat; and
5. Other natural or man-made factors affecting its continued existence.

If the species does appear to be threatened, the director immediately determines the "critical habitat"—the areas inhabited by the species that contain physical or biological features essential to the conservation of the species and that may require special management programs. "Critical habitat" may also refer to areas outside those occupied by the species which the director sees as necessary for protection of the species. He focuses on preserving key elements such as feeding sites, nesting grounds, water supplies, necessary vegetation, and soil types, attempting to nourish the species to the point where it can be removed from the endangered list.

?

How do they steer balloons?

The amazing answer to this question is, simply, they don't. Control over ascent and descent is vital, and possible, but when it comes to velocity and direction, the huge balloon and its crew are utterly at the mercy of capricious winds. It is only by the *use* of these winds that a balloonist can "steer" his craft.

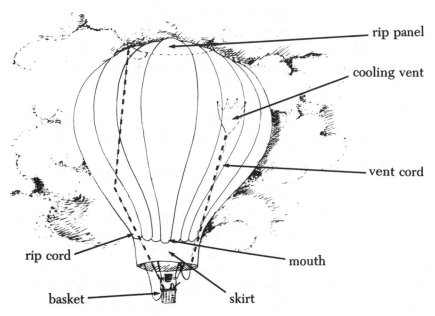

Spherical balloons may be filled with hot air or with a light gas (hydrogen, helium, or natural gas). Different operational techniques apply to the two types. When a balloonist wishes to take off in a gas balloon, he simply discharges ballast, usually in the form of sandbags. In order to descend, he releases gas from the balloon by pulling a rope that opens a small valve at the top of the balloon. Near this valve is a "rip panel," also controlled by a rope; when opened, it releases enough gas to cause the balloon to land.

Hot-air balloons are equipped with a blowtorch burner placed just below the opening at the bottom of the balloon. This burner, which supplies necessary heat, is fed by propane tanks carried in the basket. The pilot can control the rate of burning and thus the amount of ascent or descent. A cooling vent near the top of the balloon and a rip panel both enable more rapid descent.

With vertical control, then, the balloonist can try to drift at the altitude at which winds and/or air currents flow in his planned direction. Only knowledge of meteorological conditions, manipulation of altitude, and a good deal of chance can affect the course of the balloon. Nevertheless, in 1978 three Americans (Ben Abruzzo, Maxie Anderson, and Larry Newman) successfully crossed the Atlantic Ocean in a helium balloon, leaving Presque Isle, Maine, on August 11 and arriving near Paris 137 hours and 6 minutes later.

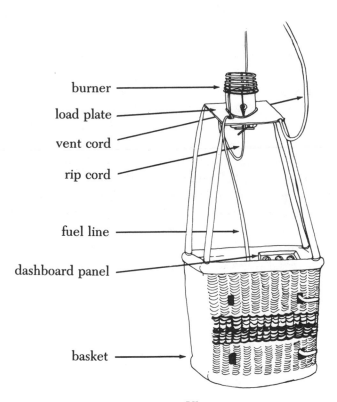

?

How does a metal detector at the airport know whether you have metal on your person?

The people at Infinetics, Inc., the manufacturer of "Friskem" detectors—which comprise over 90 percent of the worldwide market for airport metal detectors—are fearful of releasing any secrets about how their detectors operate. According to the management (who seem to assume guilt on the part of the questioner until proof of innocence is established), "Details on their technology serve only to help those who would prefer to defeat the attempted goals." So much for the curious layman.

In general terms, though, metal detectors work on a principle of induced magnetism. The primary property that distinguishes metal from other materials is its high electrical conductivity. It is possible to create a magnetic field near a metal object and to induce an electrical current in the object. This in turn sets up a magnetic field in the object that distorts the original one. Detection of this distortion leads to detection of the metal.

One of the most common forms of detectors contains two coils separately connected to two oscillator circuits having the same frequency. The coils act as inductors and produce an alternating magnetic field—until a metal object is introduced near one of the coils. This has the effect of changing the inductance of one coil and hence the frequency of oscillation. A slight discrepancy in the two oscillations results in a series of beats, just as two musical notes if close but not precisely in tune generate beats if played simultaneously. An operator hearing the beats through earphones knows there is metal nearby.

?

How do they "lift" faces?

Swayed by the high esteem in which youthful minds *and* youthful bodies are held these days, many people are turning to cosmetic surgery to smooth their furrowed brows and lift their sagging jowls. Although face lifts were first performed in Europe and the United States at the turn of the century, the process remained cloaked in secrecy, deemed unrespectable because it catered to vanity and often fostered quackery. Today, this difficult and complex surgery is considered an art, for the surgeon must not only solve the problem of wrinkles but restore the face without changing its character in the process. In short, the procedure, technically known as a rhytidoplasty or rhytidectomy, is this: a surgeon incises and detaches the skin of the face and neck, lifts and tightens the skin, trims off the excess skin, and closes the incisions.

A face lift involves surgery that requires the patient to spend three or four days in a hospital—and to have a minimum of several thousand dollars set aside for surgical fees. Perhaps because of the infinite variety of faces, there is no rigid standardization of methods. Either local or general anesthesia may be administered, and the operation usually takes about two and a half to four hours.

The surgeon begins the incision in the area of the temples, in the hair-bearing scalp where the subsequent scar will be concealed. The incision runs down to the point where the ear is attached, continues just in front of the ear, then curves around the earlobe to the back of the ear. The incision then moves into a strip of scalp on the neck hairline which has been trimmed or shaved, the precise location depending on the hair style of the patient. (Resulting scars are ideally hidden by hair.) Then the surgeon begins the incredibly delicate process of undermining, or separating the skin from the fat and muscle lying beneath it, being careful not to disturb nerves and blood vessels. In the hair area he must go particularly deep so as not to destroy the hair follicles. In general, he undermines the cheeks and the portion of the neck behind the ears, but the actual amount required naturally depends on the location of the sagging skin and the amount of "lifting" to be done. Next, he may or may not need to shift and tighten the tissues under the skin.

To actually "lift" the face, the surgeon pulls the loosened skin upward and backward, thus tightening the skin and smoothing away the patient's unwanted signs of age. Great care must be taken not to pull the skin too tightly, or to remove too much skin, for the patient might be left with a drawn or frozen expression. The surgeon tailors the skin to fit the face, makes anchor sutures above and behind the ear, and trims excess skin. Finally, he sutures the incision and proceeds to work on the other side of the face. Operating on one side at a time makes it easier for the surgeon to make the two sides as symmetrical as possible— decidedly an important factor!

If the patient wishes to be rid of an especially large double chin, the surgeon performs a submental lipectomy: he makes a transverse incision under the chin and removes superfluous skin and fat.

After a face lift the patient's head is encased in a massive bandage, which supports the tissues and helps prevent bleeding. Drains in the bandage may be necessary to draw seepage away from the wounds. After twenty-four to forty-eight hours the cocoon is removed and a new face revealed.

?

How do they grow grapes without seeds?

A seedless grapevine is grown from a bit of stem cut from a mature seedless vine. But where do we get seedless grapevines?

They originated thousands of years ago in the Middle East, in the area of present-day Iran or Afghanistan—no one knows exactly when or where. Raisins from seedless grapes are mentioned in the Bible. Early Near Eastern tribes cultivated ordinary seeded grapes to make wine and raisins. A genetic mutation must have occurred in some tribesman's grape seedlings, which gave the plant an oddity in its yearly reproductive cycle: every time its flowers were pollinated and fertilized, ready to produce seeds for a new generation of plants, the seeds-in-the-making aborted without developing the hard seed casings we have to spit out. This kind of spontaneous abortion is called stenospermoscarpy. The fruit of such a vine is seedless, and the plant cannot reproduce in the conventional way—that is, by dropping seeds. It can only produce more plants vegetatively—by growing another individual from a broken-off piece of itself.

Our tribesman must have been very pleased that such a convenient plant had arisen in his arbor, and he must have grown others by cutting off pieces of it and letting them root in the ground. Our modern green seedless grape, called a Thompson seedless, has come down to us from that first plant, passed along over the centuries by cuttings transplanted from one arbor to another. If you slice open a seedless green grape from the supermarket, you can still see the beginnings of a pit that never formed.

It would probably surprise most people to learn that if you plant the seed of any ordinary fruit grown for commerce—a seeded grape, peach, apple, blueberry, cherry, or strawberry—you will *not* get a plant that gives fruit similar to the piece you ate. A McIntosh apple seed probably won't grow a tree that makes McIntosh apples. The fruit it puts out will most likely have a noticeably different taste, shape, consistency, and size from the apple that yielded the seed. This occurs because natural sexual reproduction, which produces seeds in plants and fertile eggs in animals, makes for wide variation among the offspring: each offspring receives a different assortment of genes from each parent, and so develops its own unique set of traits. Variation is a boon to a species's survival in the wild, since it increases the chance that some members will flourish in an environment subject to violent change.

In commerce, however, genetic variation is just confusing, a grower wants to be able to depend on a characteristic taste and appearance in his fruit, so that he won't disappoint his customers. He can't very well take a bite out of each cherry to make sure it tastes all right. So all commercially sold fruit (except for citrus) is grown on trees and vines that start as cuttings taken from a plant with the qualities the grower wants to duplicate. This bypasses the sexual phase of the plants altogether and makes offspring that are genetically identical to the parent. All of a given variety of Bing cherry, McIntosh apple, Anjou pear, and Thompson grape have exactly the same collection of genes and produce nearly identical fruit.

Currently, about 90 percent of all the grapes used in United States commerce for eating fresh and for making wine and raisins are Thompson seedless grapes, which are grown in California and New Mexico. Viticulturists at the Cornell University School of Agriculture have nearly perfected a seedless variety like the Thompson which can grow in the harsher climate of the Northeast. As in the animal world, thoroughbred plants are more vulnerable to disease than "mongrel" fruit and need to be sprayed and fertilized frequently; the Cornell scientists are making their northeastern seedless as resistant as possible to insect and fungal predators.

The original Concord grapevine in Concord, Massachusetts, only recently died. One wonders if the first Thompson seedless is still putting out grapes somewhere along the Persian Gulf. . . .

?

How do they perfectly reproduce large statues in miniature?

It isn't easy to shrink the Statue of Liberty so that it fits into the hand of a tourist from Cedar Rapids, Iowa, or to make thousands of copies of a famous bust of Abraham Lincoln, each with the same wise, somber expression. The entire process calls for specialized teams of sculptors, working from the original of a statue or sculpture, photographs of the original, and an ingenious machine that looks as if Rube Goldberg invented it.

To make its copy of the Statue of Liberty, the Evelyn Hill Company, operators of a concession on Liberty Island that sells miniature replicas, collected as many photographs as it could of

100

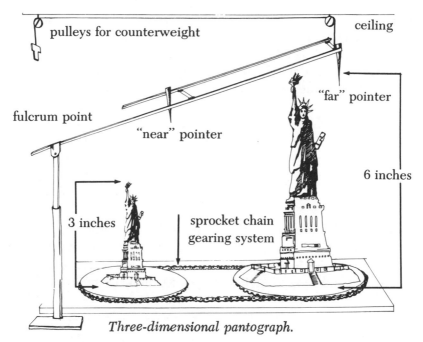

ceiling

"far" pointer

fulcrum point

"near" pointer

6 inches

3 inches

sprocket chain
gearing system

Three-dimensional pantograph.

the statue, some of them taken from ground level, some from helicopters. The company turned the pictures over to a prototype sculptor, who specializes in transforming shapes in pictures into three-dimensional objects. A prototype sculptor, using his trained eye and instinct, puts together a model made of plastic modeling clay or wax. He makes it whatever size he feels comfortable with; making a replica bigger or smaller is a separate process. He concerns himself for the moment only with getting the shape right in every detail.

To make it right does not always mean to give the replica the exact same proportions as the original; it depends on what the client wants. "If you look closely at the original statue, she's quite heavy in the bust, and also the rear. We had the sculptor take her down a little, to make it look nice," says John Silvers of Evelyn Hill.

Once the prototype sculptor has finished his model, he gives it to sculptors at the foundry where the replicas will be cast; they copy the model, in the exact size the manufacturer specifies, with the aid of a contraption called a three-dimensional pantograph. A pantograph is a movable horizontal bar with two swiveling pointers mounted on it. The pointers are linked by a second bar so that they always move in tandem—every twitch of one pointer is matched by a parallel twitch of the other. While tracing the contours of a model with one pointer, a sculptor can shape his clay replica using the other pointer, which performs the identical motions, as a guide. The apparatus is mounted on a perpendicular stand on which it can swing and turn. The two pointers project from the bar along one side of the stand, which acts as a fulcrum point, and a counterweight is suspended from the other end. The pointer farther from the fulcrum point makes larger sweeps than the near one, which describes the same shapes but on a smaller scale.

Thus the foundry sculptors can make a "reduced" copy by tracing along the original with the far pointer, while shaping the clay replica to follow the motions of the near pointer. The prototype and copy sit on turntables, to allow the pointers to reach every part. These turntables are connected by a gearing system like a bicycle's, so that they always rotate the same number of degrees.

Dave Kaye, who sculpted the prototype of Miss Liberty for Evelyn Hill, made his piece 4 feet tall. The foundry sculptors then had to "shrink" his model to the size of the replicas to be sold in the concession (6 inches, 14 inches, and 2 feet), in order to make the molds. To make a 2-foot replica, the 4-foot prototype was placed on the turntable near the far pointer; a mass of clay to form the 2-foot replica was placed on the turntable adjacent to the near pointer, exactly half as far from the fulcrum as the farther one, since the replica was to be half the size of the prototype. In addition, the near pointer was half the length of the far one, and the near turntable was half the circumference of the far table.

When a reduced replica is complete, the original prototype artist comes in to put on the finishing touches before the foundrymen make a brass mold from it, and the casting of metal alloy miniatures can begin.

?

How does *The New York Times* determine its best-seller list?

As anyone can read in the back of *The New York Times Book Review* each Sunday, the best-seller lists reflect the sales of books in 1,400 bookstores across the country. Each week those stores submit sales figures of the most popular titles, and this information is fed into a computer, which comes up with the top fifteen books in four categories: hardcover fiction, hardcover general, trade paperback, and mass-market paperback.

But where are those bookstores, and how adequately do they represent the entire country? After all, there are hundreds of bookstores in New York City alone—but pretty slim pickings across the plains of Kansas.

In 1977 the *Times* conducted a survey of all the members of the American Booksellers Association in a questionnaire about the volume of business, distribution, types of markets, and so on. From the 1,800 responses received, the *Times* made up a list of a representative sample of big, medium, and small stores in every zip code area of the country. A "big" store is one that does $50,000 or more in business in any of the four categories per year; a "small" store does less than $10,000 in any category per year. The *Times* then established seven geographic areas:

Region	Percentage of total stores
Maine, Massachusetts, Rhode Island, Vermont, Connecticut, New Hampshire	14
New York, New Jersey, Pennsylvania, Delaware	14
Maryland, Virginia, West Virginia, North Carolina, South Carolina, Tennessee, Mississippi, Georgia, Alabama, Florida	15

Region	Percentage of total stores
Ohio, Indiana, Michigan, Kentucky	10
North Dakota, South Dakota, Minnesota, Wisconsin, Montana, Illinois, Missouri, Nebraska, Kansas	14
Oklahoma, Arkansas, Iowa, Texas, Idaho, Wyoming, Utah, Colorado, Nevada, Arizona, New Mexico, Louisiana	14
California, Washington, Oregon, Alaska, Hawaii	19

Each month 1,400 stores in these areas receive a preprinted list of thirty leading titles. (There is also room on the form to mention titles not listed.) The booksellers send in this form once a week, reporting sales in actual numbers on the most popular titles. This system is sufficient to reflect hardcover sales, but mass-market paperbacks are sold in far greater quantities in drugstores, supermarkets, airports, and newsstands than in bookstores. So the *Times* consults distributors in twenty-five major markets who report the estimated sales from more than 40,000 outlets. The trade paperback figures include reports from bookstores, and from wholesalers with a total of 2,500 outlets. Another exception to the system is the largest chains, which the *Times* calls "majors." Since these chains—B. Dalton, Waldenbooks, Doubleday, and Brentano's—have stores across the country, they amass their own sales figures and the headquarters of each reports to the *Times* weekly. Although sales from the majors alone can get a book onto the bestseller list, their effect is not always so considerable, and it varies from book to book.

?

How do they know what time it is?

Man's first clock was a sundial of some kind, which told him the time with as much precision as he needed: how high is the sun in the sky, and how long will it be till dark? A sundial tells more exactly than the eye alone where our *real* clock, the sun, is. It's not surprising that people use the sun's position to give shape to the events of their lives, since all life owes its existence to the effects of the sun's energy, and indeed evolved in rhythm with its presence and absence.

The first use of time, then, is to stay in touch with one's physical environment and its cycle of light and dark, hot and cold, high tide and low tide, growth and decay: we must synchronize with the environment our own cycles of hunger, thirst, and sex. For such uses of time we must know where the sun is. But people often want to synchronize themselves not only with the physical world, but with other people: to catch trains, work in offices, eat lunch together, and so on. In order to coordinate our activities, we must give time a name that is understood by all concerned. Thus, the key difference between dealing with the natural and human worlds is that whereas the earth and sun *tell* us what time it is, we must agree with the rest of humanity on what time it is for time to mean anything.

For the entire technological world, the agreed keeper of time is the Bureau International de l'Heure (BIH) in Paris, which stays in constant contact with laboratories and observatories in seventy countries, all of which contribute to the official "correct time." The clocks at the BIH and at the headquarters of national organizations such as our National Bureau of Standards are impressive in their precision. Coordinated Universal Time (abbreviated UTC, for some reason), the standard they all keep, is exact to within a few *billionths* of a second.

The clocks used by the BIH and its members owe their regularity and accuracy to the properties of the element cesium, a silver-colored alkali metal. A cesium clock is actually a machine that produces a tone of exact pitch and frequency. An electromagnetic signal's frequency is a statement of how often the photons that make it up vibrate each second. But since it is the second we want to define and maintain, we say instead that the second is some number of photon vibrations. How can we fix vibrations within a time frame without consulting the clock we want to set? Cesium atoms perform an electromagnetic "flip"—their electrons, which spin like tops, suddenly point their axes of spin in a different direction—only at a certain frequency. If we agree that a second will be counted out at whatever frequency is required to make the cesium atoms flip, or resonate, we know that our frequency and therefore our second are as stable as the flipping property of cesium—which is very stable indeed.

The member nations of the BIH have agreed that 9,192,631,770 photon pulses—cesium's flipping frequency—is a good length of time for a second, so that's what a second is. For convenience' sake, it's very close to a second in the solar system—1/31,536,000 of the time it takes Earth to go around the sun—but the cesium atom is a more precise standard.

Having defined seconds, we can add them in computerized counters to correspond to recognizable times of day such as noon, midnight, and 4:00 A.M. But how do you tell people the time without time passing as you tell them? Countries keep their own standard cesium clocks, which they set by bringing them into phase with a portable one brought from Paris in a plane, tended by a team of technicians to keep it "ticking" correctly. Each geographical region of the world that uses exact time thus can have its own keeper of UTC and can broadcast its own time signals to users by radio. The users, in maintaining their own clocks, must allow for the time it takes the signal to reach them from its source. In the United States, the National Bureau of Standards broadcasts on station WWV in Fort Collins, Colorado. Radio waves are electromagnetic and travel at 186,000 miles per second (the speed of light), thus taking about .012 seconds to reach New York from Fort Collins.

Who needs to know the time to within billionths of a second? It is technology that has created the need for both the exact time and the hardware with which to keep it. In ship and air navigation systems, a craft's position is gauged relative to broadcast towers thousands of miles to either side of it. If a broadcast wave pattern sounds simultaneously from Washington, D.C., and Greenwich, England, and reaches a ship sailing in the North Atlantic, the ship can compute its position by calculating which "beep" traveling at the speed of light reaches it first, and by how many parts of a second. The time measurement must be accurate; an error of a hundred thousandth of a second can put the location estimate off by 2 miles.

The telephone company needs to know the exact time, too. It sends several conversations along a single wire, to save time and space, by multiplexing—breaking each conversation up into impulses much shorter than a word (in fact, lasting only a millisecond) feeding the interspersed "bits" in sequence along the wire, unscrambling the bits at the other end, and reassembling the conversations. The multiplex transmitter sending bits down the wire must be synchronized perfectly with the receiver sorting them out; otherwise, the different conversations will receive each other's bits and get hopelessly garbled.

Others who depend on exact time measurement include television and radio stations, physicists, astronomers, and the electric power companies that supply customers with 60-cycle-per-second alternating current to run their electric clocks.

The resonance of the cesium atom is one of the most regular things we know—much more accurate than the turning of Earth itself, from which man originally derived his concept of time. Earth has been slowing in its revolutions by about a second every year because the moon's gravity drags at the oceans and causes friction; in some years the effect is greater than in others. We know this by keeping track of the positions of the stars and planets relative to the turning Earth. (Paleontologists who have measured fossils of ancient coral, which made annual growth rings as trees do, say that 600 million years ago, a day on the earth was only twenty-one hours long!) A cesium clock, on the other hand, would take 370,000 years to lose a second. Thus, by the end of a year the solar system and a cesium clock can be in serious disagreement.

A compromise has been struck between the sun and our clocks: every year the BIH in Paris adjusts the time to conform to our relation to the sun, so that "high noon" in the sky remains noon on our clocks as nearly as possible. In recent years the BIH has added a "leap second" between December 31 and January 1, making one 61-second minute, to wait for the "sun time" to catch up. If the world speeds up, we may need *short* minutes every few years. Says Dr. James A. Barnes of the National Bureau of Standards in Boulder, Colorado: "When the error gets too bad, we have to reset the clocks, since it's more difficult to reset the earth."

If you need to know the time to a few billionths of a second, call the National Bureau of Standards at (303) 499–7111; but don't forget to allow for the time the signal takes to reach you at the speed of light.

?

How do they trace bullets to specific guns?

The hunt for New York's infamous "Son of Sam" killer ended when ballistics experts at the city's Police Academy Crime Laboratory examined the .44-caliber Charter Arms "Bulldog" revolver they had turned up in the car of suspect David Berkowitz. The bullets found in the bodies of the victims had all been fired from that gun; Berkowitz confessed, was convicted of the murders, and was sentenced to life imprisonment.

"Didn't give him any room to move when we identified the gun," says Detective George Simmons of the Crime Lab. "They had some other evidence—fingerprints and whatnot—but the ballistics is what put the nail in it." Detective Simmons did the matching of barrel and bullet that sealed the district attorney's case.

Fortunately for the police, every gun in the world is unique. The inside of each barrel leaves a characteristic set of stripes and scratches on the soft lead of the bullet as it passes through; those marks identify the gun as precisely as a fingerprint does a burglar. The marks are not visible to the naked eye, but for a ballistics expert with a microscope, they are as clear as a highway sign.

The pattern on the barrel comes about in the last three stages of manufacturing the gun, each of which contributes its own odd marks and scratches; together, the imperfections leave the barrel's "signature" on the bullet. The first of the steps is drilling: a barrel is made by hollowing out a solid cylinder of steel with a carbide steel drill that has a diamond tip. This process leaves a microscopically fine ring pattern on the inside, much of which will be obliterated in later stages.

Next, a hard, brittle steel gouging instrument called a broach carves long, spiral furrows along the bore. The pattern the broach leaves acts as a track to make the bullet spiral through the air like a thrown football. As with a forward pass, spiraling improves a bullet's accuracy. Every time the broach passes through another bore, sharp as it is, it gets a little duller until it is resharpened. Thus the exact width and shape of the track the broach makes are never quite the same in any two weapons.

Lapping is the final polishing step, to smooth the rough edges of the broach track and give the barrel as geometrically perfect a cylinder shape inside as possible, so that the bullets will fly accurately. Lapping leaves its own marks and scratches on the bore.

Ballistics experts examine the gun found on a suspect and fire shots of their own with it. By comparing their slugs with those found in the victim's body and applying their knowledge of barrel mechanics, a positive identification is often possible.

Says Detective Simmons, "Your suspect can always say he never fired the gun—somebody else did. But unless the bullet is too mangled up from striking the body, we can tell you which gun did the shooting."

?

How do they execute a trade on the New York Stock Exchange?

All transactions on the New York Stock Exchange take place in one of three rooms, which are known collectively as "the floor," at 11 Wall Street in New York. The largest of the rooms, built in

1903, contains twelve numbered U-shaped booths or "posts." Adjacent to this room is "the garage," built in 1911, with Posts 13 to 17; and next to that is the Blue Room, which was built in 1968 and contains Posts 18 to 22. Each post handles the stock of anywhere from 1 to 100 different companies. There are 1,550 companies listed on the New York Stock Exchange, and 1,366 members participate in the trading.

Let's say you're in Chicago and you've decided to try your luck on the stock market. Perhaps you want to buy 100 shares of U.S. Steel. First, you call your broker in Chicago and place the order. Your broker calls your order into his company's telephone clerk, who sits in one of the many telephone booths on the edge of the Exchange floor. The telephone clerk must notify the firm's broker on the floor. Each floor broker has a number. The telephone clerk pushes a button which flashes the number of the broker he wants on large, 2,000-square-foot annunciator boards which hang on a wall in each of the trading rooms. The floor broker sees his number flashed, goes to the telephone booth, and picks up the order.

He then proceeds to Post 2, where U.S. Steel's stock is handled. An indicator board at the post tells him at what price—in dollars and eighths of a dollar—the last deal was made. There the broker also sees a "crowd"—a group of other brokers and specialists who are watching U.S. Steel closely. A specialist is a member of the Exchange who coordinates the buying and selling of specific stocks, keeping track of all current bids to buy and offers to sell. Your broker approaches the crowd and asks for a quotation. "How's Steel?" he might ask, meaning "What is the highest bid on the floor right now to buy U.S. Steel and what is the lowest offer to sell?" The specialist may give him a quotation of "25 to ¼," which means that the best bid he has received to buy U.S. Steel is $25.00 and the lowest offer to sell is $25.25. Your broker now knows that he must at least top $25.00, so he can't bid lower than that. He bids 25⅛—$25.125.

"Twenty-five and one-eighth for one hundred," he says, hoping another broker in the crowd will want to sell 100 shares at 25⅛. If he receives no response for his bid, he must bid higher and meet the previous asking price. He then bids 25¼, which was the specialist's quotation. If there is more than one bid at 25¼, the specialist must decide, on the basis of priority (which bid was entered first) and size of order, which broker gets the stock.

Let's say the specialist is holding 200 shares of U.S. Steel and the first bid of 25¼ is for 200 shares. The first bid wins. If, however, the first bid is for 100 shares and then your broker enters his bid for 100 shares, the specialist divides his 200 shares between the two brokers. When bids are entered simultaneously, the larger ordinarily has priority. If simultaneous bids are equal in size, there is a "match"—a coin is flipped and the winner gets the stock.

More often, however, deals are transacted between two brokers. When your broker approaches the post to buy, it is more than likely that another broker in the crowd is trying to sell. They seek each other out and negotiate a deal. The market operates as a double auction; prices are not set by the Exchange, but by the process of bidding and offering.

No matter how a deal is arranged, a "reporter" is always on hand to watch. He records the sale on a computer card and passes the card through one of the electronic scanners set up on the floor. Within seconds the deal is recorded on ticker tape and on thousands of film projecters and Quotron machines throughout the world wherever New York Stock Exchange activity is followed. Until fairly recently, the reporter would place the order in a small plastic container, a "widget," and send it along tubing that underlies the Exchange floor to a central reporting office. There are more than 40 miles of tubing running through the Exchange.

Finally, the floor broker goes back to the telephone clerk, who sends the results of the deal to the Chicago office where you placed your order. A bill confirming details of the trade is sent to you, and you have five business days from the date of the transaction to pay for the purchase.

?

How does a hovercraft speed across the water?

When a hovercraft moves across water, it is literally floating on air—for a high-pressure air cushion is maintained beneath the hull that provides lift and allows even large vessels to whiz along at high speeds. First developed in 1959, air cushion vehicles (AVCs) are sometimes amphibious—capable of traveling both on land and in water.

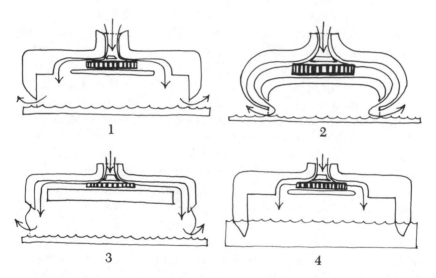

1. *A hovercraft, or air cushion vehicle, rests on a "cushion" of air beneath the hull. Air propelled by a fan down into a plenum chamber provides lift, before escaping under the wall of the ACV.*
2. *Air flows downward and inward through slits around the periphery of this vehicle, efficiently maintaining higher pressure in the cushion than in the surrounding atmosphere.*
3. *The addition of a flexible skirt provides increased clearance—and a smoother ride over choppy waves.*
4. *In a sidewall ACV, the sides extend slightly below the surface of the water; air escapes only at the bow and stern. Greater stability is achieved at the expense of increased drag.*

A substantial space, or "plenum chamber," exists beneath the vessel, into which air is pumped by fans. In some vessels, the flow of air has an annular pattern: that is, higher concentrations of air are emitted at the periphery, then act as a curtain to protect the cushion from surrounding lower-pressure air. Nozzles direct the air inward so that it pushes against the air in the cushion and maintains it far more efficiently than if the air were directed straight down. The cushion, whose air pressure is higher than atmospheric pressure, may also be protected by a flexible skirt of strong nylon impregnated with neoprene rubber. This skirt allows the ACV greater lift with less expenditure of power and makes possible travel over rough terrain and choppy water with minimal loss of air. Some large hovercraft have skirts at the bow and stern and rigid or inflatable sidewalls extending down into the water on both sides. This system vastly reduces air loss, but sidewall ACVs are practical only for traveling at slow speeds in deep water.

ACVs use an integrated lift and propulsion system, which means the same engine inflates the air cushion and propels the vehicle. Sidewall ACVs often use diesel engines, whereas most other types have lighter-weight gas-turbine engines. Air enters a duct near the top of the vessel—away from dust or spray—and flows toward one or more large fans, each with a diameter of at least 10 feet. These centrifugal fans on a vertical axis pump air down into the plenum chamber to replace air that is continuously lost. Marine propellers, water jets, or air propellers provide propulsion, and braking and steering are done aerodynamically: fins and rudders deflect airflow in the necessary direction. At slow speeds "thrust impulses" that steer an ACV are achieved with lateral propellers, and a change in the pitch angle of the propeller blades can result in braking.

Today, Bell Aerospace Textron produces three major lines of air cushion vehicles. In September 1979 the company signed a contract with the U.S. Army for construction and delivery of twenty-eight amphibious crafts—LACV-30s (Lighter, Amphibious Air Cushion Vehicle—30-Ton Payload). This vehicle is intended to move cargo and equipment from offshore ships, across beaches and marginal areas to inland points. It weighs 27 tons when empty (though its gross weight may be 62 tons) and can be deployed on container ships. This ACV averages 50 miles per hour at sea, 25

miles per hour on land. Bell Aerospace is building larger landing craft for the Navy, designed to carry tanks ashore. For commercial use Bell produces the Surface Effect Ship (SES), a nonamphibious vessel, which cruises with passengers and cargo at about 46 miles per hour in calm water, 37 miles per hour in open sea.

?

How do neon signs glow?

Neon is a colorless, odorless, inert gas, first discovered in 1898 by the British physical chemists Sir William Ramsay and Morris W. Travers, who named the gas after the Greek word meaning "new." About that time physicists were experimenting with generating radiation by striking an arc between electrodes in an evacuated tube containing only small amounts of vapor. In Paris in 1910, Georges Claude filled a tube with neon gas and found that when high voltage was applied to the two electrodes at each end, an electrical discharge occurred, which caused the tube to glow a deep red. The neon must be purified of any other gases in order for the electrical discharge to permeate it and pass through the tube. Purification is accomplished by the use of charcoal which, when cooled to -180 to -190 degrees Centigrade, absorbs impurities in the tube and is subsequently removed.

The commercial applications for neon lighting were quickly recognized in the early twentieth century, and soon other vapors besides neon were used. Mercury vapor, for example, gives rise to blue light. White fluorescent lights, developed in the 1930's, actually are filled with mercury vapor, but the inner wall of the tube is coated with material that fluoresces white under radiation.

?

How does an X ray photograph your bones but not the surrounding flesh?

An X-ray photograph of the leg you broke skiing down the expert slope with intermediate skill shows your bones most brightly because bone is dense and stops more X-ray particles than the flesh around it.

An X-ray camera fires electrons at a plate covered with silver halide crystals, which are sensitive to light. Your hapless leg is put in the way of the penetrating stream of particles. When an electron reaches the plate unimpeded, it turns a halide crystal black. The crystals that receive no electrons fall away when the plate is developed and leave that area transparent, or white under the light.

X-ray particles are so highly energized that most of them pass right through flesh, which is made mostly of water, leaving only a vague image on the film where a few of them were stopped. Bones, on the other hand, are very densely packed and contain large amounts of calcium and other heavy elements. They stop the X rays by absorbing them—the crack in your tibia shows up black on the plate because that's where bone isn't.

?

How do they come up with artificial flavors that taste just like the real thing?

To begin with, the premise of the question is debatable. Ripe bananas, for instance, have more than 150 taste components; it is highly unlikely, therefore, that a synthetic banana flavor could really duplicate the ripe banana flavor. Furthermore, the cheap synthetic flavors that consumers have been fed in recent years have made them so accustomed to an artificial taste that often they actually prefer it to a natural one. A flavor chemist for Fritz, Dodge and Alcott, Inc., reports that they've "moved away from the utilization of fresh flavor. It isn't familiar anymore. . . ." Another major flavor manufacturer admits that were they to develop a "bread" flavor, they'd imitate the taste of Wonder Bread rather than homemade!

Artificial flavoring ingredients are either imitation (a combination of natural and synthesized ingredients) or synthetic (purely chemical). In either case, the manufacturing process begins with a research chemist who attempts to isolate significant flavor constituents. He separates components of natural foods and identifies fragrances and aromas by some very complex methods. By chromatography the juice of a strawberry, for example, is allowed to seep through an absorbent in which different compounds are absorbed by different layers. Various components, thus isolated, may be analyzed further by a mass spectrometer. Here the component is spun over a magnet and at the same time bombarded by electrons. This causes the component to break down within the magnetic field, and a chemist can observe the particular pattern of breakdown. Knowing the chemical makeup of the component, he may then be able to reassemble the parts artificially.

Some components, however, have isomers, or molecules that are identical in composition but whose atoms are positioned differently. They may exist in various configurations—twisted together, for example—yet each has its own particular effect on

116

the flavor of the food. (Some cause a fatty taste, others a sour flavor, and so on.) It is thus necessary to separate them, and this process is carried out by nuclear magnetic resonance. Molecules of the substance are spun over a magnet, broken apart, and radio waves used to key on the vibrational energies emitted by the molecules. The radio waves then relate this information to an oscilloscope, which charts the pattern. Experts can then read those charts and determine the actual form of the configuration.

By these and other techniques, research chemists analyze the natural flavors in foods. The number of constituents may be overwhelming—International Flavors and Fragrances, Inc. (IFF), has detected 125 in strawberries. Some are immediately apparent; others are incredibly elusive. Furthermore, flavorists insist that were analysis all that was necessary for finding the formula that most accurately imitates nature, the creation of artificial flavors would be simple.

Charles H. Grimm, senior vice-president of IFF, insists that this matching process is an art. Like the study of wines or fine foods, evaluation of artificial flavors is done organoleptically—by actual taste and smell comparisons. A flavorist would smell and/or taste a beaker of real strawberry juice and then sample twenty, thirty, perhaps sixty other substances formulated according to the findings of the research chemist.

There are literally thousands of natural and synthetic aromatics with which flavorists construct "taste complexes." These include esters, alcohols, lactones, ketones, phenols, aldehydes, ethers, acetals, hydrocarbons with botanical tinctures, essential oils, and flower absolutes. The Food and Drug Administration has listed 800 synthetic aromatics as GRAS (Generally Recognized as Safe). Proponents of these flavors point out that synthetic flavors have greater stability and can withstand greater temperature changes than natural ones. They are more readily available, cheaper, and always the same in color and composition—a comfort to many modern consumers. Whether or not the products of food flavorists are a viable substitute for the original (in taste or in nutrients), the variety of artificial flavorings on the market is astounding. Not only can we buy food with bacon flavor, but smoky bacon, maple bacon, and mushroom bacon flavors are also manufactured. Available tomato flavors include crisp and fresh, pulpy, and

117

cooked. One manufacturer of flavors claims, "Our chicken is chickener. . . . It tastes just like Grandma's cooking."

Well, it may not have been one of Grandma's better days.

?

How does a vending machine know that the coin you inserted is the correct value and not a slug?

Vending machines are equipped with a coin-testing device that not only measures the diameter and thickness of your coin, but checks its weight, alloy composition, and magnetic properties.

The coin enters a slot, which has been carefully measured to accommodate the required coin or coins, and rolls down a chute to two hook-shaped balance arms. A coin of the correct weight presses the right arm sufficiently to move a counterweight on the left; displacement of the arm allows the coin to pass. The diameter of the coin is also checked at this point—too-small coins slip from

Coin-testing unit in a vending machine.

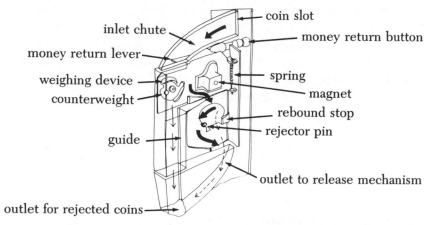

Valid coins eventually reach the outlet to the release mechanism.
Too-small coins fall to the receptacle for rejected coins.
Coins of high iron content, slowed by the magnet, fail to leap over the rejector pin; instead, they drop to the receptacle for rejected coins.

the hooks to the coin return receptacle. Those that are too large get stuck. When the coin return button is pushed, a side flap opens, allowing the coin to fall into the return receptacle.

A coin of the proper size and weight continues through the machine past a strong magnetic field. If the iron content of the coin is high, for example, the magnet catches it. The coin return button triggers a wiper that sweeps the coin away from the magnet. The speed of the coin as it moves through the machine is thus dependent on composition and on mass. The speed it accumulates must be sufficient to allow the coin to jump over a rejector pin and down an outlet leading to the release mechanism, which in turn allows the vending machine to deliver the desired product.

?

How do they roll up a roll of Scotch tape?

If you ever pull out more Scotch tape than you need, you might as well forget trying to save it by rolling it back onto the roll. It'll twist and stick to itself, your fingers, and the dispenser, and if it does actually get back on the roll it's bound to be crooked and overlap at the edges. How on earth, then, do tape manufacturers make so many millions of perfectly rolled rolls of tape that drop neatly into dispensers in offices and homes around the world?

The trick is to roll the tape before it is cut into such a small, unmanageable size. Just as a newspaper is run through a press, sheets of polyester film or cellophane several feet in width are run through a machine where, rather than being printed, they are coated with adhesive. The sticky film is fed onto a long rolling tube, also several feet in width. This super-wide roll of Scotch tape is then subjected to a slitting machine, which consists of a bar with round knives of various sizes. Almost instantaneously these sharp knives whir through both the tape and the tube to make those familiar, compact rolls.

119

?

How do they measure the size of the universe?

There are two answers to this question, depending on the definition of "the universe." One answer is that the universe is infinite—that it consists of simply everything: all matter, dust, planets, stars, energy, time, and space. Nothing could lie beyond the boundaries of "everything"; so, by simple semantics, we know the universe is infinite.

But what if one means the *observable* universe—all the matter and energy in it that you might detect if you were close enough to it? How do we know how widely those "contents" are spread? That has a more interesting answer. The observable universe is about 40 billion light-years across. One light-year is the distance light travels in a year, or about 6 trillion miles; so the total distance is about 240 billion trillion miles.

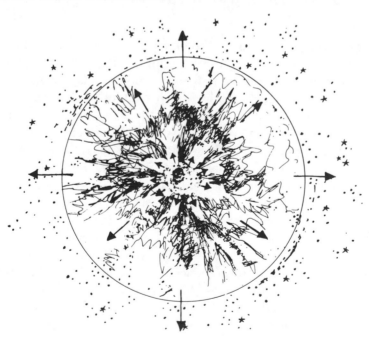

The "Big Bang," a tremendous explosion that occurred about 20 billion years ago, marked the beginning of the universe.

We know the size of the observable universe because we know when it began. Cosmologists have learned from watching the galaxies that the universe is expanding; the stars, planets, and galaxies are all moving away from one another. The current explanation is that the universe began with a tremendous explosion—the "Big Bang" theory—and that we on Earth are riding on a piece of the scattering debris. By computing the speeds of the galaxies' motions and determining the point from which they all seem to be scattering, cosmologists have figured out how long ago the explosion must have taken place for the scattering to have progressed this far. The Big Bang took place about 20 billion years ago.

Light travels faster than anything in the universe, so the remotest cosmic debris must be the pulses of light energy that shot away from the Big Bang in every direction 20 billion years ago. By now that light has traveled 20 billion light-years; light pulses traveling in opposite directions from the "Bang" are now twice as far from each other as from the point of the explosion, or 40 billion light-years from each other—and *that* is the diameter of the observable universe.

?

How do they know the universe is expanding?

The universe is blowing up. Earth is but a particle of debris hurtling through space from an awesome explosion that took place 20 billion years ago, which generated temperatures of trillions of degrees, and marked the Beginning. Ever since the "Big Bang" (see "How do they measure the size of the universe?" page 120), stars, planets, gases, and intergalactic dust have been moving away from one another like so much shrapnel.

From our vantage point on Earth, the stars don't seem to be moving. Indeed, their positions seem for us to be the most solidly predictable phenomenon we know. In Shakespeare's *Julius Caesar*, Caesar describes himself as a model of statesmanlike consistency and forthrightness:

For I am constant as the northern star,
Of whose true-fixed and resting quality
There is no fellow in the firmament.

Caesar would have been surprised to learn that the North Star, Polaris, of which he speaks is flying *toward* us through space at 10 miles per second. Astronomers assure us, however, that we and Polaris are not on a collision course. In general, the stars are moving *away* from us, especially stars outside our own galaxy. Astronomers can tell that we are all moving away from the Big Bang. The key is that light waves reaching us from the distant stars and galaxies exhibit a "red shift." To understand this, one must understand something about waves.

When a fire engine blowing its siren is coming toward you, the pitch of the siren seems to rise; as it passes and moves on into the distance, the pitch seems to descend. Sound, like light, is a form of energy, which travels in waves. Sound consists of waves of compression in the air, which bump against our eardrums in rapid succession. The diaphragm in the siren creates the pattern of waves by vibrating, sending off a pulse of densely packed air every time it is pushed out, followed by a space of loosely packed air created each time it is sucked back. The compression pattern sent through the air by one complete out-and-in cycle of the diaphragm is one wave, or pulse. The number of pulses generated in a second is called the frequency of the sound; the more waves per second our ears pick up, the higher the frequency we hear. As the fire engine approaches us, sending out hundreds of sound waves each second, each wave "catches up" a little with the next—the next pulse is emitted closer to us than the last. Each succeeding pulse strikes our ears, with less and less time between pulses; therefore the frequency of the sound waves increases, and the sound seems higher. As the engine moves away, the distance between pulses is increasingly stretched out, since the siren emits each one a little farther from us; the number reaching our ear every second is less, and thus the pitch seems to go down.

Light is another form of wave energy, and it too has different frequencies. Unlike sound, which needs a medium such as air or water through which to travel, light can travel in the vacuum of space. An astronomer analyzes starlight using a prism attached to his telescope; the prism spreads the point of "white" light from a single star, which contains many different frequencies, into a long colored band or spectrum, in which the light is arranged by frequency from left to right. The higher frequencies, which look bluish or violet, are toward the left of the band; the blue fades into green, yellow, orange, and finally red as the frequencies get lower toward the right.

When any element is burned, on Earth or in space, it gives off a certain frequency or group of frequencies of light energy. If you spread out that light with a prism, you can see the "signature" of the element as a pattern of lines in the colored wave band the prism produces. The pattern for the element calcium, for example, which is burned on the fiery surfaces of many stars, is a pair of dark lines near the high-frequency or "blue" end of the spectrum. By watching for that "signature" we can tell how a star is moving: If a star is moving away from us, the waves of light we receive from it will seem to be of a lower frequency, just as the pitch of the fire siren sounds lower as the vehicle recedes in the distance. The two lines for calcium still appear on our spectral band, but not where they should be. They are shifted to the right—toward the red or lower-frequency end of the spectrum. The farther toward the red the shift of these two calcium lines is, the faster the star or galaxy is moving away from us. With such a tool for analyzing starlight, astronomers can map out the motions of all the stars and galaxies.

The results of this mapping of the universe show that all the other stars and galaxies, except for a few relatively near ones, are moving away from ours at scores, hundreds, or thousands of miles per second. The stars that are farthest from us are moving away the fastest. The pattern is like the flight of debris spreading out from an explosion. Probably the universe will expand forever, as every star in it gets more distant from every other—there is no limit to the universe's size.

There is another possibility, however, generally considered remote, which is that in 60 to 100 billion years the force of gravity will slow down the expansion, and the stars will reverse directions and speed toward one another until they meet in another Big Bang. As it looks now, however, this second Bang is not possible, since it would take ten times as much matter as the universe now contains to generate sufficient gravitational pull to force a halt to the expansion.

A hundred billion years is pretty far down the pike as far as we on Earth are concerned. Life here in its simplest form is only 4 billion years old; man, a million or so at the most. A mere 6 billion years from now our own sun will expand into a Red Giant and burn the entire solar system into vapor. By then our descendants—if we have left any—will long before have moved on to inhabit other solar systems.

?

How do they write college entrance exams?

The anxious high school student faced with taking the dreaded Scholastic Aptitude Test (SAT) on a Saturday morning has every reason to wonder just who writes those tests and how. For in many cases the tests are the single largest factor in determining where, or even whether, a student will go on to college. Although much controversy has arisen over the effectiveness, fairness, and thoroughness of the tests, they are not taken lightly—nor are they written overnight.

The development of the Scholastic Aptitude Test, which consists of mathematical and verbal sections, is a long, careful process, taking about eighteen months from the time a question is written until it is ready for actual use. Questions are written by test specialists at the nonprofit Educational Testing Service (ETS) in Princeton, New Jersey, by high school and college teachers, and by other individuals with particular training. Although no one at ETS is employed exclusively to write questions, five out of about ten employees in the math area, and ten out of about twenty people in the verbal area, spend a substantial part of their time doing so. Many of the thirty or so free-lance test writers used by ETS are former staff members; others have attended workshops at ETS in which the ground rules for writing test questions are discussed.

Each question on an SAT is reviewed three times by the staff at ETS. First, each of various test specialists, in reviewing a series of questions, prepares a list of correct answers, which is then compared with other lists to verify that there is, indeed, agreement about the correct answer. Other reviewers judge the questions for "fairness to various minority groups and to males and females." A test editor may also make further suggestions for change which the specialists then evaluate. Furthermore, a ten-member SAT advisory committee on the outside reviews new editions of the test on a rotating schedule; three members see each test. This committee is selected with the intent to draw on the expertise and different points of view of people in diverse occupations and geographical areas. At present, the committee includes a principal of a high school in Dallas, Texas; a professor of mathematics education at the University of Georgia; an administrator at Wellesley College; a reading specialist at Columbia University; a high school math teacher from an inner-city Chicago school; and a psychometrician from Hunter College.

Questions that the various reviewers consider "acceptable" are then included in an experimental section of the actual SAT. These do not count toward the student's score. (The student, of course, doesn't know which questions are experimental; he may very well slave for ten minutes over a tricky math problem that has no bearing on his final score.) Each such question, tried out under standard testing conditions by representative samples of students, is analyzed statistically for its "effectiveness"—which is actually determined by the performance of the students themselves. For instance, if students do poorly throughout the test but answer the trial question correctly, the question is apparently too easy. Conversely, if the best students cannot correctly answer the trial question, it is probably too difficult, hence inappropriate. ETS determines the average ability level of each group taking the test, tabulates the precise number of correct and incorrect answers and omissions in the experimental section, and arrives at a computer score indicating how each group performed relative to the others. (According to James Braswell, Test Development coordinator, ETS is aware of students' "tricks of the trade"—choosing an answer because it stands out significantly from the others, for example, or choosing the longest answer; ETS tries, of course, to eliminate questions with such answers.) Finally, satisfactory questions become part of a pool of questions from which a new edition of the SAT is assembled.

At this point, one might wonder just what all those specialists, with all their checks and balances, are trying to accomplish with the SAT: what do they intend to test, and what are their guidelines for content?

ETS says the SAT is "a test of developed ability, not of innate intelligence." But they go on to deny that this "developed ability" is a direct reflection of the quality of high school education. "There is minimal dependence on curriculum in the SAT," says Braswell, "particularly in the verbal portion of the test. The mathematical portion does, however, depend heavily on first-year algebra, and to a lesser extent on geometry taught in junior high or earlier." The test, then, attempts to draw on abilities developed both in and out of school. Critics, however, feel the tests simply evaluate a student's ability to take tests, which may derive from intelligence, background, ambition, fear of failure—or, simply, quick metabolism.

?

How do slot machine operators keep the odds in their favor?

All slot machines are built to take in more than they give back, but buyers of the machine can request (within limits) that the machine always retain a certain percentage. In other words, when ordering a particular model, the operator can request a "tight" or a "liberal" machine. There is a recent trend toward liberal machines because hard-core slot machine players know which machines are generous; they simply won't play on the mean machines—and word spreads. The slot machines in Las Vegas and Reno are reputed to be among the most liberal anywhere in the world, but the generous amount the machines return is compensated by the high volume of gamblers attracted to the machines in those cities.

The standard slot machine has three reels. Each reel tape contains 20 symbols, the famous oranges, cherries, and the like. To win, of course, one must get 3 of the same symbol across the board. But since there are 20 symbols on three tapes, there are

8,000 possible combinations (20 × 20 × 20). By use of simple mathematics and sophisticated electronics, the machine is programmed to retain a certain percentage of money over this cycle of 8,000, and to give back a certain percentage. Slot machines worldwide generally hold from 3 to 20 percent of the intake and give back 80 to 97 percent. Not every player who puts $100 into a 90 percent machine will get $90 back, of course; success lies in hitting the cycle and the right moment.

?

How do they get the foam into a can of shaving cream?

If you've ever actually noted how long one can of shaving cream lasts, you'll know that a lot of foam is somehow packed into a small 11-ounce can.

The fact is, the soapy solution expands as it comes out of the can because it contains hydrocarbon propellent, which vaporizes as it hits the air. The hydrocarbon has a pressure above that of the atmosphere, so at normal temperatures it turns into a gas. Emulsified in the liquid soap, it is kept in the can under pressure, until your finger on the valve presses down on a spring which releases the material—and foam spurts out.

Hydrocarbon propellant constitutes about 3 to 5 percent of the total contents of a can. The soapy solution, which includes lubricants and perfumes, is first mixed and then put into the can as it travels along a filling line. The propellant is then added by one of two methods. The top of the can (valve and valve cap) may be installed and crimped first. Then a gasing machine pushes propellant through the valve under pressure. Or the propellant may be added before the valve has been attached. A machine descends over the top of the can and presses a metered amount of propellant into it. Immediately the valve and cap descend to close the can, sealing the soap and propellant inside.

?

How do the musicians in an orchestra know what the conductor wants them to do?

Perhaps you have watched the impeccable movements of George Szell, the nuances of Seiji Ozawa, the romantic drama of Leonard Bernstein, who flails his arms and occasionally leaves the ground, and been at a loss to see how any musician really knows what the conductor wants him to do, and further, how any musician could possibly change orchestras and not be totally perplexed. Within the multitude of styles, which are probably as various as the conductors themselves, there are certain basic motions in common.

A conductor generally uses his right hand to keep the beat, a downstroke indicating the first beat of a measure, an upstroke marking the last. A piece in 3/4 time is counted by lowering the arm down (1), to the right (2), and up (3). The diagrams illustrate the movements for two, three, four, six, and nine beats.

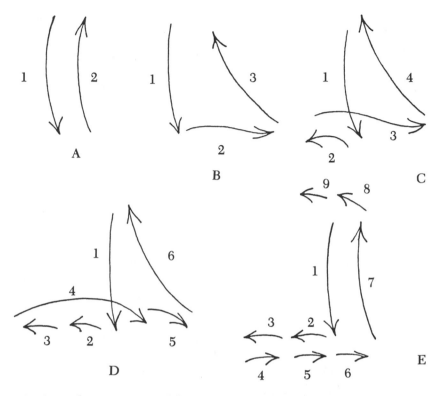

It is rarely necessary with a professional orchestra to mark every beat, so a conductor does not keep rigidly to those motions. While never losing the beat, he incorporates a wide sweep of natural expression to bring out his interpretation of the piece. The left hand is especially important for marking shadings of dynamics and entrances of other instruments or voices. The conductor needn't cue everyone, however. In a piano concerto, for instance, the solo player undoubtedly knows where to come in, so the conductor might concentrate on bringing in the violins at the right moment, or on toning down the cellos. Small movements tell the orchestra to play softly, and larger, grandiose gestures obviously indicate a crescendo. A conductor uses short, abrupt motions for fast passages; long, sinuous strokes are appropriate for those to be played slowly.

Most conductors use a baton to keep the beat. Others have recently abandoned the baton to free both hands for evocative gestures. Choral conductors frequently use two hands to keep the beat. Techniques may vary, and musicians may rely a good deal on intuition, but the conductor is essential for coordinating the orchestra and for effecting a single interpretation of the piece. The system is far from new; Sumerian and Egyptian reliefs from about 2800 B.C. show figures with hands raised leading players of harps and flutes.

?

How do they rate movies?

Movie ratings are determined by a board of seven—six members and a chairman—within the Classification and Rating Administration (CARA), under the auspices of the Motion Picture Association of America (MPAA). The six board members are full-time, paid employees based in Hollywood, where they watch movies nearly all day long. "The members are selected," says Chairman of the Board Richard D. Heffner, "with two goals in mind: flexibility and stability." Thus, two members holding long terms are "old-timers" who are well acquainted with film history; no one, however, is granted tenure. Two others are people on one- or two-year leave from their regular professional involvements—one, for instance, is a writer. Being more recently involved with the outside world, these members reflect changing attitudes and social mores, particularly those of parents. The other two members are generally younger people with three-year appointments, who will move on, usually to pursue careers in the film industry.

The Motion Picture Association of America's president, Jack Valenti, formulated the voluntary rating system in 1968 with two other organizations: the National Association of Theater Owners (NATO) and the International Film Importers and Distributors of America (IFIDA). Their stated purpose was and continues to be to advise parents in advance of what they are likely to consider suitable for their children, so that they may make an informed decision about whether their kids should see it. But the rating system was also designed to safeguard artistic freedom—by not making value judgments and by acting in lieu of government controls, which the motion picture industry fears would undoubtedly be more rigid.

The concerns involved in classifying a film include theme, language, nudity and sex, and violence. The categories established in 1968 are basically the same today, though the cutoff age for R and X ratings, which used to be 16, is now 17. The categories are:

G: "General Audiences." The board applies this rating to films that contain nothing that might be offensive to parents even when their youngest children view the film. MPAA says, "Some snippets of language may go beyond polite conversation, but they are common everyday expressions. . . . The violence is at a minimum. Nudity and sex scenes are not present."

PG: "Parental Guidance Suggested." These films may contain some profanity, some violence, and brief nudity, but no extended or severe horror or sex. The PG rating acts as an alert to parents to take responsibility for their children's moviegoing.

R: "Restricted, under 17s require accompanying parent or guardian." Here the "language may be rough, the violence may be hard, and while explicit sex is not to be found . . . nudity and love-making may be involved." Parents must be there to take the edge off a youngster's film experience.

X: "No one under 17 admitted." These patently "adult" films may contain an "accumulation of brutal or sexually connected language, or of explicit sex or excessive and sadistic violence." Apparently many producers of particularly violent or sexual films never even submit their films to the board for ratings, but simply apply an X themselves, hoping to attract those on the lookout for as much excitement as they can get. (No other rating, however, can be self-applied.)

The ratings are not comparative or imitative. The board claims to classify each film individually, taking note of what elements are present, to what extent, and for how long, so that the rating usually reflects a summation of the film, not a particular scene. One exception is the appearance of any harsh, sexually derived words, which automatically drive the film into the R category. Otherwise there is no predetermined set of rules. Richard Heffner (who is a historian, teacher, and author of *A Documentary History of the United States* as well as chairman of the ratings board) said, ". . . there is no pretense that *all* of one kind of film content . . . must go into one classification rather than another. That would be unrealistic, a denial of the nature of contemporary films—and their audiences." Each board member first applies an over-all rating, then fills out a rating form giving his or her reason for rating in each of several categories, and then applies an overall rating. The final rating is decided by majority vote.

Because of the flexibility of the system and the absence of absolute criteria, there is much debate about the ratings—and many an irate producer who feels he will lose half his audience because of an R rating, say, on a film he considers PG (and vice versa!). Such disgruntled producers may revise their film and resubmit it, which means the board must sit through two, three, sometimes eight versions of the same film. If disagreement persists, the producer may appeal the decision to a Rating Appeals Board, composed of twenty-four members from MPAA, NATO, and IFIDA. Such was the case with the producers of *Dogs*, rated R. Heffner, however, remained steadfast in his defense of the rating board's decision:

> . . . the Rating Board feels that most parents of young children would consider it inappropriate to classify *Dogs* as "PG," given its many scenes both of vicious dog attacks upon human beings and of their bloody results.
>
> Dogs are not, after all, seldom-seen denizens of the deep or of the wilderness that children generally encounter only in fictional situations. They are house-hold pets, the favorites of American children. And we believe that most American parents will find the results of their frenzied attacks upon human beings—as depicted so forcefully in [the] film—far too heavy for their younger children to see unaccompanied by an adult.
>
> We . . . appreciate the fact that the fearsomeness upon which we base our "R" for *Dogs* is considered basic to the film's essence and purpose. But we believe that that fearsomeness also takes the film far beyond what most parents will anticipate or accept in the "PG" classification.

?

How does a Polaroid picture develop in broad daylight?

Each frame in a pack of Polaroid film is a self-contained unit that serves as film, darkroom, and finished print. It works its sorcery in the seventeen chemical layers crammed with great precision under the surface of a square image area less than .002 inch thick. Migrating among these layers are the dyes that make the picture, the developing agents that bring the colors out, and the opacifier dye, which protects the image as it develops.

After you take a shot, the camera sends your picture-to-be through a set of rollers that squeeze it like an old-fashioned clothes wringer. This breaks open a pod lining one side of the image area and forces liquid reagents (chemicals that cause reactions) to flow among the film layers and make your picture emerge. These include white pigment, water, developers, opacifiers, and alkalis. The entire process goes on under the surface. The white pigment in the reagent makes the white areas in the print; the colors rise from beneath.

The opacifier spreads with the other reagents all the way across the emulsion to prevent any further exposure of the film; it is a whitish dye that keeps light from bombarding the sensitive layers below by absorbing it before it can penetrate further; the dye absorbs light only when in an alkaline solution, however. The reagents squeezed in with the opacifier are themselves alkalines so as the processing finishes and the reagents are used up, the solution becomes less alkaline, and the opacifier stops absorbing light and turns transparent. This lets the colors of your new picture shine through.

Colors are made in a photographic image by mixing only three basic dyes: cyan (blue-green), magenta (purplish red), and yellow. Combinations of these can make any color in nature. The three colors work together because each of them is in a way the opposite of something: yellow is the color you get by mixing all the colors of the spectrum except blue; magenta is everything but green; and cyan is the spectrum minus red. Thus, to get a certain area of film to show up green, all the magenta dye at that spot must somehow be concealed while the cyan and yellow are brought forth.

In Polaroid film, developers attached to the dye molecules themselves, called dye developers, make a certain color appear by immobilizing the dyes that *aren't* needed for it. The immobilized dyes stay concealed under the many chemical layers, and the needed dyes float to the top where you can see them.

The dyes begin in separate layers at the bottom of the stack of seventeen. Each dye layer is overlaid by a thin covering of silver halide, a chemical sensitive to light. The halide above each dye is sensitive to a different color of light. For instance, when light from a green object strikes an area of the film, the green-sensitive halide molecules—which cover the magenta dye—change their shape. As the reagent flows in, the exposed green-sensitive silver halide reacts with the magenta dye underneath it and holds it in place. Meanwhile, the unexposed halides over the cyan and yellow layers at that spot (which aren't sensitive to green light) haven't changed their shape, and they *don't* react with the dyes they cover; so cyan and yellow float freely up to a positive upper layer to make the green you see in your picture. They are trapped there by another chemical, to keep them from migrating any more and spoiling the image.

A clear plastic top layer protects the finished print from damage and even makes it look brighter, as light from the room bounces back and forth between the glossy emulsion and the plastic coat.

The exact processes and chemical names involved in Polaroid photography are still cloaked in fierce industrial secrecy and are protected by several hundred unreadable patents (patents are written to obscure deliberately what the invention in question is to be used for, to make it harder for competitors to benefit from any of the information in them). This incredibly intricate technology is the result of forty years of continuous research and invention in light theory, machine engineering, and organic chemistry. Several hundred compounds new to the planet Earth were whipped up specially in the effort to perfect instant photography—all for the sake of those 60 seconds of magic, and for the image that preserves a moment of your everyday life.

?

How do they get corn off the cob and into the can?

When truckloads of freshly picked corn arrive at a processing plant, the ears are dumped onto a conveyor belt that transports them to a husking machine. Rotating rollers with fluted surfaces strip the foliage and stalk from the randomly fed corn and send it on for inspection. Immature or diseased corn is removed by hand; in some plants the most perfect ears are selected to be marketed as frozen corn on the cob. The remaining healthy ears are then sent along a conveyor belt to the cutters. Workers must stand on either side of the belt and line up the corn by hand so that it enters the machine straight on, butt end first. Some machines have rotating blades that remove the kernels of corn; in others the blades are stationary and the ears are simply pushed through. Small ears are accommodated by automatic adjustments in the blades, which open and close radially like the aperture on a camera. The blades

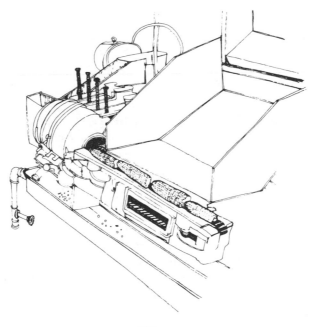

on older machines were set by a spring-loading device to a minimum opening, so that the ears would push them open to the necessary degree. On newer machines, the ears pass between rollers that gauge the size of the ear, and a linkage to the blade head opens it accordingly. Corn is stripped from the cob as fast as the workers can line up the ears, which is about 100 ears per minute. The machines themselves are capable of cutting 120 to 140 ears per minute.

The completion of the packing process is surprising: the corn is vacuum-canned and sealed *before* it is cooked. The cans then go to a retort, or huge steam pressure cooker, where they stand while the contents cook. Some plants have a spiral running the length of the retort, which rolls the cans continuously to allow better penetration of heat and more even distribution inside the can. Finally, rollers on a conveyor pass transport the cans from the cooker to a machine that stacks them in the "shine state"—labels may be added at the plant or later at a distribution center.

?

How do they make mirrors?

Whether out of curiosity, vanity, or a motive as yet unexplored, people throughout the ages have wanted to see their own reflection. As early as 2500 B.C. the Egyptians had mirrors of highly polished metal, usually of bronze, occasionally of silver or gold. The first commercial glass mirrors were made in Venice in 1564; these were made of blown glass that was flattened and coated with an amalgam of mercury and tin. The Venetians proceeded to supply Europe with mirrors for centuries. It wasn't until 1840 that a German chemist named Justus Liebig came up with the method of silvering that we use today. By this technique, silver-ammonia compounds are subjected to the chemical action of a reducing agent, such as invert sugar, Rochelle salt, or for-maldehyde, and the resulting metallic silver is spread evenly over the back of a smooth pane of plate glass.

Although scarcely noticeable in everyday use, plane mirrors actually produce multiple images: a slight reflection from the front as well as the stronger reflection from the back. The distortion, caused by small amounts of light passing through the glass, becomes extremely significant in scientific use, for which precision is imperative. The mirrors used in telescopes, therefore, are coated on the front as well as on the back. Aluminum, or aluminum and chromium, has replaced silver, which tarnishes rather easily. The coating is formed by vacuum deposition, a method in which the metal is heated on a coil in a vacuum chamber. The resulting vapor deposits a very thin film—a few millionths of an inch thick—onto glass ground to the proper spherical or paraboloidal shape.

?

How do camels go without water?

The notion that camels can go without water completely is a myth, nor do they use their extraordinary humps as storage tanks for water. The fact is, camels are able to make long, burdened treks across blazing deserts where oases are few and far between because of their uncommonly economical use of water. They are able to tolerate a greater depletion of body water (30 percent) than human beings, who can stand to lose only about 12 percent, because camels lose water from their body tissues alone, leaving the water content of the blood fairly constant. Most mammals, on the other hand, lose water from the blood, which becomes increasingly viscous and sluggish until it no longer carries away a sufficient amount of metabolic body heat and leads to heat prostration, collapse, and possible death.

Camels can also consume up to 25 gallons of water in a very short time, taking in as much as they have lost and thoroughly diluting their body tissues without dying of water intoxication (a condition in which the cells are overly flooded) as would other mammals.

Camels can tolerate not only wide variations in water content, but also a rather broad range of body temperatures, which helps them use water economically. During the summer in North Africa, for example, a camel's temperature might be 93 degrees Fahrenheit in the morning and rise to 105.3 degrees Fahrenheit in the afternoon. The camel does not begin to sweat, however, until the higher temperature is reached, which means water loss by sweating is limited. The coarse hair on the camel's back helps block some of the sun's heat, but it is well ventilated enough to allow cooling by quick evaporation of sweat.

Little water is lost in the camel's feces. The rate of urine flow is low, and, to compensate, the kidneys secrete a very low amount of urea, particularly when protein is scarce. To help them survive in the torrid deserts of Central Asia, India, and North Africa, the camels' metabolic rate is low, allowing these phlegmatic animals to live on low-grade, dry food and to stay away from water holes for stretches of two weeks or more.

?

How do they measure the elevation of a city or mountain?

In addition to the networks of highways, railroads, and telephone wires that connect the farthest sections of the country, another, less visible system exists by which elevations of towns, cities, mountains, and lakes have been determined. Points of reference are marked by thousands of bench marks from coast to coast, the work of state surveys, the U.S. Geological Survey, the U.S. Coast and Geodetic Survey, and others. "Monumented" bench marks (which appear on maps as oblique cross symbols with the letters *BM*) are identified by standard tablets set in concrete or stone posts, firm rock, or buildings. Nonmonumented bench marks may consist of chiseled squares or crosses in masonry structures, metal pins or nails in concrete, or copper nails and washers in tree roots. This ever spreading network is the means of arriving at our most precise determinations of elevation. Such

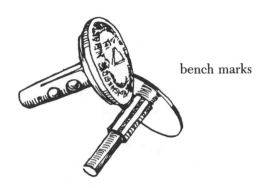

bench marks

determinations are not only a matter of general interest to the public; they are highly important for control of topographic mapping and necessary for many surveying and civil engineering operations.

In the United States, geodetic elevations refer to mean sea level, which is the average height of the sea measured hourly over a period of nineteen years. (In this length of time the earth completes a cycle incorporating the full sweep of tidal variations.) The first transcontinental line of precise levels started in 1878 at a tidal station in Sandy Hook, New Jersey, which was intended to provide a vertical control along the 39th parallel. Measurements along this line, taken across the entire continent, were described as being on the "Sandy Hook Datum." The first ties to the Pacific coast were made at Seattle, Washington, in 1907 and at San Diego, California, in 1912.

In 1929 increased knowledge about sea level resulted in a so-called special adjustment. Mean sea level apparently slopes upward to the north along the Atlantic and Pacific coasts, and to the west along the Gulf coast. It is also somewhat higher on the Pacific coast than on the Atlantic. New data were obtained from twenty-six tidal gauges at twenty-one United States sites and five locations in Canada. It is on the basis of those measurements that the elevations we know today were determined.

With a known elevation in hand, surveyors may advance the line of controls by several methods. By far the most common is leveling, which is classified in four orders of decreasing accuracy. (First-order leveling, for example, extends over a distance of .05 to 1 mile, measures to an accuracy of .017 foot per mile, and establishes bench marks at least every mile. Third-order, on the other hand, is slightly less precise; monumented bench marks are placed within 3-mile limits.) The U.S. Coast and Geodetic Survey is responsible for most first- and second-order controls. Whenever possible, points are identified and measured along highways and railroads, the most accessible sites available.

A leveling crew consists of a levelman, a recorder, and two rodmen. The standard level is equipped with a telescope for sighting and a leveling device for making and maintaining a horizontal line of sight. This device is either a sort of pendulum, which operates quickly and accurately by the force of gravity, or a cylindrical vial containing a bubble, which must be adjusted manually. The levelman first sights a rod (graduated in hundredths of a yard) held on a point whose elevation is known. He adds the rod reading to this elevation in order to determine the height of his instrument. He then turns the level in the direction he wishes to progress and sights another rod, usually about 50 feet away. In the most precise leveling, the two rods must be exactly equidistant from the level to prevent any distortion due to refraction or the curvature of the earth. The elevation at the point of the second rod is found by subtracting the new rod reading from the height of the instrument. The level is then advanced to a new setup and the procedure repeated, using the newly determined elevation as a reference. Various checks are made to prevent errors, which can be magnified greatly over substantial distances.

A leveling crew may progress quite happily down a highway or across a field, but dense forests, steep inclines, and mountains present new sets of problems. Siting points step by stepup a massive, icy peak such as Mount McKinley would, of course, be tricky. In such a case a method of determining a low-order elevation without ascending the mountain may be employed. In the most widely used technique, a surveyor starts at Point A of known elevation at the base of the mountain. If he knows the latitudinal and longitudinal coordinates of that point and the coordinates of the peak to be measured, he can calculate the distance between the two points. Another method of determining the distance to the peak is to observe the horizontal angle at Point A from Point B to the peak, observe the horizontal angle at Point B from the peak to Point A, and determine the distance between Point A and Point B. The distances from Point A and

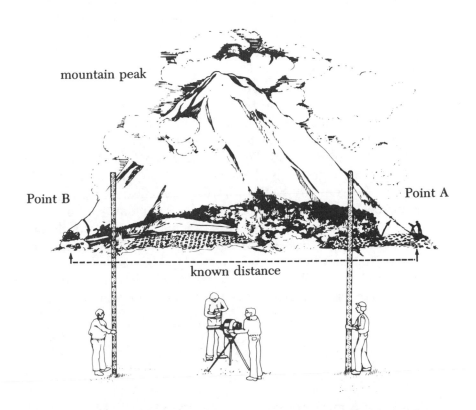

mountain peak

Point B

Point A

known distance

In the foreground, a leveling team made up of a front rodman, recorder, levelman, and rear rodman advance along reasonably flat terrain, determining new points of elevation from points where the elevation is known. In the background, a surveyor sights the mountain peak with a theodolite in the process of determining its elevation, using angle measurement and the distances between the three points: A, B, and the peak.

Point B to the peak can then be computed. Using a theodolite—an instrument that measures both horizontal and vertical angles—the surveyor then sights the mountain peak and measures the vertical angle. With these two figures (distance between the points and vertical angle measurement) he can determine the mountain's elevation trigonometrically. This technique, which measures the vertical angle in one direction only, makes use of what is called a nonreciprocal vertical angle.

Reciprocal vertical angles can be used if one can get to the top of the mountain and perform the same procedure in reverse— sighting Point A and/or Point B at the base of the mountain and measuring the vertical angle to it. Also, if one gets to the top of the mountain, the distance to Point A and/or Point B could be determined by measuring them with an Electronic Distance Measuring Instrument (EDMI). (This sophisticated instrument has a mirror that reflects light to another instrument—in this case at Point A or B—and the distance is calculated automatically on the basis of the speed of light.) Elevation differences computed from both top and bottom are then compared, and if they are within the allowed tolerance, they are combined to arrive at a more accurate trigonometric elevation of the mountain.

?

How does a microwave oven cook food from the inside out?

In 1945 Edison General Electric introduced the first microwave oven for popular consumption; since then the commercial and domestic use of these ovens has been steadily increasing, largely because of the speed with which they cook food. Microwave ovens cook food by friction: the oven emits short radio waves (micro-waves range from 1 millimeter to 30 centimeters in length) which penetrate the food and cause its molecules to vibrate. This motion creates heat, which in turn cooks the food.

Glass, cardboard, and even china containers can safely be placed in the oven while it is on, for microwaves pass through

142

without heating them. Also, microwaves bounce off metal without altering its temperature.

A microwave oven contains an electronic vacuum tube called a magnitron which converts electrical energy into high-frequency microwave energy by oscillation. In most ovens the microwaves travel through a metal tube to the metal blades of a stirrer (which resembles an electric fan), which then scatters the microwaves throughout the oven; they strike the walls, bounce off, and penetrate the food. Because of the finite number of microwaves produced by the magnitron, microwave cooking is less efficient than conventional ovens for cooking large quantities of food. For instance, a regular oven takes about an hour to bake one, or many, potatoes; a microwave oven can bake one potato in 3 minutes—but 2 minutes more are needed to bake each additional potato.

?

How does a thermostat know your house has cooled off?

Thermostat means, literally, "heat constant." Temperature changes have a great effect on matter, including the matter human beings are made of; being too hot or cold can do the body great damage. A thermostat keeps the temperature of a house constant by using the response of matter to temperature change to throw switches in a heating system on and off.

Most thermostats are based on a bimetallic strip that expands and contracts with changes in temperature. A bimetallic strip is a strip made of two different metals, bonded together, that have different rates of thermal expansion. Heat is the random motion of the atoms making up a substance as they collide with one another. All matter expands as it is heated, because its atoms have more collisions and knock one another farther and farther away. Some substances expand more than others. For example, a strip of brass expands more quickly than a strip of iron heated to the same temperature. If you heat a strip of iron and brass that have been bonded together in a metal "sandwich," the strip as a whole curls

143

toward the iron layer, as the brass seeks to expand while attached to the less volatile iron. If you cool the strip, it curls the other way, since brass also contracts faster than iron.

If you run an electric current through the strip, which powers an electromagnet to hold your furnace switch in the "on" position, a thermostat will turn off the furnace every time the house gets too hot and thus keep the temperature within a narrow range. At a "cold" temperature—say, 50 degrees Fahrenheit—the strip, carrying a current, touches a metal contact to keep the magnet working and the furnace on. With the brass side facing the contact, every time the temperature rises above, say, 65 degrees Fahrenheit the brass expands more than the iron and curls toward the iron half of the sandwich—away from the contact. This breaks the circuit, leaving the electromagnet without power, which lets the furnace switch go to "off." If the temperature drops again, the brass contracts and the strip curls back to the contact, switching on the furnace.

You can also adjust the temperature you want to maintain: by sliding the contact toward the tip of the strip, you can lower the "threshold" temperature at which the furnace kicks off, since the tip moves first as the strip curls.

A thermostat to control a cooling system has the iron side of the strip touching the contact, so the cooler goes off as the brass contracts and pulls the iron away.

?

How do glasses correct nearsightedness or farsightedness?

The range of eye problems is vast, and the methods of correction are highly refined and complex, but the basic principle behind the correction of nearsightedness or farsightedness is quite simple. If you have either of these conditions, the purpose of your glasses is to converge or diverge the light that enters your eyes so that it will focus the image at the right place: on the retina.

The human eye is spherical. Its outer layer, the sclerotic coat, is

white except in the front, where light passes through the cornea, whose curved shape bends the light rays in order to focus them. The middle or choroid coat, containing pigment and blood vessels, forms the iris in front of the eye, with its opening, the pupil. The pupil opens or closes in accordance with the amount of light to which it is exposed, allowing you to see as clearly as possible in the dark while protecting you from intense, direct rays on a hot summer day. A lens behind the iris, held in place by suspensory ligaments, focuses the incoming light. Contraction of muscles attached to the ligaments causes the lens to bend from a flat to a

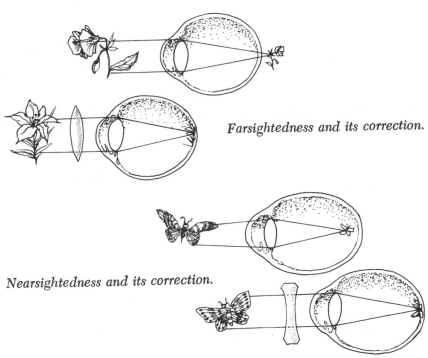

Farsightedness and its correction.

Nearsightedness and its correction.

more spherical shape, which in turn shifts the focus of images. In a normal eye the lens causes the rays of light to converge on the inner coat of the eye, the retina, which contains light-sensitive rods and cones.

If you are farsighted, however, the light doesn't converge enough to bring nearby objects into focus, either because the distance from the pupil to the retina is too short or the lens too flat. A convex lens in your glasses, which causes the light to converge somewhat before it enters the eye, can correct this problem, also helping the eye itself to converge the light more quickly. Conversely, if you are nearsighted, your eyeball may be too long or your lens too spherical, and as a result the image of a distant object comes into focus before it reaches the retina, falling out of focus again by the time it strikes the retina. A concave lens in your glasses should diverge the light sufficiently to compensate.

?

How do they determine from the rubble the cause of a building's collapse?

If the rubble always contained the secret of why a building collapsed, the work of investigating engineers would be greatly facilitated. As it is, digging through and photographing the rubble is only a part of the work entailed. Thorough examination must be made of the building's history from the time it was conceived by an architect. This means locating and studying the architect's and engineer's drawings, the engineering calculations, the shop drawings of contractors and subcontractors for each part, and the quality control records kept during the building's construction. An investigating committee would search for any documentation of a problem that was never corrected, although if an engineer or contractor were aware of such an error, he might not have kept the document around.

As is apparent, determining the cause of a building's collapse is a task for an intuitive Sherlock Holmes with a comprehensive education in engineering. When lawsuits are involved (and they generally are when millions of dollars are at stake), you can be sure the investigators won't leave a single beam, rock, or page unturned.

Buildings fail because of one or a combination of the following: design errors, construction errors, material deficiencies, or a natural disaster that exceeds the safety risk determined by a code, which usually is based on what might happen once in a hundred years. The first three factors are what concern an investigator, and they generally derive from ignorance, carelessness, or greed. For example, if an engineer misconstrued the architect's intention and used beams that are too thin to support the roof load or an expected snow load, the building suffers from a design error. If the contractor failed to use enough guys, or supporting wires, while building, the collapse is the result of faulty construction. Another possibility is that someone along the way tried to cut costs by using concrete that doesn't meet the strength requirements necessary for the building. A sample of concrete is taken at the outset of construction and tested for twenty-eight days; as the building is begun during this time, "shores" are used to support it until the concrete is fully dry and has been proved adequate. Early removal of these shores by hasty contractors is a prevalent cause of collapse.

Not all collapses are as spectacular as that of the Hartford Civic Center Coliseum, which fell on January 18, 1978. Nor are investigations always so extensive as that done by Lev Zetlin Associates, Inc., an engineering firm that did an exhaustive study of the entire project. But a glimpse at some of their proceedings gives an idea of what is involved in determining the cause of a building's collapse.

From the start there were investigators in the field, examining and photographing the roof structure, a space truss specifically designed for the Coliseum. (The space truss consisted of 120 inverted pyramid modules, each 30 feet square, with intermediate bracing members.) Initially, 15 feet of rubble from the roof lay in the middle of the Coliseum and obscured what later aerial photographs revealed to be a line of buckling right down the middle of the building. Findings in the field were constantly compared and contrasted with independent studies of architec-

147

tural, structural, and mechanical drawings; electrical, plumbing, and space truss architectural drawings; and steel shop drawings for the space truss. Especially useful were computer analyses of the roof, which simulated its structural behavior in various sequences of failure. For example, a series of pictures was drawn simulating how the space truss would react under different roof loads. Although many Hartford residents thought that snow caused the roof collapse, the committee found that the snow load on January 18 was only 17 pounds per square foot, and the design allowed for 30 pounds per square foot. On the other hand, the roof load (excluding outside factors such as snow) was designed for 40 pounds per square foot, but the actual load was found to be 53 pounds per square foot. On a total load basis, the roof structure was supporting (or trying to support) 1.5 million pounds more than it was designed to sustain. In addition to all this, a metallurgical report was drawn up evaluating materials used and their conformity to safety codes.

By studying the computer drawings and photographs of the Coliseum that indicated the direction of collapse, the committee realized that failure was progressive, that individual members had given way, causing others to fail—a dominolike process that began at the time the space truss was erected. A highly technical, mathematical analysis of the pyramid modules showed the bracing to be inadequate. Collapse was primarily caused by miscalculation of the buckling capacity of certain members of the space frame.

?

How do they get natural gas to your house?

When you flick on your gas stove to make a cup of coffee, you may be at the receiving end of a delivery system reaching more than 1,000 miles.

Natural gas, created by the decomposition of organic matter, becomes trapped in pockets hundreds of feet below the earth's surface. Shafts are drilled into those pockets to obtain the gas, which is fed into transmission lines as large as 42 inches in diameter. The gas is pumped at high pressures over great distances through an extraordinary network of pipelines that supplies the entire country. New York City's gas, for example, comes all the way from Texas and Louisiana, traveling for five days at 15 miles per hour.

When the gas arrives at its destination, the pipeline companies route it to metering control stations operated by the local gas company. Pressure in the pumped gas is reduced and a chemical added to give gas the distinctive smell we associate with it. Natural gas is in fact odorless, and dangerous leaks could go undetected if the scent chemical were not added.

Metal or plastic pipes—mains and service pipes—carry gas underground to your house or apartment building. These pipes are embedded in sand and surrounded by fill at least 3 feet underground. Checkpoints occur at regular intervals throughout the system, consisting of two manholes, 25 feet apart, each equipped with a filter to clean gas of any dirt particles and a regulator to increase or decrease the rate of flow. The manholes are on the same main, but an alternate pipe can divert the gas before the first manhole and return it after the second in the event that problems arise with the regulators. The pressure in some gas lines also may be monitored at a central control office. Mains branch into smaller service lines with control valves to supply each house or apartment building. These in turn channel the gas to the heaters, air conditioners, or stoves in your home.

In order to meet high demand for gas in winter, some companies store huge quantities in steel tanks in the form of liquefied natural gas (LNG). Gas is taken directly from the pipelines, cleaned, and chilled to an extremely low temperature of −260 degrees Fahrenheit. As it cools, the gas shrinks. In liquid form it occupies only 1/600 of the space it does as a vapor, making it convenient to store and to transport over land.

?

How do they splice genes?

Gene splicing, a truly revolutionary feat of molecular biologists in recent years, has the potential to make new life forms from different organisms and to synthesize cheaply the scarce substances needed to cure disease. Among those is the potent antiviral protein interferon, which may at last cure the common cold and may provide effective treatment of cancer.

To understand gene splicing, one has to go back to the 1950's and 1960's, to the research done on the structure of genes. In 1953 James Watson and Francis Crick discovered the molecular structure of DNA, or deoxyribonucleic acid. Some years later they discovered that the genes within the nucleus of a cell contain long, twisting strands of DNA—a sort of double spiral staircase, or "double helix"—and that each strand contains four series of smaller branches. It is these four subunits, which are randomly

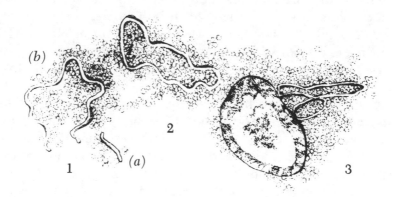

1. *A DNA gene (a) moves toward a plasmid (b), which has been cut with the help of enzymes and lies open to receive the new link.*
2. *The DNA gene has latched on to the sticky ends of the plasmid to form a new DNA molecule.*
3. *The new plasmid is on the verge of penetrating the bacterium membrane. Once inside, it will alter the future of the bacterium with its new genetic code.*

repeated, that provide the master plan, the unique code, for a specific protein; and proteins—in a variety of forms—make up the entire human body. Another nucleic acid, RNA (ribonucleic acid), is the messenger that carries the genetic code. RNA has one strand, with four subunits that arrange themselves to match perfectly those of a DNA strand. The RNA then moves out of the cell, gathers biochemicals, and formulates protein, the third essential ingredient—the stuff of which we are made.

In the seventies biologists learned that certain enzymes, called restriction enzymes, can be used to cut a DNA strand at certain places. Bits of DNA actually can be taken out and replaced in a different order, or new bits introduced, to provide a brand-new blueprint for the RNA to follow.

Biologists engaged in such research have been working with the *Escherichia coli* bacterium, a single-celled organism that lives in the human stomach and intestines. They chose this bacterium partly because it contains a thousand times less DNA than a human cell. (If unwound, the DNA in a *single* human cell would stretch a mile or more!) First, the *E. coli* is chemically treated to release its DNA. Biologists then isolate a plasmid, a ring of DNA integral to the structure of the bacterium. A restriction enzyme cuts the plasmid, and the enzyme actually leaves the cut ends of the plasmid slightly sticky. When a new DNA gene, which has also been treated by the restriction enzyme, leaving it somewhat sticky, is introduced, it latches on to the plasmid. The new molecule is then returned to the *E. coli* bacterium, whose membrane has been softened with a chemical to allow the plasmid to reenter. No matter how foreign the introduced protein may be, the bacterium adapts and multiplies according to its new code.

A hormone called somatostatin was the first protein to be synthesized in *E. coli* by recombinant DNA. Later came insulin, then a growth hormone from the pituitary gland, and most recently interferon. The tricky part in many instances is locating the gene in the first place. Sometimes biologists find the RNA first and use it to form DNA. If the RNA is abundant and easy to collect, as with insulin, the process is facilitated; if it is scarce, as in the case of interferon RNA in the white blood cell, the arduous search is for one molecule among thousands.

?

How do they transmit pictures by telephone?

The transmission of photographs over telephone wires is extremely useful—especially for newspapers and magazines which may require photographs instantly—and it is not as complicated as one might think.

First, a positive photographic image is illuminated with a small light. The whiter the image, the greater the reflection; darker images reflect less light. A photocell picks up the reflected light and converts it into an electronic signal, which is then transmitted over the telephone system. If one were to view with an oscilloscope a picture signal being transmitted over the phone line, it would look very much like that of voice or music transmission.

At the other end, a receiver takes this modulated picture signal, extracts the information, and translates the electrical code back into an image. There are several different types of receivers, but the most common is an electrostatic unit, in which paper charged with the appropriate voltage is sent through a toning station that produces the image. Older equipment uses ordinary negative film, and the recovered electronic signal is used to drive a lamp that exposes the negative. The negative is then taken into a darkroom and processed just as is ordinary photographic film.

?

How do they actually transfer money from your checking account to someone else's?

When people wrote checks in England as early as 1762, the banks hired delivery clerks to run back and forth between banks to collect the money. To expedite matters, banks developed clearinghouses, organizations in the bank's locality through which checks were exchanged and net balances settled. Woodrow Wilson organized this system on a nationwide basis in the United States when he signed the Federal Reserve Act in 1913, which provides a national clearing mechanism for checks. A Federal Reserve bank acts as a check-clearing and collection center for the banks in its district. There are twelve main Federal Reserve banks (and twenty-six branches) in major cities across the country. Individual banks have deposits at their Federal Reserve (or correspondent) bank, where transactions are settled by crediting the sending and debiting the receiving banks' accounts. The Federal Reserve banks then must pay each other daily by settling the net balances of each day's transactions on the books of an interdistrict settlement fund in Washington.

If you send a check from Chicago, for example, to a friend in California, the transfer of money isn't quite so direct as it might appear. First, the friend goes to his local bank in Berkeley and deposits your check. The local bank deposits the check for credit in the Federal Reserve Bank of San Francisco, which then sends it on for collection from the Federal Reserve Bank of Chicago. The Federal Reserve Bank of Chicago forwards the check to your own local bank, which deducts the amount from your account (assuming you aren't bouncing checks) and then tells the Reserve Bank of Chicago to deduct the same amount from its deposit account with the Reserve Bank. Next, the Federal Reserve Bank of Chicago must pay the Federal Reserve Bank of San Francisco by payment in its share of the interdistrict settlement fund. The Federal Reserve Bank of San Francisco may then credit the local bank in Berkeley, which in turn credits your friend's account.

In 1979 Americans wrote approximately 34.14 million checks, and each year the volume of checks is estimated to increase by 7 percent. Fifteen billion of these checks passed through Federal Reserve banks; the others—particularly those representing large transactions between banks—were processed by correspondent banks, city clearinghouses, and so on. Most Federal Reserve banks are equipped with IBM 3890 processing machines, which, at a rate of 100,000 per minute, sort checks into compartments representing single banks or groups of banks, at the same time weeding out forgeries, checks improperly endorsed or dated, and checks drawn on accounts with insufficient funds. In 1979 more

153

than 4,000 full- and part-time employees of the Federal Reserve were involved in the national operation of check clearance.

?

How do they make dry ice?

This strange substance—ice so cold it burns—is an excellent refrigerant, of course, and also a useful source for the ghoulish vapors in vampire and mystery movies. Dry ice is actually composed of carbon dioxide, which at normal temperatures sublimes, or becomes a gas.

The carbon dioxide is stored and shipped as a liquid in tanks at pressures approaching 1,073 pounds per square inch. In order to make dry ice, the liquid is withdrawn from a tank and allowed to evaporate at a normal pressure in a porous bag. This rapid evaporation consumes so much heat that part of the liquid CO_2 freezes to a temperature of -109 degrees Fahrenheit. Looking something like snow, the frozen liquid is then compressed by machine into blocks, which can be shipped and sold, and which will, in time, melt away to a gas.

?

How does radiation therapy help cure cancer?

Radiation works on cancer because it damages cells; by and large, normal cells recover from the bombardment better than malignant ones.

"Radiation" in this case refers to ionizing radiation—a flow of energy that tends to split the molecule it strikes into ions, or particles with an electrical charge. For example, when a water molecule is ionized, it is rearranged from the familiar H_2O

154

molecule into a positive ion and a negative ion: H^+ and OH^-. Ionizing a cell's contents with an outside force disrupts its functioning.

The radiation used in cancer therapy consists of either X rays—high-frequency light that penetrates flesh easily—or particle radiation—a flow of tiny particles given off by the atoms of certain elements. Both kinds of radiation ionize what they strike. X rays are beamed at a tumor through an electrically powered X-ray tube, whereas pieces of radioactive elements such as radium or radioactive phosphorus are implanted directly into cancerous tissue to disrupt the malignant cells.

Tumor cells are dangerous because they get in the way of normal bodily functions: they begin as normal cells, but because of a change, or mutation, in their genes, they stop performing their usual tasks and start reproducing wildly. They use up the nutrients and blood supply around them and push vital organs aside as they grow. Radiation tends to kill rapidly multiplying cells more than others, for some reason, and also damages the blood vessels supplying malignant cells. If the therapy works, the tumor stops growing or slows down. This gives the body's own defenses a better chance at destroying it and makes other treatments such as surgery and chemotherapy more effective.

As with any procedure using radiation on the body, radiation treatment incurs some risks, since it does damage normal cells as well as defective ones. Doctors minimize the risks by limiting the area of the body bombarded to the tumor itself, as much as possible, and by spacing radiation doses over time to give normal tissue time to recover between treatments. Radiation therapy is used when the long-term risks of cancer and birth defects caused by the radiation are outweighed by the imminent threat to the patient's life posed by a cancer in the body.

?

How do they suspend a suspension bridge?

Although modern suspension bridges dazzle the eye as awesome feats of technology, the engineering form is nearly as old as man himself. Vines were the source of cables on the earliest suspension bridges. In the fourth century A.D. plaited bamboo and iron cables were used on bridges in India.

The first truly modern suspension bridge was constructed in the mid-nineteenth century by John Augustus Roebling, a German-born American engineer. His bridges, which still stand, have towers supporting massive cables, tension anchorage for the stays, a roadway suspended from main cables, and—a vitally important innovation—a stiffening deck below or beside the road deck to prevent oscillation. Roebling's first grand success, a bridge with four suspension cables and two decks, spanned Niagara Falls in 1855. The determined engineer soon undertook a still more

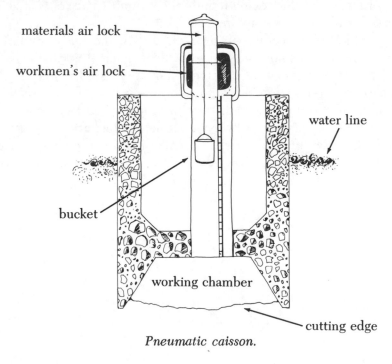

materials air lock

workmen's air lock

water line

bucket

working chamber

cutting edge

Pneumatic caisson.

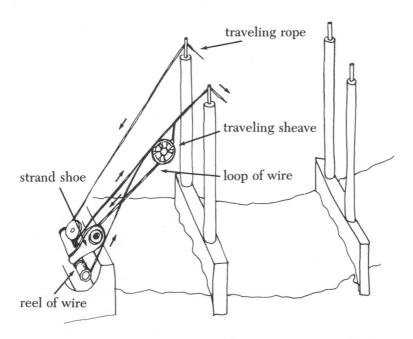

traveling rope

traveling sheave

strand shoe

loop of wire

reel of wire

Suspending parallel wire cables on a suspension bridge.

ambitious task: construction of the Brooklyn Bridge connecting Long Island and downtown Manhattan, a distance of 1,600 feet across the East River. In 1867 Roebling had the revolutionary idea of using steel wire, more resilient than iron, for the cables. Six iron trusses would run the length of the bridge's floor for stability. Aesthetics, too, were a consideration, as evidenced by the beautiful stays and broad walkway. Roebling had a tragic accident and died in 1869, but his son Washington Augustus Roebling assumed responsibility for construction, which was not completed until 1883.

In order to dig the foundations and sink the towers of the Brooklyn Bridge, Roebling used pneumatic caissons, a method still very much in the experimental stage in his day. A pneumatic caisson is a huge box or cylinder with a lower cutting edge, closed at the top and filled with compressed air to prevent soil and water from pouring in. The vessel contains an internal, airtight deck, with pressurized chambers below, where workers excavate the water bed. Mud and rubble are hauled out through another air lock, and concrete is lowered in. Pneumatic caissons today are constructed of reinforced concrete; Roebling's caissons (which measured approximately 100 by 160 feet) were made of yellow pine, coated with pitch on the inside, with tin on the outside. Furthermore, no one in the mid-nineteenth century understood the necessity of decompressing slowly after working in the chambers of the caisson; more than 100 workers—and Roebling himself—suffered severe cases of "the bends." Today, the length of time one can spend underwater and the rate of decompression are regulated by law.

Roebling's two pneumatic caissons suffered a series of disasters—floods, fires, and blowouts—as the cutting edges gradually sank into the riverbed. Working three shifts of eight hours each for more than two years, 360 men removed mud and gravel, exploded the hard clay bottom, and removed traprock and gneiss—all by the light of gas burners and calcium lights.

Erecting the cables occupied another twenty-six months. After the 271.5-foot towers were constructed, the first wire connecting the banks was towed across by scow and hoisted into position between the towers. A second rope was dragged back and the two ends spliced together, forming a continuous rope, or "traveler rope." On each bank the rope was looped around driving and guiding wheels attached to the anchorages. (In all suspension bridges, anchorages secure the ends of the cables and may be made of masonry, concrete, or natural rock.) Next, other ropes were drawn across and a planked footbridge built from which to regulate the placement of cables. Large wheels of wire were positioned near the anchorages on the Brooklyn side. A loop of two wires was hung around the light wheels of a "traveling sheave," which in turn was fastened to the traveler rope. Thus one trip of the sheave carried two wires from the Brooklyn to the New York bank, where they were fastened to a horseshoe-shaped structure called a shoe. The sheave was returned empty to the Brooklyn side, and a second sheave brought two more wires across. A total of 286 wires, bound parallel, went into each strand, and nineteen strands, in turn, made up each of the four massive cables.

The modern method of suspending a suspension bridge, although faster and more efficient, is not very different from that instigated by the Roeblings. Tower and anchorage foundations are laid first by underwater excavating, driving piles, use of pneumatic caissons, or cofferdam (a wall that isolates the area of work)—depending upon the condition of the water bed. Next, the concrete pier tops are leveled. Steel slabs nearly 5 inches thick are attached to the piers with steel dowels, and bottom sections of the towers are welded to the slabs. Steel platforms, equipped with cranes and other hoisting gear, are slung between the low towers, which are gradually built up. Cables of high-tensile steel, with individual parallel wires or twisted wires, may be as massive as 1 yard or more in diameter. Lengths of cables are put onto huge reels bearing nearly 30 miles apiece, the ends of the cables being carefully spliced together. A carriage motivated by a pulley system bears the reel over a fixed cable, from one anchorage up over the towers to the opposite shore. There the loop is anchored and a new one placed on the wheel. In order for the construction crew to have access to the cables, a temporary catwalk of cross timbers is erected. Another machine binds the cables together with wire. Finally, a coat of corrosion-resistant paint is added.

The road deck is built out gradually from both sides of the river. Or sections of it may be floated out and raised into place. There is always a certain degree of distortion, so chords of the stiffening truss are added only when the bridge is nearly complete. Until that time it remains vulnerable to strong winds.

The main span (the length between the two towers) of the Verrazano-Narrows Bridge, connecting Staten Island and Brooklyn, New York, reaches 4,260 feet—the longest in the world—and the spectacular Golden Gate Bridge in San Francisco stretches a total of 8,981 feet, with a main span of 4,200 feet. The strongest suspension bridge is New York's George Washington Bridge, designed by P. H. Ammann and constructed in 1931. Each of the four original cables, almost 1 yard in diameter,

contains 26,474 galvanized steel wires, giving the bridge a live load strength of 5,080 pounds per foot. A second road deck was added in 1962, and the bridge now accommodates fourteen lanes of traffic.

?

How do they get catgut for tennis rackets?

Ailurophiles around the world would have protested long ago if catgut were truly from cats. Although the ancient Egyptians, Babylonians, and later the Greeks and Romans made the tough cords we call catgut, it is doubtful that cats were ever the source. Today, at any rate, catgut is actually sheepgut.

The intestines of a sheep are washed and cut into ribbons. After the muscle tissue has been scraped away, the ribbons are soaked in an alkaline bath for several hours. They are stretched on frames, then removed while still moist to be sorted by size and twisted into cords. Finally, they are smoothed and polished.

Although catgut is increasingly being replaced by nylon or steel in the manufacture of tennis rackets, it remains a major source for the strings of violins, cellos, guitars, and other musical instruments. The combination of strength—gut is one of the toughest of natural fibers—and flexibility makes it ideal for producing warm, crisp sounds. Traditionally, the best catgut for musical instruments was made in Italy; today the Pirazzi family, who moved north to Offenbach, Germany, and who made strings for Paganini, make the finest strings anywhere in the world.

Catgut has surgical uses as well. About 50 percent of all suturing is done with catgut. The material, though sturdy, can be absorbed slowly by the body after the tissues have healed.

Finally, most of us have *eaten* catgut—probably unawares. An ever larger proportion of the supply is being used for the casings of sausages, which in turn raises the cost of stringing one's violin or tennis racket.

?

How do they match fingerprints?

In 1883, before fingerprint science was clearly understood as a viable means of criminal identification, Mark Twain was on to the system—a thumbprint leads to the detection of a murderer in *Life on the Mississippi*. And in *Pudd'nhead Wilson*, a novel Twain

published ten years later, a dramatic court trial highlights the infallibility of fingerprint identification. Twain's tipster was probably Sir Francis Galton, an English anthropologist who first established the individuality and permanence of fingerprints in the 1880's; his findings led to the installation in 1901 of official fingerprinting for criminal identification in England and Wales. A system of classification was devised by Edward Richard Henry, who became commissioner of London's Metropolitan Police, and it is the Henry System, with modifications and elaborations, that the Federal Bureau of Investigation uses today.

The Identification Division of the FBI was formed in 1924 by combining records from both the National Bureau of Criminal Identification and Leavenworth Penitentiary. Its purpose was to establish a national repository of criminal identification data for law enforcement agencies. Today the records have expanded vastly to include aliens, armed services personnel, and civilian employees. As of October 1, 1976, there were 165 million fingerprint cards on file, more than 74 million belonging to the criminal division.

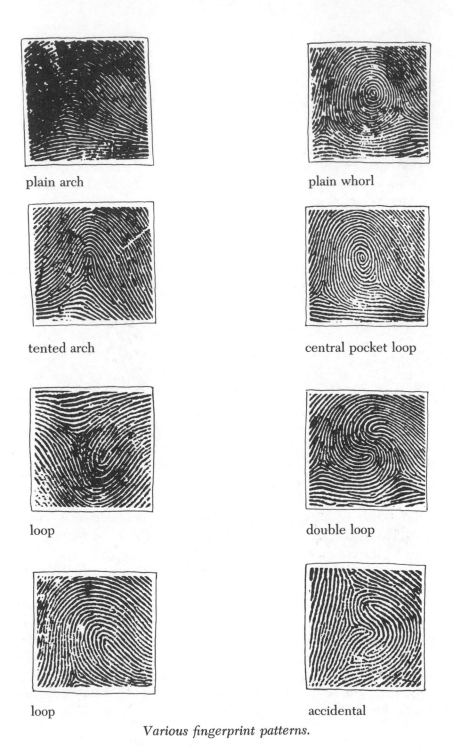

plain arch

plain whorl

tented arch

central pocket loop

loop

double loop

loop

accidental

Various fingerprint patterns.

Thousands of prints related to arrests are sent daily to the FBI. Each passes through a lengthy and complex "assembly line" of processes that date the prints, cross-index the name, classify the type of print, and frequently compare the print with existing files to make sure the new print is not in fact a duplicate. (Sixty-eight percent of persons fingerprinted because of arrests have previous records on file.) The preliminary classification (using the Henry System) is based on the existence of particular patterns in finger impressions, which include loops, arches, and whorls; each of these types is subdivided further. An arbitrary value is affixed to the appearance of certain characteristics on each finger, and the addition of those values results in a formula consisting of code letters and numerals. The initial classification, written in the upper right-hand corner of the card, directs each print to the appropriate file.

Because of the vastness of the fingerprint files, a fragment of a fingerprint from a fraudulent check, for example, cannot—as the movies would lead us to believe—lead to discovery of the criminal. But if law enforcement agencies provide a list of several or even a hundred suspects, the FBI can pull its files and make an identification from a tiny fingerprint fragment no bigger than the eraser tip of a pencil.

Various processes, including laser treatment, may be used to examine latent prints on crime-related objects. A fraudulent check, for example, can be sprayed with a reagent called a ninhydrin solution to develop latent impressions. Metal, glass, and smooth wood are dusted with a powder that sticks to the smallest oily residues left by the skin. After photographing the fragment, the technician "lifts" the powder tracing with a flexible tape to which the powder adheres. The pattern is then sealed under a transparent cellophane cover, and the technician compares this sample with fingerprints of known suspects.

The technician bases his identification on the details of fingerprint ridge characteristics. The ridges in a fingerprint have typical directions and forms. Most common are the "ridge ending" and the "bifurcation." The "dot" is another basic characteristic; the "short ridge" and the "island" are also recognized. With the aid of magnifying equipment, technicians make comparisons based on the number of ridges lying between ridge details, the linear

163

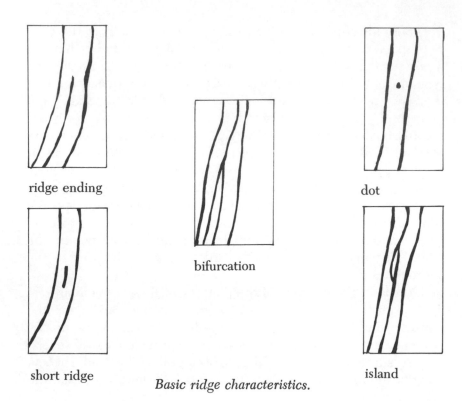

ridge ending

dot

bifurcation

short ridge

island

Basic ridge characteristics.

elevation or spacing of the details, and their direction. Opinions vary about how many points in common between a latent and a known print must be found in order to make an absolute identification—and the courts do not specify. An acceptable number is somewhere between twelve and seventeen, with twelve being most frequently quoted, as a result of the French criminologist Edmond Lucard's insistence that this figure is sufficient.

Fingerprint identification has other purposes besides tracking criminals. Lost and bewildered amnesia victims often turn to the police for help in discovering who they are. Although the FBI will not disclose specific names and places, it reports, for example, that in a southwestern state, police received a call from a man in a phone booth. He had a gun in a shoulder holster, and no idea of his name or where he came from. A set of his prints was sent to the FBI, where his U.S. Navy fingerprints, taken elsewhere years before, led to his identity.

?

How does Frank Perdue kill chickens?

As the company slogan says, "It takes a tough man to make a tender chicken," and Perdue prides itself on the efficiency with which it processes all those chickens, slaughters them, and prepares them for the marketplace in a matter of hours.

If a chicken passes the examination for quality, it is lucky enough to be caught by hand from a crate and hung by its feet on processing shackles, side by side with hundreds of others. The shackles, attached to a conveyor chain, consist of metal loops several inches apart into which the legs are hooked. Soothed first by red lights, the chickens pass through a tank of water and saline solution containing an electrical charge that stuns them. The conveyor then advances to a rotating blade that slices their necks, killing them instantaneously. Plucking is accomplished by machines called pickers: after immersion in very hot water to loosen the feathers, the chickens are passed between a series of rotating metal drums covered with short rubber fingers that pull off the feathers. An assembly line further prepares the chickens for market, and they are finally shipped off to a Perdue distributor or chain warehouse in a carton that reads: "Any squawks? Call . . ."

?

How does Ivory soap float?

In 1879, when Ivory soap was first developed by Procter and Gamble, it sank just like any other brand. It had never entered anyone's head to make it float. The soap's "floatability" actually came about by accident.

According to Procter and Gamble, one day, in the early days of Ivory soap manufacture, a worker went off to lunch, forgetting to turn off the machine that mixed the solution of soap. When he returned, he discovered a curious frothy mixture. Various workers and undoubtedly Mr. Procter himself took a look at the bubbly concoction and decided it was still usable—there was no need to throw it all away. Not long after the soap hit the market, the manufacturer started receiving letters from excited consumers asking for more "floating soap." The idea was novel, and the floating soap certainly had its uses—especially if one had to bathe in the nearby muddy Ohio River.

Once the company traced the floating soap to the frothy solution, it realized all it need do was to beat air into the mixture as it was being made. This made the soap lighter than water so that it would float. And that's exactly what Procter and Gamble does with Ivory soap today—though some consumer advocates point out that this technique gives less soap for the dollar.

?

How do they transplant hair?

According to Dr. Michael Greenwald, one of the nation's leading hair and skin specialists, hair transplantation was developed in the early 1950's by New York dermatologist Dr. Norman Orentreich, and his technique remains today the only safe and permanent way to replace hair: a minor surgical office procedure in which hair plugs from normal areas of the scalp, such as the back and sides, are moved to bald areas. Each plug transplanted has seven to fifteen hair follicles and is about the size of a pencil eraser. The transplanted hair should last a lifetime, or at least as long as the hair would have remained in the region from which the transplant was taken.

The operation itself is fairly simple. The donor area of the scalp is deadened with a local anesthetic similar to that used by a dentist. The desired number of hair transplants (each measuring about 5/32 inch in diameter) are then removed with a special instrument, which penetrates the scalp about ¼ inch, or to just

166

beneath the hair follicle. Next, the bald areas are deadened, and small plugs of the same diameter are removed and discarded. The hair transplants are carefully placed into the previously prepared bald areas a fraction of an inch apart and in such a direction that they will grow in a natural manner. A cosmetically acceptable dressing is then applied, which is removed the next morning. There is no more discomfort than one would experience at the dentist's office; the local anesthetic produces a smarting sensation, but there is seldom any pain after the procedure.

The transplanted hair is sometimes shed within four weeks after the operation, because of the trauma of surgery. But about eight weeks later new hair begins to grow from the healthy follicles, and it continues to grow at the normal rate of approximately ½ inch per month.

As for the portion of the scalp from which the transplants were taken, there remain only small scars that are hidden by surrounding hair. In fact, as many as 1,400 transplants from the back of the head can be removed without leaving a cosmetic defect.

?

How do they know whether your phone is bugged?

A phone-bugging detection service (or, as it's known in the trade, "intelligence sweeping") is one of the most secretive businesses in the world—topped, perhaps, only by the phone-bugging business itself. Phone-bugging detection equipment is usually changed by the service every three months, and often sooner—but then, so are the phone bugs.

Intelligence sweep engineers employ a wide variety of equipment. Although no functional countermeasures can be used to prevent the original placement of a bug—which consists of a small radio transmitter—the intelligence sweeper utilizes microwaves to determine whether or not a phone is bugged and, if it is, where in the immediate vicinity the bug resides. The bugs themselves operate on a particular radio frequency which allows the conversation to be broadcast to another party; the intelligence sweeper's microwaves are used to try to spot the exact location of the radio waves. Using a hit-or-miss system of triangulation (determining a position by taking bearings to two fixed points of a known distance apart and computing the dimensions of the resultant triangle), the sweeper eventually, arduously, pinpoints the location, and then simply performs a physical search to discover the transmitter.

An alternative to contracting for a private, secretive intelligence sweep is to call up the phone company. American Telephone and Telegraph provides, free of charge, a phone-bugging detection service for all its customers. Ask the company to check your phone and it will. Last year 10,000 subscribers called for this service, and AT & T in turn detected about 200 listening devices.

?

How do astronomers know where one galaxy ends and another begins?

When Galileo turned the first telescope toward the heavens, he recorded that the Milky Way (the galaxy in which Earth spins) is a stretch of innumerable stars grouped together in clusters. Those star clusters are, in fact, groupings of solar systems, composed of many suns, some with planets revolving around them. Webbing all the clusters together, creating a cloud effect, is interstellar gas (hydrogen and helium combined with more complex molecules), which spreads, in varying densities, across the galaxy.

The Milky Way is 1,000 light-years thick and 100,000 light-years across at its widest. There are approximately 100 billion solar systems in the Milky Way, comprising 100 billion to 200 billion suns. Those suns release light, which can be seen, and electromagnetic energy, which can be detected with radio telescopes.

The boundaries of a galaxy are marked by the absence of bodies (solar systems, star clusters) to attract one another and by the thinning of interstellar gas. Between galaxies are enormous voids filled only with intergalactic gas—either hydrogen or helium.

irregular galaxy

elliptical galaxies

spiral galaxies

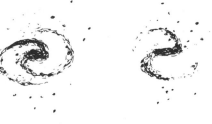

barred spiral galaxies

One way astronomers know where one galaxy ends and another begins is by observation of the forms of the galaxies. A galaxy known as Messier 31, which is 2.2 million light-years away, can be seen with the naked eye. Others require the aid of binoculars and small telescopes. Five hundred million galaxies, spanning a distance of 5 billion light-years, are within the reach of large reflecting telescopes.

The galaxies appear in a variety of forms. Spiral galaxies have well-defined arms tightly wound around a nucleus, whereas barred spiral galaxies are characterized by arms emanating from both ends of a luminous bar running through a nuclear region. Some galaxies, which contain fewer luminous stars, are elliptical; another category, called irregular galaxies, includes all those having no characteristic pattern.

It is also possible to photograph galaxies with an optical telescope. The instrument collects the galaxy's light with a mirror and reflects it onto a photographic plate from which a photograph is made. Large clusters of stars transmit light to the plate, whereas the dark spaces between galaxies cast no light, thus defining a galaxy's boundaries. One of the largest optical telescopes in the world is the Hale reflecting telescope on Mount Palomar in California. Its mirror, measuring nearly 5½ yards in diameter, collects 1 million times more light than the eye.

A more reliable, and now more widely used, device used to observe the galaxies is the radio telescope. Like optical telescopes, most radio telescopes can be positioned to "look" at different points in the universe. Some are shaped like large dishes; others consist of a group of antennae; several are actually built into natural craters in the earth. The paraboloidal dish of a typical radio telescope reflects and focuses radio waves to a "feed antenna," or pickup device, at the center of the telescope. After amplification by a receiver, the signals are conveyed by cable to a computer, which reads the intensity of the radio waves thus received from various points. A computer printout shows how radiomagnetic energy is concentrated and dispersed throughout a galaxy. At the boundaries of the galaxy, radio waves, like light waves, become very weak, and thus does the printout show where a galaxy begins and ends.

The largest radio telescope in the world lies in the hills near

Arecibo, Puerto Rico. Its vast reflector dish, lined with aluminum panels, measures 1,000 feet in diameter. The most powerful radio telescope, however, named the Very Large Array (VLA), has a series of fifteen dish-shaped antennae, each 82 feet in diameter, spread in a Y shape across the plains near Socorro, New Mexico. When all twenty-seven antennae act together electronically, the telescope has the resolving power of a single dish 17 miles in diameter.

?

How do they produce hashish?

In the thirteenth century, Marco Polo observed Chinese farmers smoking hashish as they tended their rice fields. The *Arabian Nights* of the early sixteenth century paints mysterious and dreamy scenes of Arabs getting high for days and nights on end. But the magical recipe for making hashish was known centuries before that. A Chinese doctor, writing in 2747 B.C., prescribed hashish as a cure for malaria and absentmindedness. Since hashish lowers one's body temperature slightly, it might ease a malarial fever; but as a solution to absentmindedness—the advice certainly seems questionable today!

Hashish, like marijuana, comes from the hemp plant, *Cannabis sativa*. The active ingredient in both is tetrahydrocannabinol, or THC. The effects of the two are similar, but hashish is much stronger, having a higher percentage of THC—10 to 15 percent as opposed to 1 to 3 percent in marijuana.

Marijuana comprises leaves, flowers, stems, and seeds that have been dried and chopped, but hashish comes only from the very top of the plant, where a rich resin oozes from the budding flowers and seed heads. In various parts of Asia, the female cannabis plants—which are more potent than their male counterparts—are collected before they have flowered fully. The resin, which provides the liquid base of hashish, is separated from buds and

171

leaves by beating the plants against burlap until small lumps congeal. Sugar is usually added later for weight.

The most potent hashish anywhere in the world comes from India—but you won't find this *charas* in the United States; the crumbly cakes of hashish are too fragile to be transported easily. In India, resin containing an exceptionally high percentage of THC is wiped from the female plants and is then mixed, but not chemically combined, with other ingredients. Only the Indian hemp plant, *Cannabis sativa*, produces pure *charas*. *Cannabis indica* of Africa and Asia and *Cannabis americana* of South America, Latin America, and the United States do not.

Hashish may be bought in liquid form, which is simply resin mixed with water or syrupy glucose. In North Africa a white powder type of hashish is used, consisting of resin that has been dried in the sun. Although never exported, it shows up in the notorious "green cookies" (which are actually tan) made in Marrakesh.

The most common type of hashish comes in the form of a block or lump and is produced in Lebanon, Nepal, and North Africa. The resin and a very small proportion of other ingredients, particularly sugar, have been stirred together over heat and dried in intense heat so that the different elements combine. This hashish is often quite dark, but it's a myth that the darker the hashish the better—some manufacturers add iodine to deepen the color.

?

How do they create spectacular fireworks?

As far back as the tenth century the Chinese were making fireworks, using saltpeter, sulfur, and charcoal. With the invention of gunpowder (which is actually composed of those same ingredients), the manufacture and display of fireworks came under military control in Europe until the eighteenth century, when the Italians, notable enthusiasts of fireworks, took the lead in using

172

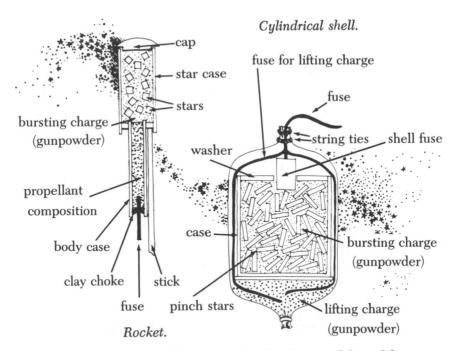

Cylindrical shell.

cap

star case

stars

fuse for lifting charge

fuse

bursting charge (gunpowder)

string ties

shell fuse

washer

propellant composition

case

bursting charge (gunpowder)

body case

clay choke

stick

lifting charge (gunpowder)

fuse

pinch stars

Rocket.

them at festivals and celebrations. (Today the rapid fire of dizzying rockets and pinwheels reflected in the canals near Venice's San Marco each July in celebration of the Feast of the Redeemer surpasses any show here on the Fourth.) The nineteenth century brought some stupendous shows in England, initiated by the manufacturers themselves. Charles Thomas Brock sponsored shows at the Crystal Palace near London using lances, or tiny, brightly burning tubes, to trace out words, pictures, and portraits of famous people—with some 35,000 lances per piece.

Fireworks contain excess fuel so that after the initial blast, some remains to burn in the air. Most are made of potassium nitrate, sulfur, and finely ground charcoal. Others contain potassium nitrate and salts of antimony, or arsenic and sulfur. Gunpowder provides the lift and explosion, and potassium chlorate creates brilliant colors.

The different patterns created by fireworks in the air are determined by variations in composition, arrangement, and casing. Roman candles, for example, packed in a case ¾ inch in diameter, have three layers, each with three different types of material: a "fountain" charge of sulfur, charcoal, saltpeter, and

173

other metal particles that give off sparks; "stars"—white or colored compounds that burn for a few seconds; and gunpowder. In each layer the fountain burns and lights the star, which is shot out by the gunpowder. Other types, such as shells that are filled with stars, have smaller shells inside that produce successive blasts after the first. The casing for pinwheels has a nozzle at each end and a central nail around which the explosive material revolves. Rockets have a paper cap on a cylindrical case tightly packed with stars and gunpowder. When the fuse is lit, burning occurs in a lower conical cavity. A propelling charge sends the rocket soaring, then ignites the gunpowder and stars for a breathtaking spectacle in midair.

?

How does Planters shell all those peanuts without breaking them?

Shelling peanuts may not seem like a difficult or very interesting task, but when you're talking about cleaning, sizing, and shelling 100,000 pounds of peanuts an hour (which the Planters plant in Aulander, North Carolina, can do), the process is a major operation.

To begin with, peanuts are extremely dirty, for they grow in the ground and arrive at the processing plants along with sticks, rubble, and clods of dirt that often bear a dangerous resemblance in both size and color to the peanuts themselves. The entire load of peanuts (and accompaniments) is dumped into a reel machine that removes some of the rocks, dirt, and sticks clinging to the peanuts. What's left is conveyed to a louver deck with 2-inch square openings, through which the peanuts fall; the larger, alien materials are "floated" off and discarded. A second deck screen with small openings does exactly the opposite: there the dirt fragments and grass slip through the screen and the peanuts remain behind. Then the peanuts are sent across a series of screens that separate the peanuts into five different sizes. The smallest drop through the screen with the smallest holes, those that don't fit pass on to the next, and so on.

The peanuts are then roasted in their shells and sent along a conveyor belt, where an electric eye sorts out discolored ones; workers pick out the remaining rejects by hand.

Finally, the good, healthy peanuts head for the shellers. These consist of semicircular baskets with openings of different sizes to accommodate the different-size peanuts. The openings are measured in sixty-fourths of an inch: a "$30/64$" is used for the largest peanuts. Four bars bolted onto a central hub turn at a rate of 200 revolutions per minute. The beaters, which have sharp edges, are precisely placed at a specific distance from the basket so that as the peanuts are struck, they are forced down through the holes—and as they go, the shells crack. Peanuts and broken shells alike tumble through, and large suction fans draw off the hulls, leaving the heavier peanuts behind.

Now that the peanuts are shelled, they are again sized by rolling them back and forth across screens, and the peanuts that have made it through still in their shells are sent back to a smaller-size shelling unit. Remaining shells and sticks are cleaned out by a machine that throws the peanuts up an incline; bizarre as it seems, the peanuts move up but sticks, grass, and the like never reach the top. (This makes sense if you consider that a hurled stone goes faster and farther than a feather thrown with the same force.) Another electric eye then scans the peanuts for dark or discolored skin, and a final visual inspection is made by workers who look over the peanuts on a series of tables and pick out any damaged ones and any lingering foreign matter. Ultimately there are five edible grades, and a remaining group of small, immature peanuts to be processed into peanut oil.

And how long does the entire complicated process take? Barely 30 minutes.

?

How do they give you fresh air in a 747, flying at an altitude of 40,000 feet?

The airlines seem to compete with one another to make flying at 30,000 or 40,000 feet above the earth as comfortable, homey, and as similar to life on the ground as possible. They boast good food and wine, provide magazines and pillows, and—something we take for granted wherever we are—supply us with air at a comfortable temperature and pressure. Remarkably, this air comes from right outside the airplane, but before it reaches you it passes through a complex pressurization and air-conditioning system, which in turn has several backup systems to assure maximum safety.

Fans in the engine of a Boeing 747 suck outside air into the engine's compressor. A small percentage of this air is issued directly into the pneumatic system for air conditioning and pressurization, avoiding the combustion chamber so as not to pick up noxious exhaust elements. Since the air reaches a temperature of about 400 degrees Fahrenheit in the compressor, it is necessary to cool it with new, cold air from the outside. Scoops under the fuselage draw in outside air ("ram air"), which at an altitude of 45,000 feet has a temperature of approximately −70 degrees Fahrenheit.

The 747 can control and maintain different temperatures in four different zones of the jet: the flight deck, main deck nose, main deck center, and main deck aft. Three air cycle packs, each consisting of a fan, a compressor, and a turbine on a common shaft, work in unison to cool the air in the pneumatic system. They are adjusted to cool the air to the maximum required by the zones; this air then feeds into a common "cold plenum," or storage tank. From there air goes directly to the zone calling for the coldest temperature. For zones requiring warmer temperatures, hot air may be added along the way to raise the cool air to the appropriate temperature.

The air cycle packs provide 8,000 cubic feet per minute of fresh

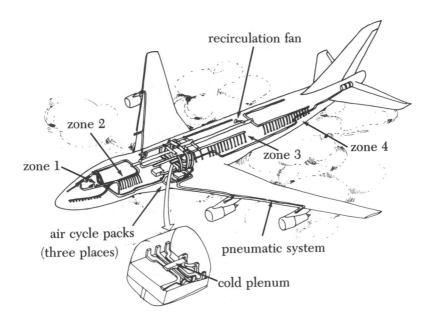

recirculation fan

zone 2

zone 1

zone 3

zone 4

air cycle packs
(three places)

pneumatic system

cold plenum

air, and a distribution system adds another 2,000 cubic feet per minute of recirculated air. Electrically operated valves control the amounts of hot or cold air entering the ducts and can route the air through any combination of engines and any combination of packs; that flexibility ensures safety in the event one or even two packs should become inoperative. In the main cabin, air enters along the side walls at hat-rack level. About 20 percent of the air goes up into the ceiling area, where fans direct it back into the supply ducts. Exhaust air leaves through side wall openings just above floor level and is circulated down to warm the cargo compartments, which are usually at 40 to 65 degrees Fahrenheit.

Just as heating, cooling, and recirculating are performed constantly while the plane is in flight, pressurization is maintained and, again, carefully monitored. The pilot has a selector on the flight panel by which he may control cabin pressure manually, or it may be controlled automatically. Air pressure drops as the plane ascends; in order to counteract this, the aircraft must be "pumped up" to provide necessary comfort. Since the thin air pumped in from the stratosphere contains less oxygen, nitrogen, and other gases than we are accustomed to, more air is continuously pumped in, compressed, cooled, and released through the air-conditioning system. A fully automatic system measures the amount of pressure required to avoid structural damage or passenger discomfort. At 45,000 feet, the atmosphere inside the airplane is comparable to that at 8,000 feet, which is perfectly comfortable since extreme and prolonged physical exertion isn't necessary. Upon descent, a system of valves releases the inside pressure gradually, so that passengers and crew are acclimated to the airport landing altitude, and the doors of the airtight airplane can be opened safely without air rushing in or out.

?

How does an airplane land in fog?

It may not settle your queasy stomach to know, but an interconnected network of electronic devices makes the landing of an aircraft in "blind" weather conditions at least as safe as driving home from the airport.

The key to your return to the earth from 20,000 feet in a pea-soup fog is the instrument landing system, or ILS, which can bring a trained pilot right to the runway threshold without his so much as glancing outside the cockpit.

In a blind landing, the pilot first uses radar navigation equipment to seek out a radio beacon called the outer marker, located from 5 to 7 miles from the runway. As he passes over the marker, a purple light on the instrument panel glows for a few seconds; meanwhile, a distinctive tone is sounded. Once oriented in this way, the plane descends along an imaginary "chute," or glide path, whose dimensions and location are relayed by a pair of radio signals. One comes from a transmitter, called a localizer, set beyond the far end of the runway, which tells the pilot whether he's to the right or left of the runway centerline. The other signal comes from a transmitter to the side of the runway which describes the glide slope path; it tilts at an angle of 2½ to 3 degrees from a height of 475 feet at the outer marker to the runway threshold itself, like a giant imaginary ramp.

As the plane descends through the fog, the pilot trains his eyes on his approach instruments—usually a cross-pointer pattern with a vertical and a horizontal needle. If both needles are centered, the plane is in the "chute"; if either strays, the pilot corrects up, down, or sideways to put the aircraft perfectly back on track.

About a minute and a half past the outer marker, a second light blinks amber for a few seconds and a beeper is again heard. This tells the pilot he is passing over the middle marker about half a mile from touchdown. By now he should be about 200 feet above the runway, and the runway lights ought to be visible directly ahead. If not, he hits the throttle to go around again—or to another airport.

In the unlikely event that the ILS should fail, there is a backup method for getting down. Tower controllers, using precision radar, can "talk" a blind-flying pilot right down the chute.

Aviation planners a decade ago thought pilots would be routinely landing in zero-visibility fog by now. That dream is still in a holding pattern for several reasons. Chief among them is the problem of taxiing blind, because—rolling along the runway at 150 miles per hour in dense ground fog—a pilot can't make his way safely with only runway lights as a guide.

?

How do they mop up oil spills?

In 1973 the National Academy of Sciences Ocean Affairs Board reported that each year *5 to 10 million metric tons* of crude oil and its byproducts (fuel oil, kerosene, gasoline, and lubricants) go into the sea. Sources range from expended ocean transport fuel to the much publicized and controversial oil spills.

Although big spills near populated beach areas receive widespread headlines and arouse considerable public outrage, smaller, confined spills in marshlands and harbors are far more grave and dangerous. In such places the oil cannot disperse, and continued release of oil can cause whole classes of plant or animal life to sicken and die, resulting in permanent changes in the ecosystem.

179

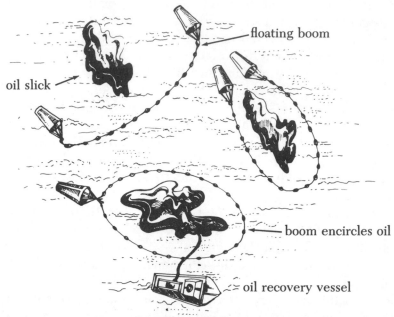

oil slick

floating boom

boom encircles oil

oil recovery vessel

Open sea spill booming.

If the oil is light—gasoline or kerosene, for example—some evaporates, whereas heavier oils tend to break down into small, hard tar balls. In either case, some soluble elements always dissolve in the water, creating an invisible threat to the life in that area. Bacteria in the water may eat some of the oil, but nature cannot rid itself entirely of the huge amounts of oil going into the sea, and we are dependent on technology to help with the job.

One of the best and most widely used methods for containing oil so that it may be mopped up is the use of oil spill booms. A boom acts as a mechanical barrier to obstruct surface water and oil, while allowing subsurface water to pass. An upper barrier of poly- urethane, polyethylene, foam, or compressed air covered with plastic reaches above the water and is supported by a float. Below this tubular float hangs a "skirt" made of plastic, rubber, canvas, or plywood, which blocks the oil. The boom is stabilized by a lead ballast. Two boats may "boom off" an area by towing a spill boom between them at a rate of 1.5 miles per hour, or a boat tows one end while the other end is anchored. The slow speed is necessary to prevent water from slipping under the boom; furthermore, the

180

method is often impractical in open ocean, for waves more than 2 or 3 feet high can cause oil to rush over the top of the boom.

To actually remove oil from the water, a variety of skimmers may be employed. A floating suction head, which is simply an enlargement of the end of a suction hose, can be immersed in thick oil slicks. Powered by a hydraulic pump, the hose draws in oil and water, and the two are then separated by gravity or other means. A floating weir—usually in the form of an inverted cup, 18 to 24 inches in diameter, supported by floats—has a straight edge that separates oil from the surface of the water and, in most cases, another weir inside *it* to further separate the two. Weirs, obviously, are impractical in strong winds and choppy water.

A drum or disk is another type of skimmer, which operates by rotating in and out of the oil slick. As the drum comes out of the water, coated with oil, it is wiped clean, then reimmersed to pick up more oil. The most efficient types consist of two counterrotating drums: one placed near the surface of the water moves rapidly with the water flow, while the other, immersed at a deeper level, moves slowly in the opposite direction. The former is coated with polyethylene, which works well with heavy oils; the latter has a

Belt skimmer.

water-wetted steel surface, which is more effective on lighter oils. Oleophilic belts—long belts covered with a material such as polyurethane foam which absorbs oil and repels water—may be set loose in a slick and harvested later by hand, or dragged behind a boat, or mounted on an inclined plane between two rollers. The oleophilic fibers soak up oil, which is then squeezed out and the belt reused. Like other skimmers, the belts do not work well in rough water, which can wash oil off before the belts are removed.

A very good method for cleaning up small, well-contained spills and vestiges of large spills involves the use of sorbents, which float in the water and soak up oil by capillary action or cause the oil to adhere to a large surface area. Inorganic sorbents include vermiculite, perlite, expanded perlite, and volcanic ash, which absorb four to eight times their own weight in oil and can then be recovered with dip nets or pool skimmers. If the wind is not too strong, organic sorbents such as peat moss, straw, milled corncobs, wood cellulose fiber, and milled cottonseed hulls can be spread on the water. In contact with oil these materials become heavy, fibrous mats which must be collected by hand or with sewer-vacuuming equipment. Synthetic organic sorbents are also used. Although costly, these materials, which include polyurethane foam, urea formaldehyde foam, polyethylene, and polypropylene, can be reused several times. Since they are persistent in the environment, they must eventually be recovered.

Chemicals, under very strict control of the Environmental Protection Agency (EPA) and similar agencies, are also useful in cleaning up spills. If placed with a spraying device around the perimeter of a spill, chemicals containing a complex alcohol that repel oil can actually move it and concentrate it into a smaller slick. Other chemicals, such as detergents, disperse oil by breaking it down into small globules that spread out through the water. Dispersants must be thoroughly mixed with the water in order to be effective. If there is sufficient wave action, the chemical may be sprayed from a plane; otherwise, it is discharged by a device dragged behind a boat. Sinking agents spread by dusting from a plane that cause oil to sink to the bottom to be degraded by biological action are illegal, according to EPA and U.S. Coast Guard regulation, subsequent to the Federal Water Pollution Control Act of 1972. The sinking agents themselves—

sand, for example—may be innocuous, but heavy oil on the ocean bottom may be harmful to fish and plant life, or the oil may escape and resurface, thus re-creating the initial problem. Sometimes oil is burned, and certain chemicals are used to provide wicks or sorbents that insulate oil from water and allow it to burn—though not always successfully.

All these methods are helpful, but none is completely effective, and each has its drawbacks. Oil spill research continues, and one of the most exciting breakthroughs derives from nature itself: the use of petrophilic bacteria—bacteria that eat hydrocarbons. Since several different species of bacteria are required to consume oil efficiently, Dr. Ananda M. Chakabarty of the General Electric Research and Development Center used genetic engineering to come up with a single strain having the eating capabilities of four different bacteria. This super strain—the patent for which was recently upheld in a landmark Supreme Court case—consumes oil far more rapidly than any other natural organism. Experiments at the University of Texas have resulted in another remarkable development: several different strains of natural bacteria may be dried and stored indefinitely as a powder, ready to be spread on a spill at a moment's notice. Researchers have conducted a test in which the powder was spread on a 10-gallon spill contained by booms; within six hours, not a trace of oil remained.

?

How do they measure the ratings that reveal on Tuesday morning what Americans watched on TV Sunday evening?

The A. C. Nielsen Company's Nielsen Television Index (NTI) is one of the most important and powerful rating services in the country, as the entire commercial television industry relies upon the ratings to determine both its programming and its advertising rates. Nielsen, founded in 1923, originally performed surveys for manufacturers of industrial machinery and equipment. But by 1950 the company had expanded into communications and developed the NTI system for network television. By 1954 the company was providing the Nielsen Station Index for local stations.

Today the Nielsen TV service includes over 1,200 households in more than 600 counties across the United States. NTI statisticians, using U.S. Census figures on the number and location of households nationwide, select representative households on the basis of location alone. The specific demographics within each household become known only after the selection process, when each member is asked to fill out a form including such information as age, sex, race, income, and occupation. Nevertheless, Nielsen claims that its sample reflects, within 2 percent, the national figures on population diversity as collected by the U.S. Census. In November 1979, for example, the Census reported that, of the entire population, 23 percent were men between the ages of eighteen and forty-nine; 24 percent were women in the same age bracket. NTI's sample included precisely those percentages. Each year 20 percent of the representative households are replaced by another group; one household could thus contribute information for five years.

The base of the Nielsen Television Index network is the Storage Instantaneous Audimeter (SIA). The SIA, which can be placed out of sight in a cabinet or in the basement away from the television set, measures all TV set usage within a household. According to Nielsen, the SIA "stores in its electronic memory exactly when each TV set in the household is turned on, how long it stays on the channel tuned, and all channel switchings."

The members of the NTI household are required to do nothing for Nielsen except watch TV. Each SIA unit is connected to a special phone line used only by NTI. At least twice a day, a Nielsen computer "dials" each home unit and retrieves the stored information. These data are then immediately processed in Nielsen's central TV research computers and, because the phone hookup is foolproof and immediate, ratings for, let's say, "60 Minutes" on Sunday evening are returned to the computer promptly, processed, and printed out. By Tuesday at 11:00 A.M. the ratings are released to terminal outlets in Nielsen's clients' offices and made available to the press.

?

How do they make rain?

For centuries dance, magic, invocation of the gods, the lighting of fires, and the ringing of church bells have all been used in one place or another by various cultures in attempts to produce rain. But it wasn't until 1946 that two pioneering scientists working for General Electric evolved ways to make rain based on knowledge of the physical processes of rain formation. Vincent Schaefer experimented with dry ice (solid carbon dioxide) chilled to −70 degrees Centigrade. He found that if he dropped a fragment of dry ice into a chamber filled with very cold cloud matter, several million ice crystals formed; the ice crystals would capture excess moisture and thereby sufficient weight to fall to the ground. Bernard Vonnegut came up with the idea of using silver iodide, which, like dry ice, acts to convert cool water into particles of ice. Guided by ground radar, planes could fly above very cold clouds (−5 to −15 degrees Centigrade) and spray a smoke of tiny silver iodide crystals produced from burning or fireworks. Basically, the silver iodide releases energy and moisture latent in droplets of water—it doesn't actually create the water that becomes rain.

Objective testing of these symptoms is difficult, and many scientists insist that we still don't know enough about clouds to prove that seeding is a valid means of producing rain. Nevertheless, the methods exploit the processes involved when rain occurs naturally. The air contains particles of water in liquid and gaseous states. The production of a visible cloud results from condensation of vapor to a liquid or solid state, wherein the vapor molecules actually penetrate the liquid molecules. Additional nuclei in the atmosphere attract the moisture and aid condensation. In fact, without those particles, droplets of water would never grow large and heavy enough to fall to the earth—or, if they did fall, air resistance would prevent the tiny drops from arriving. The atmosphere would become supersaturated and the earth stricken with drought.

In nature, these additional nuclei come from a variety of

sources. Seawater evaporates and leaves salt particles in the air; other nuclei come from the products of combustion, active volcanoes, dust raised by wind, and cosmic dust from meteorites. Although so tiny as to be invisible to the naked eye, these particles fill the air and capture excess vapor, which condenses, provides additional weight, and eventually falls. These special nuclei are also necessary for freezing. For although the temperature in the atmosphere above 15,000 feet is usually at or below freezing, the freely moving liquid droplets cannot gather and freeze to become ice crystals unless a larger particle attracts them. Without such a particle, freezing cannot occur until the temperature falls to about − 40 degrees Centigrade.

?

How do they take photographs of the insides of the human body?

Using strands made of 100,000 hairlike glass fibers drawn into a bundle, medical scientists can see around corners and even take pictures in the darkest reaches of the human body. The technology is called fiber-optic endoscopy, and with it doctors can photograph the inner surfaces of the esophagus, stomach, intestines, lungs, arteries, and sometimes the heart, kidneys, and pancreas.

An individual optical fiber is about one-tenth the diameter of a human hair and has a peculiar ability to carry light from one place to another without losing much of it on the way. The fiber has two parts: an inner core and an outer cladding. The core and cladding are made of two different grades of clear glass. The core glass has a higher refractive index, which is to say it is denser and bends light rays more, than the glass of the cladding—in the same way that water has a higher refractive index than air, which is why a spoon stuck into a glass of water looks bent. The effect of the fiber core's greater density is to keep light inside the fiber: light projected into the core strikes the cladding around it, but instead of leaking away, its rays are bent at such an angle that they bounce back to the fiber's core. Thus light can be sent along a clear, flexible fiber without losing strength, no matter how many twists and turns it takes.

To get an image of an internal organ, a doctor sends an endoscope into the body, either through one of its natural openings or through one made especially for the purpose. An endoscope is a flexible tube containing two separate bundles of fibers, each serving a different purpose. One carries light into the opening, to illuminate the area being examined; the other picks up light reflected off the tissues and carries it back to the physician's eye or to the camera. The second bundle has a wide-angle lens— less than ⅛ inch in diameter, with a field of view of 60 to 100 degrees—attached to the remote end and an eyepiece, photographic lens, or viewing screen on the doctor's end. Each fiber in the receiving bundle acts like a single tile in a mosaic, to form ¹⁄₁₀₀,₀₀₀ of the image. Also inside the tube are pathways alongside the glass strands through which a doctor can insert instruments or fluids.

Using fiber-optic "image bundles," surgeons can watch and photograph many of the body's internal processes in their natural colors, to check for problems and locate tissues more accurately for surgical repairs. The film is slightly more sensitive than ordinary color film; this allows for fast shutter speeds, so that moving organs don't blur the image.

Optical fiber is made by fitting a foot-long glass rod about ½ inch in diameter inside a glass tube of a lower refractive index and heating the two until they bond. Then, in a "drawing tower," the softened glass cylinder is stretched like taffy into a wispy fiber nearly 1 million feet long; the machines that do the stretching can turn out 1,000 miles of fiber in an hour. A hundred thousand or more fibers are bundled together to make a strand ⅛ inch in diameter, capable of carrying an image.

Fiber-optic technology is actually used more for examining patients than for photographing them. Its special advantage as a diagnostic tool is that the body is not disturbed as much as it is by other methods of information gathering. In exploratory surgery, the body is traumatized by being cut open, and the patient is exposed to the danger of infection; X-ray photography fires potentially harmful ionizing radiation at the body, which carries long-term cancer risks. Optical fibers make many examinations less painful, and less risky.

?

How does a jewel thief know whether a string of pearls is worth stealing?

There may be more ways than one, but the great Arthur Barry, a big-time thief in the twenties who averaged half a million dollars in thefts per year, had a unique and quick technique. In the Plaza Hotel robbery of 1925, Barry made off with $750,000 in jewels belonging to Mrs. James P. Donahue, daughter of F. W. Woolworth. Not only was the theft executed in broad daylight, but Barry stealthily removed the jewels from a dressing table while Mrs. Donahue sat in the bathtub a few feet away. Among the objects stolen was a rope of pearls valued at $450,000. But the drawer containing the pearls had not one rope but five—four were imitations that the police captain later called "good enough to fool an oyster." Was Barry's choice pure luck? Not at all—he rubbed the pearls gently across his teeth. Fakes are smooth and slippery, he later said, but real pearls give a slightly rough, grating sensation.

?

How do they make pictures big enough to put on billboards?

Billboard painters do it, with brushes and oil paint.

"We're probably the fresco painters of the modern era. In the Renaissance, the Church had the money; now it's the ad agencies. Our stuff isn't as creative as other art, but it's real craftsmanship that goes into these signs," says billboard painter George Martin.

To make the truly huge billboard ads of the kind you see on the ultramodern highways and beltways of our major cities—the ones that show a sparkling gin-and-tonic with a lime peel floating in it and beads of condensation glistening on the glass—requires the services of a team of hardy painters willing to climb 50-foot scaffolds in 100-degree heat or subzero cold and splash on photographic-looking images in oil paint. Photography and lithography are too expensive or inadequate to produce the colorful brilliance of these signs (called spectaculars) on such a Gargantuan scale—35 by 100 feet.

The first step in making a "spectacular" takes place at an advertising agency: the art department photographs the product and lays out the ad, including any headline, just as it wants the billboard to appear, on a normal-size piece of paper. The ad is then given to a graphics company that specializes in "outdoor advertising." Along with the scale drawing, the agency specifies the shades of color it wants. "Bulletin painters," as the billboard artists call themselves, have a repertoire of six reds, four yellows, three greens, and two blues, plus one each of orange, brown, and black. They use real oil paint instead of acrylics, because acrylics are dull and dry too quickly. They tend not to mix colors on a billboard, since the colors would lose the intensity essential for maximum effect.

With the sketch in hand, the painters can proceed in one of two ways. The more mechanized approach is to put the ad into an opaque projector and beam it onto huge sheets of paper on the wall of a large room. A painter walks up to the image and pokes little holes in the paper along all the important lines. Then a team of painters takes the hole tracing of the ad, which is divided into several sections, and mounts each section on an area of board. The tracing is then pounded with a bag of charcoal; the charcoal leaks through the bag and through the holes in the paper to leave guidelines on the board. This is called a pounce pattern. Checking against the photograph for color and details, the painters fill in the finished ad in sections, and the sections are put together at the roadside.

There is another common method which is very close to what the old fresco painters used—which George Martin refers to as simply a pattern. The painter works from a desk-size image of the

ad, but instead of projecting it, he draws a ¼-inch-square grid over it. With nothing but the sketch, a brush, and a yardstick in hand, and his buckets of paint by his side, the artist can now climb the scaffold and lay out a perfectly proportioned oil painting 60 feet long or more. Each ¼-inch square on the sketch corresponds to a 1-foot square on the finished sign. Using his yardstick, Martin marks reference points in charcoal and paints his oeuvre in manageable 1-foot squares. So practiced is Martin that he paints the curves of his 3-foot letters freehand.

"Everybody thinks Michelangelo just lay on his back and painted the Sistine Chapel. He didn't; he worked from a pattern, same as we do."

What are the subjects of the modern bulletin painter's artistry? "There's no imagination in 'em," George Martin laments. "Now it's just cigarettes and booze. Mind-rot stuff. You used to get a face now and then, a bathing beauty, something with a challenge to it. But since the cigarette companies got kicked off TV, they've been pouring all their money into billboards and drove the price of an ad up. Now they're the only ones who can afford it. Too bad, really, but what can you do?"

?

How do they restore a valuable painting?

Many of us are unaware that modern paintings as well as those of the Old Masters must be cared for periodically. If you have an oil painting in your home that has been subjected to smoke or intense light from a southern exposure for 10 or 20 years, the colors may have darkened gradually, the varnish yellowed or deteriorated, the canvas itself became flaccid. Extreme temperature changes also may be harmful, causing the painting to expand and contract and the varnish to crack. Over the years oil paints oxidize and grow increasingly hard and rocklike. A lump of paint might actually lose cohesiveness and come loose from the painting.

Within the past 150 years the conservation and restoration of paintings has become a serious concern of specially trained professionals, rather than a task occasionally carried out by the original artist, or a later artist who felt he could improve upon the original. Frans Hals and Jan Gossaert are among the artists who felt free to restore the paintings of others, which often meant changing certain details of the picture. This procedure was not frowned upon or considered an intrusion in the seventeenth and eighteenth centuries. Today, of course, we would all be horrified if a masterpiece were altered by restoration or conservation, and conservators always take extensive photographs of the art in question before beginning to work, just to protect themselves from such accusations.

Restoration nowadays is as much a science as an art, using such scientific aids as photomicrography, infrared rays, X rays, and spectrophotometry, as well as the restorer's intimate knowledge of pigments, canvas, and varnish. (Professional conservators are in fact divided about how scientific they ought to be: European restorers accuse the Americans of being scrupulously scientific to the point of being cold and unfeeling. Our method of laying a painting down flat and going to work with chemicals and scalpels goes against their tradition of inspired art.)

Dana Cranmer, a skilled conservator at the Guggenheim

Museum in New York City, explains the difference between conservation and restoration: "Restorers concentrate on appearance and cosmetics, whereas conservators are concerned primarily with the health and longevity of a painting." Periodically she actually *washes* the museum's paintings by a slow and painstaking method. Using small swabs of cotton wound around a little wooden stick (the instrument resembles a Q-Tip, although the cotton can—and must—be changed frequently) and working systematically in a grid pattern across the painting, she wipes away the old layer of varnish from the painting with the aid of various solvents such as petroleum benzine, toluene, and acetone. If the work doesn't have a protective varnish, she cleans the pigments themselves, using cotton swabs dipped in distilled water. After the cleaning process, a new layer of varnish is applied (to those paintings that had varnish previously). The Guggenheim uses synthetic varnishes which can be sprayed on with a spray gun, rather than the older natural resins such as dammar or mastic, which are painted on with flat brushes. Applying the latter is a tricky procedure, for irregular brushstrokes can cause a change in the reflectance of light—which alters the appearance of the painting—whereas too much varnish levels out all nuances of light and shadow.

Another standard task of the conservator is to reinforce the canvas, which inevitably sags with time. This is accomplished by placing a new liner on the back of the canvas. Relining is also a useful technique for preventing deterioration and blistering in old paintings. The risk involved may be considerable, however, as was the case with Anthony Vandyke's *Rinaldo and Armida*, which was restored in the late 1950's. There was an area in the front where a paint layer had separated in small cleavages from the old supporting fabric. Conservators feared that when they scraped away the old adhesive from the back, using small knives, the paint would crumble and come loose. But, after much debate, they faced the painting with thin mulberry paper and a layer of cotton gauze and proceeded with the task of relining.

Some conservators use the traditional method of affixing a new liner with an electric iron, but the Guggenheim has a special "heat table"—a table covered with an aluminum sheet that can be heated—for precisely this purpose. The painting is placed face up on the table, and the new liner, coated with an adhesive, is put in place beneath it. A protective sheet is spread over the face of the painting. Finally, a plastic sheet is laid on top and a vacuum created between it and the painting by means of a vacuum pump. The painting lies under even pressure for approximately an hour, usually at a temperature of 160 degrees Fahrenheit. (Tests are performed beforehand on tiny sections of the painting to determine its heat tolerance.) The heat activates the adhesive, which then holds solidly to the canvas as the painting cools for three hours. Next it is stretched on a stretcher, a wooden frame with movable joints. This type of frame is very efficient for adjusting the tautness of the canvas, but partly because of high cost, most artists simply use strainers—frames without adjustable joints—to frame their work.

A painting with chipped or cracked paint requires specialized care. Retouching is an extremely taxing procedure that draws on the artistic capabilities of the restorer. How could anyone dare take a brush to a Vermeer? One consolation is that all restoration—and particularly repainting—is reversible.

If a chip of paint is missing, the conservator or restorer uses a method called inpainting. First the spot to be repaired is coated with varnish. Then it is filled to the perimeters of loss with gesso or putty—usually the same material as the ground of the painting (the preparatory layer originally used to prime the canvas). Using very fine pins or scalpels, the restorer sculpts the gesso to match the contours of the surrounding paint. When this is dry, the area is again coated with varnish and at last painted with watercolors (some restorers use egg tempera followed by a glaze of transparent oil paint). As one can imagine, mixing the watercolors to match not only the precise color but also the tone of the oils is an extraordinary feat. Although a restorer might come upon it in an hour, the same task could take a week. All inpainting—being of a different material and age than the surrounding paint film— inevitably discolors and must be renewed periodically, usually every century.

How does the restorer know what color to use if the painting is very old and has faded or darkened over the centuries? Removal of the varnish is the secret, for it is the varnish that changes, not the pigments. (A look at the exquisite, often brighter pigments that

193

appear when varnish is removed has led many conservators to believe that the Old Masters did not, in fact, intend their paintings to have that old, sepialike appearance, which became so valued by later generations.)

Occasionally great paintings have been damaged to a degree that seems irreparable. In 1914 Velasquez's *The Toilet of Venus* was slashed by a brazen suffragette, outraged at Venus's provocative pose. Rembrandt's *Night Watch* was first cut by a maniac in 1911; in 1975 a mental patient rushed into the Rijksmuseum in Amsterdam and slashed the painting with a knife. There were a dozen cuts and scratches—some more than a yard long—and a triangular piece of canvas actually fell out completely.

The museum's chief restorer, Luitsen Kuiper, organized and carried out the massive task of repairing the painting, which took six months and cost $37,300. Immediate measures were taken to prevent the edges of the canvas from stretching or sagging: the missing piece was repositioned and held with transparent tape on the back, and the front was strengthened with Japanese rice paper and glue. Next the lining, which had been put on in 1947, was removed with small knives. Kuiper then had to bridge the cuts with many small linen fibers. One by one the threads of the canvas were pasted to the short linen fibers with glue and synthetic resin. Extra fibers were shaved away. Kuiper then applied a beeswax and resin mixture and ironed on the lining with flatirons. Next the rice paper and glue residue (which looked alarming) had to be removed from the front with alcohol.

In order to retouch, Kuiper had to remove a layer of varnish that had been applied in 1947. He didn't stop there, however, but went on to remove a much older layer of varnish—while many around him fretted that the paint would come off, too. As he worked, he discovered some areas of overpainting, apparently executed by another artist in the eighteenth century! (Rembrandt had completed the painting in 1642.) Throughout, extensive examination of the painting's structure and areas of damage were made with X rays, infrared photographs, and a stereomicroscope (a microscope with a set of optics for each eye, which allows an object to be viewed in three dimensions).

Kuiper treated the entire painting with oil of turpentine to create "an even glimmer," and finally he began the arduous job of retouching. Tinted chalk and glue were used to build up the ground where the paint was slashed. Then Kuiper mixed his paints, using more colors than had Rembrandt, who required only six to ten. Kuiper used oil paints on top of a wet varnish. When the paints had dried thoroughly, he applied a final coat of varnish and allowed it to harden behind a glass, which protected the painting from climatic changes, for a full eight months. The results of the restoration are outstanding; art historians, restorers, and the general public who inspect the painting come away duly impressed.

Every now and then restoring a painting entails *taking away* paint rather than adding it. In the mid-sixteenth century Agnolo Bronzino painted *An Allegory*: Venus in all her natural splendor lies in the woods surrounded by naked Cupids with their curvaceous bottoms in full view. Some 50 to 200 years later a more modest generation decided to veil the nudity, cover Venus's nipple, and place bushes in "appropriate" places. The overpainting was detected much later, and some fortunate restorer had the happy task of stripping away Venus's veils.

?

How do they keep the ice in a skating rink from melting?

Skating rinks maintain their frozen surfaces even in warm air because the temperature *beneath* the ice is so cold that the ice is not affected significantly by moderate temperatures *above* it. Thus a burst of sunshine over an outdoor rink, which allows skaters to shed their sweaters, cannot succeed in melting the ice.

In a figure-skating rink the ice is generally about 2 inches thick; permanent ice hockey rinks use slightly thicker ice. It lies on a concrete floor through which runs a maze of ¾- to 1-inch-diameter pipes. The pipes are placed crosswise rather than lengthwise and lie no more than 2 inches apart; an Olympic-size rink of 185 feet by 85 feet has 7 to 11 miles of pipes embedded in its concrete floor. A very cold brine solution, or a glycol solution similar to the antifreeze used in cars, is continuously pumped through the pipes. The solution draws off heat from the floor, as chillers run by compressors cool the soltuion to −5 to −15 degrees Fahrenheit each time it circulates. The warmer the air above the ice, the more solution is pumped through the pipes.

?

How do they put the lines under an ice hockey rink?

The ice in a hockey rink ranges in thickness from 3 inches to a mere ⅝ inch in places such as Madison Square Garden, where ice must be made and taken up in a matter of hours. (This thin ice is a trial to professional players who make abrupt turns or screeching stops and sometimes scrape the floor below with their blades.) Depending on the time factor and the thickness of the ice, a variety of methods may be used to get those mysterious blue and red lines, circles, and insignias under the ice—and to erase them again when necessary.

If all the ice is removed from the rink, a water-base paint may be applied to the concrete floor that lies below. The entire floor is painted white with 6-foot-wide squeegees pushed by hand; then the lines and circles are painted on with the help of wood stencils. A second method, which is a bit trickier but more common, involves building up a thin layer of ice about ¼ inch thick. After the entire surface of the ice is painted, a machine called a Thompson edger is used to cut shallow grooves ⅛ inch deep into the ice, thereby marking the placement of the lines. Red or blue paint is applied by hand with brushes or simply poured into the grooves, which prevent it from running. As soon as the paint dries, a layer of clear water is spread over the ice to provide a coating. When in a few hours this coating has frozen, more ice may be built up to the usual level of 2 or 3 inches.

This process, which may take two days, is obviously impractical in a stadium where a horse show is scheduled for Friday night, a National Hockey League game on Saturday. A method used with increasing frequency these days substitutes plastic or paper for paint. The material is simply spread right onto the floor, and ice is then made over it. After the game both the ice and the lines may be taken up to make way for the next event.

?

How do they make tall buildings perfectly vertical?

Next time you're near a particularly tall high-rise building, stand at the base and look up, sighting along a corner. It will undoubtedly surprise you to see that the building really isn't perfectly vertical; it may even jag in and out in some places. It would be entirely too time-consuming and costly for engineers and construction crews to make each building absolutely plumb (or straight); and besides, it isn't necessary. The strong materials of which the buildings are constructed have a certain amount of flexibility and give. On a very windy day, for example, a skyscraper might sway as much as several inches without cracking or causing damage. Some imprecision may also arise from human error in the construction process—without grave consequences. Nevertheless, various precautions are taken to keep a building plumb as it is going up.

The simplest building has four supporting members, or columns, one at each corner. The columns are set on base plates that are secured by grout (high-strength concrete) lying underneath. The first step in making a building vertical is to check the elevation of the base plates to make sure all four are equal. The construction crew erects columns with a "splice elevation" of two tiers, which means the members extend just above the level of the second floor. While the columns are supported with heavy steel cables called guy wires, the builders lay the horizontal members, or beams, on which the first and second floors will be built. It is only at this point that they check to see whether the building is going up straight. Two workers stand on the second beam, one with a measuring rod, the other with a level (or a transit, which contains a level). The rod, which is graduated in hundredths of a foot, has a movable metal target that can be clamped wherever desired. The transitman, holding the level, "shoots" with his telescopic sight at the rodman, who holds the rod successively at each corner of the building. The team can then determine whether the splice level is equal all around.

The next step is so obvious and basic, one wouldn't suspect it in this era of advanced technology. The crew dangles a "plumb bob," a weight on a string, from the second tier to the ground. Since the pull of gravity naturally draws the string into a straight line, the crew simply measures the distance between the building and the string at the top and base of each column. An alternate method requires the use of a transit. The key instrument in any surveying operation, a transit can be used to measure horizontal angles to any required accuracy, vertical angles to about plus or minus 10 seconds of arc, differences in elevation, and distances. The transitman stands on the ground a certain distance from the building and shoots at a point, say, 3 inches outside the column near the bottom and then 3 inches outside the column at the second tier. If those points are aligned, the building is plumb. If not, the heavy guy wires supporting the columns must be adjusted. Since bolts connecting the members have not yet been fully tightened, the whole structure can be shifted the necessary amount to make it plumb. The construction crew must, of course, repeat the procedures at each splice level—usually every two floors.

Whereas gravity is an aid in making a building vertical, the curvature of the earth can produce some startling results with an apparently plumb building. This factor is a consideration only in the case of exceptionally tall or wide buildings, but engineers have been known to overlook it, thinking that the measurements for a small building can be transferred precisely to a large one. Picture imaginary lines extending toward the center of the earth from the columns of a terribly high building, or one that covers a large area, if the columns are perpendicular to a tangent of the earth at the point of contact. In either case, lines pointing down into the earth would eventually meet and form an angle, which means that although the columns may be inherently straight, they are not exactly parallel to each other.

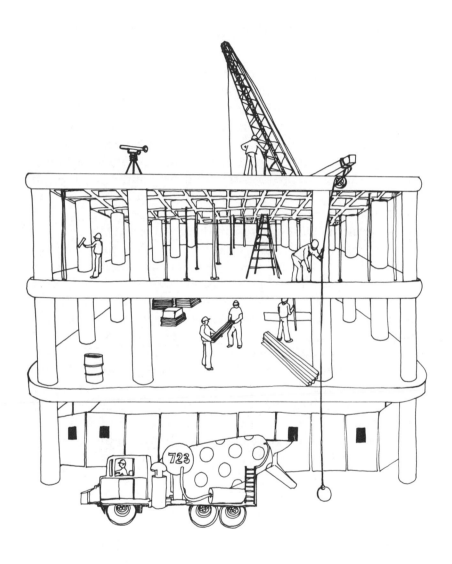

?

How do they tune a piano?

When a piano tuner arrives at your house, all he needs is a tuning fork, a crank, a damping wedge, and a finely trained ear. He sounds the fork simply by tapping it and causing it to vibrate. The sound produced is the A above middle C, the first note to be tuned in the central octave of the piano. The standard pitch of this A, throughout the Americas, Europe, and the Soviet Union, is A-440. The number represents the frequency of the pitch, or how many times (cycles) per second the string vibrates back and forth when struck.

Since the pitch of a single key on the piano is actually generated by three strings (except in the bass, where each note has only one string), the tuner uses a felt wedge to dampen (deaden) two strings of A while he plays the note and listens to hear whether or not it's in tune with the fork. If the two pitches are close but not precisely the same, he'll hear a series of pulsations, or beats, arising from the discrepancy in frequencies. The farther apart the pitches of the two notes, the more rapid the beats. As the notes are brought in tune, the beats slow and eventually stop. The pitch of a string is determined by its length, so the tuner adjusts this length by turning with his crank the wrest pin that secures the string. When the left-hand string of A has been tuned precisely to 440, the tuner no longer needs the fork. He moves the wedge and tunes the other two strings of A to the corrected first.

The remaining notes of the central scale are then tuned by interval (the distance between two notes: A to B is a second, A to C is a third, and so on). The most usual sequence starts with the fifth below A (D), then proceeds with the fourth above D (G), other fifths and fourths within the octave, and then the thirds, until all twelve notes of the octave are brought into their proper relationships with one another. One string at a time, the tuner eventually tunes every string on the piano—a total of 235. (This number varies because some pianos have more bass strings than others.)

You might assume that your piano is being tuned perfectly, but if it were, it would grate on your ear and in places seem drastically *out* of tune. On a well-tuned piano, each note is actually slightly out of tune with the others, yet the modern ear (since the time of Bach) has become totally accustomed to the "errors," so that this tuning sounds correct. As irrational as it may seem, when the notes of a scale are tuned to be acoustically correct according to the pure system worked out by Pythagoras, certain keys and small ranges of tone are perfect, but others, especially chromatic tones, sound terribly wrong. The solution, based on systems devised more than 250 years ago, is to divide the octave into twelve equal semitones and to spread the discrepancy evenly over the semitones. Ultimately, no interval except the octave is acoustically correct. This system underlies Bach's famous *Well-Tempered Clavier*, the forty-eight preludes and fugues—one for each major and minor key—which can be played equally well in every key.

When a piano is tuned in modern fashion—to "equal temperament"—each fifth must be flattened (lowered in pitch) by one-fiftieth of a semitone, or two "cents." The tuner knows the proper discrepancy exists when he hears one beat per second when tuning the fifths. With other intervals the discrepancy is greater. The tuner knows to listen for faster beats with progressively smaller intervals. An equal-tempered third is sharpened (raised in pitch) by one-seventh of a semitone, or fourteen cents, and eight beats per second should be heard when a third—G to B, for example—is played. Ultimately, with the equal temperament system, no interval is precisely in tune, but each interval of a certain kind is out of tune by the same amount.

Although you hear only one pitch when you press a key on your piano, each note is actually made up of composite tones, or harmonics. This is because as the whole string vibrates, sections of half, one-third, one-quarter (and so on) the length of the string vibrate simultaneously. Each note thus has a series of harmonics: the first is the octave above the note, the second is the fifth above that, then the fourth above the fifth, and so on. You can test this system of harmonics by trying an experiment on your piano: depress middle C silently, then play the C below and, magically, you'll hear the higher note as well. The middle-C string, half the length of the lower C string, is set in sympathetic vibration. Other notes in this harmonic series can be produced by depressing G above middle C (fifth), C above that (fourth), then E (third).

Harmonics are significant in the tuning of a piano because they form the basis of relationships between notes. Certain notes of a scale have certain harmonics in common, for example, and the pitches of the scale actually derive from the pitches of the harmonic series. As described above, the notes within the central octave are adjusted slightly to best represent pitches to the human ear, so they are only approximations of the "pure" pitches of a C harmonic. But these notes are in fact harmonics of lower notes on the piano. When this central scale, the one heard best by the human ear, has been tuned, each note of the two octaves above and below it are tuned one by one to its pitches. The farthest octaves are, in turn, tuned to them.

?

How do they charm snakes?

Charming snakes, though totally alien and perhaps horrific to Westerners, is an ancient and venerated tradition in India, dating from the third century B.C., and in Egypt, where mention of it appears in the early *Book of the Dead*.

The "snakers" (as they like to be called) in India regard themselves as a distinct caste, with spiritual beliefs integrally bound up with the snakes. They begin their training at the age of five or six, learning to handle snakes and to develop snake charming as an art, a way of life, and, most important of all, the means of carrying on the sacred traditions of their forefathers. Adult snakers—all of them male—have no other source of livelihood. They therefore plan their performances to have as much impact as possible on audiences, whose donations tend to be larger when the danger seems considerable. The favorite snake to use is the cobra, famous for its dramatic arched position. The image passed down to us is of a turbaned man "charming" a snake with his flute and causing it to rise out of its basket. But snakes don't have ears, and the cobra actually does not hear the flute at all. The snaker lures the snake, or rather threatens it sufficiently to make it rise up in a wary position, not with music but with physical gestures. He may splatter cold water on the snake to alarm it and then blow his flute near enough that the air rushes annoyingly over the snake's back. (The flute is not like the conventional Western one but is rather a reed instrument with a gourd, two bamboo pipes, and occasionally a brass pipe.) The trick is to keep the snake interested enough to remain arched, yet not anger it so much that it strikes or runs away. The snaker may pass his hand before the snake's head to keep its attention, or shift the instrument back and forth. Other snakes, usually nonpoisonous ones, may be loose around the snaker—just to add to the show.

?

How do they know when man was born?

The controversial question of when man evolved to a large extent remains shrouded in mystery. To start, we have no clear-cut biological definition of a human being, nor do we have a precise behavioral definition. Some of us would like to forget our animal ancestry altogether; others admit the descent from apes but allow a good 15 million years in between for evolution and progress to the point where we seem to have little in common with monkeys. Anthropologists have unearthed clues to the past, but a complete and final answer is yet to be found—perhaps buried in a remote recess of the earth, perhaps embodied in man himself.

A recent breakthrough, reported in *Smithsonian* magazine, derives from a comparison of our own blood proteins with those of various species of apes and monkeys. In 1967 Vincent Sarich and Allan Wilson of the University of California measured the similarities by first injecting rabbits with human albumin, which caused them to produce antibodies. Sarich and Wilson then mixed the albumin proteins of various primates with the antibodies. The stronger the reaction of the antibodies, the closer the relation between the human and animal albumin proteins. In the case of monkeys, the reaction was 80 percent. The antibody reaction for gibbons was 88 percent; for orangutans, 92 percent. The closest of all were the African apes—the chimpanzee and gorilla—whose albumins caused a 96 percent reaction. We now know that—in addition to strong similarities between certain human and chimpanzee blood proteins—almost 99 percent of the DNA in chimps is *identical* to our own! Sarich and Wilson went on to hypothesize that the rate of evolution of the blood proteins is constant. Given the known differences today, they calculated that man's divergence from the African ape occurred a mere 5 million years ago.

Another party, working in the field rather than in the lab, found in the flat-topped volcanic craters of Ethiopia's Afar Triangle the bones of hominids that lived 3 or 4 million years ago. (One expedition was led by F. Clark Howell of the University of California and Yves Coppens of the Musée de l'Homme in Paris; a second was organized by Donald Johanson of the Cleveland Museum of Natural History and Maurice Taieb of the Centre National de la Recherche Scientifique.) The bones of thirteen individuals were uncovered, and many were pieced together. The formation of a knee joint indicated that the hominids, called *Australopithecus afarensis*, walked upright. And they had human feet that pointed straight ahead, rather than to the side as do those of apes. Many anthropologists (particularly Owen Lovejoy and Richard Lee) now believe that the upright position evolved not so that the primate could use tools, as Darwin believed, but rather so that the male could carry food back to the female. This was the result of a long period of evolution in which early primates experienced longer periods of time between births and longer periods of infant dependency. To enable the species to survive, the male assumed the role of provider, ranging far and wide to gather food, while the female remained with her vulnerable infant.

A system of monogamy thus arose out of necessity and apparently was used by the mysterious *afarensis*. Not only did they look like human beings, then, with their upright stature, but some patterns of social order may have been similar to ours. Is this enough to call them early men? Not quite, for in the area of brain power the *afarensis* doesn't hold up. The size of the skull of the hominid shows that its brain was similar in size to that of a chimpanzee: 300 to 500 cubic centimeters compared to modern man's 1,000 to 2,000 cubic centimeters. (The overall height of *afarensis* was only about 3½ to 5 feet.) Johanson and Tim White of the University of California believe that *afarensis* split into two branches: one favored muscle power and large jaws and became extinct; the other developed increasingly larger brains and perhaps led to the genus *Homo*.

The earliest traces of *Homo erectus* date from about 1.5 million years ago. Their brains ranged from 800 to 1,300 cubic centimeters, and they are particularly distinguished by their tools—not just sharp edges for cutting, but symmetrical, carefully shaped hand axes. These hominids may have ventured out of Africa to Eurasia.

In eastern Greece an ancient skull was recently found, by accident, which has turned out to be the earliest trace of *Homo sapiens,* our immediate ancestors. Clark Howell and Christopher Stringer of the British Museum of Natural History analyzed the skull and reported it to be 500,000 years old.

These findings, summarized by John Pfeiffer in *Smithsonian,* provide hints of the evolutionary process, but the question of just when the early primates left off being apes or hominids and emerged as man—or just where we decide to draw the fine line of distinction—remains open to debate, speculation, and wonder.

?

How do cable cars clang up and down steep San Francisco hills?

The motive force for cable cars is provided by a moving cable generated from a power station. The system was conceived in 1867 by the American mechanic Andrew S. Hallidie. By 1873 the first cable railroad, built by the Clay Street Hill Railroad Company, was in operation in San Francisco. This remarkable system, which aroused considerable excitement at the time, is basically the same

today and continues to draw admiration from visitors to the city. Many cities followed San Francisco's lead in the 1870's, but abandoned the system for practical electrical power in the twentieth century.

The first cable car line in San Francisco extended 2,800 feet over a 307-foot incline. A grip device on the car ("Hallidie's grip") clamps onto a continuously moving subsurface cable between the rails, which draws the car along. An operator stops the car by releasing the grip and applying brakes.

On exceptionally steep inclines a funicular system employing two cars connected by cables is most efficient. As one car ascends, the other descends and provides a counterbalance. This works best on a single track, except, of course, in the middle, where a double track allows the cars to pass each other.

?

How do fireflies flash?

The firefly is a nocturnal beetle whose rhythmic flashes of light are perhaps a means of sexual attraction, perhaps a warning signal for protection. Although scientists are still uncertain about its use, they do know how the light is created.

The greenish-white "fire" contains little infrared or ultraviolet light and is thus known as "cold light." It is produced in the abdomen of the firefly by almost instantaneous oxidation of a chemical called luciferin, when an enzyme, luciferase, is present. Luminescence occurs when adenosine triphosphate (ATP) reacts with luciferase, magnesium ion, and luciferin to form a complex (luciferase-luciferyl-adenylate) and pyrophosphate. This complex reacts with oxygen, producing sufficient energy to convert the complex from a low- to a high-energy, excited state. The luciferase-luciferyl-adenylate complex disperses its new energy by radiating a photon of visible light—the flash that we see—and thereafter returns to its original state.

The lighting occurs in cells called photocytes, which are supplied with oxygen by air tubes (tracheae). The nervous system, in combination with the photocytes and tracheal end organs (cells at the ends of the tracheae), controls the rate of flashing. The excitation stimulus is conveyed by a nerve to the photocytes, through the tracheal end organs, and a chemical mediator is quickly secreted by the nerve to stop the light. Other types of beetles, whose luminescence is long and lingering, apparently do not have these tracheal end organs.

Common fireflies emit a green or bright yellow light, but in Paraguay there exists a 3-inch wingless beetle, known as the railway beetle, that produces red lights at both ends of its body and green lights at different points in between.

?

How do they determine the cause and time of death from an autopsy?

The Chief Medical Examiner's Office in New York City operates twenty-four hours a day to determine how people die. Twenty-four percent of the 72,079 deaths in the city in 1979 were not certified by a private physician and were referred to the Medical Examiner's Office. Most of those were caused by criminal violence, accidents, and suicides. Other categories that call for autopsy include "unusual" cases—the sudden death of someone in good health, death as a result of therapy or surgery, and so on. Any noncertified death after which cremation is requested must also be examined, for obvious reasons.

A museum on the sixth floor of the Medical Examiner's Office houses all sorts of evidence from autopsies, from weapons to bones. One specimen is the skull of a man who was thought to have died from a stroke, until examination revealed a wound track in the deepest recesses of the brain. The examiner traced the wound to the membranes covering the brain, and then to a small hole in the side of the skull which was concealed by hair. An assailant had plunged an ice pick into the man's head.

In a typical case, an examiner might be called to the scene of a homicide. He investigates the area, the position of the body, and other conditions. Blood droplets radiating around the body might suggest that the man was shot there; the absence of such telltale clues might indicate that the body was dumped at the site long after death. A jagged wound surrounded by scorched skin means the assailant shot at close range.

The time of death is usually problematic, and no single test is dependable. If rigor mortis has set in, the victim is likely to have died at least five or six hours previously. If his limbs are not yet completely cold, he has probably been dead fewer than twelve hours.

The examiner brings the homicide victim to the office, where the entire body, not just the area of the wound, is examined. Radiographs are used to look for a bullet or bullet fragments. Urine and stomach contents are analyzed for alcohol or drugs. Blood samples are taken to be compared with possible evidence found on a suspect. Fingernail scrapings are examined for the same reason. In the Easter Sunday killings of 1937 such a scraping was enough evidence to indict twenty-eight-year-old Robert Irwin for three murders. Irwin had been jilted by Ethel Gedeon and went to her apartment enraged. He found Ethel out, and turned on her mother instead. He strangled Mrs. Gedeon, who scratched his face as she struggled. The desperate Irwin, finding Ethel's sister and a boarder also at home, murdered them, too. Irwin was seen near the apartment and became a suspect, and the autopsy, which detected stubble from his face beneath Mrs. Gedeon's fingernails, confirmed his guilt.

208

In the famous case of the Crimmins children, murdered by their mother, Alice, in July 1965, the contents of the little girl's stomach held a vital clue to the time of death. Dr. Milton Helpern, then Chief Medical Examiner, performed the autopsy. Tiny hemorrhages in the eyelids and larynx, as well as congested lungs, suggested asphyxia. (The girl, Missy Crimmins, had in fact been found with her pajamas knotted around her mouth.) Although the cause of death could thus be verified, the autopsy unearthed other factors essential to the case. Alice Crimmins had said she fed the children at 7:30 P.M. and saw them after midnight; they were abducted in the predawn hours, she claimed. Helpern, however, found fresh food in the child's stomach—which was full—indicating that Missy had died within two hours of a meal. In cases of physical or mental disturbance hours or even days before death, which can alter drastically or even stop the digestion process, analysis of stomach contents may be misleading. But in Missy's case, since death was rapid, the evidence was significant, leading Helpern to believe that Alice Crimmins was lying. Courtroom scenes that dragged on for years have proved him right.

When in 1933 Helpern was new in the position of Chief Medical Examiner, he investigated the death of a heroin addict—and, in the process, turned up a dozen cases of malaria. The man, a seaman, was thought to have died from encephalitis, or brain infection. Helpern did an autopsy and found purplish patches in the white matter of the brain, caused by thousands of small hemorrhages. Microscopic examination revealed red blood cells infested with malarial parasites blocking capillaries to the brain; the man had died of malignant tertian malaria (the estivo-autumnal type). But Helpern didn't stop there. Having learned that outbreaks of malaria had occurred among other addicts, he visited the city prison and the correction hospital on New York's Welfare Island, where he talked with and examined addicts who took the drug intravenously. Eleven of the 110 addicts had malaria; each had been infected by an injection apparatus that was used communally. A drop of blood would get through the needle and into the syringe; thus were malarial parasites transferred to the next user.

Determining the cause of death from autopsy is not always foolproof, of course. Cases arise, for example, in which examiners fail to distinguish between an injury inflicted before death and one that was incurred after death. Nevertheless, autopsy can reveal valuable information—findings to make or break a courtroom case—when performed with the proper knowledge and expertise.

?

How do they make gasohol?

The market for gasohol is still very small and its production costly, but this promising alternative to gasoline has a higher octane than the real thing and cuts down on the consumption of oil. Conservationists are particularly excited about gasohol, for in the final analysis, it is solar energy that drives your car through the organic raw materials of gasohol, such as corn or sugarcane.

Gasohol is a blend of 10 percent ethyl alcohol (ethanol) and 90 percent unleaded gasoline. Ethanol is produced by fermentation of starches and sugars. By far the largest source for this is corn, which is the most abundant of cereal grains grown in the United States. Oats, barley, wheat, and milo can be used, as well as sugarcane, sweet sorghum, and sugar beets. Potatoes and cassava (a starchy plant) are possible sources, as is cellulose, which can be broken down into fermentable sugars.

Just about any fuel can be used to power the fermentation plant in which ethanol is made: coal, agricultural and industrial wastes, natural gas, solar or geothermal energy, and oil.

The corn is ground and cooked so that the starch can be processed further. Enzymes are added to convert the starch to sugars, which in turn are converted to alcohol by reacting with yeast. The alcohol is distilled until it is 190 proof—that is, 95 percent of the substance is alcohol. Finally, any vestiges of water are removed so that the alcohol is totally dry—200 proof. This ethyl alcohol is then blended with unleaded gasoline.

The yield of ethyl alcohol from one acre of produce varies. An acre of corn yields 250 gallons; an acre of sugar beets, 350 gallons; an acre of sugarcane, 630 gallons. Producers of gasohol are anxious that land be set aside solely for growing crops for production of ethanol, but the depletion of food supplies, nutrients, and organic soil constituents remains a matter of concern.

Since alcohol is an excellent solvent, it is essential that all equipment handling gasohol be clean. Mechanical problems have resulted from clogged filters, especially in old cars, in which gasohol loosens accumulated dirt. Oil companies report that mileage improvement is questionable, but, in general, engines that run on gasohol tend to foul less and to run cooler and cleaner. And, of course, in a time of dwindling oil imports and limited supplies, the fact that gasohol contains less oil than gasoline is certainly appealing.

In the future it may become economical to produce gasohol from garbage. The cellulosic portion—paper and wood—of municipal waste, although readily available, must be subjected to radical treatments before the yeasts can act upon it. First, the lignin, which forms a hard shell around the cellulose, must be cracked, either in pressure cookers or by explosion from high-pressure jets into low-pressure areas, which causes the lignin to swell. Then the cellulose cells, containing thousands of units, must be broken down into single or double sugars by addition of water and treatment either by sulfuric acid—this method is rapid but costly—or by enzyme action, which requires two days. When these processes are made less cumbersome and expensive, however, we may be running our cars on old newspapers.

?

How do they know how many stars are in the universe?

Astronomers know how many stars are in the universe because they are pretty certain they can tell how big it is. They know how big it is because they think they know how old it is—although there is some disagreement on that point. And estimates of the universe's age in turn depend on estimates of the speeds and distances of the farthest stars we are able to detect. This question's

211

answer is a good example of the interconnectedness of astronomical knowledge.

The reasoning goes something like this. The farthest galaxies whose energy reaches our telescopes on Earth are flying away from us at nearly the speed of light. This is shown when their light is broken down in a spectrograph, an instrument that measures the wavelengths of the light reaching it: there is an extreme "red shift" in the spectral lines made by the various elements making up the stars. (For an explanation of the red shift, see "How do they know the universe is expanding?" page 121.) Astronomers have concluded that this means the universe is expanding, blowing up before our eyes. The amount of the red shift from the far galaxies tells us both *how fast* they are receding from us and *how far away* they are (see "How do they know how far away the stars are?" page 213). If we know how far from one another the pieces of the universe are, where they are heading, and how fast they are moving, we can apply the laws of motion and determine *when* they must have exploded to be flying away at their present speeds. The commonly accepted estimate for the Beginning, the Big Bang that created everything, is between 10 and 20 billion years ago. How wide is a universe that blew apart, say, 20 billion years ago? Nothing we know of travels faster than light, so the light energy from the Big Bang itself must be scattered the farthest of anything in the universe. Since light travels at 186,000 miles per second, or one light-year in a year (6 trillion miles), the light generated at the moment of Creation must have progressed 20 billion light-years in all directions since then. So the matter and energy in the universe must have a radius of at most 20 billion light-years, or a diameter of 40 billion light-years.

By judging the vast distances of space, astronomers have found that the galaxies they are able to detect are on the average 100,000 (10^5, or $10 \times 10 \times 10 \times 10 \times 10$) light-years in diameter, and that the distance between stars is about 5 light-years. So the number of stars that can fit in a galaxy of an average spiral shape is about 100 billion (10^{11}).

The galaxies are about 2 million light-years apart in our corner of the universe. It seems reasonable to assume that the universe is approximately spherical, if it was formed by an explosion, and that its debris is distributed with approximate uniformity. Thus, in a spherical universe with a maximum diameter of 40 billion light-years, there is room for about 10 billion (10^{10}) galaxies. So in 10^{10} galaxies, each containing about 10^{11} stars, there are at most $10^{10\,+\,11}$, or 10^{21} stars; or about a thousand billion billion stars in the universe.

?

How do they know how far away the stars are?

It sounds like a simple question, but in many ways it's not. How can we know how far away something is if we can't touch it? By comparing the way it appears to us with the appearances of things whose distances we know. If we assume that the same physical laws apply everywhere, we can use reasoning to find our way from things we measure with our hand out to the farthest stars in the universe. For mankind, the first link in the chain stretching to the stars was finding the distance from Earth to Mars.

By observing the paths of the stars and planets as they moved across the sky over the centuries, Western astronomers came up with an accurate model of how the solar system was constructed, with the sun at its center and the planets making elliptical orbits around it. By counting the months or years it took for each wandering planet to return to its original position in the sky, astronomers could tell which planets were more and less distant from the sun—those that took the longest to go around were farthest from the center. But they had no idea of the actual distances in miles. In 1671 two Frenchmen, using a measuring technique common in surveying called trigonometric parallax, found the distance in miles to Mars, and from that they figured all the distances in the solar system.

A ship carrying one astronomer, Jean Richer, set out for the port of Cayenne in French Guiana, which is in the Western Hemisphere. Richer's colleague, Giovanni Domenico Cassini, stayed behind in Paris, which is in the earth's Eastern Hemisphere. On the same night (which they had agreed upon before

Richer left France), at nearly the same moment, both astronomers thousands of miles apart pointed their telescopes toward Mars and took down its position relative to the stars around it. Each man saw Mars in a slightly different position; the difference was caused by a phenomenon called parallax.

If you look at something from two different places, it appears to move in relation to its background. You can demonstrate parallax yourself: hold one finger up about a foot from your face, against the background of objects in a room. Look at your finger with your left eye alone, and then with your right eye alone. The finger will seem to move; through one eye it might be next to the lamp, and through the other it may line up with the chair leg. This happens because you're looking through eyes 2 to 3 inches apart; it's only 12 inches out to your finger, so the change in vantage point makes a big difference. If you look at the avocado plant 20 feet away through each eye, however, it *won't* seem to move. The parallax you observe with your eyes gives you depth perception for nearby objects; the use of parallax on a larger scale in astronomy gives us depth perception to find the distance of relatively near objects in space.

In Richer and Cassini's experiment, Paris and Cayenne are the two eyes, and Mars is the finger. To Richer in Cayenne, Mars's perimeter lined up in front of one set of stars, and to Cassini it seemed to lie slightly east of that position. When they were able to get back together and compare readings, they measured the amount of the discrepancy in degrees of arc. Surveyors and astronomers use degrees to measure how much of their field of vision an object takes up—each degree is 1/360 of the circle you see turning completely around while watching the horizon. Richer and Cassini were able then to draw an imaginary triangle in space, between Paris, Cayenne, and Mars. They knew the length of the base of the triangle: 4,000 miles; that was the distance between Paris and Cayenne—which had been measured by sailing ships— minus a calculated amount to allow for the earth's curvature. They could find the angles of the triangle from the degree measurement they had made: the triangle's top angle equaled the number of degrees' parallax shift in Mars's position. Using trigonometry, they could then find the height of the triangle: the distance to Mars from Earth, about 49 million miles.

Parallax measurement has also been used to find the distance of some of the nearer stars, such as Alpha Centauri and Sirius. Since stars are so much farther away than the planets, sightings taken from different points on Earth are not far enough from each other to show a measurable parallax. Astronomers instead take down the position of the star twice from the same spot, six months apart. The second sighting is thus made when Earth is on the other side of its orbit of the sun. So when sighting a star trillions of miles away, instead of trying to measure the minute parallax shift from vantage points only 4,000 miles apart, we can use points separated by twice the distance from Earth to the sun: 2×93 million miles, or 186 million miles. With a triangle base of that size, we can find by parallax that the distance to Alpha Centauri, the nearest visible star to our solar system, is about 24 trillion miles (4.3 light-years) away, and to Sirius about 52 trillion miles (8.8 light-years).

The universe is unimaginably vast. Stars are so far apart just within one galaxy that if the sun were the size of an orange, the nearest star would be represented by another orange 1,000 miles away. A journey from our solar system to neighboring Alpha Centauri in the fastest rocket known to man would take 1 million years. Thus, parallax sightings taken from the far points of Earth's orbit are useful only for finding the distance to stars 100 light-years away or less. Most of the galaxy is much farther from us than that, and we must use other methods of reckoning. There are many, and they draw on a wide assortment of facts scientists know about the stars.

One way of finding the distance to a star more than 100 light-years away is by spectroscopic parallax—analyzing the color of the light that reaches us from the star with a spectroscope, a device that very precisely spreads out the spectrum from a beam of light the way a prism does, arranging the frequencies the beam contains from highest to lowest. The brighter the "blue" or high-frequency end of the spectral band, the hotter the star. Heat is the motion of particles; the faster the atoms of a star vibrate, the more frequently (per second) they emit waves of energy in the form of light, and the more high-frequency waves show on the spectrum.

Astronomers have noticed among the near stars, whose distances they can measure by trigonometric parallax, that the hotter stars have the most mass and the greatest luminosity—they send

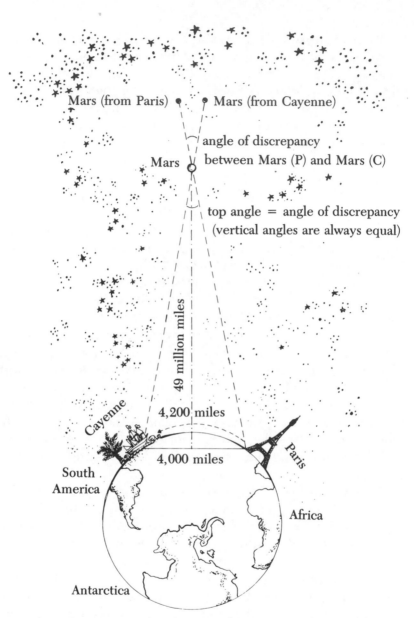

Mars (from Paris)   •   • Mars (from Cayenne)

angle of discrepancy
between Mars (P) and Mars (C)

Mars ◉

top angle = angle of discrepancy
(vertical angles are always equal)

49 million miles

Cayenne

4,200 miles

4,000 miles

Paris

South
America

Africa

Antarctica

*Viewed from two different points on Earth, Mars appears to occupy
two different places in the heavens. From each point the planet seems
to sit in front of a different arrangement of stars. Astronomers can
measure this parallax shift as some number of degrees on a circle.
Using this degree measurement and the actual distance between the
two vantage points on Earth, scientists applying elementary trigonometry can figure the distance to Mars.*

out the most total light. They conclude that the trend applies to all stars, that temperature always has the same relation to luminosity. Thus from the bright blue spectrum of Epsilon Orionis in the constellation Orion (the Hunter), which shows it to be burning at the fierce temperature of 24,800 Kelvins (about 44,000 degrees Fahrenheit), scientists estimate that it must have a radiating power 470,000 times that of the sun—the sun's temperature is only 5,800 Kelvins. If we can accept the estimate of Epsilon Orionis's true brightness and compare it to how bright it *appears* to us on Earth, we can then figure its distance, since light always dissipates at the same rate the farther it gets from its source. A photometer, analogous to a photographer's light meter, attached to a telescope measures the apparent brightness of a star by counting the light particles that reach us from it per second; the formula for apparent brightness is luminosity $\div$ 4π (distance)^2. From the color of Epsilon Orionis, which indicates its temperature, which in turn tells its radiating power, we conclude that it is 1,600 light-years away.

Spectroscopic parallax, however, is useful only out to the edge of our own galaxy, 100,000 light-years away. The Milky Way, which contains 100 billion stars like the sun, is only one of 10 billion or so galaxies in the universe. As wide as the void is between stars in the Milky Way—5 light-years—the distance between galaxies is an even more staggering 2 *million* light-years. The light we see coming from our closest neighboring galaxy, Andromeda, was emitted 2 million years ago, when mankind's prehistoric ancestor *Australopithecus* was busy chasing gazelles near the Olduvai Gorge in East Africa.

To judge the distance to another galaxy, astronomers scan its stars for a type known as a Cepheid variable. The brightness of a Cepheid varies regularly; some give off twice as much light in the bright phase as in the dim. Polaris, the North Star, is one of the Cepheid variables in our own galaxy. By measuring the distance to the nearer Cepheids by spectroscopic parallax and other short-range methods, astronomers have found that the length of a variable star's period of pulsation—its complete cycle of bright and dim—is related to its mass and luminosity. The longer the period, the greater the peak luminosity. Polaris has a four-day cycle and is 2,500 times as bright as the sun.

Applying the principle to a Cepheid in another galaxy, we can tell its luminosity from the length of its period and compare the star's apparent brightness with its luminosity to get the distance, as with spectroscopic parallax.

Beyond 10 million light-years things get more approximate: we know the luminosity of the entire Milky Way Galaxy; when we sight a distant galaxy, we assume it is about as intrinsically bright as our own and again estimate distance from apparent brightness.

But how about galaxies near the far ends of the universe—2 billion to 20 billion light-years away? The only way now known to determine how far it is to a galaxy so distant is to measure the amount of its red shift (see "How do they know the universe is expanding?" page 121); those with the greatest red shift are receding the fastest. Their trajectories suggest that the universe consists of the fragments of a cosmic explosion scattering into space.

In an explosion, the fastest-moving particles fly the farthest from the blast; that is what astronomers see happening in the universe. Among stars whose distances can be measured by Cepheid or galactic luminosity, it seems the farther away they are, the faster they are receding from us—and the more pronounced is their red shift. Thus for the very farthest galaxies more than 3 billion light-years away—for which we can barely pick up a spectrum—we must figure that the distance is proportional to how fast a galaxy is flying from us, as shown by its red shift. The extreme shift of a galaxy in the constellation Hydra shows it to be receding at 38,000 miles per *second*, which is more than 20 percent of the speed of light. That would indicate that the galaxy is 3.6 billion light-years away.

?

How does a polygraph detect lies?

Police have used polygraphs extensively since 1924. The machines have no particular magic of second sight which enables them to probe the twisted emotions of a suspected criminal;

rather, they measure blood pressure, pulse rate, and respiration simultaneously by means of a pneumograph tube around the subject's chest and a pulse cuff around the arm. Impulses are picked up and traced on moving graph paper, which is driven by a synchronous electric motor. The theory is that respiration, blood pressure, and pulse are involuntary actions—not subject to the person's conscious will—yet they are bound up with the person's emotional state. Fluctuations from the norm, generally a heightening of those actions, signify emotional tumult and, the police deduce, a lie.

Giving a lie detector test is an involved procedure that requires the expertise and sound judgment of a specially trained administrator. It would, of course, be ludicrous to ask the subject only the key question, such as "Did you murder your wife?" The subject must also be asked a series of control questions; for example, "What is your name?" or "Did you ever steal anything in your entire life?" If he answers no to the latter, chances are he is lying, and any change in his pulse or breathing can be observed. In some instances the subject may actually be told to lie so that the administrator can note the degree of curve in the lines appearing on the graph paper. When the key question is asked, the administrator must compare the degree of change in the line with the lines corresponding to other answers—some truthful, some not.

Because the outcome of a lie detector test is so dependent on the abilities of the test giver, polygraphs are absolutely forbidden in courts, nor can test results be used in testimony. Psychologists are far from convinced of the validity of polygraphs, but the police, who use trained people to give the test, consider them an invaluable aid.

?

How do sword swallowers swallow swords?

In an age of sophisticated movie effects and skillful stuntmen, we usually conclude that dangerous exploits on the screen or stage are somehow rigged—especially if the feat is as daring as sword swallowing. But the fact is that most performers of this uncanny act do not fake it or use gimmicks. Admittedly, some magicians today insert a tube along the neck and chest under their clothes, with an opening near the mouth concealed by a fake beard. Others use a sword that retracts into the hilt when pressure is put on the tip. But the original sword swallowers and many today do indeed swallow the blade, which is carefully measured to extend to the base of the stomach—and no farther. In the nineteenth century, a street juggler—originally a Zouave, or member of a French

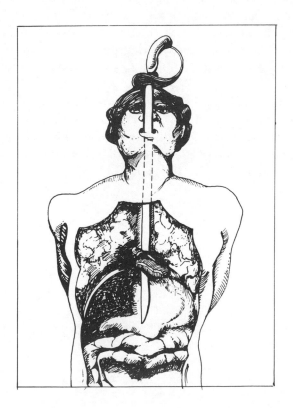

infantry unit noted for its quick-spirited drills—used to allow spectators to touch the projection of a saber pressing against his stomach wall below his sternum. He was a braver fellow than most, for many performers of this feat swallow a guiding tube beforehand and retain it, partially swallowed, throughout the performance. Composed of thin metal, 17 to 19 inches long and just under an inch wide, the tube protects the path along which the sword will descend.

In order to gradually overcome the gag reflex, a sword swallower begins practicing with smaller objects, such as spoons and forks, being careful not to drop them and swallow them whole. With head tilted back, mouth open wide, he aims to align with the descending object his mouth and pharynx (4 to 4¾ inches), esophagus (10 to 11 inches), cardiac opening of the stomach, and distended stomach (7¾ to 8½ inches). The total distance is about 21½ to 24½ inches; the length of the flat blade of the saber is generally 21½ to 23½ inches. Needless to say, the sword swallower must fast before such a performance.

?

How do they tell how smart you are from an IQ test?

Because most people refer to an IQ, or "intelligence quotient," as a fixed score, with the power to determine one's education, career choices, and even self-respect, you'd think it must be derived from a single, standardized test. Quite the opposite is true. There are numerous tests, with varying fundamental principles and of course different gradations of complexity depending on the age of the test taker, that can be used to determine an IQ score.

This kind of testing began in France in 1905 when the French government commissioned Alfred Binet and Theodore Simon to develop a test that could be used to separate the children who should attend regular school from those who should go to special schools for slow learners. In other words, Binet's test indicated

221

whether or not a child would succeed academically by comparing his rate of learning with that of others his own age. This test, composed of 54 questions, was revised and expanded in 1916 and became the widely used Stanford-Binet test, which underwent further revisions in 1937 and 1960. It involves tests of analogs and opposites, comprehension, vocabulary, verbal and pictorial completion, and memory.

The other widely used measure of intelligence is the Wechsler Scale, first used in 1939 to evaluate patients at Bellevue Hospital, New York. The Wechsler Intelligence Scale for Children (WISC) was standardized in 1949 on a sample of 2,200 English-speaking white children whose fathers fit into nine occupational categories. Today the scales have been revised to measure people of all ages, with a test for preschool ages four to six and one-half, children six to sixteen, and adults sixteen to seventy-four.

Unlike the Stanford-Binet, WISC divides a child's intelligence into categories. An IQ score is derived from measuring each subtest and formulating an average. The subtests are designed to call upon a wide scope of the child's abilities, from concentration and alertness to practical knowledge and moral sensibility. (Critics of the tests, however, say they fail to measure a child's creativity.)

An "Information" section, composed of 30 questions on a broad range of general facts, measures how much information a child has gotten from his environment. Such questions as "How many pennies are there in a dime?" which draw on everyday experience are mixed with others requiring information learned in school, such as "What is the capital of Greece?" or "Who wrote *Romeo and Juliet*?" A "Comprehension" section of 14 problem questions has been devised to evaluate social and moral behavior patterns acquired in everyday learning, as well as to measure emotional stability. Practical judgment is required to answer such questions as "What is the thing to do when you cut your finger?" or "Why are criminals locked up?" An "Arithmetic" subtest of timed problems calls upon the ability to manipulate number concepts, requiring alertness to carry out the four basic operations of addition, subtraction, multiplication, and division. These problems are used to indicate a child's cognitive development. "Similarities" involves identification of likenesses, for Wechsler believed the ability to develop classificatory relationships to be an excellent test of human intelligence. These questions require associative thinking—"Lemons are sour and sugar is . . ."—and reasoning—"In what way are a pound and a yard alike?" A "Vocabulary" subtest contains a list of words to be defined, with special attention paid to the semantic character of the definition. In this category, educational and environmental influences are obviously significant factors in the child's chances of success. "Picture Arrangement" consists of cut-up pictures or picture sequences to be assembled. This test, which is timed, is designed to measure perception, visual comprehension, and understanding of causal connections. Other subtests include "Block Design," "Picture Completion," "Object Assembly," and "Coding."

Proponents of IQ tests believe that 80 percent of intelligence is inherited and only 20 percent stems from conditioning, and that the tests adequately measure pure intelligence. Critics, whose numbers are increasing, hold that no one has ever actually proved that an IQ test and intelligence are precisely related. They point to culturally biased items that result in higher scores for average-income whites than for poor urban blacks. All too many questions draw on how much a child has learned in school, an inadequate indication of potential or basic mental ability. Another criticism is that an individual's IQ score often fluctuates, depending on emotional state, age, and the desire of the child or adult to succeed.

?

How does a gun silencer silence the shot?

When a thug on TV sneaks up behind his unsuspecting victim, skillfully attaches a silencer to his revolver, and nails him with a few soundless shots—you're watching pure fiction. First, no silencer completely eliminates the sound of a gunshot; at best, it partially suppresses the loud crack from the explosion of gases behind the bullet. (In Europe silencers are more appropriately called "sound modulators.") Second, a silencer is ineffective on a revolver, for as the bullet jumps from the cylinder to the barrel in this weapon, the sound escapes out the side.

In the early part of this century, when shooting was a popular sport, the ecologically minded inventor Hiram Percy Maxim disliked all the noise so intensely that he developed both the silencer for firearms and the muffler for automobiles. By 1934 the United States viewed the silencer as a weapon unto itself; a Treasury act controlled silencers and placed a high tax on them. Today each state has its own laws; silencers are illegal in New York, for example, but permitted in Connecticut and Massachusetts.

A silencer functions on the same principle as a car muffler. When placed at the end of the barrel of a firearm, the silencer absorbs heat and pressure from the explosion. Spiral veins of steel or bronze wool inside the tube of the silencer actually catch gases behind the bullet. As the gases rotate along this longer spiral path, they are broken down, cooled somewhat, and emitted more slowly; the explosion of gases is thereby suppressed and the sound modified. Silencers vary in size, depending on the model of gun for which they are required, but they tend to be larger than those you see on TV: 2 to 3 inches in diameter and 9 to 15 inches long for a .38 or .357; 1 inch in diameter and 6 to 8 inches long for a .22 handgun or automatic.

Silencers may be hard to come by, but quiet murders are not. By simply wrapping the nozzle of an automatic pistol in a pillow, a gunman can achieve a cheap and very effective means of muffling the sound.

?

How do they make fake cherries?

There are bright red cherries, sometimes found in pie fillings and cakes, that have nothing in them remotely resembling a real cherry. In the 1940's a synthetic cherry was created, comprised of a sodium alginate solution, artificially flavored and colored with a red dye. Drops of the solution are allowed to fall into a bath of calcium salt. A "skin" of insoluble calcium alginate clings to each drop. The drops are allowed to cure and eventually, as calcium ions penetrate the center, they gel into sweet, unwholesome "cherries."

You may be tempted to shove aside the cherry on your ice cream sundae with disdain, but your fears are needless—this is a maraschino cherry, a real cherry that has simply been dyed.

?

How does a dentist perform a root canal?

You know there's a cavity in that upper molar (your tongue keeps returning unconsciously to the unfortunate spot), but you can't bring yourself to make an appointment with the dreaded dentist—just the sound of his drill makes your skin crawl. You continue to procrastinate. Then you bite down just the wrong way on a hard candy, the tooth cracks, and you despair. You may not lose the tooth, but you face extensive root canal work, which makes filling a cavity seem like a breeze.

The outer coating of your teeth is enamel. Beneath the enamel, dentin, a living substance, fills the crown and roots. This material in turn protects the sensitive nerve or pulp chamber in the crown, which narrows as it extends down into the roots. A tooth may have one, two, or three roots. When a dentist does a root canal, he actually removes the pulp, composed of nerves and small blood vessels, from the chamber right down to the roots and fills the empty cavity—the canal—with another substance.

If all the nerves in your tooth have not been destroyed, the dentist gives you a local anesthetic. Then he clamps a thin sheet of rubber over and around your tooth to prevent saliva and/or the side of your mouth from touching the tooth and exposing it to germs. Using a drill, he really goes to town, drilling right down into the pulp chamber and below. Using fine wire broaches, reamers, and files, he removes pulp and infection, enlarges the canal slightly, and smooths the walls. X rays are useful for guiding the instruments to the tip. The canal is then irrigated with 3

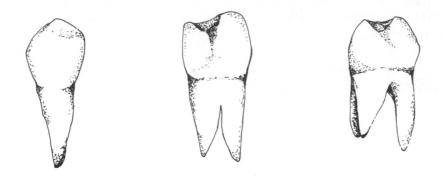

One-, two-, and three-root teeth.

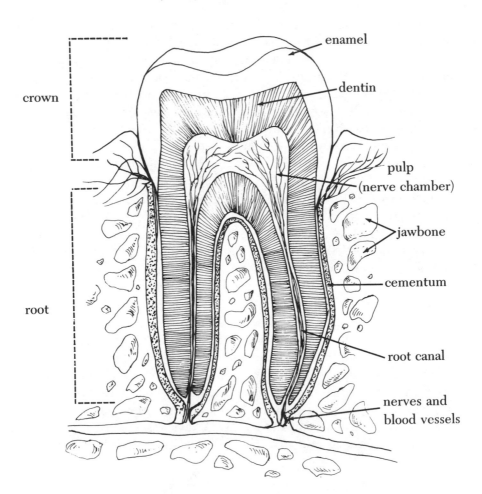

enamel

dentin

crown

pulp
(nerve chamber)

jawbone

cementum

root

root canal

nerves and
blood vessels

percent hydrogen peroxide to kill germs and sealed with medicaments. The tooth is not filled, however, until it is completely free of germs, which requires several visits to the dentist. When there is no sign of infection, the dentist fills the root with a special cement. He inserts a gutta-percha stick or silver point into the cement to the tip of the canal and then fills the rest with cement. Again, X rays help to ensure that the entire canal is filled. Only then does the dentist put a regular filling in your weary tooth and, perhaps, add a crown or porcelain jacket for support.

Root canal work can save not only a severely damaged or diseased tooth, but even a tooth that is completely knocked out—if you get to the dentist within a half hour after your accident. The dentist can put your tooth back in place, and the thin covering of the tooth eventually will reattach itself to the jawbone. In the meantime the tooth is wired in place and cannot be used. The dentist may do a root canal immediately, as he holds your tooth in place, or may wait until it is more secure before replacing the damaged pulp.

?

How do they know how cold "absolute zero" is?

There isn't any limit to how *hot* something could be, if an infinite supply of energy were available. But cold is just the absence of heat, and there is, theoretically, a state of "no heat" or *absolute zero,* which is the coldest anything can be anywhere in the universe— −273 degrees Centigrade, or about −459 degrees Fahrenheit. That is far colder than the Siberian steppe, where winter temperatures dip to an invigorating −100 degrees Fahrenheit, and colder than any temperature ever reached in a laboratory. Scientists know what it is, though, by measuring how gases expand and shrink with changes in temperature.

Heat is the motion of the atoms or molecules making up an object. Any substance—solid, liquid, or gas—contains some heat, its particles somehow moving: vibrating, rotating, or bumping into one another. When we say, for instance, that one pot of water is hotter than another, we mean its molecules are colliding more often than those in the other pot. Objects expand with heat because their particles move around more, propelled by collisions with other particles. Thus a cold automobile tire looks flatter than one that's been driven on for an hour.

Scientists use gases at various temperatures to study heat, because the behavior of gases demonstrates the action of particles, which are the "stuff" of heat, very clearly. If you confine a gas in a container and heat it, its molecules collide more and more frequently, raising the pressure on the container walls as the gas tries to expand. If you cool the gas, the pressure drops. If you confine the gas in a *flexible* container that changes its volume in response to the volume of gas, keeping the pressure constant, the gas expands or contracts at a constant rate with every change in temperature, corresponding to its molecular motion.

By measuring its volume at 0 degrees Centigrade and then at other temperatures, it can be determined that any gas shrinks by $1/273$ of its volume for every degree Centigrade that its temperature is lowered. Scientists reason that the coldest possible temperature must be one at which there is so little molecular motion that a gas takes up no volume at all. If the volume of a gas sample is 2 liters at 0 degrees Centigrade, and it drops by $1/273$ of that (.0073 liters) for every degree Centigrade that its temperature is lowered, it must take a drop of 273 of those degrees Centigrade to reach zero volume. If volume in a gas is caused by heat, the temperature at zero volume must be "zero heat" or absolute zero: -273.15 degrees Centigrade. Absolute zero is also called 0 degrees Kelvin or 0 Kelvins, after Lord Kelvin, who established the idea of absolute temperature. The Kelvin scale, which is commonly used in physics and astronomy, defines all temperatures as a given distance from absolute zero.

Absolute zero can never actually be reached, according to cryogenic physicists, who specialize in producing very low temperatures in the laboratory. Any refrigeration process gets less efficient as a substance approaches absolute zero, since refrigeration uses molecular motion itself to slow down molecular motion. Using such tools as magnetic fields and liquid helium, however, experimenters have achieved temperatures only .0001 degree above absolute zero in samples of copper. Individual particles smaller than a copper atom have been cooled to .000001 degree above 0 degrees Kelvin.

What is the use of producing such low temperatures? One use is making a revolution in computer technology. Computers built to take advantage of a process called superconductivity, which occurs only below 7 degrees Kelvin, will be ten times faster than today's machines, use a fraction of the electricity, and fit nicely into a box a few inches long on each side. The new computers will use a type of superconducting switch in their circuits called a "Josephson junction." This switch operates with *no* electrical resistance, unlike any electronic device now available. It can go from "on" to "off" in 6 *trillionths* of a second, defying classical physics.

Superconductivity is possible when certain substances get so cold that their larger particles, such as molecules and atoms, hardly vibrate at all; this allows the smaller electrons to flow smoothly without getting "bumped" by nearby atoms. It is the disruptive vibration of large particles that causes electrical resistance and wastes time and energy in an electrical system. A Josephson junction computer would contain about 1 million superconducting switches and could work only while submerged in a bath of liquid helium at a temperature of 4 degrees Kelvin, which keeps the circuits cold enough.

?

How do astronauts relieve themselves in space?

When an astronaut, dressed in an elaborate spacesuit, is in his capsule hurtling through space at a tremendous speed, and perhaps consuming one of the hydratable delicacies prepackaged for him, relieving himself is not the problem it appears to be. Toilet facilities on the spacecraft are quite simple. The astronaut attaches a plastic bag with an adhesive lip near his anal opening. When full, the bag, which contains a germicide to prevent bacteria and gas formation, is sealed and stored in an empty food container for analysis after the flight. To urinate, the astronaut uses a fitted receptacle connected by a hose to a collection device where urine may be stored. In some NASA flights, urine was simply dumped overboard.

?

How do they measure continental drift?

When Alfred Wegener, a brilliant German meteorologist working in the early part of this century, came up with a theory that until 150 million years ago there was only one continent on the earth, geologists around the world were skeptical. It took until the 1960's for man's knowledge about the lithosphere (the earth's outermost crust) to advance to the point at which the revolutionary concept of plate tectonics was accepted.

By studying the ocean basin floors, geophysicists had discovered that the earth consists of plates constantly in motion toward or against each other, that the hard, brittle lithosphere is constantly moving above a soft asthenosphere. The ability to measure this movement involves study of the earth's magnetic field, its normal and reversed epochs, and the ocean floor, in which different epochs can be detected over a certain distance and then correlated to a magnetic reversal time scale. This entire analysis is as brilliant as it is complicated.

The earth's basaltic lavas contain iron and titanium, which, when extremely hot (1,100 degrees Centigrade), are not naturally magnetized. As they cool, however, they pass a critical point known as the Curie point, after which they become magnetized in alignment with the earth's magnetic field. A startling fact known to geophysicists is that approximately every 100,000 to 1 million years, the earth's polarity actually reverses itself. (This means that a needle on a compass that points north in a normal epoch would make a symmetrical switch and point south in a reversed epoch.) Our own normal epoch began 700,000 years ago, but geophysicists have discovered many polarity reversals preserved in the ocean basin floors, the earliest occurring some 160 million years ago.

Those reversals are discovered by examination of an axial rift on the ocean floor, where over the ages basaltic lava has welled up, formed a crust, split, and slowly moved outward. The lava of a

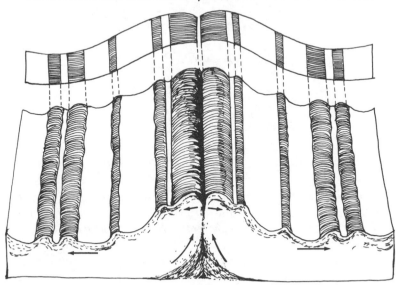

millions of years before present

4.0 3.5 3.0 2.5 2.0 1.5 1.0 0.5 0.0 0.5 1.0 1.5 2.0 2.5 3.0 3.5 4.0

Basaltic lava pushes upward and splits, forming an axial rift on an ocean floor. As the upwelling continues, newer lava spreads outward on both sides, pushing older lava farther from the rift. Thus is the lava of a particular age divided and separated farther over time. The symmetrical, striped pattern on either side of the rift denotes normal (shaded) and reversed (white) epochs, as identified from the magnetic polarity of the lava, or oceanic crust.

particular age thus forms two lines or strips on either side of the rift, which grow steadily farther apart as newer lava wells up and pushes outward. The result is a wonderful mirror image, symmetrical with respect to the rift.

Oceanographic surveys have confirmed this pattern by the use of a magnetometer towed through the water which measures the earth's magnetic field and detects normal and reversed epochs. (Basically, the instrument consists of a bottle containing distilled water and a wire coil, which are polarized and made extremely sensitive to intensity of magnetism.) Oceanographers measure the total intensity of the earth's magnetic field, about 95 percent of which is generated in the earth's molten core and the remaining 5 percent resulting from the permanent magnetization of the

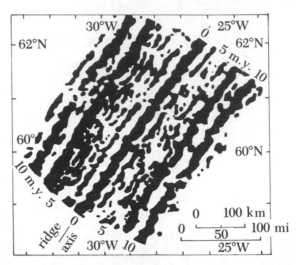

Minute variations in the earth's magnetic field picked up by a magnetometer can be resolved into a pattern. This magnetic anomaly pattern for a section of the Mid-Atlantic Ridge southwest of Iceland shows the anomalies—like the lava strips—to be symmetrical with respect to the axis of the ridge. Study of the magnetic values across the mid-oceanic ridge leads to identification of normal and reversed epochs. Rock ages are given in millions of years (m.y.).

oceanic crust. If the crust is normally magnetized, its magnetic field is parallel to and runs in the same direction as the earth's magnetic field, thus adding to the total measurement. If, on the other hand, it is reversely magnetized, the crustal field runs parallel, but in the opposite direction, to the earth's magnetic field and thus reduces the overall measurement. Over hundreds of miles, the magnetometer registers a long-wavelength pattern which indicates total field intensity. Then, using a computer, oceanographers subtract the "carrier wave," which represents the magnetic field generated in the earth's core. What's left are the departures from this norm, magnetic anomalies that result from permanent magnetization of the oceanic crust. After several surveys, the magnetic anomalies can be resolved into a lineated pattern and, in accordance with the lava strips, they too are symmetrical with respect to the mid-oceanic ridge.

The next step is to measure the width of the lava strips by modeling the anomalies into a pattern that represents normal and reversed magnetic areas over a certain distance. This pattern is then correlated to a magnetic reversal time scale (in millions of years), derived in part by radiometric determination of the age of the rock in a particular strip. Knowing that x kilometers of normal and reversely magnetized lava strips occupy y millions of years, geophysicists can then, of course, calculate the rate of drift: distance ÷ time = rate of drift. For example, if a span of 10 million years is determined in the ages of the crust found within 440 kilometers on one side of a ridge:

$$\frac{440 \times 10^5 \text{ centimeters}}{10 \times 10^6 \text{ years}} = 4.4 \text{ centimeters per year}$$

This 4.4 centimeters per year of movement is the rate of drift on one side only; the total rate is double that amount. The average, or worldwide, rate of total crustal separation, however, is only about 2 centimeters—less than an inch—per year.

?

How does a ship move uphill through a canal?

When a canal or other waterway passes over rough terrain with steep inclines, a lock or series of locks is built to enable ships to travel safely. A lock is a watertight enclosure equipped with gates at both its upstream and downstream ends. Its size depends on the size of the ships using the waterway. Small locks, 72 feet long and 7 feet wide, are found on canals in England; the Mississippi and Ohio rivers contain massive 1,200-by-110-foot locks.

If a ship is traveling upstream, the water level within the lock must at first be the same as that on the downstream side of the lock, in order for the ship to enter. Once the ship is inside, the gates swing shut, and the water level in the lock is raised by pumping in water through conduits that open into the bottom or sides. When a water level equal to that on the upstream side is reached, the gates at that end open, and the ship proceeds. This procedure may be repeated through as many locks as are necessary to lift the vessel to the water level of its destination.

Locks have distinct disadvantages, however. The process is extremely slow and requires huge amounts of water. Alternate methods include inclined planes, which enable substantial differences in water level to be overcome within relatively short distances. Ships are removed from the water and transported on trucks up or down planes to the desired level of the canal. An inclined plane at the Big Chute of the Trent Waterway in Canada spans 58 feet, and one at Krasnoyarsk, Russia, can accommodate a 1,500-ton vessel.

Lift locking, in which the lock itself is raised or lowered mechanically, is common in Europe. Vertical lifts operate by means of high-pressure hydraulic rams, or by a system of counterbalances and ropes, with electrically driven gearing. The Anderton Lift in England and Les Fontinettes in France are among those that enable ships to move uphill without undue delays.

?

How do Polaroid sunglasses block out the glare but not the rest of the world?

Polaroid glasses cut out the glare from your field of view by filtering out all the horizontal light waves, which happen to be what "glare" is made of. The lens that performs this feat was invented by Edwin H. Land at the age of eighteen, working in a laboratory he set up in his rented apartment on New York's West Side. Land later founded Polaroid, invented the Polaroid camera, and became quite wealthy.

Light, like all energy, travels in waves, just as the energy of motion travels in waves through the ocean. Ocean waves oscillate (vibrate) vertically, describing an up-and-down motion as they move toward the shore; anyone who has been clobbered by a six-foot breaker can attest to this. Light waves from the sun and from ordinary light bulbs vibrate at all different angles: horizontally, vertically, and at every angle in between.

When you look down a brightly lit roadway, with the sun's glare reflecting off your car's hood and blinding you, the light reaching

57-degree angle

Polaroid glasses filter out all horizontal light waves—the waves that cause glare. Light comes from the sun in all directions; some light waves hit the hood of your car at a 57-degree angle—Brewster's angle. The horizontal waves that bounce off the hood at Brewster's angle appear to your eyes as glare.

Polaroid lens
material

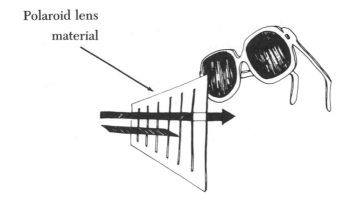

Polaroid glasses have vertical slits so that vertical waves can pass through; horizontal waves—glare—can't fit.

your eye from the glare spots contains a large percentage of horizontal waves; this happens because light that strikes a shiny surface at the special angle of 57 degrees (called Brewster's angle) is filtered or polarized by the surface so that only waves that vibrate parallel to the surface bounce off and reach your eye. In the case of a car hood, horizontal waves reach you, since the hood is horizontal. This polarized light has not penetrated the paint on the hood or been changed by it—it simply bounces—so it appears the same color as the sun that generated it: blinding white.

Polaroid sunglasses contain vertical ribbing as fine as the height of a single light wave—about a millionth of an inch—which polarizes light vertically, stopping all but the vertically vibrating waves. The ribbing is made by stretching a sheet of heat-softened plastic, which makes parallel "stretch marks" or stress lines in the sheet. A light-absorbing dye is applied to the plastic, which settles along the minute lines to form the ribbing.

This material wipes out glare from horizontal surfaces because the horizontal light waves coming off at Brewster's angle can't fit through the Polaroid ribbing, which runs crosswise to them. Most things that are important for us to see move on horizontal surfaces, such as roads, floors, and bodies of water, so a vertically polarizing lens takes out the worst glare. We see clearly through the lens because there are enough vertical waves that do get through to light the scene for us.

You can test polarization for yourself at the drugstore racks where the glasses are sold. Put on one pair, and hold another pair in front of you as if you were about to put it on. The second set of lenses looks as clear as the set you have on—through it you're seeing vertical waves that have made it through both polarizers. Now, swing the second pair sideways so that its lenses line up one above the other instead of side by side. The second set of lenses now looks black. Turned on its side, set 2 transmits only horizontal waves, whereas set 1 cuts out all of them, transmitting only vertical ones. Thus nothing can reach your eyes through both pairs—between them they have polarized out all the light.

?

How do they measure the gross national product?

The gross national product, or GNP, is the primary indicator of the pace of economic activity within a nation. It is defined as the sum of the money values of all final goods and services that are produced in a certain period of time, usually a year.

The money value of a thing is its market value, what people are willing to pay for it. You might purchase a pair of shoes that you think are worth more than the $30 you pay for them, or you might feel the price is too high for imitation leather and you're being ripped off, but those considerations don't count. What you pay is what is recorded.

A final good means the good has been purchased by its ultimate user. Intermediate sales are not counted; if all steps were included, the output of the economy would appear to be double, triple, or even more what it actually is. For example, when a gas company buys gas from a pipeline company, the sale isn't counted; but the sale of gas from the gas company to you, the final user, is included.

Similarly, GNP reflects only the goods and services produced in a given year. If, for instance, you buy a 1970 Ford in 1980, it won't be counted by a national statistician, nor will the resale of a house be tabulated. GNP would, however, include the car dealer's markup and the real estate agent's commission.

Statisticians do not, or cannot, count goods and services that don't pass through an organized market, such as gambling in Chicago—but not Las Vegas—and work you do for yourself in your spare time.

What about all the goods that a company produces but does not sell—the inventories that linger in the warehouse? Those goods are added, as if they'd been bought by the companies that produced them.

Investment goods present another problem. The machines and tools that factories use are not sold to consumers, but are nonetheless considered final products, used by the companies that purchase them.

The usual method of measuring GNP is to add the following four amounts:

1. Consumption of final goods and services.

2. Gross private domestic investment, which is business investment in plant and equipment, residential construction, and inventory investment.

3. Government purchases. This includes what the government pays its employees, purchases of military equipment, typewriters used in government offices, and so on. Transfer payments, which make up a large share of government spending, are not included, for they simply involve shuffling money back and forth, for example, in grants to state and local governments, Social Security, unemployment compensation, and public assistance.

4. Net exports, which is the total of exports minus imports.

Coming up with these four figures is another matter altogether. The enormous numbers of facts and figures collected monthly and annually from various sources are compiled by a small group of people in the National Income and Wealth Division of the U.S. Department of Commerce's Bureau of Economic Analysis (BEA). This group relies heavily on other agencies, such as the Census Bureau and its several thousand employees, and on thorough nationwide surveys. Every five years—the years ending with a 2 or a 7—the Census Bureau sends out questionnaires to wholesalers, retailers, manufacturers, construction companies, agricultural industries, and so on, to get extensive information about the type and quantity of goods produced, and about intermediate and final sales. The Census data provide the basic bench marks for the GNP components. More than five-year figures are necessary, however, for politicians, economists, businessmen, and the general public to keep abreast of the nation's rate of productivity, and figures are accumulated annually and also quarterly at 15-day, 45-day, and 75-day intervals. In general, data collected over a one- or two-month period go into the 15-day estimates, but two or three months are necessary for the 45-day estimates. The 75-day estimates generally use data from all three months of the quarter.

In the area of personal consumption expenditures, the Department of Commerce gets most of its information from the Census Bureau's Monthly Retail Trade Survey and from trade sources, such as trade publications. In order to estimate the sales of new cars, for example, statisticians record unit sales from trade sources for three months—average unit prices for two months make up a 15-day estimate; three months of prices go into the 45-day estimate. The average unit price is based on trade source list prices and on Bureau of Labor Statistics data on discounts. Sales to government and to business are estimated separately and subtracted to obtain sales to consumers. The 45-day and quarterly figures are used to interpolate and extrapolate annual estimates. Quarterly figures on tobacco products are determined from Internal Revenue Service (IRS) excise tax collections and price data of the Bureau of Labor Statistics. Hotels and motels are services whose receipts are estimated quarterly by the Census Bureau, annually from records drawn out of trade sources. In the area of utilities, water and other sanitary services may be estimated quarterly by "trend"—old figures are used and updated when new ones are unavailable or deemed unnecessary. Gas, telephone, telegraph, and electricity are measured by revenue data from trade sources. Regulatory agencies, tax data from Census surveys of state and local government finances, and the U.S. Treasury also aid in measuring sales of utilities.

The government represents another vast network with goods and services to be recorded. Many of the data used by the BEA are obtained from the Bureau of Accounts of the U.S. Treasury Department. The Bureau of Accounts computes monthly Treasury statements (MTS) from the total expenditures of different departments. Reports with detailed breakdowns of spending are compiled by each department and agency annually. For example, yearly defense reports tell just how much was spent on tanks, planes, ships, and so on.

Changes in business inventories are recorded by the Census, or in the case of farms, by the U.S. Department of Agriculture. The Census Bureau also keeps track of imported and exported merchandise. Then, too, there's the net interest you earn on your savings account—of which the IRS keeps careful count and then, like so many other agencies, channels the information to the BEA.

?

How does a pipe organ generate sound?

When an organist strikes the first chord of one of Bach's majestic chorales and the very arches of the cathedral seem to tremble, it's incredible to think all that sound is being generated by *air*. A pipe organ sounds when the column of air enclosed in the pipe is disturbed and set in vibration. Before the advent of electricity, someone with a set of bellows stood by to supply the air; today, the same effect is accomplished electrically by a rotary blower that delivers a steady amount of air under constant pressure.

The simplest organs have only one set of pipes, one pipe for every key on the keyboard. But in order to produce a rich variety of colors and tones, most organs have several sets, called stops or registers, set in a wind chest. When a key is pressed, a valve in the chest beneath the appropriate pipe opens, letting a stream of air into the bottom of the pipe. It is this vibrating column of air, whose molecules move up and down parallel to the length of the pipe, that produces the sound. As with piano strings, the longer the pipe, the lower the note; the pipe for C below middle C is exactly double the length of the pipe for middle C itself.

?

How do they pick the Pope?

The election of a new Pope by traditional methods passed down through the centuries occurs in the Vatican in Rome, where the College of Cardinals gathers behind closed doors under strict vows of secrecy. This tradition of secrecy arose so that the selection process could take place without interference from powerful secular governments. Precisely what occurs during the time the cardinals are cloistered there thus remains shrouded in some mystery. Still, some elements of the process have become known.

After waiting a minimum of fifteen days after the death of the previous Pope, the three orders of cardinals—cardinal bishops, cardinal priests, and cardinal deacons—meet and begin talking among themselves about potential candidates. Outright electioneering (as for a U.S. President) is not believed to occur, but the cardinals probe each other's feelings about the strengths and weaknesses of candidates; and although they rely on prayer for guidance, they are not immune to politics.

The Sacred College of Cardinals, of which there were 111 members when John Paul II was elected in 1978, gathers at the Hall of Congregations and first proceeds to the basilica of the papal palazzo to celebrate mass. The cardinals are locked for an indefinite amount of time within the Vatican walls, along with confessors, physicians, janitors, cooks, and barbers. Only the cardinals, of course, convene in the Sistine Chapel to elect the new Pope; the others work to make the cardinals' stay comfortable, or simply remain on hand, ready to be of service. The museum and library are cleared of tourists, and the members of the conclave, under rigorous security, stay in private cells in the papal palazzo and attached buildings. Because of a scandal in the thirteenth century when the conclave remained for thirty-three months banqueting and carousing, the food is plain at best. Most phones are disconnected, and mail is censored. Periodic searches are made for radios or other devices for transmitting messages to the outside.

At the first congregation the cardinals must swear an oath, under penalty of excommunication, "to observe with the greatest fidelity and with all persons, including conclavists, the secrecy concerning everything that in any way relates to the election of a Roman Pontiff and concerning what takes place in the conclave or place of election, directly or indirectly concerning the scrutinies . . . not to break this secrecy in any way, whether during the conclave or after the election of a new Pontiff, unless . . . given a special faculty or explicit authorization from the same future Pontiff." The cardinals must swear to elect the man they hold most worthy of being Pope and ignore any influence of secular governments. All others present within the Vatican must swear, under penalty of excommunication, a similar oath of secrecy about everything relating to the election.

Traditionally, no voting occurs on the first day, which is reserved for prayer, consultation, and a meeting of the conclave to hear the constitution for the election of a new Pope. On the second day the conclave meets in the Sistine Chapel to begin the election. The constitution of Pope Paul VI allows for three methods of selection. The first is by inspiration: a cardinal may be moved to call out the name of a candidate, and if the others unanimously call out "I elect," the matter is settled. Usually, however, the election is by scrutiny, or secret ballot, which calls for a majority of two-thirds plus one in support of a single candidate. Balloting occurs twice daily for three consecutive days. No speeches or conversations are permitted while the cardinals are gathered for balloting. Each writes a name on a formal ballot, goes to the altar, prays, makes a vow of secrecy, and drops the ballot onto a plate that covers a chalice. He then tips the plate so that all may see the ballot fall into the cup. Three elected cardinals act as "scrutinizers" to count the votes and read them aloud. Another committee of three cardinals recounts them. If there is no majority of two-thirds plus one, the balloting is done a second time. If again a majority is not reached, the ballots are burned in a stove along with a chemical pellet that turns the smoke black. Those anxiously waiting outside the Vatican see the puffs of dark smoke, which signify that no Pope has yet been elected. After three days of balloting the cardinals recess for several days of prayer, meditation, and spiritual exhortation.

In the event of an impasse, which is extremely rare, the Sacred College may decide to vote only between the two leading candidates or opt for the third method of election: by an appointed delegation of nine to fifteen cardinals. (The number must be uneven.) The College decides whether the delegation's vote must be unanimous or a simple majority, whether the candidate must be from the College or from a wider field, and how long the delegation may take to reach a decision. For centuries, though, it has not been necessary to pursue this course of action.

When at last a new Pope has been elected, the ballots are burned in the stove with a chemical that emits white smoke to alert the waiting world outside.

?

How can they tell what a dinosaur looked like from a single bone?

When dinosaur expert Dr. James Jensen of Brigham Young University unearthed the "Ultrasaurus," the biggest creature ever to walk the earth, in an ancient Colorado riverbed, all he really found was a shoulder blade. How could he know what the rest of the animal looked like, much less that it was the biggest monster on land?

"You've got to understand something about the body: it really is a machine," Jensen said. "The muscles act like cables, and the nerves are literally an electrical system. You look at a bone and see how thick it had to be, where the muscles and tendons were attached (they leave grooves in the bone), where there are holes for nerve passageways; you look at the joint on the end to see how it moved. You ask yourself, 'What did this machine part do?' It's

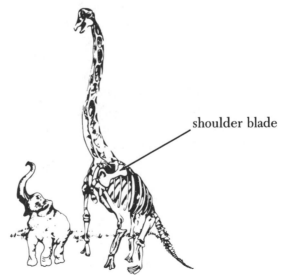

shoulder blade

"Ultrasaurus," the tallest dinosaur ever to walk the earth, carried its head 60 feet high. An elephant, by contrast, stands only one-fourth as tall. Scientists deduced the titanic proportions of "Ultrasaurus" from a single 9-foot-long shoulder blade.

really just like everyday life: you can tell a pencil sharpener from an egg beater, can't you?"

When Dr. Jensen, called "Dinosaur Jim" by his colleagues, made paleontological history in 1979 by finding the 9-foot-long scapula of a brachiosaurid, he nicknamed the creature "Ultrasaurus." He says it was a vegetarian, weighing 80 tons and standing 60 feet high—tall enough to poke its head casually into a fifth-story window. Jensen deduced its dimensions by extrapolating from a more complete skeleton of a smaller species of brachiosaurid, which had similarly shaped shoulder blades.

"You have to be a good parts man; it's something that comes with experience. Same way a good mechanic can look at a carburetor and tell you how big a car it ran." A shoulder blade does a certain job in a skeleton, supporting a certain amount of weight; knowing the size and shape of the smaller brachiosaurid, which Jensen dubbed "Supersaurus," he could tell that a larger scapula must have come from an even larger "Ultrasaurus."

Many things are known about extinct creatures from observing the animals in today's world: the shape and strength of bone used in a given area of the body, which indicate the shape and function of the flesh covering it; joint structure, as a clue to eating habits— vegetarians tend to munch using the head alone, whereas carnivores often have forelimbs that can bend toward the head, to enable them to put bits of flesh into their mouths; size, as a clue to metabolism—very large animals can afford to move slowly, effortlessly absorbing heat from the sun with their huge bodies, instead of generating it themselves as a small animal must. Small creatures tend to move fast to keep warm, whereas larger ones, such as elephants, bears, crocodiles, and big snakes, are lazy by comparison. Dinosaurs moved very slowly indeed, according to Jensen, and were cold-blooded—generating no heat in their own bodies and depending on the environment for warmth.

?

How does a thermos keep coffee hot, or lemonade cold, for hours on end?

According to Prévost's Theory of Exchange, the colder of two bodies always absorbs heat waves until both bodies are the same temperature. By this theory, it would be natural for scalding coffee or ice-cold lemonade in a thermos to lose heat or gain it, respectively. But a thermos is designed to cut down the exchange of heat between the inside and the outside of the bottle by hampering the three ways in which heat can travel: conduction, convection, and radiation.

A standard thermos, made of metal or plastic, has an inner container consisting of a double glass bottle. A near vacuum exists between the two layers of glass, and the lips of the bottles are sealed by melting the edges together. Glass is used because it is a poor conductor of heat, which means that in glass heat does not pass rapidly from molecule to molecule as it does in a better heat conductor such as copper. The stopper and pads that hold the bottle in place in the outer container are generally made of cork, also a very poor conductor of heat. The near vacuum between the two layers of glass limits the possibility of heat escaping from or penetrating the thermos by convection—the transmission of heat by means of the movement of heated matter from one place to another in a liquid or gas. Since, however, heat can travel through a vacuum by radiation, the facing surfaces of glass are coated with a silvery solution of aluminum which reflects heat waves and does not absorb them.

Sir James Dewar invented the thermos or "vacuum bottle" in 1885 to keep heat from the liquid gas with which he was experimenting; the happy byproduct of his ingenuity has made July picnics and December football games more pleasurable ever since.

?

How do they embalm a corpse?

Since ancient times, disparate cultures have been fascinated with the idea of preserving the bodies of the dead. We usually associate embalming with the elaborate funeral rites of the kings and queens of ancient Egypt, but it was also practiced by the prehistoric Paraca Indians of Peru and the Guanches of the Canary Islands. Tibetans today still embalm by the same formula used in that part of the world for centuries.

Embalming in Egypt was a long, expensive process probably reserved for royalty. The brain, intestines, and vital organs of the deceased were removed, washed in palm wine, and placed in vases with herbs. The body cavities were then filled with powder of myrrh and aromatic resins. After the incisions were sewn shut, the body was placed in niter (potassium nitrate or saltpeter) for seventy days, at which time the body was washed, wrapped, and placed in a coffin.

The modern principle of embalming by arterial injection was understood by William Harvey in the seventeenth century, but the technique as a way to preserve bodies for burial is usually attributed to the Scottish anatomist William Hunter, working a century later. In 1775 Hunter and his younger brother, John Hunter, embalmed Mrs. Martin Van Butchell, whose will stipulated that her husband could retain her fortune only as long as her body remained above ground. Hunter injected oil of turpentine and camphorated spirits of wine into the arteries, and Mrs. Van Butchell stayed in a glass-topped coffin in her husband's living room for years.

Since the Civil War, embalming has been an accepted practice in the United States. Today most bodies that are not cremated and are retained for some days before burial are embalmed. The process involves draining the blood from the veins and replacing it with a formalin-based fluid containing other ingredients such as phenol or dialdehydes. The percentage of formaldehyde is specified by state public health law. After disinfecting the skin and hair, the embalmer injects this formaldehyde solution into a main artery. Hand or electric pumps provide the necessary pressure to circulate the fluid. By an older technique, the fluid is simply allowed to flow through the arteries by means of gravity. In the event of arterial blockage, the fluid is applied locally. Next, the embalmer removes cavity fluid with a long, hollow needle called a trocar and inserts a stronger formaldehyde solution into the abdominal and thoracic cavities—areas not reached by the arterial fluid. The longevity of embalming varies considerably—from several months to thirty or forty years, depending on the thoroughness of the procedure and the nature of the body and of the soil in which it is buried.

?

How do "electric eye" elevator doors pop open for you if you walk through them as they start to close?

Two of the "fathers of the atomic bomb," Albert Einstein and Max Planck, are also responsible for the development of elevator doors that reopen automatically if they start to close as a person steps into the car. The two men explained how light falling on some materials can change them from poor conductors of electricity into good conductors. Research into the nature of electricity that followed from the discoveries of Planck and Einstein when they described the "photoelectric effect" led to the invention of the photocell—the device that cues a motor to reopen the doors without your having to touch them.

As you step into an automatic elevator, you'll notice a thin beam of electric light shining at about thigh level across the threshold; it leads to a little receptor on the right. When you put your hand or body in front of that beam, the doors won't close. The receptor is made of a type of metal called a semiconductor. Semiconductors include silicon, cadmium, arsenic, and germanium; they sometimes resist an electric current and sometimes conduct it efficiently, depending on the frequency of the light striking them.

247

Electricity is the flow of free electrons. Ordinarily we think of an electron as a tiny particle orbiting a particular atom the way the moon goes around Earth. In some metals, however, the nuclei of the atoms bond closely with each other in a rigid, regular pattern called a crystal, with loose electrons moving at random through the entire structure. Metals such as iron and copper arrange themselves this way and are good conductors of electricity, because the electrons drifting through the crystal lattice can easily be made to bump into each other and flow from one point to another—through a wire, for example.

Other metals, however, are made differently. When they crystallize, they do not leave any electrons adrift, but keep them bound with the nuclei in particular atoms. Thus they are poor conductors, since there aren't free electrons to conduct a flow of current. The element germanium solidifies in this nonconducting form under ordinary conditions; but if the right frequency of light strikes its atoms, electrons can be "kicked" free by the force of the energy and made available to conduct electricity.

Max Planck's discovery, which Einstein confirmed, was that light consisted of packets or particles of energy called photons, which vibrate at different frequencies. Planck said that the higher the frequency or speed of vibration a photon has, the greater its power to "kick" an electron free from a nucleus. Substances have different thresholds of energy needed for the kick to take effect, below which their electrons can't be moved.

The sensors in automatic elevator door mechanisms generally respond to frequencies close to visible light. One common arrangement works like this: the elevator doors' "at rest" position is closed; it requires the action of an electric motor to open them. The current supply for the door-opening monitor is controlled by a conventional switch. Most of the time this switch is off, with no power reaching the doors. Two different mechanisms, however, can throw it to "on" under different circumstances, to make the doors open. The most obvious is a timer that opens the doors for a certain number of seconds when the car reaches each floor; the other is the photocell safety device.

The safety device is a switch controlling another switch: the door switch springs to the "on" position and opens the doors unless it's held "off" by an electromagnet called a relay. Power for the relay magnet must pass through the germanium crystals in the photocell receptor on the right of the doorway. While the light across the threshold is reaching the receptor and keeping its electrons "kicked" and excited enough to conduct current, the power to the relay keeps flowing, which keeps the door opener off, which means the doors can close whenever the timer lets them. When the beam is blocked by a person entering the elevator, however, the electrons in the germanium lose their energy and are recaptured in its crystal structure; the germanium suddenly loses its conductivity and breaks the relay circuit. The electromagnet stops working and no longer holds the door motor off. The motor therefore switches on, the doors pop open instead of crushing you, and you can step through the door into the elevator.

?

How does a dollar-bill changer know whether your dollar is real?

If you've ever tried to cheat a dollar-bill changer by inserting a piece of notepaper, newspaper, or whatever's on hand when your money runs low, you'll know the machine is no fool. More than the correct size note is necessary to set off the circuits that send four quarters into a change receptacle. A common design, the one-dollar-bill validator made by Micro Magnetic Industries, Inc., performs no fewer than five authenticity tests on your dollar bill, so you might as well leave the Monopoly money at home.

This machine consists of a solid-state system of control and sensing circuits and a motorized dual-belt drive system that transports the dollar bill. The first test—a gross density check—occurs as the forward part of the bill enters the machine: a light shines on the bill, and a photocell measures the amount of light passing through it. If the bill is too thick or too thin, it can't enter the validator.

Inside the machine a second, more elaborate optical test is performed, using a moiré grid pattern, a stable light source, and a silicon photovoltaic cell. The moiré grid pattern contains lines designed to correspond to the very fine lines that run diagonally through the words "ONE DOLLAR" on the back of a dollar bill. As this section of the bill passes in front of the grid, a light shines through the grid, and the lining up of the lines (or the disparity between them) creates an optical wave pattern. A photovoltaic cell, in turn, transforms this pattern into frequency information. The optics circuits consist of an electronic frequence filter and an integrator. If the bill is real, a single frequency appears at the output of the filter, to be integrated and converted into "time-presence information." Depending on the presence and duration of the signal from the optics scanning unit, the integrator accepts or rejects your bill. This interferometric scheme allows the machine not only to weed out play or foreign money, but to distinguish between a one and a five-, ten-, or twenty-dollar bill; different printing patterns produce different optical "signals."

Meanwhile, the bill is also being scanned by a magnetic pickup transducer. Magnetic characteristics, resulting from magnetic ink used in the printing of all valid bills, are transformed into an electronic signal. Again, depending on the presence and duration of the signal, your bill may be judged an acceptable candidate or a reject.

The bill must then travel on to interrupt a light path between another optic pickup cell and a light source. This triggers the validator to evaluate the results of the previous tests—the density, optic, and magnetic circuits. If any of those circuits is in the reject mode, the machine rejects the bill.

If the bill passes, it activates a circuit that measures its length and a circuit that "remembers" that the previous tests produced acceptable results. At last, a "credit" signal is activated to give you your change in return. Once inside the machine, electromechanical interlocks prevent the retrieval of the bill by devious means.

?

How do they notate choreography?

Until the twentieth century, specific dances were passed on by observation and oral tradition. Although a variety of dance notation systems have since been formulated, two in particular are widely accepted and used with increasing frequency. The first, Labanotation, invented by the movement theorist Rudolf Von Laban in 1928, uses symbols on a vertical staff which is read from bottom to top. Joan and Rudolf Benesh, on the other hand, formulated a system known as Choreology in 1956, in which the spaces in a five-line staff correspond to parts of the body, as if the body were superimposed on the staff; it is read from left to right. This system was immediately adopted by the Royal Ballet in England, but today there is much debate about which system is superior. Many feel that Labanotation is more detailed and hence more accurate. Proponents of Benesh, however, say their system is widely applicable to different kinds of movement and, being more pictorial than Labanotation, is easier to read.

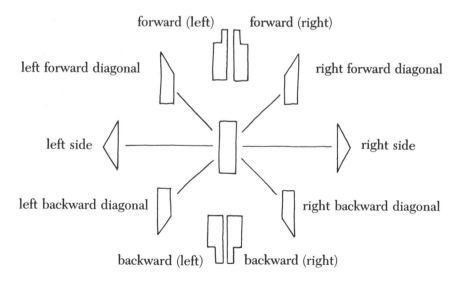

Direction symbols.

Any dance notation system must take into account three major factors: where the body is moving in space, what part of the body is moving, and how long it takes to complete the movement.

Labanotation has a set of direction symbols based on a rectangle. The rectangle itself implies the dancer is stationary, but variations in the shape (a triangle, for example, pointing to right or left) indicate which way to move. The symbols are in this sense pictorial.

It is possible to include simultaneously in the direction symbol an indication of the level of the movements: steps to be executed at low level (with knees bent) are shaded, those for the middle level (with legs straight, feet flat on the floor) contain a dot, and high-level movements (on the balls of the feet) are indicated by diagonal lines.

Basic levels (shadings).   low level / middle level / high level

The symbols are placed on a vertical staff composed basically of three lines, the center one being, as it were, the dancer's spinal cord. Columns to the left and right represent parts of the body on the left and right sides; a symbol written in the left arm column, for example, tells a dancer how and where to move the left arm. Columns immediately to the left and right of the centerline indicate progressions of the whole body by means of transference

Enlargement of staff.

left arm gesture | torso—if needed | left leg gesture | left support | right support | right leg gesture | torso or parts | right arm gesture of weight, jumps, or falls. Next to these "support" columns are columns for leg gestures. Outside the three-line staff are columns for body movements (torso, chest, pelvis), and adjacent to these are the arm columns. Additional columns may be added as needed for symbols modifying the main movements.

Also contained in this intriguing system is a measurement of time. The length of a symbol indicates how long the movement takes, with longer symbols representing slower movements and shorter ones faster motions.

| slow | medium | fast |

In addition, the vertical staff is marked off into bars, or measures, that match the horizontal measures of a musical score. Small dots on the center line indicate beats. The following shows two measures in 3/4 time:

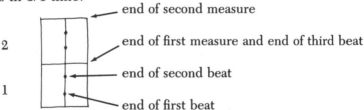

end of second measure

end of first measure and end of third beat

end of second beat

end of first beat

Other symbols supplement these fundamentals, allowing Labanotation to account for any motion one can imagine. Different types of hooks show which part of the foot is in contact with the floor, and a system of pins can (among other things) indicate the degree of a turn.

Degree of turn.

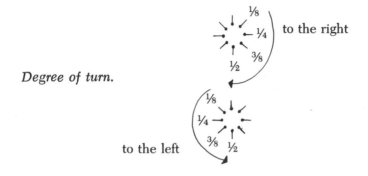

to the right

to the left

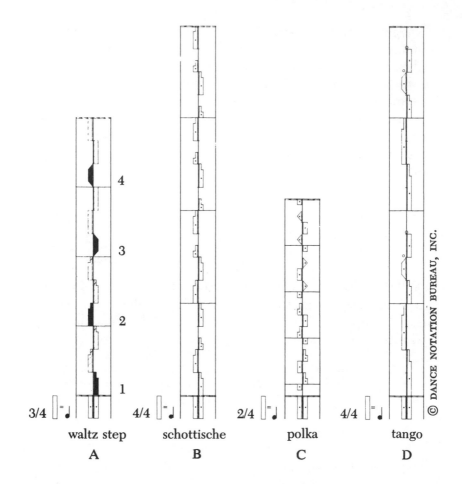

3/4 | ♩ = ♩   waltz step   4/4 | ♩ = ♩   schottische   2/4 | ♩ = ♩   polka   4/4 | ♩ = ♩   tango

A   B   C   D

© DANCE NOTATION BUREAU, INC.

The movements of four dances are expressed in Labanotation, which uses symbols on a vertical staff (shown here in ⅗ scale of the actual size of the notation). Reading from bottom to top, a dancer following the above four measures of the waltz step would (1) step forward with the right foot, leg bent; then forward on the ball of the left foot; and forward on the ball of the right foot. A dance teacher would say simply: down, up, up. (2) This measure repeats the first, but beginning with the left foot. (3) The dancer takes a step to the right, at low level (leg bent), brings the left foot to meet the right, and takes two steps in place on the balls of the feet. (4) The dancer moves to the left, then takes two steps in place—down, up, up. Throughout, the symbols are quite long, indicating a slow tempo. They are of equal length, which means that the three movements within each ¾ measure are of equal duration.

Until recently Labanotation had to be painstakingly written out by hand. But in the sixties New York City's Dance Notation Bureau collaborated with IBM to develop a means of typing the notation. By 1973 IBM developed a typing element with eighty-eight separate characters that can be used on an IBM Selectric. The Dance Bureau has also published volume 1 of an extraordinary book entitled *Doris Humphrey: The Collected Works,* which contains the choreography of three of Humphrey's works, scored in Labanotation.

In the dance notation invented by Rudolf and Joan Benesh, a five-line staff acts as a matrix for the human body. The top of the head touches the top line and the feet touch the bottom line; the three lines in between intercept the body at the top of the shoulders, waist, and knees. Lines and dots are employed as the basic signs to note the exact spot occupied by the extremities—hands and feet. These signs, plotted in the appropriate place on the staff contain information about positioning of the limbs in relation to the torso: a horizontal line means level with (or parallel to) the body; a vertical line, in front of the body; a dot, behind the body.

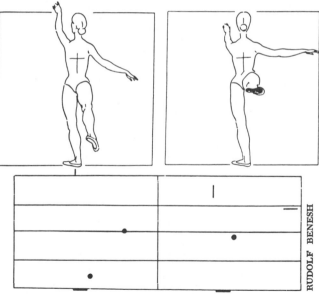

Benesh notation describes an arabesque on a five-line staff which, as illustrated above, corresponds to the figure of a dancer. The lines and dots indicate placement of the hands and feet, their height, and their position in relation to the plane of the body.

The position of a bent knee or elbow is denoted on the staff by a cross:

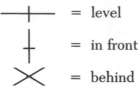

    = level

    = in front

    = behind

Foot position is indicated by where the basic sign is placed in relation to the bottom line of the staff: on top of the line means on point; through the line indicates demi-point; below the line is a flat foot.

The movement of an arm or leg is shown by a movement line drawn from the point at which the limb starts to the point at which it arrives. A basic sign is plotted at the finishing point, but not at the starting point, thereby indicating the direction in which the hand or foot should move.

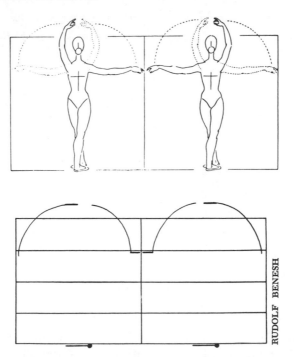

RUDOLF BENESH

Movement lines, together with symbols for positioning of the hands and feet, express side to side arm waving in Benesh notation.

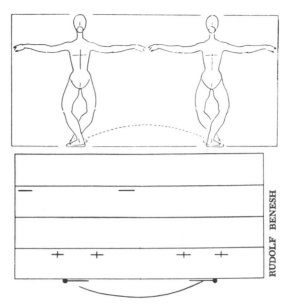

A curved line beneath the staff indicates the leap required in this changement.

Locomotion, or traveling movements such as jumping, stepping, and sliding, is shown by movement lines drawn along or under the bottom line of the staff. A curved line beneath the staff indicates a jump of some kind; a straight line denotes a slide.

The pins placed below the bottom line of the staff tell the dancer which direction to face in relation to the audience. Furthermore, a system of arrows and hooks is used to show the direction of travel and the dancer's relationship to it, for example, whether one faces or has one's back to the line of travel.

Finally, it is essential that the system incorporate a measurement of time. A number at the beginning of the staff tells the number of beats per bar, and signs written above the staff mark the beats and half beats appropriately:

ϕ = half beat λ ϕ = quarter beats

As one reads from left to right, these rhythm signs mark points in time, while the notation of the staff denotes points in space.

257

?

How do they put 3-D movies on television?

For some, TV has assumed a reality more meaningful than the actual world; others simply delight in the technical advances that have provided, say, better color. But for whatever reason people are enamored of their television sets, a desire to make programs still more lifelike continues: interest in three-dimensional TV images is widespread in Japan and Australia already, and it is gaining in the United States.

Our eyes perceive depth because each eye sees a particular image from a slightly different angle. Since our eyes are approximately 2½ inches apart, two images are reflected on our two retinas and then fused by the brain into a single perception. The earliest 3-D movies in the United States employed two synchronized projectors which showed two pictures of a scene as viewed from two positions. Those positions were approximately as far apart as our own eyes, and the viewer fused the images in his mind just as he would an object in the real world. The two pictures were superimposed on each other, however; one projector had a red filter, the other a green. Viewers, in turn, wore cellophane glasses with red on one side, green on the other. The eye watching through red cellophane would be blind to the green image created by the green filter, and vice versa. This system enabled a viewer to separate the image pairs cast by the projectors sufficiently to see the scene in 3-D.

Later, polarized filters and glasses replaced the cellophane. A polarizing filter blocks all light waves except those running in the same direction as its own particular "grain." A vertically polarized filter is placed on one projector, a horizontally polarized filter on the other. Glasses containing one vertically polarized and one horizontally polarized lens separate the stereoscopic pairs created by the superimposed images on the screen and provide a sense of depth.

Systems used abroad for 3-D television rely on illusion rather than on stereoscopic vision. A simple psychological illusion which provides the basis of 3-D in Japan uses the Pulfrich pendulum effect: if one eye is covered with a gray filter, a pendulum swinging back and forth, strangely enough, appears to be making an elliptical path. Viewers must wear glasses with one blank lens and one gray filter. The drawback, of course, is that the subjects on the screen must be in constant motion. An actor or actress at a standstill loses an entire dimension!

Australia is adopting an inexpensive Digital Optical Technology System, which also establishes 3-D by illusion. While the central subject of the film is in focus, the background is deliberately blurred. In addition, the background colors on one side are given a reddish edge (achieved through color separation), those on the other side a cyan, or greenish-blue, edge; the fringe colors of the subject in the foreground are reversed. The scene looks two-dimensional until the viewer puts on red- and cyan-tinted glasses. The variations in color are subsequently translated into variations in depth.

In the future, holography, which uses beams of laser light to produce startlingly realistic images, will undoubtedly be a source for the most sophisticated and refined 3-D TV ever.

?

How do they dig tunnels underwater?

There are two fundamental methods of tunneling underwater that have enabled men to overcome the problem of floods and collapsing walls.

The Thames tunnel was built in the mid-nineteenth-century by a system that ensured that the air pressure within the tunnel exceeded the water pressure without, thus preventing the inflow of water. First, the face of the tunnel is sealed with heavy airtight gates. Necessary equipment—shields, conveyors, dump cars, and segment erectors—are placed within the tunnel, and workers pass back and forth through air locks and a decompression chamber used for acclimatization. Air is pumped into the tunnel until the

259

pressure inside is higher than that of the water pressure outside. In addition, pressure grouting with cement, bituminous emulsions, or gelling salt solution is usually necessary. When loose gravel presents a problem in the tunnel, temporary jetties may be built above from which are lowered tubes that inject a bentonite-silicate cement mixture, forming an impervious strip on either side of the digging. Any water leaking into the tunnel is pumped out, and eventually a waterproof lining is constructed.

The second, and newer, method of tunneling underwater involves first constructing the tunnel, then lowering the prefabricated sections into the water. The section of the Paris Métro that runs under the Seine, built in 1910, was constructed in this way, as were the Chesapeake Bay Tunnel and the Ij Road Tunnel in Amsterdam. Concrete or steel sections, generally nearly 200 feet in length, are floated out and sunk into dredged trenches. Temporary end walls are then removed, and the joints are sealed. The trench holding the tunnel is filled in to secure its position. Pile foundations help support the tunnel, and it is essential that their tops be made level so that weight is distributed evenly across the long sections. This was accomplished in Holland's Rotterdam Metro by first sinking each tunnel section onto four piles. Other piles to support the section had been driven in slightly farther, but were topped with false heads, each containing a nylon-sleeved cavity. When cement grout was pumped into the sleeves, the false heads rose to the level of the tunnel.

?

How do they get air into a 2-mile-long tunnel?

When as many as 5,000 cars, trucks, and buses may pass through a tunnel in an hour, it is essential to dilute exhaust gases, which include hazardous carbon monoxide, by means of mechanical ventilation. Approximately 150 cubic feet per minute of fresh air is required in a two-lane tunnel, and twice that amount is necessary in a four-lane tunnel.

The ventilation system in New York's Holland Tunnel, completed in 1927, set the pattern for many long vehicular tunnels in the United States and other countries. The 1.6-mile, twin-tube tunnel runs under the Hudson River between Manhattan and New Jersey at a depth of 93 feet. Four ventilation towers, two on each side of the river, contain enormous blowers that force fresh air through louvers in the sides of the buildings and into ducts running beneath each roadway. Air enters the ducts at a velocity of 60 miles per hour and is diverted into expansion chambers that run the length of the tunnel. By an upward system, fresh air is emitted at curbside through a series of slots. The slot openings can be regulated from a central control point so that the amount of ventilation in the tunnel varies according to traffic conditions. Exhaust fumes and air escape through ducts in the ceiling of the tunnel, travel to chimneys in the buildings at either end, and empty into the atmosphere. In peak traffic, this efficient system changes all the air in the tunnel every 1.5 minutes.

Other methods of ventilating a tunnel include a longitudinal system, used in the Saint-Cloud Tunnel in Paris: air is drawn in through ducts from the ends of the tunnel and issued out in the center with fans. By the upward transverse system, found in the Mersey Tunnel in Liverpool, England, the inlet is at curbside (as in the Holland Tunnel), but exhaust is channeled out through shafts at both ends. The Velsen Tunnel in the Netherlands employs yet another method—a cross-flow system—in which blowing ducts and exhaust ducts are situated on opposite sides of the tunnel to ensure proper ventilation.

?

How do they know whether an object dates from 1000 B.C. or 3000 B.C.?

When an archaeologist examines an artifact, knowledge that the object belongs to a certain period sometimes suffices. But in many cases he requires a chronometric, or absolute, date: a quantitative measurement of time with respect to a given scale. Chronometric dating techniques, of which there are a variety, are based on change in natural phenomena. Knowing the rate of change and the amount of change enables one to calculate the number of years that have elapsed since the process of change began.

The most widely used technique since the late 1950's is radiocarbon dating. The principle behind it originated with Nobel laureate Willard F. Libby's examination of effects of cosmic rays on the earth and the earth's atmosphere. Neutrons are produced when those rays enter the atmosphere; the neutrons then cause a transmutation in the nucleus of any atom with which they collide. Although the neutrons are themselves uncharged, they react with nitrogen-14 to produce a heavy isotope of carbon, carbon-14, which is radioactive. This newly created carbon-14 reacts with the atmospheric oxygen to become carbon dioxide, which in turn enters the biological carbon cycle. Carbonaceous material is dissolved in the oceans; carbon dioxide enters plants by photosynthesis; and the plants are ingested by animals.

When organic matter dies, however, carbon-14 atoms can no longer be assimilated or supported, and disintegration into nitrogen-14 occurs. The half-life of carbon-14—the time required for half of the radioactive carbon to disintegrate—is 5,730 years. As it dissolves, the carbon-14 emits a beta particle. (A beta particle is an electron or positive electron ejected from the nucleus of an atom during radioactive decay.) It is by counting the number of beta radiations emitted per minute per gram of material that the half-life is measured. Modern carbon-14 emits 15 counts per minute per gram; carbon that is 5,730 years old should emit 7.5 counts per minute per gram.

Because of the high carbon content of organic matter, it is most suitable for the radiocarbon technique of dating, and lesser amounts need to be examined than of material that is low in carbon. Laboratories can calculate a reliable date from an examination of charcoal, wood, shell, bone, basic alloys of iron, peat, paper, cloth, animal tissue, leaves, pollen, pottery shards, carbonaceous soils, and even prehistoric soot from the ceilings of caves.

When a sample of material containing carbon is brought to a lab, it is first examined carefully and all contaminants removed. Next it is converted to a gaseous form—carbon dioxide, methane, acetylene, or benzene—by burning or other methods. A complex vacuum system then removes radioactive and electronegative impurities derived from the original material. The sample is taken to a proportional counter that counts the beta particles emitted from the carbon, so that this rate can be compared with a modern standard for the same material and an age determined. The proportional counter produces, and measures, electrical pulses in proportion to the energy of the beta particle initiating each pulse. Because it is necessary to shield the material being analyzed from any background radiation coming from the earth, 8 inches of iron surround the counter.

The dating sample is generally counted for at least two separate 1,000-minute intervals. After a final count has been obtained, a "radiocarbon date" can be calculated by means of a complex mathematical formula involving the activity of the sample, the activity of a modern sample, and the decay constant.

Radiocarbon dating can be used to date an object anywhere from 500 to 50,000 years old. Comparative dating by other methods has shown that radiocarbon dates are not entirely precise; that is, some discrepancies exist between radiocarbon dates and astronomical dates. This is especially true in the case of extremely old objects dating from between 5500 B.C. and 9000 B.C. Radiocarbon dates are thus given with a standard deviation, such as 1200 ± 100 B.C., meaning the object probably dates from somewhere between 1300 B.C. and 1100 B.C.

?

How does a diamond cutter cut a diamond?

For centuries mankind has prized the brilliant, precious stones that were first collected in India, possibly as early as 800 B.C. Pliny the Elder called diamonds the "most highly valued human possessions," and in recent years they have been put to multiple uses ranging far beyond the ornamentation of crowns and wedding rings. The National Aeronautics and Space Administration uses an extremely thin diamond disk to help determine the temperature of the stars, and surgeons are able to remove cataracts with sharp diamond knives.

Diamonds are actually made of carbon—the same atoms that compose coal and graphite—the difference arising from how the materials were formed. Millions of years ago carbon in the earth's upper mantle beneath the crust, subjected to extreme heat and pressure from molten rock, crystallized into rough diamonds. Those crystals grew into various forms, all in the cubic system of crystallization. Most rough diamonds occur in the form of octahedrons, but twin crystals, known as macles or twins, dodecahedrons, and cubes are also found.

Diamonds have a perfect cleavage grain parallel to the octahedron faces, making it possible to divide large crystals and macles along any of four cleavage grains. But the diamond, whose etymology stems from the Greek word *adamas*, meaning "unconquerable," is the hardest substance known and can be cut only by another diamond.

Diamond cutting, the process by which a rough crystal is transformed into a polished stone, calls upon the skill and expertise of perhaps five different craftsmen. The history of diamond cutting stretches back to the late Middle Ages, when craftsmen first reduced the angles of pyramidal stones to form the first "point cut." By the mid-fifteenth century, more than 250 cuts had been developed, among them the symmetrical and relatively plain table cut and the exquisite rose cut, with its domed crown of triangular facets meeting in a point at the center. Out of a series of logical developments, the rough was fashioned in various ways, until finally the modern brilliant cut was developed. In 1919 Marcel Tolkowsky mathematically determined the optimal angles and positioning of the 58 facets that would ensure maximum reflection of light through the top of the diamond. The principal cuts today are divided into two categories: the brilliant cuts—round, oval, marquise, pear-shaped, and heart-shaped—and the

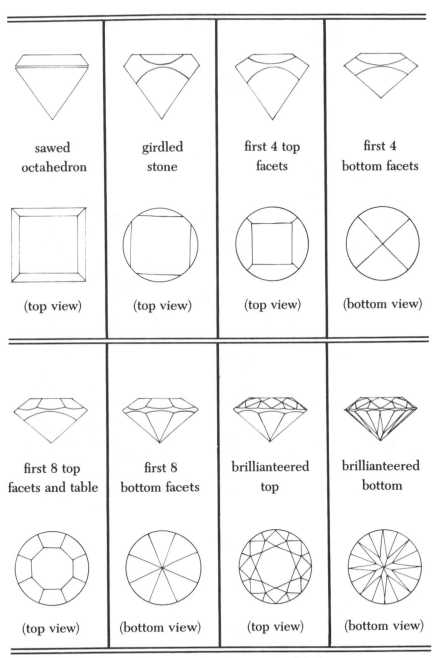

sawed octahedron	girdled stone	first 4 top facets	first 4 bottom facets
(top view)	(top view)	(top view)	(bottom view)
first 8 top facets and table	first 8 bottom facets	brillianteered top	brillianteered bottom
(top view)	(bottom view)	(top view)	(bottom view)

Some of the stages in cutting a modern brilliant diamond from an octahedral crystal.

step cuts—notably the rectangular emerald cut and the tapered or straight baguette.

Before beginning to cut, a craftsman studies a rough stone under a 10-power magnifying loupe to determine whether or not the stone should be cut at all, and if so, what is the best way to get maximum value from the rough. Usually he polishes one facet, which allows him to peer inside the stone and take note of any inclusions (trapped foreign matter) or interior features. For weeks he might weigh the factors that will determine the finished stone's value: cutting, clarity, carat weight, and color. He determines whether size, clarity, or a fine cut (which might mean considerable weight loss, but a more brilliant stone) is of primary importance.

If the stone is to be cleaved, the cutter marks it with india ink exactly along the cleavage grain. He cements it to a 10-inch-long cleaving stick, then takes another diamond, called a sharp because of its sharp edge, and rubs it back and forth along the line marked with ink. When a small notch or "kerf" of the required depth has been formed, he anchors the stick in a lead box. He places a thin, flat-edged, steel cleaving knife into the kerf and with a mallet gives the back of the knife a sharp blow, which splits the crystal. This procedure demands exceptional skill.

A more common method of making two or more diamonds out of one crystal is sawing. The stone is held firmly by two steel dops and positioned before a rotating phosphor bronze disk, whose cutting edge is coated with a paste of olive oil and diamond dust. Although the saw rotates at 5,500 revolutions per minute, it will cut only .05 inch in an hour. Today there are factories for diamond sawing in which one craftsman might oversee twelve machines cutting at once.

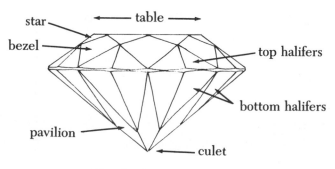

The finished stone.

Next, the diamond must be shaped. This is done by cementing it to a cylindrical dop or holder and then mounting it on a lathe. A second diamond on a dop at the end of a long stick is held by hand against it. By this process, called bruting, the stone is girdled or rounded at its greatest width.

Finally, the complex task of grinding and polishing is accomplished by holding the diamond, again in a kind of dop called a tang, against a rotating horizontal disk. The disk is made of relatively soft iron and is covered with a mixture of olive oil and diamond powder, which acts as an abrasive. The first facet to be cut is the table, or upper flat surface. Its position is of utmost importance, for all of the other symmetrical facets depend on its placement. The diamond is held in the dop at the end of the tang, and careful adjustments are made so that the facet will be ground in the proper position. After 8 more facets are cut or "blocked" on top, and 8 on the bottom, the diamond is bruted again. The stone is then passed on to the brillianteer, who makes the final 40 facets and the culet facet (opposite the table). The brillianteer must ensure that all facet junctions—points at which 4 or 5 facets meet—are precise. All told, when the polished gem at last is finished, it may be less than half the size of the original rough, uncut stone.

In recent years, lasers have proved a remarkable and very useful means of sawing diamonds in any direction desired. The intense light of the laser, which heats the diamond and turns it into graphite, can actually saw through the stone with pulsating, progressive shots of laser light along a line. A laser can also minimize black inclusions: a laser bores a hole down to the inclusion, and a strong chemical oxidizer is forced into the hole, which dissolves the inclusion and turns it white. With such impurities less visible, the value of the diamond can be increased, and the damage done by the laser is no worse than a white inclusion left in the diamond.

?

How do they select contestants for the Miss America Pageant?

Miss America is not chosen on the basis of beauty alone—although this was the case back in 1921 when the pageant originated as a showcase for Atlantic City bathing beauties who paraded the Boardwalk on Labor Day weekend. Today the pageant has become a scholarship foundation, with such other factors as talent and poise brought into consideration by the contest judges. The Foundation, a nonprofit civic corporation sponsored by the Gillette Company, Nestlé Company, and Kellogg Company, awards $2 million in scholarships annually, with $20,000 going to Miss America.

A candidate for Miss America must be a United States citizen and a high school graduate between the ages of seventeen and twenty-six. She must never have been married and be of "good moral character." With these qualities—and an ambition for fame and glamour—she is eligible for a local pageant held in her state. The Miss America Pageant grants a franchise to a "responsible organization" within each state, which in turn enfranchises other organizations, generally civic and service clubs, to conduct the contest on local levels. The headquarters in Atlantic City provides the clubs with a complete kit—how to hold a Miss America Pageant in your own backyard, as it were. Local pageants are informed about judging procedures and balloting, budgets, advertising aids, and publicity.

At every level—local, state, and national—the contestants are judged in four separate categories: private interview, evening gown, talent, and swimsuit. Points are accumulated in each division and added at the end, with extra weight awarded for talent. First, the contestant meets alone for 7 minutes with a panel of judges who form an evaluation of her personality, mental alertness, and general knowledge. Mature vocabulary, pleasant voice, good manners, and sincerity are all winning attributes in this category. In the opening stage competition, contestants wear evening gowns of their own choice, walk before the judges, and speak for 15 seconds. Poise, grace, and an overall attractive appearance are key factors here. Next is the talent competition, in which the women sing, dance, act, or in some way dramatize a hobby or career. The judges are instructed to look for potential as well as already trained and accomplished talent. Then comes the procession of contestants in swimsuits, when the judges look for fine figures, poise, and posture to select the next beauty queen of America.

?

How do they decide whether a steak is Prime or Choice?

It won't satisfy your curiosity about just what kind of meat you're eating to learn that the decisions about gradations are, when it comes right down to it, quite subjective. Government inspectors (the only ones permitted to make such decisions) rate the meat right at the slaughterhouse, an entire cow at a time. The overriding factors are color and amount of marble. The brighter the meat and the more tiny flecks of fat, the higher the grade. The inspector stamps as Prime the meat he considers of highest quality, after which come the categories of Choice, Good, and Ungraded. No fixed standards exist, however, and decisions vary not only from inspector to inspector but from day to day, depending on how a particular inspector feels. If he has indigestion from too much steak the night before, it might have some bearing on what lands on your own table.

?

How does detergent cut grease?

Detergents make use of the fact that water sticks to itself. Like soap, detergents are surfactants; water jams surfactant molecules between the surfaces of dirt and clothing fiber to pry the dirt particles loose and keep them from sticking again. Unlike soap, detergents can work in "hard" or mineral-laden water almost as well as in soft water, but their basic cleaning action is the same as that of soap.

The cohesion of water is the key to the surfactant process. Water molecules stick together because they are dipolar—each one has two poles, positive and negative. A water molecule (H_2O) is laid out like a triangle, with an oxygen atom at one end and the two hydrogen atoms at the other. The oxygen atom, the triangle's vertex, has a negative electric field around it, and the hydrogen base of the triangle has a positive field. The molecule as a whole is electrically neutral—with equal numbers of positive and negative

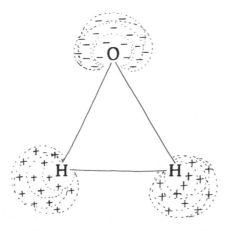

A water molecule has two magnetic poles: negative at the oxygen end, positive at the hydrogen end.

charges—but its positive and negative parts are comparatively far apart, and this affects how water behaves. Like charges repel each other and opposite charges attract; dipolarity makes water stick to itself because the hydrogen "base" of one molecule is attracted to the negative oxygen "vertex" of another molecule. Thus water molecules are always trying to stay next to other water molecules; this self-attraction or surface tension makes water an inefficient cleaning agent without a surfactant, and a very efficient one with a surfactant. By itself, water does not "wet" other materials very completely; it draws itself into little spheres or droplets instead of spreading out into the fabric fibers. A surfactant molecule has parts that allow it to reduce water's surface tension so that it can penetrate fabric better; it also *uses* water's surface tension as a force to dislodge dirt in the fabric.

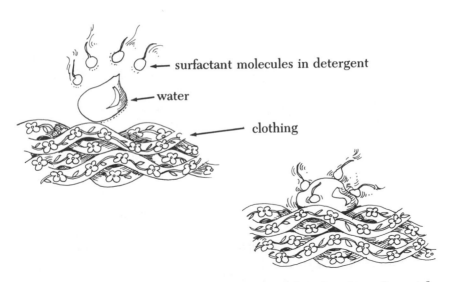

surfactant molecules in detergent

water

clothing

For detergent to work efficiently, the material to be cleaned must be wet. Here, a water droplet, pressed by hydrophilic surfactant molecules, is squashed flatter against a clothing fiber, wetting it more thoroughly. Continued pressure will break the droplet into smaller drops, distributing it further.

As soon as it is mixed with water, the detergent molecule sodium alkylbenzenesulfonate drops its sodium atom, but one of the sodium's electrons stays attached to the molecule. The sodium thereby becomes a cation, or positively charged particle, because it has lost one (negative) electron. The remaining larger part of the molecule keeps the extra electron and is therefore a negatively charged particle, or anion. Sodium alkylbenzenesulfonate is an anionic surfactant, because it is the anion that does all the work of cleaning.

The anion has two parts, a "head" and a "tail," that act together to pry grease particles loose. The head, made of sulfur and oxygen, is hydrophilic, or attracted to water, because its arrangement of electrical charges complements an opposite pattern of charges found in groups of water molecules. This works similarly to the way water attracts itself. The tail, a long chain of carbon and hydrogen atoms, has no particular affinity for water and is called hydrophobic ("water-hating").

As soon as the sodium ions drop off, the remaining anions spread quickly throughout the solution, led by their eager hydrophilic heads seeking water. At the same time, the water molecules, permeated and overrun by anions, continually try to regroup and stick back together. Their affinity for each other is greater than their affinity for the anions' heads. As the water sticks back together, the anions are forced outward toward all the surfaces: where the water meets the air and the sides of its container, and into the clothes in the washing machine.

At the same time the hydrophilic heads of the anions are pushing back at the water, drawn by electrical attraction. The effect on the water is to spread it out, flattening the spherical droplets that have formed on the clothing, breaking them into smaller droplets and flattening them again, spreading them deep into the clothing fibers. This pressure from the anions forces the water into contact with a greater area of fiber, the way pressing an inflated balloon on a tabletop with one's hand increases the area of the balloon that touches the table.

The water, however, keeps regrouping, always forcing the

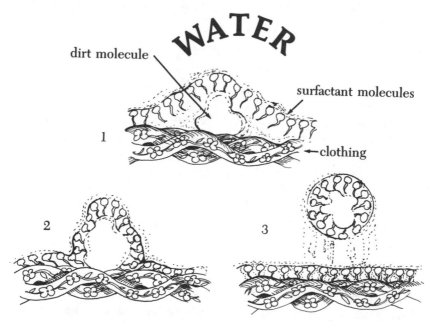

Surfactant molecules in detergent successfully lift dirt from clothing. The cohesive or "self-sticking" force of water presses surfactant molecules into the crevice between a dirt molecule and clothing fiber (1, 2). Finally, the water molecules come together between them, further separating dirt and clothing and carrying the dirt away (3).

anions outside itself. Most importantly, it forces them, hydrophobic tails first, far into the crevices between fiber and greasy dirt. Pressed on all sides by the water, the anions pry the dirt loose and surround it, hydrophilic heads all pointing out into the water like hairs standing on end. Once the dirt particles are removed and surrounded this way, they cannot restick to the fibers, since there are now anions coating every surface—anions all have negative charges, and like charges repel each other. So the dirt stays suspended until it is thrown away with the rinse water.

The major difference between soap and detergent is that detergent contains special additives, usually phosphates, that electrically soak up stray minerals such as calcium ions from the wash water. Calcium ions are positive and can attach themselves to the heads of the (negative) surfactant anions, making them useless for cleaning. By adding phosphate anions to the water, one can draw off the calcium cations and keep them out of the way while the surfactant molecules clean the clothes.

?

How do they collect caviar?

At the home of the Romanoff Caviar Company in Teaneck, New Jersey, resides a monumental stuffed and mounted Beluga sturgeon caught in 1911 which weighed over 2,000 pounds. This giant fish was the source of about 350 pounds of caviar, which at the time was sold for $10 a pound. Today the prized Beluga has become increasingly scarce, and prices have soared to an astronomical $350 a pound—were that sturgeon alive today, she'd be worth $122,500.

True caviar is the salted roe (eggs) of the sturgeon family. The largest of sturgeon, Beluga, averages 800 pounds and takes about fifteen years to mature; its roe brings the highest price. The Osetra is slightly smaller, and the Sevruga, the smallest of all, requires eight to ten years to reach its full size. The roe usually constitutes 15 to 20 percent of the gross weight of the fish.

The sturgeon are caught in sturdy nets (although large fish often tear right through them in a dash for freedom) by experienced fishermen who know the species and its habits well. Brought immediately to shore, the fish are gutted and the roe processed under the supervision of a "caviar master." He separates the eggs from the sac on a wire mesh, cleans them, and decides how much salt to add—a crucial decision. The best caviar requires the least amount of salt, and "little salt" is denoted by the Russian word *malossol*; thus Beluga Malossol or Sevruga Malossol is Number 1 grade. Machines are never used to handle the roe—only careful hands, for the eggs should not be broken. Although the Romanoff Company buys only the caviar, the fish itself is purchased by others and marketed fresh, frozen, or smoked.

When caviar arrives in bulk at Romanoff, it must pass an exacting test by the master taster, Arnold Hansen-Sturm, fifth-generation president of the company. He examines it visually (although color does not necessarily signify grade), and he smells it—though some samples, Hansen-Sturm says, he'd prefer not to get so close to. The ultimate test, however, is taste. And the taster gets his fill of caviar. (When Hansen-Sturm takes a break to go on vacation only a Russian who has been with the company for forty years is entrusted with his job.)

Samples are then taken to a lab to be tested for PCB, mercury, or other contaminants, according to Food and Drug Administration regulations. Fortunately for caviar addicts, if a fish has been in polluted water, the contaminant lodges first in the fatty tissue under the skin, and the eggs are rarely affected.

The best caviar is only sold fresh, packed in salt; the rest is sterilized by a pasteurization process and put into vacuum-sealed jars. This type has a shelf life of one or two years, whereas fresh caviar must be eaten within a few weeks.

Most of us think of the Caspian Sea as the major source of sturgeon, and for many years it was. But only a century ago, the Delaware River and other United States waterways teemed with sturgeon. The Romanoff Company actually was first established to *export* caviar to Europe, at a rate of 100,000 pounds a year. Largely because of overfishing, the supply of sturgeon dwindled. However, now that imports from Iran have been terminated (and the sturgeon population in the Caspian Sea seriously threatened by industrial waste), the sturgeon industry in this country is cropping up again. Sturgeon weighing about 250 pounds are caught in the Atlantic Ocean, the Columbia River, and various inland waters.

The roe from other fish cannot compare with that from sturgeon, but the difference in price is high enough compensation for many people. The "caviar" you find in the supermarket comes from lumpfish caught in Canada, Norway, and Iceland, or from the salmon of Alaska. Lumpfish roe is a pinkish color, but red or black dye is added to simulate the roe of salmon or sturgeon.

?

How does a heat-seeking missile find its target?

Most modern jet fighter planes are armed with heat-seeking missiles—9-foot-long rocket-powered "darts" that pursue enemy aircraft as if they had wills of their own. By staying pointed toward a source of heat, such as an enemy jet's tailpipe or wing, a missile like the American Sidewinder (named after the western sidewinder rattlesnake, which finds its prey by sensing the victim's body heat) can follow the target jet even if the enemy pilot turns, rolls, or dives to get his craft out of the way. Heat-seeking or infrared missiles were developed in the 1950's; their first combat use was in 1958, when a Nationalist Chinese fighter shot down a Red Chinese jet.

Everything in the solar system contains some heat; that is, molecules and atoms everywhere are colliding with each other and vibrating. To say that something is hotter than something else means that its particles are colliding more frequently. As the particles vibrate, they make electromagnetic waves which emanate from the object in all directions. The sun, for example, is quite hot (11,000 degrees Fahrenheit), so its particles vibrate very frequently and give off the greatest amount of radiation in the visible light range, where the waves vibrate about one quadrillion (10^{15}) times a second. Cooler objects than the sun, such as jet tailpipes, give off the most radiation at lower frequencies, in the infrared range, where the waves vibrate around 100 billion times a second. A Sidewinder's controls make it follow the object in its path having a peak radiation in the infrared.

275

The pursuit mechanism is based on a phenomenon called photoconductivity. Certain substances called semiconductors won't conduct an electric current under most circumstances, but will do so when they are struck with a particular frequency of electromagnetic energy. A substance is able to conduct electricity when the electrons in its atoms can get far enough away from the attraction of their nuclei to wander about and flow as a group from one object to another. Ordinary conductors like copper and platinum conduct under most conditions without any extra energy. Semiconductors like germanium, silicon, and arsenic compounds must have their electrons "kicked" away from their nuclei by a shot of light of the correct frequency before they are able to flow. This property makes them useful in switches.

The nose of an infrared air-to-air missile has a special "window" that receives light waves as the rocket travels and directs their energy to the guidance circuits. Semiconductor junctions in these circuits let current pass through only when they are struck by infrared light. The nose cone is covered with semiconductor cells; if the target jet dives to escape, the cells on the underside of the nose receive more radiation, switch to their conductor phase, and pass current to computer circuits which tilt down the rocket's tail fins so that it follows the jet into its dive. Any maneuver the target makes is registered by the semiconductors in the nose cone, which signal the computer to adjust the rocket's course. The warhead, meanwhile, sends out radar waves (microwaves), which bounce off the target and return to a receiver in the rocket. A computer logic circuit measures how long each wave takes to leave the transmitter and return. As the missile gets nearer the enemy jet, the period gets shorter; when the echo is almost instantaneous, the computer gives the signal to detonate, and the 25-pound warhead explodes, destroying the jet.

The sun gives off vast amounts of infrared radiation; why doesn't every Sidewinder go spinning off into the sun? For several reasons. First, the rocket senses waves only from in front of it and is not "aware" of the sun unless it points toward it—and pilots try to avoid firing toward the sun. In addition, computer logic systems correct for such background "clutter" when the target lies in the direction of the sun. The sun gives off a great deal of visible-wavelength light as well as infrared, much more of it than a jet; so the computer can be instructed to ignore any infrared source that also gives off more than a certain proportion of visible light.

Often jets carry infrared decoy flares, which they release when a missile is pursuing them to distract the rocket's sensors. Many jets also give off confusing countercommand radio signals to the approaching rocket's guidance system to muddle its navigation. Naturally, rockets are now designed with built-in *counter*-counter-measures to distinguish between its own commands and counter-measure signals and to help it tell the difference between infrared flares, the enemy jet, and the sun.

?

How do art conservationists remove a fresco from a wall?

Many highly valued frescoes, such as those by Giotto in the Scrovegni Chapel at Padua or the Byzantine wall paintings in Greece, are in grave danger of deteriorating. Frequently, the damage is caused by dampness, which rises through the walls of the building, or penetrates from the outside, or condenses on the inner surface if, for example, the church is heated on weekends but left cold during the week. Another more serious problem stems from the increasing amounts of sulfur dioxide in the air—the product of industry and cars. This has an effect on murals painted in lime mortar, which over the years becomes calcium carbonate. In the presence of moisture, sulfur dioxide causes the calcium carbonate to become calcium sulfate, which has a far greater volume than the carbonate. The walls—and the murals—then start to crumble and disintegrate under the pressure of expansion. Solutions to these problems range from simply guarding against leaks and providing uniform heat to—the most drastic course of action—actually removing the fresco from the wall.

When a fresco was first painted, it was likely done by one of two methods or a combination of both. In *buon fresco* (true fresco), pigments mixed with water are applied while the plaster on the wall is still wet, whereas in *fresco secco*, pigments mixed with egg, lime, or glue are painted onto plaster that has dried and hardened. Lime mortar underlies the plaster, and guide drawings, or *sinopia*, in red earth pigments are made on the first rough layer.

As this is covered each day with a wet plaster called *intonaco*, the *sinopia* drawings are retraced. How, then, do conservationists go about removing such a painting without its crumbling away to nothing?

A common technique, *strappo*, involves gluing a canvas to the painting and gradually pulling away a thin layer of pigments, with the help of very thin spatulas. The glue binding the canvas to the painting must, of course, be stronger than the internal cohesion of the plaster. After excess plaster has been stripped away, the pigments are fixed by a rigid support with synthetic resins. By another method, *stacco*, a thicker layer of plaster is removed—so much, in fact, that the original *sinopia* drawings may be revealed. The plaster on the back of the fresco is smoothed and then attached to a board. In both methods the fresco is taken down in strips or sections, which have been carefully marked out before work begins.

An astounding act of art conservation took place on the remote Greek island of Naxos in the old Church of the Protothronos several years ago. There an entire Byzantine dome painting was removed in one piece—a first in the annals of preservation.

The painting (which had been done in semifresco, a combination of the two techniques described above) was suffering from water seepage, which caused the paint to peel. Candles and incense used in services had left a coat of grease and soot on its surface. And a yet more important factor in the decision to remove the painting for restoration was that another, older painting was discovered beneath it. A decision was made to remove only the newer painting—a tricky business even on a small scale—but to preserve the form and plasticity of the original, conservationists decided to attempt to lower the entire dome painting at once in its proper shape.

First, the painting was covered very carefully with cotton gauze. A protective fabric was added. Then the dome was marked out with concentric circles and great circle arcs. Thin stainless-steel wires wrapped in gauze and soaked with adhesive were placed along these latitudinal and longitudinal lines. Wherever they crossed, they were soldered together. Sections of paint around the windows were detached with metal spatulas, but most areas were loosened by means of traction. A central wooden structure was built, positioned vertically below the dome. This king post had

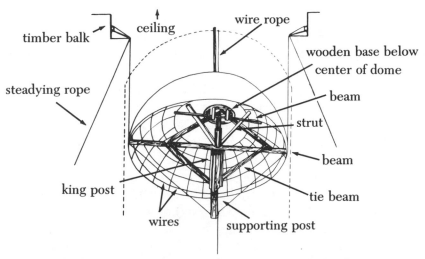

Labels in figure:
timber balk — ceiling — wire rope — wooden base below center of dome — steadying rope — beam — strut — beam — king post — wires — supporting post — tie beam

A supporting structure and pulley system lowered the dome painting from the ceiling of the Church of the Protothronos on Naxos.

two horizontal crossbeams at right angles to each other. The ends of the crossbeams were attached to the tops of four windows. Next, tie wires (thin wire rope adjusted by bottle screws) were connected to the king post. The other ends of the wires were fastened by means of an **S**-hook to the wires inside the dome, where the latitudinal and longitudinal pieces crossed. Two wires, diametrically opposed, were pulled simultaneously by tightening the screws and thus shortening the tie wires.

After the surface painting was eased away from the one beneath it, it was lowered gradually by means of a pulley system, resting temporarily on the king post. Steadying ropes were attached to various anchor points in the church, and the supporting scaffolding was disassembled. Finally, the painting reached the floor, to be removed for retouching and restoration.

How do they stop an oil-well blowout?

On June 3, 1979, a Mexican oil well, Ixtoc 1, blew out when an undersea drill hit a volatile pocket of oil and gas. The immense pressure of the gas caused the well to throw out an overwhelming

30,000 barrels per day of oil. Some of the oil burned at the surface, some was sucked into cleanup ships, but a great deal spread out over the Gulf of Mexico, eventually stretching to the shores of Texas.

The celebrated oil-well fire fighter Red Adair was hired to try to solve the problem. His divers, working at a depth of 160 feet, tried to repair damaged pipes, while 1,500 men and twelve planes and helicopters tried to contain the slick. Adair's efforts were not entirely successful, and the slick continued to spread. The underwater gauges and wellhead were partially blocked by debris from the shattered rig, and one diver said the morass of broken drill pipes resembled a "platter of spaghetti."

It was then decided that the best solution was to drill two intercepting relief wells to tap the oil below the escape point, thereby relieving the pressure. The Mexican oil company Pemex began to drill Ixtoc 1A and Ixtoc 1B, but the drilling would require months; meanwhile, thousands of barrels of oil continued to spew into the sea. A steel pipe was attached to the kill valve (which was blocked), and Pemex began pumping mud, gelatin, salt water, and then cement into the well, hoping to stanch the flow. In late June another break occurred farther down the wellhead, and Pemex had to ignite the oil on the surface of the water to prevent its spreading. The drilling inched along. It wasn't until the end of July that Pemex managed to reduce the flow from 30,000 barrels per day to 21,000 barrels per day, and they went on pumping huge quantities of heavy drilling mud, steel and iron balls, cement, and chemicals into the bore well. By August 20, Ixtoc 1A was 8,612 feet deep, with 3,000 feet to go before reaching the depth of the runway, and Ixtoc 1B was 6,237 feet deep.

September brought a new plan, called Operation Sombrero, for crushing the blowout. This involved placing a huge, 300-ton inverted steel funnel—which, indeed, looked like a sombrero—over the well. It would collect about 80 percent of the oil at the wellhead, divert this oil into collection vessels, flare the gas, and return the seawater to Campeche Bay. Mechanical flaws halted the operation for several weeks, and although the "sombrero" eventually helped somewhat, it couldn't stop Ixtoc 1.

The story of the blowout continued far longer than anyone anticipated. The leakage was reduced to a dribble by October, but only in March 1980 did the two directional wells finally shut off

Ixtoc 1. Then the hole, which had received so many tons of metal balls and mud, was finally plugged with cement. Pemex had employed just about every known method for controlling an oil-well blowout—and spent $131.6 million along the way.

?

How do they paint the straight lines on streets?

Traffic problems are severe enough without the additional hazard of zigzagging lines on city streets or unevenly spaced lanes on a superhighway. To ensure that the lines are straight and to expedite an otherwise painstaking operation, machines are used to apply the paint.

Before the actual painting of a small road or city street, the three or four men who make up a highway crew must "spot," or outline with chalk or string, the precise placement of the lines, at 20-foot intervals, according to an engineer's plans. To apply the paint, a small, gasoline-powered machine resembling an oversized lawn mower may be handled manually by one person. Air compression forces paint out onto the road while the operator concentrates on holding the machine in a straight line. This small machine is especially useful for making the lines at crosswalks, and also for laying down hot plastic instead of paint, which the larger machines cannot do. Hot plastic is an excellent substitute for paint, lasting from eighteen months to three years, whereas paint must be applied every three to six months on a busy street.

Generally, this small machine is too slow for big highway jobs, so a large truck moving at about 5 miles an hour is used. The crew does not have to "spot" the lines as with city streets, but rather the truck has a pointer in the front which the driver lines up very near the median strip so as not to swerve from side to side. The crew then lowers the carriages—two rams that extend to either side behind the truck and run along on their own little wheels. (When not in use, they are kept folded up inside the truck.) These elaborate carriages hold spray guns and other equipment for applying the paint. The crew measures the width of the highway and sets each carriage accordingly, spanning the entire width if the outside line is to be painted, half the width for the centerline, and so on. Preheated paint is shot out onto the road by compressors and the guns on the carriages, which are operated from the truck.

One person drives, two operate the guns, and another drives behind to make sure the lines are correctly placed. The driver tries as much as possible to move in a straight line, but if he shifts to one side, those in back can compensate by moving horizontally a guide arm that directs the guns. This task requires six months to a year of training as well as good concentration.

?

How do instruments in the cockpit tell a pilot how fast he is flying?

Along with an altimeter and vertical velocity indicator in the cockpit of a plane is an airspeed indicator (ASI), which registers the speed at which the aircraft is flying. The instrument has two needles, one indicating hundreds, the other tens of knots—but from where do its readings derive?

Outside the plane, usually placed on one of the wings, is a thin cylindrical tube, or Pitot tube, originated by Henry Pitot (1695–1771) to measure the flow velocity of air or water. Always positioned parallel to the axis of the plane, this tube projects forward into the airflow. As the plane accelerates, an increasing amount of air is driven into the open-ended tube, thus raising the air pressure inside. A second tube—this one sealed at its forward-facing end—is also attached to the frame of the plane, sometimes along with the Pitot tube, sometimes in a more protected area. A series of holes along its length provides access of air, but the air pressure inside it is not affected by the plane's forward motion. This static tube thus allows a reading of the atmospheric pressure outside the plane. Both tubes are connected by pressure lines to an expandable diaphragm inside the airtight case of the ASI. As the aircraft accelerates, increased air pressure causes the diaphragm to expand; it contracts, of course, as the plane decelerates. The needles of the ASI are attached to this diaphragm and move according to its expansion or contraction. Through mechanical linkage, then, the differential in air pressure readings of atmospheric air and air driven into the Pitot tube is measured as airspeed.

?

How do salmon, after years of migration over vast distances, return to the rivers in which they were spawned?

The extraordinary process of salmon migration begins when an adult female salmon lays her eggs on a gravelly riverbed, forming a nest by swishing her tail from side to side. The best location is in shallow water at the head of a riffle, where fast water spills over the gravel and brings nourishing oxygen to the eggs. Only about 5 out of 5,000 of these small pink eggs (each about the size of a buckshot) actually hatch, and these are then threatened by hazards such as predators and polluted water. Since the female dies soon after laying her eggs, the young alevins are equipped with a large yellow sac attached to their bellies which nourishes them for several months. At an age of one to three years the smolts—still quite small—go downstream to the sea, sometimes traveling as much as thousands of miles to do so. In the oceans they feed voraciously on plankton and small fish for at least a year, generally three or four. Pink salmon from the rivers of British Columbia travel northward, paralleling the North American coast, sweeping along the southern coast of Alaska, then turning south, making a huge 2,000-mile elliptical path back to the mouth of the spawning river. While the pink salmon make one circuit, chum and sockeye may complete two or three, traveling 10,000 miles before seeking their natal streams. Although various species of salmon may mix while swimming and feeding far out at sea, they consistently separate when their sex cells ripen, triggering the response to go home to spawn.

How do the salmon know where to go? Some biologists suggest that the fish are guided by celestial cues, in particular by the position of the sun; but since cloudy days are hardly the exception—in the Pacific Northwest and Gulf of Alaska at least—

this theory seems unlikely. Each body of water has its own inherent chemical composition and thus a particular smell, and many biologists believe that salmon, on arriving near the mouth of their natal river, proceed to smell their way home. But this idea fails to explain the ability of salmon to return over vast distances, especially when in experiments they have been taken out and dumped into totally unfamiliar waters. Dr. William F. Royce at the University of Washington feels that the migratory cues are inherited rather than memorized, that the salmon discern tiny electrical charges generated by ocean currents and orient themselves according to the earth's magnetic field. The path is in some way imprinted on the chromosomes and passed on through the generations.

However the salmon rediscover their natal rivers, the journey upstream is another awesome feat. They travel night and day, swimming in a series of spurts, with intermittent rests in quiet pools. They flap their strong tails in wide strokes to propel them upstream—up swift currents and waterfalls that may be 10 or more feet high. No matter how long the arduous swim takes, the salmon eat nothing the entire way, surviving only on the oxygen in the water. One of the longest runs is in the Yukon River, where chinook travel nearly the river's entire length of 2,000 miles to spawn in Nesutlin Lake. Beginning at speeds of 10 or 20 miles a day, they later accelerate to 50 or 60 miles a day. After a month of travel the battered, emaciated fish arrive home and prepare to spawn, but within days after the female deposits her eggs and the male, hovering nearby, releases his sperm, both will die.

Salmon populations have been dangerously reduced not only by fishing industries and river pollution, but by construction of dams that have prevented their inland journeys. In the eighteenth century salmon were so abundant in the Connecticut River that they were considered common, even lower-class, fare. In 1798 the Upper Locks and Canal Company built a 16-foot dam across the river at Hadley Falls, Massachusetts, and by 1810 the occasional salmon caught was so rare that the lucky fisherman had little idea what sort of fish he'd hooked. Similarly, the Grand Coulee Dam built on the Columbia River in the 1930's had harmful effects on chinooks and bluebacks from that area. Laws today frequently require that fish ladders, or steps, be built on any dam in a river containing salmon.

Index

Dollar-bill changer, weeding out fake or foreign money by, 249–250

Dry ice
manufacture of, 154
and rainmaking, 185

Dynamite, invention of, 47

Early man, evidence of, 42–43

Earth's magnetic field
and honeycomb building by bees, 54
navigation of homing pigeons and, 20

Educational Testing Service (ETS), 124–126

Eggs, sorting by size, 61–62

Electric elevators, 41

"Electric eye" elevator doors, method of working, 247–249

Electricity, generation of, 73–74

Elevation, measurement of, 138–142

Elevators
"electric eye" doors of, 247–249
high-speed, 41

Embalming, 246–247

Encyclopaedia Britannica, method of writing, 31–33

Endangered species, determination of, 92–93

Ethanol, 210

Evolution of man, 203–205

Eyeglasses, correction of nearsightedness or farsightedness with, 144–146

Face lifts, 97–98

Farsightedness, 146

Fastball, measurement of speed of, 39

FBI, Identification Division of, 161, 163, 164

Federal Reserve banks, 153–154

Fetus, sex determination, 21–23

Fiber-optic endoscopy, 186–188

Filters, cigarette, 39

Fingerprint matching, 161–164

Fireflies, creation of light by, 206–207

Fireworks, method of creating, 172–174

Fish, counting of, 90. See also Salmon

Flavors, synthetic, 116–118

Floating of steel ship, 27–28

Food
and artificial flavors, 116–118
bees' method of locating, 56–58
fake cherries, 224–225

Forgery. See Art forgeries

Freeze-drying method, 52–53

Frescoes, removal from wall, 277–279

Frozen sperm, 67–68

Fruit trees, 99–100

Galaxies
boundaries of, 168–171
distance to, 217–218

Garbage, gasohol from, 211

Gasohol, manufacture of, 210–211

Genes
and honeycomb building by bees, 53–54
splicing, 150–151
See also entries under Genetic

Genetic disorders, and amniocentesis, 21

Genetic engineering, and petrophilic bacteria, 183

Genetic variation, and fruit growing, 99–100

Global crop forecasting, 43–47

GNP. See Gross national product

Grapes. See Seedless grapes

"Green cookies," 172

Gross national product, measurement of, 237–239

Gun silencer, method of working, 223–224

Guns, tracing bullets to, 108–109

Hair transplants, 166–167

Hartford Civic Center Coliseum, collapse of, 147–148

Hashish, production of, 171–172

Heart, and artificial pacemaker, 28–30

287

Heat-seeking missiles, method of finding target, 275–277

Heredity
and salmon migration, 284
and selection of sperm donors, 69
See also Genes

Holography, 259

Homing pigeons, theories on navigation by, 20–21

Homo erectus, 205

Homo sapiens, 205

Honeycombs, reasons for bees building, 53–56

Hot-air balloons. *See* Balloons

Hovercraft, operation of, 112–114

Hurricanes
predicting path of, 26
speed of, 24–26

Ice hockey rink, lines under ice in, 196–197

Ice skating rinks, prevention of melting in, 195–196

Illusion
sawing woman in half, 23–24
and 3-D television, 258–259

Infrared missiles. *See* Heat-seeking missiles

Infrared photographs
and detection of art forgeries, 51
and global crop forecasting, 45–47

Infrasounds, navigation by homing pigeons and, 21

Insect population, 91

Instant coffee, manufacture of, 52–53

Instrument landing system (ILS), 178–179

Intelligence
measurement with IQ test, 221–223
and tests, 126

IQ test, 221–223

IRS, decision on auditing, 79–80

Ivory soap, floatability of, 165–166

Labanotation, 251–257

Landsat satellites, 43, 45–47

Large Area Crop Inventory Experiment (LACIE), 46–47

Lasers, and diamond cutting, 267

Laundry, differentiation of clothing in, 75

Laws
on conservation of salmon, 284
on gun silencers, 224
on inscription on coins, 35
on lie detector tests, 219

Lead, method of placing in pencil, 36

Lie detector tests, 218–219

Light
definition of, 72
and electric eye doors, 247–249
and solar temperature, 71–73
See also Light, speed of; Polarized light; Ultraviolet light; Visible light

Light, speed of
determination of, 70–71
and estimates of number of stars in universe, 212–213
and size of universe, 120–121

Lincoln penny, 34–35

Lizard population, counting of, 90

Macropaedia, 32–33

Magicians, method of sawing person in half, 23–24

Mail sorting, 17–19

Man, first, 203–205

Mark II facer canceler, 17–18

Measurement
of continental drift, 230–233
of distance to stars, 213–218
of elevation, 138–142
of gross national product, 237–239
of speed of airplane, 282–283

Meat grading, 269

Medical Examiner's Office, 207–210

Medicine, time-release capsules for, 74–75

Mercury vapor, 114–115

Metal detectors, 96

Micropaedia, 33

288

Vending machine, coin-testing device of, 118–119
Ventilation of tunnels, 260–261
Very Large Array (VLA), 171
Visible light, 73
Vision, correction with eyeglasses, 144–146

Water
  camels and, 137–138
  and detergent action, 270–273
  flotation and, 27–28
Weather prediction. *See* Hurricanes
Wechsler Intelligence Scale for Children (WISC), 222–223

X-chromosome-linked disorders, 21, 22
Xerox machine, copy-making by, 63–66
X rays
  of bones, 115
  compared with fiber-optic endoscopy, 187–188
  and detection of art forgeries, 51

Y chromosome, 22

Zip code, 18, 19

MORE

HOW DO
THEY DO THAT?

Wonders of the
Modern World Explained

Caroline Sutton
and
Kevin Markey

Illustrated by Tom Vincent
A Hilltown Book

It is the policy of William Morrow and Company, Inc., and its imprints and affiliates, recognizing the importance of preserving what has been written, to print the books we publish on acid-free paper, and we exert our best efforts to that end.

Library of Congress Cataloging-in-Publication Data

Sutton, Caroline.
    More how do they do that? / Caroline Sutton and Kevin Markey.
        p.   cm.
    Includes bibliographical references.
    ISBN 0-688-13221-9
    1. Questions and answers.   I. Markey, Kevin.   II. Title.
    AG195.M34   1992
    031.02—dc20

                                                                    92-22201
                                                                         CIP

Printed in the United States of America

ACKNOWLEDGMENTS

WE WOULD LIKE TO THANK the following writers who contributed to the book: Allison Adato, Renée Bacher, Lynne Bertrand, Freda Garmaise, Denise Lovatt Martin, Jennifer Wolff, and Ariel Zeitlin.

Contents

?

How do they detect counterfeit bills?

ALTHOUGH THE AVERAGE PERSON might be slipped a counterfeit bill and accept it unawares, someone trained in detection can nearly always spot it instantly and effortlessly. Why? Because the government has made it all but impossible to precisely copy the real stuff. The distinctive markings of legitimate money are printed by steel engraved plates on unique paper, all of which gives Federal Reserve notes a visual sharpness unmatched by imitations. Counterfeit bills are detected either because they lack certain visual design details, attributable to poor draftsmanship or faulty printing techniques, or because they are printed on the wrong paper.

Even an exact-scale, line-by-line copy of a bill—and anyone with access to a photocopier can, but not legally, make such a copy—would fail to pass muster. It would come off looking flat in comparison to money printed on the official government plates. The most common method of counterfeiting is by photo-offset, whereby a printing plate is made from a photograph of a real bill. The effect is like a poster of a painting: visually similar, but obviously not the same thing. On a photo-offset counterfeit, the portrait fails to stand out distinctly from the background; the saw-tooth points of the Treasury seal are usually uneven; the scroll work around the border is often blurred; the background appears mottled.

Regardless of the level of printing sophistication achieved by a counterfeiter, a phony bill is always given away by the paper it is printed on. The paper used for U.S. currency, manufactured

15

exclusively for the government by Crane and Company, a paper company headquartered in Dalton, Massachusetts, is easily identified by the tiny blue and red fibers woven into it, fibers which are visible to the naked eye. Such paper cannot legally be manufactured by anyone but Crane. Ersatz bills often have superficial blue and red markings, but upon close examination it can be seen that the faint squiggles are printed *on* the paper and not embedded *in* it.

The United States first took a serious look at counterfeiting in the early 1860s, when it is estimated some thirty percent of the currency in circulation was phony. The problem was that there were 1,600 state banks designing, printing, and issuing 7,000 varieties of notes, a practice that led to widespread confusion. It got to the point where no one really remembered what all the different bills were supposed to look like. In 1863 the government decided to simplify things by adopting a national currency. Far from being deterred, however, counterfeiters set about duplicating the new national currency with the same vigor that they had previously shown in faking the old state-bank notes. It soon became apparent that the only way to stop counterfeiting would be to actively suppress it, and in 1865 the United States Secret Service was established for that purpose.

The Secret Service has enjoyed great success in its efforts, but new printing technology, in the form of high-quality color copiers, is making counterfeit detection increasingly difficult. What clever counterfeiters are doing these days is bleaching out the printing from a one dollar bill and then using a color copier to give the blank bill a higher denomination make-over. Singles become tens, twenties, fifties, or hundreds; not pure profit, but a healthy return on a small initial investment. Since the bogus high-denomination bills are printed on good paper and have accurate designs, a person might not realize he has been passed one unless he is already looking for it. To make things easier for unsuspecting clerks, the government changed paper money at the end of 1991. (The last change was in 1928 when the government reduced the dimensions of bills from 3.1 inches by 7.4 inches to the current size, about 2.5

16

inches by 6.6 inches). The new currency has a clear polyester thread woven into the paper; this vertical thread (appearing to the left of the Treasury seal on high-denomination bills, between the seal and the portrait on singles) states the correct denomination of the bill. The money, called "denominated distinctive currency," will allow store and bank employees to check instantly a bill's legitimacy by holding it up to a light and reading the thread. The anticounterfeit bills will be phased in gradually, allowing time for the old, unmarked bills to be reclaimed and destroyed.

?

How do they keep you from registering to vote in more than one jurisdiction?

"WE WOULD HATE FOR YOU to say so," reports a Federal Election Commission official, "but basically there is no way to do it." So, now that we've spilled the beans, what's to keep you from registering to vote in every district from here to Kalamazoo? Well, a couple of things, foremost among them your unwavering honesty.

Each state of the union handles its own voter registration. A voter registration card typically requires that you state your current address, which to qualify you for the vote must lie within the district you are registering in, and also your previous address. Election officials can easily check the truth of the recorded addresses by referring to town census and tax lists. When you register after moving from one district to another in the same state, a town official asks if you were registered in your last community; if you respond positively, a postcard will be sent to your last town's civic officials, telling them to strike you from their voter registration list. A person wanting multiple registrations would first have to establish residency in a number of jurisdictions and then deny prior registrations (previous addresses are harder to conceal because of readily available information such as tax records and automobile registrations). Even so, there is a chance that town officials would send a courtesy notice to the old district anyway. Also, a few states maintain a central voter registration computer that contains the name and district of every registered voter and quickly catches duplicates.

Interstate registration fraud is a bit harder to detect. States are not legally required to notify other states when they pick up one of their voters, and only about two thirds of the states currently do so. Conceivably, a resident voter of say, California, could move to Texas and register to vote there while maintaining and denying his registration in California, thereby gaining an extra presidential ballot and the ability to vote for two governors and a large number of state and local office seekers. Of course, that person might end up paying all sorts of extra taxes as well.

Most people do not lie about their registration history, and most voter registration personnel are inclined to trust anyone whose sense of civic duty is strong enough to make him get out and vote. As the Federal Election Commission official put it, "They're so happy when people come in to register, they're not going to make it difficult."

?

How do they get ships through the Panama Canal?

A REMARKABLE FEAT of engineering, the Panama Canal covers a distance of fifty-one miles and lifts a ship as high as a nine-story

Going Up...

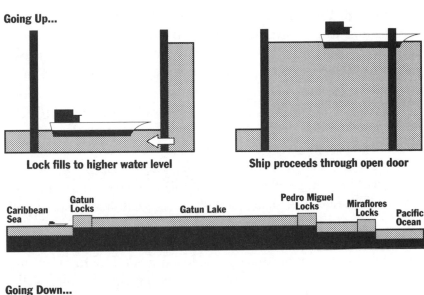

Lock fills to higher water level   Ship proceeds through open door

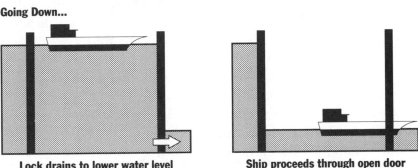

Caribbean Sea   Gatun Locks   Gatun Lake   Pedro Miguel Locks   Miraflores Locks   Pacific Ocean

Going Down...

Lock drains to lower water level   Ship proceeds through open door

When a ship enters the Panama Canal, water flows into the lock to raise the craft to the height of a nine-story building. To passengers, the lift feels like an elevator ride. At the other end of the canal, water drains from the lock to lower the ship to sea level.

building in order to overcome the high terrain of the Isthmus of Panama. The canal was built to provide a shortcut for ships traveling from the Atlantic Ocean to the Pacific or vice versa. No longer would they have to make the arduous 7,500-mile voyage around Cape Horn, the southernmost tip of South America.

The original plan for the canal called for cutting through the isthmus with a sea-level channel, and the huge undertaking began that way in the late 1800s. But the rocky continental divide that

19

cuts through Panama turned out to be a formidable barrier, and the cost of cutting down through it was too high. So three sets of locks were built instead—one near the Atlantic Ocean and two near the Pacific—to lift and lower the ships. The locks are massive chambers, into and out of which water flows. They are built of concrete, and are large enough—at 1,000 feet long, 110 feet wide and 70 feet deep—to accommodate all but the world's largest military ships and supertankers. The locks are paired so that ships can pass in both directions. Three man-made lakes—particularly the huge, dam-held Gatun Lake—were built to supply the locks and the channels with water. The immense project was completed in the summer of 1914.

A ship that begins at the Caribbean, or Atlantic, end of the canal enters the Gatun Locks at sea level, guided by tugboats and electric towing locomotives called "mules" on the chamber walls. Steel gates close behind the boat, lake water flows in through valves in the bottom of the chamber, and the ship rises. About ten minutes later the water has risen to the level of the water in the second chamber, and the gates in front of the boat swing out. (The steel doors are nearly silent as they move, says David McCullough, who wrote *The Path Between the Seas: The Creation of the Panama Canal, 1870–1914*. And, he says, you feel you are riding a slow elevator, except that the elevator is your whole ship.) In the second chamber the water rises again, delivering the ship into a third chamber, where the process is repeated a final time. Ultimately, the boat rises in three steps to a height of eighty-seven feet above sea level.

After passing through the Gatun Locks, the ship travels across Gatun Lake and the isthmus until it nears the end of the canal and the Pedro Miguel Lock. Here, and in the next set of locks called Miraflores, the boat is lowered back to sea level as water pours out of the locks. The ship then takes up its voyage on the Pacific side of Central America, in the Gulf of Panama. There is often a backlog of ships waiting to move through the Panama Canal, but once en route, ships only need about eight hours to make the passage from ocean to ocean.

?

How do they make a breed of dog "official" at the American Kennel Club?

AS THE SELF-ORDAINED ARBITER of canine society, the American Kennel Club maintains standards that would be the envy of the Gilded Age's Newport set. Of the four hundred and fifty or so dog breeds that exist in the world today, the AKC deigns to recognize only one hundred and thirty. For a breed to gain official recognition, it must prove that it is genetically chaste; its bloodlines must be untainted by mixed marriages. For individual dogs, admission to the exclusive club depends on two factors. First, Rex must produce pedigree papers that show his bloodlines have been pure for at least three generations; and second, a witness must attest that the hopeful dog conforms to the stringent written standards of his breed. These standards regulate such cosmetic features as eye color, ear shape, overall size, coat thickness, and tail length, but disregard entirely the applicant's ability (or inability) to hunt, swim, or fetch. The American Kennel Club is not a meritocracy.

Breed standards, the ideal against which individual dogs are measured, are written by AKC member clubs devoted exclusively to a certain type of dog. The chow chow club, for instance, decides what a chow chow should look like. By codifying a breed's desirable physical traits, the "parent" clubs make it easy to recognize a "champion" dog: the champion is the one that conforms most exactly to the written standard. Once a dog has been judged a "champion" at a show, it becomes the living aesthetic yardstick

21

by which all other members of its breed are measured, and, consequently, a busy stud or brood bitch as breeders scramble to take a dip in its gene pool.

Breeds are produced by a process of genetic winnowing that limits variability by making matches among dogs that possess similar favorable traits. To get popular "purebreds," many commercial breeders employ a method called "linebreeding," a euphemism for inbreeding: desirable dogs are mated with their desirable grandparents or even parents to produce cosmetically perfect litters. Natural variability is curtailed, but even so, experts admit that the only way to really recognize a "purebred" dog is to examine its pedigree. Hence the necessity of the AKC registry, a sort of canine Mayflower Register.

Rigorous inbreeding creates dogs whose only function is to conform to the highly arbitrary breed standards maintained by the AKC. As a result, some heavily sought-after breeds have been genetically altered. Cocker spaniels, for example, have pretty much exchanged their hunting ability for nice, long coats. Even worse, inbreeding can endorse recessive traits in a dog, leading to a variety of health problems such as skin conditions, organ defects, and mental instability.

The American Kennel Club was formed in 1884 by a group of sport hunters who wanted to organize various existing breed-specific clubs. The original AKC registry listed about five and a half thousand dogs of impeccable pedigree. The idea caught on among the dog-buying and -showing public, and in the 1950s, when more than five million dogs were being registered every year, the AKC adopted strict procedures for recognizing breeds. To be recognized by the AKC, a breed needs first to have been registered domestically for a few decades or, in the case of a foreign breed, for thirty years. Second, there must exist a club devoted to the breed, and the club must have at least one hundred members who own among them at least one hundred of the animals, all of which meet the sponsoring club's physical specifications, as approved by the AKC. Once a breed meets these requirements it must pass through a development period, typically lasting from two to five years, during which it is allowed to enter, but not score, in AKC dog shows. Barring any mishaps or lack of commercial interest, the AKC will make the new breed official—i.e., raise its status from registered to recognized—at the end of the trial period.

Some breeds, such as the Australian kelpie, remain unofficial breeds for years and years, never receiving official status. Usually, however, such a snub is the choice of the sponsoring club, whose members want to cash in on the visibility to be gained from AKC registration, but don't want to engage in the harmful overbreeding necessary to receive official recognition.

How do they write headlines at the *New York Post*?

HEADLINES SELL THE *New York Post*. A good one can boost sales by thirty thousand copies in a single day. At forty cents an issue, that's $12,000 in additional revenue for Manhattan's highest-street-sale-circulation tabloid. Even more, a well-received "wood"—an idiom dating back to when headlines were carved from blocks of oak—massages the ego of whoever writes it, which could be one of many reporters and editors who gather around the news desk every weekday evening, or even a copy clerk who happens to walk by and proffer an offhand suggestion. Headline writing at the *Post* is a team sport; old-timers remember each one and the person who wrote it the way veteran baseball announcers recall stats of retired outfielders.

The best way to explain how headlines are written at the *Post* is to take you to the large red-carpeted city room near the southeastern tip of Manhattan where dozens of reporters and editors sit opposite each other at gray metal desks. The day is December 9, 1991. The time is about seven-thirty P.M. Breaking stories include the following: hostage Terry Anderson's return home to New York after six years of captivity in Lebanon; CIA director Robert Gates's warning of pending civil war in the Soviet Union; the conviction of four teens in the fatal subway stabbing of Utah tourist Brian Watkins after the U.S. Open in September 1990; the attempted shakedown of Woody Allen's film crew by a black activist; the crumbling of the beleaguered empire of Robert Maxwell, late owner of the *Post*'s chief competitor *The Daily News*; and finally, William Kennedy Smith's defense testimony in his Palm Beach rape trial.

Succumbing to a temptation they have resisted for the nine days since the well-publicized (and well-covered) trial began, Managing Editor Jimmy Lynch and Executive Editor Lou Colasuonno decide to put Smith on page one. While his testimony was unemotional and smug, it was still credible. Moreover, he has offered stark details of his sexual activity on the night in question. The *Post* can't resist.

The initial layout reads "WILLIAM'S LAST STAND," but editors quickly decide it sounds as if the defendant is losing, which by most accounts is not the case. In jest, Colasuonno offers "WILLIE'S WET DREAM," a tame turn-of-phrase in comparison with his earlier bid, "MISTER SOFTIE." Metro Editor Richard Gooding suggests a film theme: "SPLENDOR IN THE GRASS." A light applause fills the room when Gooding then suggests "WILLIE WHIPS LASCH," but the suggestion is soon scrapped because no one knows if most readers are familiar with the name of the Florida prosecutor trying the case.

The winner: "WILLIAM TELL," an earlier recommendation by Day City Editor David Ng. Pushing his luck, Ng suggests superimposing an arrow through Smith's head—no go.

24

A kicker below the headline lets readers know what to expect inside the paper. In this case, it is four brief but telling lines:

- Kennedy Grilled 4½ Hrs.
- Says They Had Sex Twice
- Denies That It Was Rape
- Prosecutor Gets Nowhere

According to Colasuonno, *New York Post* headlines are like the windows at Macy's. "If you don't like what you see," he says, "you're not going to come into the store." The *Post*'s subscription base is minuscule. Without a provocative headline, an issue will rot on the stands.

Colasuonno admits that there are some stories that merit appearing on page one, but cannot be said in few enough words. In such an instance, this story is teased on the bottom of the front page in a small box called a tracer, which tells the reader where it is covered inside. "If we can't find the right words for it," he says, "it's just not a wood."

Although the *Post* has been accused of insensitivity to delicate issues, Colasuonno insists that he and other editors try to be compassionate toward human tragedy. "We don't laugh at dead bodies, crime and murder," he says.

But if there is a chance to have some fun with a page one story, Colasuonno and the rest of his jeans-and-turtleneck crew are more than happy to twist the truth for a good laugh. During the week in February 1990 when Donald and Ivana Trump's divorce became public fodder, the *Post* broke sales records with such woods as "GIMME THE PLAZA," and "THEY MET IN CHURCH," the latter an unsubstantiated rumor that The Donald met his then unknown girlfriend in a house of God, which was untrue.

But, as Colasuonno says, sex, along with politics and celebrities, sells papers. And any combination of the three will help the tabloid fly off newsstands during the morning commute to work.

"Sex is sex," he says, "and the temptations are the same for the beer-drinking working man as they are for the most highly paid athlete and celebrity or the most powerful politician. They all put their pants on one leg at a time."

?

How do they find arbitrators for baseball contract arbitrations?

LIKE ANY OTHER BIG BUSINESS, professional baseball is divided between labor and management. Players are labor; they belong to the Major League Baseball Players Association, a trade union. Baseball team owners represent management. The Commissioner of Baseball oversees an organization called Major League Baseball, which acts as the governing body of the professional sport. Basically, a player who has been on the same major league team for three years, or who has been playing in the big leagues for six years, is eligible for arbitration if he cannot reach an agreement with his team when his contract expires.

Generally, the way salary negotiation works in baseball is that the player, through his agent, requests a certain fee, say $1 million a year for three years. The team's general manager then makes a counterproposal, say $750,000 a year for two years, with a signing bonus of $200,000. If the player and the team are unable to reach an agreement, and the player has put in the requisite years of service, the player can elect to arbitrate. This means both he (labor) and the team (management) will be given an opportunity to present their cases to an unbiased third party, the arbitrator. After hearing each side's arguments, the arbitrator must pick the figure he thinks is most fair. He must choose either the figure

26

submitted by the player, or the figure submitted by the team. No compromises are allowed.

Where does one find an arbitrator? The American Arbitration Association, founded in 1926 and based in New York, maintains a roster of eligible, professional arbitrators. Its self-described function is to "provide administrative services for arbitrating, mediating, or negotiating disputes, and impartial administration of elections." The association provides panels of arbitrators for parties involved in contract disputes. Its services are called upon not just for baseball, but for disputes in any business. In fact, baseball contract disputes make up only a small portion of the association's work load.

When the association receives a request for an arbitrator, it submits a list of qualified candidates to the parties involved in the dispute. The list includes comprehensive biographical and professional data for each individual. In a baseball contract dispute, the Players Association and Major League Baseball, acting on behalf of the owner, must jointly select an arbitrator. They start by eliminating from the list of candidates anyone who might have a conflict of interest or who might in any way be prejudiced. Major League Baseball, for example, might object to an arbitrator who has heard disputes in the past and always taken the side of the players. The Players Association might harbor reservations about an arbitrator who has a lot of corporate executives for friends. After whittling down the list, the Players Association and Major League Baseball decide on an arbitrator to hear their cases. Hearings occur during the first two weeks of February, after which the designated arbitrator hands down his decision. The decision is legal and binding; no further appeal is allowed.

?

How do they make margarine taste like butter (almost, anyway)?

"EVERYBODY HAS A DIFFERENT interpretation of butter flavor," says Dr. Peter Freund, manager of product applications at Chr. Hansen's Laboratory, Inc., in Milwaukee. Your interpretation is influenced by the butter you were raised on, the type of dairy cows bred where you grew up, the fodder they ate, and even the amount of time butter was allowed to sit during processing.

While butter is derived from animal fats, margarine—butter's close imitation—is made from the oils of vegetables. In an attempt to minimize the difference in taste, margarine manufacturers buy from laboratories such as Hansen's a host of pastes and liquid flavor additives. (Hansen's offers "theater butter," "buttered corn-on-the-cob," and so on.) These flavor combinations are added in trace amounts to margarine to produce what taste specialists call flavor and aroma "notes." The "top notes" are made of quickly evaporating compounds that work as much on your sense of smell as on your sense of taste. The "bottom notes" are derived from butterfat and free fatty acids. These provide the round, rich taste you associate with butter, a flavor you sense in the back of your throat.

The strongest top note in butter comes from a yellowish-green liquid called diacetyl—one of the products of bacteria fermentation of dairy foods. Butter naturally contains "friendly" bacteria and diacetyl, but margarine doesn't, so flavor companies make up bottles and drums of the liquid in combination with other flavors.

One common method for doing this uses a "starter distillate": first, bacteria are grown in milk and then the diacetyl and other flavors are steam-distilled off in highly concentrated form. Another method uses bacterial fermentation on a nondairy medium; a third synthesizes the diacetyl chemically.

The free fatty acids added to margarine to replicate butter's strong bottom notes often come from real cream or butterfat. But before you health enthusiasts gasp in horror, let it be said that the fat is treated with an enzyme called lipase to break off fatty acids, which in the right combination give the taste you recognize as buttery. The source for the lipase has a lot to do with getting that combination—a favored one is the salivary glands of kid goats.

Finally, salt makes up about one and a half percent of butter, and is usually added in about that percentage to margarine. You'd notice a difference without it, except that extra amounts of diacetyl are commonly added to low-salt and no-salt margarines to jack up their taste even more.

?

How do so many Japanese play golf in a country with so few golf courses?

GOLF HAS BECOME something of a national pastime in Japan, claiming more than 12.5 million enthusiasts. They vie for playing time on the land-starved country's few courses, which offer about as much elbow room as Grand Central Station at rush hour. These Japanese golf courses are unfathomably expensive—membership at Koganei Country Club in Tokyo runs in the neighborhood of $2.5 million, plus annual dues.

On weekends, foursomes begin lining up as early as two in the morning and by dawn, when the first group starts, crowds numbering into the hundreds are not unusual. And these are the lucky men (many courses exclude women) with reservations. Even the most rag-tag courses are booked up to three months in advance.

Japanese business policies further aggravate the weekend congestion problem. Executives are expected to play golf, so much so that they are considered corporate liabilities if they don't. Many companies, however, will not permit employees to play during the week. Not to golf is a grave dishonor, but to have a low handicap is worse. It means you've been neglecting work to practice.

To satisfy their yen for the sport, most Japanese golfers frequent the multitiered driving ranges that have sprung up in densely populated urban centers. State-of-the-art Shiba Golf, in downtown Tokyo, can accommodate 155 people on its three-story range. After golfers hit their shots into a 280-yard rubber field, the loose balls are funneled onto conveyer belts and fed into the basement where they are cleaned and dried before being recirculated by means of a giant pneumatic pump.

At less technologically advanced ranges, usually built on rooftops, golfers drive shot after shot into hanging safety nets, and the ball never actually travels more than twenty feet.

Japanese department stores, recognizing a lucrative trend, have pulled out all stops to cash in on the golf craze. In addition to offering complete lines of accessories and clothing—no self-respecting duffer would be caught dead without the traditional polyester trousers and short-sleeved shirt—some stores now feature indoor practice ranges. At the Sheibu Big Box, on the fifth floor of a Tokyo clothing and sports shop, there is a glass-enclosed sand trap, where real balls are blasted out of real sand and into nets.

Video golf, played live with equipment against a projected backdrop, is another popular simulation of the real thing. Players hit off a tee into a large movie screen on which is projected an image of a world-famous golf course, like St. Andrews or Pebble

30

Beach. Three cameras record the speed, spin, and trajectory of the ball as it leaves the club, and feed the information into a computer that calculates where the ball would have landed on the actual course. After the image is readjusted, the player again tees off into the screen, repeating the process until he reaches the green, after which he putts the ball into a cup in the floor.

To squeeze in extra practice time during the morning commute, Japanese businessmen have taken to swinging their umbrellas on crowded subway platforms as they wait for their trains, a practice that has resulted in a number of personal injury suits.

Despite the golf craze, called *golf-kichigai* locally, only a small fraction of the enthusiasts ever really play. According to one story making the rounds, during a recent trip to Japan, a professional player stopped in at one of the urban driving ranges and spotted some guy swinging perfectly.

"What's your handicap?" the pro asks him.

"I don't know," the guy says.

"Come again?" asks the pro.

"I've never played on a golf course," the guy says.

How do they set the price on a new public stock offering?

WHEN BILL GATES III WANTED to cash in on all the work and effort he put into Microsoft, the computer software company he founded, he took advantage of something called an initial public offering, or IPO. Today the thirty-five-year-old Harvard dropout is worth $3.9 billion.

What is an IPO and how does it work? An IPO is a corporation's first offering of stock to the public. It is also almost invariably an opportunity for the existing investors and participating venture capitalists to make big profits, since for the first time their shares will be given a market value reflecting expectations for the company's future growth.

When a private company decides to sell shares to the public, it usually hires an investment banking firm, such as Morgan Stanley or Goldman Sachs. This firm assumes the risk of buying the new securities from the corporation at a fixed price and selling them to the public at a markup, the markup representing the firm's profit. The investment banking firm often diffuses the risk among a number of other underwriters called a syndicate.

Determining the share price of a new issue is tricky business. The company and its investment banker often use a Wall Street formula called a price-earnings ratio, or P/E, which is the price of a stock divided by its earnings per share. A company, for instance, whose stock was selling for $20 a share and had annual earnings of $1 a share would have a P/E of 20.

In layman's terms, the P/E indicates how much investors might be willing to pay for a company's earning power. A stock going public with a high P/E means the company going public has good future earnings potential. High P/E stocks—those with P/Es over 20—are typically young, fast-growing companies. Low P/E stocks are quite the opposite and tend to be in mature industries or sectors of the economy that have fallen out of favor with investors.

Setting the IPO price involves a lot of guesswork on the part of the investment banker. If the investment banker believes that investors will perceive the company as a rising star, he will set a price with a high P/E. If he thinks investors will be only lukewarm about the company's future earnings potential, he'll have to consider a lower P/E and thus a lower stock price. If, for example, a hot, young biotechnology firm with high earnings potential is going public, investment bankers would argue that the stock deserves a high P/E. If they expect the stock to earn, say 50 cents a share next year, they might set the share price at $15, or a

P/E of 30. For the investor, that's only about a 3 percent return on each share of stock. But if the company's earnings keep growing quickly in the years to come, that high price may be well worth it.

Private companies like to go public when the stock market is doing well. That way they'll be able to raise more money for each dollar of projected earnings. If, however, the market is in a slump, companies usually wait to go public until a bull market returns.

Once a company decides to go public, it's the underwriters who take most of the risk. That's because the underwriters make the profit on the difference between the price they pay to the issuer for the new stock and the public offering price. When there's strong demand for an IPO, the underwriter will sell all the new stock and make a handsome profit. But if there's weak demand for the stock—perhaps the price was set too high—then the underwriters are stuck with stock worth less than what they paid for it.

?

How do they know Jimmy Hoffa is dead?

AT ABOUT TWO in the afternoon on July 30, 1975, former head of the Teamsters Jimmy Hoffa left his suburban home in Bloomfield Hills, outside Detroit, and drove to a nearby restaurant called Machus Red Fox. Some forty-five minutes later, witnesses say, several gentlemen in a maroon Mercury sedan arrived at the restaurant, picked up the erstwhile union boss, and drove away. Hoffa has not been seen since.

The FBI maintains that Hoffa met his maker that day, and the courts, which in 1982 declared Hoffa "presumed dead," take the FBI at its word. This is somewhat problematic, since the best way to prove death is to produce a corpse, and in Hoffa's case the authorities still have not done that. Lack of corporeal evidence, though, can be explained. In 1981, Charles Allen, a mafia hit man, testified before the Senate that, "Jimmy was ground up in little pieces, shipped to Florida and dumped in a swamp," in which case there would be no body. Another theory, favored by investigators, is that after slaying Hoffa, the men in the maroon sedan delivered his body to a mob-controlled sanitation plant in Hamtramck, Michigan, where it was eliminated. A number of variations on the disposal theme have been forwarded at one time or another. One claimed Hoffa's body was incinerated in Detroit; a second offered that Hoffa was first garroted and then run through a meat processing plant. As recently as 1989, a former organized crime associate announced that Hoffa was interred under the football field at Giants Stadium, in East Rutherford, New Jersey. The fact that no one quite agrees on the whereabouts of the corpse, or the method of disposing of it, suggests not Hoffa's survival but rather the morbid cleverness of mob executioners.

One point on which everyone does agree (except, perhaps, the suspect who swore Hoffa "ran off to Brazil with a go-go dancer") is that Hoffa was murdered. And for that crime, the feds have a motive: they argue that Hoffa planned to knock off Frank Fitzsimmons, the man who replaced him as head of the Teamsters in 1967 when Hoffa was sent to prison for jury tampering. The mob got wind of Hoffa's plot and, since they did not want the former honcho interfering with lucrative new friendships, killed Hoffa before he could get to Fitzsimmons. The prime suspect is Anthony "Tony Pro" Provenzano, a mafioso and ex-Teamster vice-president from New Jersey who was supposed to meet Hoffa at Machus Red Fox the day Jimmy vanished. Tony Pro had never shown up for the meeting. Provenzano, who in 1978 was convicted of ordering the murder of another union official, is now in prison. The FBI also has evidence strongly suggesting foul play: traces of Hoffa's blood and hair were detected in the recovered abduction car. All of this was good enough for the courts, and in 1982, at the petition of Hoffa's son, they declared Hoffa "presumed dead." In Michigan, where the younger Hoffa filed the fateful petition, it takes three years for a presumed dead person to become officially dead, and so in 1985, ten years after he was last seen, Jimmy Hoffa legally died.

How do they get rid of gallstones without operating?

GALLSTONES DEVELOP when bile in the gallbladder, a muscular little digestive organ tucked away behind the liver, becomes oversaturated with cholesterol. The gallbladder stores digestive bile from the liver, and too much cholesterol causes the bile to crystallize, a condition that leads to gallstones. Without treatment, gallstones can reach a size of two inches in diameter. Each year, about half a million of the twenty million or so people in the United States who suffer from gallstones require serious medical attention for their attacks. Surgical removal of the gallbladder remains the most common procedure, but in recent years some less painful and less expensive treatments have been developed. Lithotripsy gets rid of gallstones by pulverizing them with shock waves; ether dissolves gallstones when it is injected directly into the gallbladder; a drug called ursodiol can be taken orally to dissolve gallstones.

Lithotripsy, a word whose Greek roots mean "stone grinding," was developed in the 1970s in Germany to treat kidney stones, and has since been adapted for use on gallstones in this country. The treatment works on the same principle as earthquakes: shock waves move by displacing particles in their path; if shock waves displace enough particles when they pass through a solid object, the object will collapse. With gallstones, it generally takes about an hour and as many 1,400 shock waves to crush the stones into grains of sand small enough to pass through the gastrointestinal tract.

Before shock waves can be aimed at a patient's gallstones, the exact position of the stones within the gallbladder must be mapped by ultrasound. Once the doctor has located the offending stones, the patient, usually under mild sedation but not anesthetized, is connected to the lithotripsy machine via a water cushion. The machine generates shock waves, which pass easily through the cushion and the patient's body (human tissue has roughly the same density as water) until they reach the stones. The stones offer more resistance to the shock waves than healthy tissue does; as a result, the gallstones are jarred violently. Eventually, the gallstones collapse. The patient remains fully conscious throughout the procedure and can usually feel a jolting sensation within the abdomen, but no pain. Recovery from lithotripsy is virtually immediate, whereas it may take a patient more than a month to recover from surgery.

Ether treatment, whereby a patient's gallbladder is cleaned by direct injection of liquid ether, requires hospitalization for the duration of the treatment, usually a few days, but is still far less severe than surgery. It is an efficient procedure, akin to saving a dirty cooking pot by scrubbing it with a cleansing agent rather than throwing it away. Ursodiol treatment, like ether, dissolves gallstones; while ether does it almost instantly, ursodiol treatment takes six to twenty-four months, the advantage being the patient need not be hospitalized.

?

How do they make telephones for the deaf?

A TELECOMMUNICATION DEVICE for the deaf, or TDD as they are commonly called, allows a conversation to be typed over the phone lines, permitting people with impaired hearing to read incoming messages. The devices, which resemble portable electric typewriters, are equipped with keyboards, light-emitting diode (LED) character displays that show the text electronically, and modems that convert TDD impulses into acoustic tones. Instead of talking into the phone receiver, a TDD user places the telephone handset in the TDD modem and types out his message. The modem converts the typed message into electric impulses and sends them through the phone line to a receiving TDD, which translates the impulses back into words and displays the message on the receiver's screen. The recipient can then type out a response and send it back to the person on the other end of the line. The setup is akin to a personal Western Union, enabling a deaf person to send and receive telegrams at home.

Like other electronic appliances and computers, TDDs are plugged into ordinary wall outlets; they can be connected to any phone. Most of the newer models are battery operable, a feature that enables them to go and be used anywhere, even at public pay phones, where there might not be a wall socket. The latest portable units are only slightly larger than a calculator, small enough to slip inside a jacket pocket or a purse.

In the United States, the two largest manufacturers of TDDs are Krown Research and Ultratec, each of which produces a wide variety of machines. Depending on the model, a TDD might include such functions as a built-in printer for producing hard copy of conversations, and "direct coupling"—linkage through a standard modular telephone cord—which eliminates the need for a traditional telephone set. Some of the more advanced devices can be hooked up to computers or television sets to display more lines of type.

A phone system, no matter how advanced, is useless if it doesn't inform the owner of incoming calls. To get around the obvious problem of how to let a deaf person know when the phone is ringing, TDDs are commonly used in tandem with signaling devices that cause lights to flash when a call comes in. The signaler is a small free-standing box, about the size of a transistor radio, into which a lamp can be plugged. When the phone rings the lamp begins to flash. The main signaler, which must be plugged in near the phone, can also transmit messages to receivers arranged throughout the house, setting off multiple blinking lamps.

The biggest restraint to TDD use is that the devices can communicate only with other TDDs, a considerable dilemma for the nation's twenty-one million deaf and hard-of-hearing people. Through the efforts of such groups as the National Association for the Deaf, though, more and more businesses and public facilities, like airports, are installing TDDs. The devices range in price from about $200, for a basic unit, to $650, for a top-of-the-line model.

?

How do banks make money off of credit card purchases even when you don't pay interest?

SINCE MOST PEOPLE DON'T pay their credit card bills in full each month, the bank that issued the card usually *can* charge interest, and that money, called finance charges, constitutes by far the greatest percentage of income for the bank. But let's say you are conservative with your credit, don't run amok by overspending, and don't let the bills slide. You won't provide the bank with any interest on your tally of purchases, but it is assured of other income nonetheless.

The next two biggest sources of income for banks that issue credit cards are the annual fee and the merchant discount rate. The bank may charge you anywhere up to about $50 per year just for the privilege of having the card. However, in a society glutted with plastic, some banks are trying to lure customers by literally giving their cards away, with no annual fee. American Express, on the other hand, which is a company and not a bank, continues to charge a "membership fee" of $55 a year. It must charge a higher rate because the American Express card is a charge card rather than a credit card: you must pay your entire bill each month, so the company receives no income from finance charges.

In order to draw the largest possible number of consumers, most industries and services today, from restaurants to furniture stores, allow you to pay by credit card. The merchant himself gives up a small percentage of his income for this service. Here's how it works. A merchant who wishes to let his customers pay with Visa or MasterCard first makes an arrangement with a merchant bank. This bank in turn works with a card-issuing bank, say, Chase. The two banks may in fact be one and the same, but the functions are different and independent of each other. The merchant bank decides, within a fairly narrow range, what percentage of the face value of the purchase will be retained by the card-issuing bank. It may also lease the credit-card verification equipment to the merchant, especially if his business is small and he can't afford to buy it outright. Exactly what the merchant's "discount rate" is (i.e., what percentage he pays), depends on a number of factors, such as type and volume of industry. Obviously, a large chain such as Macy's will pay a lower percentage than an independent merchant with a single store. The type of data transmission facilities also have a bearing: if the merchant reconciles his books and accumulates his drafts only every few days and submits them by mail, he will pay a higher rate—the "paper rate"—than if he submits them electronically by computer, which performs the function daily, even instantly. (One reason banks prefer the faster service is it helps prevent fraud.) Typically, the merchant discount rate for MasterCard or Visa is 1.8 percent.

Now let's say you buy a sweater from a small boutique for $100.00 with your Chase Visa card. The owner of the store submits a draft to the merchant bank for $100; it keeps a very small amount—about 35 cents in this case—as a fee for processing the draft and delivers the transaction to the card-issuing bank. Chase retains the balance of that 1.8 percent—$1.45 out of the $100.00. This fee is intended to cover Chase's costs of posting and processing your account, billing you, and so on. Chase is not making a profit, though. "It's a break-even scenario at best," says David Anglin of Visa U.S.A. And MasterCard's president Alex Hart admits, "The fees we charge merchants don't even cover our costs."

Not so at American Express. That company charges merchants a whopping 3.98 to 4.5 percent, which comfortably covers the company's costs and then some. The significantly higher rate is why some merchants don't subscribe.

Finally, card-issuing banks accrue some income from "service fees." If you exceed your credit limit, the computer sends out a red alert and the bank charges you some five or ten dollars. If you bounce a check to the bank or fail to pay the minimum amount on time, again you'll be charged. The amount of these nuisance fees—so called by consumers—bears some relation to how much it costs the bank to handle the problems. The big profits still lie in the finance charges.

How do they choose cartoons for *The New Yorker*?

COSMOPOLITAN CARTOONS have long been a trademark of *The New Yorker*. You can find the cartoonists' names listed modestly at the end of the magazine's table of contents under the heading "Drawings." The term is a holdover from the late 1920s and '30s, when *New Yorker* cartoons were sometimes written by one person and drawn by another. Now, of course, this is no longer the case; each drawing is created by a single artist. And art editor Lee Lorenz, himself a contributor, comfortably refers to them as "cartoons."

The New Yorker has a group of about sixty-five artists who contribute regularly to the magazine. Each artist submits twelve to thirty cartoons every week to Lorenz, who narrows the field and shows his choices to the magazine's editor. Together they settle on the best, selecting some for immediate use and others to be published later. Each weekly issue contains about two dozen cartoons. The choices for future use are stored in a reserve bank, filed under seasonal themes or categories such as "heaven and hell," "married couples," "cocktail parties," "olden times," "talking animals," and so forth.

Some of the cartoons in the magazine—albeit a very small percentage—are created by artists outside the regular group. Lorenz himself reviews all unsolicited submissions, which pour in at a rate of hundreds and even thousands a week. He's on the lookout for new talent, in the form of "a recognizable, individual graphic style and personal point of view." If he likes the work in a new portfolio, he meets with the artist and starts buying one cartoon at a time. Eventually he may invite the artist to sign on with the magazine—but not very often. He has offered only eight new contracts for cartoonists in three years, and the established artists tend to stay on. William Steig and George Price, for example, have been keeping *New Yorker* readers in stitches since the late 1920s.

"People at *The New Yorker* tend to dismiss the suggestion that there is such a thing as a *New Yorker* style," wrote Louis Menand in *The New Republic* magazine in February 1990. "The requirement for a story, they say, is that it be well written; the requirement for a drawing is that it be funny."

Lorenz would agree. Asked to describe the humor in *New Yorker* cartoons, he replies, "I can't. . . . It's too subjective." He disagrees with the term "highbrow"—although he agrees the magazine is aimed at the well-educated, well-heeled, upper-middle-class reader. The humor ranges, he says, and "the audience [for cartoons] extends beyond people who love *The New Yorker*. People can go to the magazine and get a laugh even if they're not interested in fact, fiction or reportage."

New Yorker cartoons do in fact range more widely than ever before. "The world has changed a lot," Lorenz says. "You can't outrun your audience, but you certainly have to keep up." To that end, he has introduced cartoonists with new styles. Roz Chast, for example, contributes some wonderful cartoons with a very personal, postcard-like sensibility. And in his cartoons, Danny Shanahan makes hip verbal and visual puns: "Chicken à la King," the caption reads beneath a picture of a chicken dressed as Elvis Presley.

How do they make rechargeable batteries?

ALL BATTERIES WORK by converting chemical energy into electric energy. The difference between primary, or nonrechargeable, and secondary, or rechargeable, batteries lies in the specific chemical reactions each battery type uses to produce an electron flow, which in batteries is electricity. In primary batteries the chemical reactions cannot be reversed, thus a primary battery can be discharged only once; the chemical reactions that give a secondary battery its power are reversible, allowing electricity to be regenerated after each discharge.

A battery cell is composed of an anode, which is a negative electrode, and a cathode, a positive electrode. The two electrodes are separated by an electrolyte, a chemical medium through which electrons can travel from the anode to the cathode. The cathode is usually made of a metal that naturally releases oxygen ions, while the anode is usually made of a type of metal capable of oxidizing, or mixing with oxygen. The oxygen released by the cathode is absorbed by the anode; such oxidization in the anode generates excess electrons, which produces a chain reaction: the flow of excess electrons from the anode to the oxygen-losing cathode. The flow of excess electrons from anode to cathode triggers the cathode to release more oxygen, which in turn causes the

43

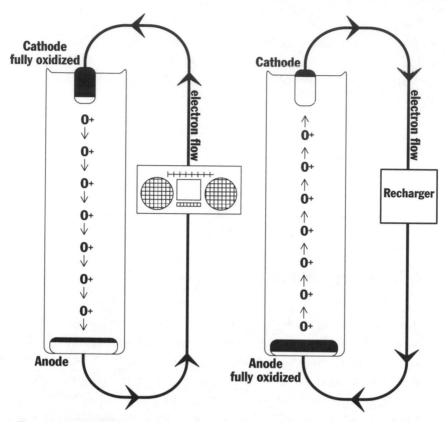

The chemical reactions that power rechargeable betteries are reversible. As the battery discharges (left), the cathode releases oxygen to the anode, causing it to generate electricity. Once the anode is fully oxidized, the battery must be recharged. In recharging (right), the anode releases oxygen back to the cathode.

anode to oxidize, thereby generating more electrons. Think of a battery as a microcosm of a self-contained university: the cathode is like an undergraduate college which continuously graduates students (oxygen) who enroll in graduate school (the anode) where they are transformed into professors (electrons), who stream over to the undergraduate college (the cathode) to find jobs.

In a primary battery, the migration of electrons can only occur in one direction, from anode to cathode. When the anode has absorbed all the available oxygen, it stops producing electrons, and the flow of electricity ceases. In a secondary battery, once the fully oxidized anode has stopped producing electrons, the chemical reactions that produced the electron flow can be reversed, thereby returning the anode to a deoxidized state in which it can once again absorb oxygen and produce electricity.

A nonrechargeable battery is sort of like a really inexpensive, disposable videocassette (if there were such a thing) that cannot be rewound: after such a cassette had been played there would be no way to get back to the beginning. A rechargeable battery discharges and recharges just as a standard cassette plays and rewinds.

The two most popular types of rechargeable batteries are lead-acid and nickel-cadmium. Lead-acid batteries, of which the typical car battery is the most common example, have lead (Pb) anodes and lead dioxide (PbO_2) cathodes. Nickel-cadmium batteries have nickel (Ni) anodes and cadmium (Cd) cathodes, and come in the full range of standard sizes—triple A to nine volt—for use in all the familiar battery-operated devices. Alkaline batteries, the standard throwaway kind, have zinc (Zn) anodes and manganese dioxide (MnO_2) cathodes.

A battery's voltage is determined by the materials used for its anodes and cathodes. Zinc and manganese dioxide combine to produce a voltage of 1.5 volts, slightly higher than 1.2 volts achieved by nickel and cadmium in the standard rechargeable battery. Voltage, however, is reduced with use, and whereas an alkaline starts at 1.5 volts but steadily loses power, a nickel-cadmium battery maintains its 1.2 volts through 90 percent of its discharge. This means rechargeable batteries, although they run down faster than alkalines, provide consistently more power while in operation.

A single charge of an AA nickel-cadmium battery lasts only 25 to 50 percent as long as the total discharge of an AA alkaline battery, which means that a nickel-cadmium battery might go through four cycles before matching a throwaway's life span. But since a nickel-cadmium battery can be recharged as many as a thousand times, its total longevity equals about 250 generations of alkalines.

?

How do they set the minimum bid on a painting that is up for auction?

BEFORE PUTTING A PAINTING on the auction block, the auction house responsible for selling it and the consigner (the owner of the painting) decide upon a reserve price. A reserve price is the price below which the owner is unwilling to part with his painting. It is frequently set at about 60 percent of the low estimated value of the painting. For example, if the estimated value of a painting is a minimum of $1,000,000, the reserve price might be $600,000. There is no universal formula for establishing the reserve, and sellers enjoy some flexibility in setting their bottom line. Legally, the reserve cannot exceed the low estimated value of the painting being sold.

To come up with the reserve price for a painting, an auction firm must first arrive at an estimate of the painting's worth. In the parlance of the trade, an estimate is a determination of the amount a painting is likely to fetch at auction. An estimate differs from an appraisal, which is a written document used for insurance and tax purposes.

A number of factors, including the quality, rarity, condition, and provenance (history of ownership) of the painting, influence the final estimate. Market conditions also come to bear: the art market, like the stock market, tends to be either bearish or bullish. Nineteen eighty-seven, for instance, was a bullish year—one that saw the van Gogh still life *Irises* sell for a record $72 million. Since 1989 the market has quieted down. It's possible that if

Irises was auctioned off today, it would fetch less than what it did in the gaga market of 1987. Another important factor in determining the worth of a painting is historical precedent, that is, the prices attained during the last six months to a year in sales of similar paintings.

Let's say you are a businessman and art collector. You've taken a bath on some ill-advised real estate investments and need to raise cash to cover your debts. You decide to "de-acquisition" (art-world doublespeak for sell) an Old Master painting. The first thing you would do is contact one of the big auction firms like Sotheby's and tell them you want to sell, say, a Titian. Because you are famous and a painting by this sixteenth-century Italian painter is significant, the auction firm will probably send a staff appraiser to your house rather than making you ship the painting to them, which is how it usually works.

The appraiser will examine the painting for integral quality: how it stacks up against other Old Master works and, especially, against other paintings by Titian. Is it a good painting by Titian or not one of his best? Major work or relatively minor? In terms of rarity, any painting by Titian is automatically first-class, because few of his works are in circulation. Then the appraiser will examine the condition of the painting. A work of art that has been damaged in any way is not worth as much as one in pristine condition. If the painting is impaired, the appraiser will have to decide whether the damage is reversible. A slight tear in the canvas, for instance, can probably be fixed; damage caused by sloppy restoration efforts, on the other hand, is permanent and will devalue the painting.

After examining the painting, the appraiser will usually come up with a preliminary estimate. Before the final, pre-auction estimate is made, however, he'll check the going rate for Titians. Probably no Titians will have come on the market in the last six months to a year, so market analysts will look for other Old Master paintings of comparable quality and find out what they sold for and when. The subject matter of the painting will also influence the estimate: the market is always better for top-quality mythological love scenes than for gory crucifixions, two favored Renaissance subjects.

Once you receive an estimate for your painting, you will set the reserve price. The reserve is between you and the auction house; it is not released to the buying public. A number of factors, such as how much money you need, how long you are willing to wait to sell the painting, and the number of bidders expected to turn out for the auction, will influence where you set the reserve. You can set it at any price up to and including the low estimate, but you cannot legally set it higher than the low estimate. This means that if your painting has been estimated at between $20 million and $25 million, the reserve can go up to $20 million. If at the auction bidding fails to reach the reserve price, the painting will be removed from the block and either held by the auction house to be re-auctioned at a later date, or returned immediately to you, depending on what you and the auction house decide to do.

How do antilock brakes work?

AT THE MERCEDES TEST TRACK in Stuttgart, Germany, workers drive these elegant autos at high speeds through slalom courses. Going ninety miles an hour, the driver slams on the brakes and nimbly maneuvers the car through a series of orange pylons. Why don't these pricy vehicles flip off course like so many Matchbox cars in the hands of a four-year-old? Because of the quick response of antilock brakes.

Today it is not only luxury models that can give you the addi-

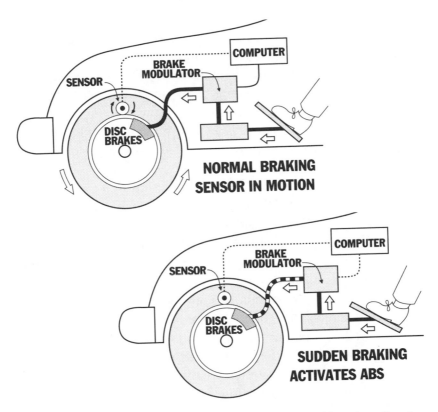

During normal braking, the sensor on the wheel moves smoothly and monitors how fast the wheels are turning. When you slam on the brakes for a sudden stop, the sensor informs the computer, which in turn signals the brake modulator to initiate a rapid braking action—the antilock brake system.

tional safety of antilock brakes. General Motors, for instance, includes them as standard equipment on many of its Pontiacs, Cadillacs, Buicks, and Chevrolets and offers them as optional equipment on other models.

The heart of the antilock braking system (ABS) is a computer inside the vehicle. A sensor located on the inside of the wheel monitors how fast the wheels are turning and feeds this information continuously to the computer. The sensor has calibrations, or small teeth, that run smoothly when the wheels of the car are turning properly. If you brake gradually, your brakes will perform on their own as usual. But if you suddenly jam on the brakes— regardless of how fast you may be going—the sensor in milliseconds registers that the teeth are not moving uniformly and signals the computer that the wheels are about to lock. The computer, in turn, activates a hydraulic modulator that forces hydraulic fluid to the braking system, initiating a sort of stuttering effect. The brake disks clamp and unclamp incredibly fast—up to fifteen times per second. The result is a rapid pumping action, like that which you may have practiced yourself on slippery snowy roads, but of course much faster. The point is, the wheels continue to roll slightly, preventing the hazardous lockup that can send you spiraling off the road. With this system, too, you can generally stop in a shorter distance and also maintain your ability to steer.

The concept underlying ABS arose back in the early fifties when Dunlop Tire Company in England developed an antilock braking system called Maxaret for aircraft. In the sixties the Japanese incorporated the system in some of their high-speed trains. Today, in automobiles, these brakes are becoming widespread and are gradually being phased in as standard equipment.

Any drawbacks? It's fine if your car has them, but in the event of a quick stop on a congested highway, you'd better hope the driver behind you has them too.

How do they know television viewers don't cheat during the Nielsen ratings?

NIELSEN MEDIA RESEARCH, the company responsible for compiling information on America's television viewing habits, employs a device called the Nielsen People Meter to get its figures. The electronic meter, which is about the size and shape of a small cigar box, is attached to each of a sample family's television sets, and whenever a set is turned on, the meter automatically records the time and the channel. The meter also documents channel switches and the time at which the set is turned off. Since the meter communicates directly with the television set, going over the head of the fallible viewer, the possibility for cheating is all but eliminated. The machine remembers what people watched until Nielsen technicians collect the data, and if someone was to detach the machine from the television set, it would remember that, too.

Nielsen maintains a field of four thousand sample viewing households, a demographically representative sample of the entire country, and applies the information it receives from them to the country as a whole. If 15 percent of Nielsen sample viewers tune in to a program, the company assumes that 15 percent of the national television audience tuned in along with them; the program would then be assigned a rating of 15. Since 92.1 million U.S. households have televisions, a rating of 15 translates into 13.8 million households. The math works like this: 15 percent (rating) × 92.1 (U.S. households with television sets) = 13.8 million (number of households tuned in).

In order to obtain viewer profiles, the Nielsen People Meter is equipped with a number of personal viewer buttons, one for each sample household member. When a sample viewer turns on the TV set he is supposed to identify himself to the meter by punching his button. Button number one, for example, would belong to Bob, a thirty-five-year-old father, while button number two would belong to Shirley, Bob's thirty-year-old wife, and button number three would belong to their five-year-old daughter, Susie. The viewer identification buttons do allow for the possibility of deception, as there is nothing to prevent little Susie from punching Bob's button every time she turns on *Sesame Street*. Even so, while such deception might throw off the demographic breakdown slightly, it would not affect a show's rating.

Another source of error arises when someone turns on the set and then goes into another room, say, to prepare dinner; since the show is on, it gains rating points even though no one is watching it. If a sample viewer is really intent on disrupting the ratings, he could secretly buy an extra TV for private use, all the while keeping the metered set tuned in to talk shows and late-night movies. Admittedly, such behavior, if it exists at all, is extreme, and Nielsen doesn't waste time worrying about infiltration by the odd crank.

Nielsen collects the information stored in its People Meters nightly by means of a direct phone line to each box. The company usually does this around two o'clock in the morning when everyone is asleep.

The four thousand sample households, selected randomly from a pool maintained by Nielsen, remain pretty much constant. Changes occur when the members move and leave the meter behind, or when a household tires of participating in television research and asks Nielsen to come remove the meters.

?

How do they manufacture genes?

MAN CANNOT MAKE A GENE. He can only emulate one. In fact, scientists are less interested in reproducing actual genes than they are in copying the stuff genes are made of—clumps of DNA that are the blueprints for manufacturing proteins and chemicals imperative for life.

Formulated in 1985, the polymerase chain reaction (PCR) has enabled scientists to make millions of copies of a single strand of DNA in a matter of hours. The technology both hastens and consolidates the more onerous tasks of genetic mapping and se-

1. ORIGINAL DNA FRAGMENT.

2. HEATING "UNZIPS" DNA INTO TWO STRANDS.

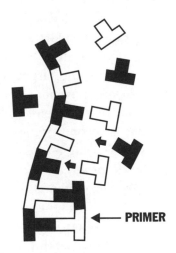

← PRIMER

3. PRIMER ATTACHES TO ONE END OF EACH DNA STRAND AND BEGINS BUILDING NEW COPIES....

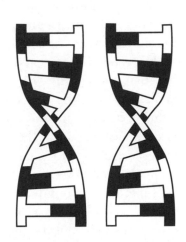

4. RESULTING IN TWO NEW DNA FRAGMENTS READY FOR NEXT HEATING CYLCLE.

Scientists can alter the blueprint of a DNA fragment by this process called polymerase chain reaction, in which a new DNA fragment is introduced and two new DNA fragments are created.

quencing that once could take several years to complete. According to an article in *U.S. News and World Report*, PCR has been used to find genetic defects that cause some types of cancer, to design diagnostic tests for such illnesses as Lyme disease and AIDS, to identify criminals through samples left at crime scenes, and even to recover DNA from frozen mammoths, mummies and other long-dead organisms.

PCR works simply and efficiently. It takes its cue from a process already perfected by every living system: with the aid of an array of enzymes, a cell divides and makes an exact copy of itself—a phenomenon that occurs in the human body millions of times every second. By heating a strand of DNA inside a test tube, a technician separates the DNA molecule and thus creates two complementary strands of the original double-stranded DNA. Next, short, synthetic DNA molecules known as primers are added to the test tube, at which point the process goes beyond the natural function of a living system. When the test tube is cooled, these primers anneal to one end of the targeted DNA fragment, and with the addition of nucleotides, instruct a DNA-building enzyme where to begin copying. The result is two new double-stranded pieces of DNA with one end of the target fragment indexed by the primer. Thus there are now four target strands of DNA: the two parentals and the two progenies. The heating and cooling process is repeated and a second primer earmarks the other end of the targeted DNA, yielding an exact duplicate. Since the process is one of geometric progression, where the number of DNA produced is multiplied exponentially with each repetition, one million copies of the DNA fragment are generated from twenty to thirty such cycles, enabling scientists to implement other tools of genetic engineering to research the specific makeup of the gene.

Transgenic manipulation is another method of producing new DNA. Using a microscope and microsyringe, foreign DNA is injected into animal egg cells so that it can be incorporated with human genes coded to produce either enzymes or proteins and so that its genetic performance can be studied. In what some analysts believe will grow into a $1.5 billion industry, transgenics are expected to help produce leaner livestock and to cultivate animals into "living factories" that manufacture protein-based drugs.

Surely the most ambitious and hopeful sign for the future of genetics is gene therapy, a process that permits "healthy" genes to be injected into the body to combat faulty ones. According to Dr. Michael Blaese, a researcher at the National Institutes of Health (NIH) who is conducting the first human trials in gene therapy, by the middle of the twenty-first century the technology will "be used for treating everything from cardiovascular disease to senility to cancer as well as for many of the more than four thousand recognized inherited diseases, many of which have no effective treatment at all."

Gene therapy brings scientists into the nucleus of the cell, where they can manipulate genetic material and explore methods of treating disease at its source. The ultimate goal of gene therapy is to treat inherited metabolic diseases prophylactically—in other words, to treat genetic deficiencies while a child is in utero so that chances of developing ailments such as cancer and heart disease are completely wiped out. This would be accomplished by repairing a defective gene or adding one which would correct instructions delivered to the cells. Though still in an experimental phase, gene therapy is used to treat such diseases while they are in progress. Some experts believe that in utero gene therapy will be as common as amniocentesis, and instead of just learning about what deformities a child will be born with, or will be predisposed to, the disorders will be corrected before an infant takes its first breath.

As it exists today, gene therapy permits genetically altered DNA to be attached to a disarmed virus which serves as delivery truck to targeted cells. The NIH recently received government approval for what might result in the world's first cancer vaccine. The vaccine will be made from the patient's own genetically altered cancerous DNA, which is then reinjected into the body. This form of gene therapy has been proposed for the treatment of advanced skin cancer, gastrointestinal cancer and kidney cancer.

How do they stop you from getting a credit card under a false name?

CREDIT CARD FRAUD WRENCHES millions of dollars every year from the credit industry. And even though that's only a fraction of a percent of credit card issuers' profits, most issuers, such as banks, are careful to review applications. Hypothetically you could call yourself Spot, so long as you paid your bills. But in reality, it's illegal to take a phony name, and you'd get caught: your bank wants to know the real you. The real you is a lot more likely to pay.

Credit card cheats can be pretty creative. Their scams using false names vary considerably. Sometimes they read the obituaries and apply for credit using the name of a dead person. And some actually *have* tried using their dogs' names or made-up names. But the most common ploy by far is to steal somebody's wallet and credit cards, then apply for credit under the victim's name. This works nicely because it gives the thief access to his victim's driver's license, social security card and possibly even such things as a job ID card. The thief fills out an application for credit under the victim's name. He uses the victim's address as "previous address" and uses his own address as "current address." That way, of course, the new credit card gets mailed straight to the thief at his address, which is usually a post office box he can change in a pinch.

Criminal groups tend to apply for credit many times a year using this very method, with all sorts of assumed names. A high number of applications coming from the same address is one clue to a credit card company that something is amiss. In the early days of credit cards decades ago, at least one man collected thousands of cards under false names before he was caught.

So how *do* banks and credit card companies stop you from getting a card under a false name? Using computers and telephones, they monitor your application patterns and catch your slipups. Visa and MasterCard—the two biggest credit card companies in the world—have a joint "Issuers' Clearinghouse Service," which keeps millions of computer records of addresses, phone numbers, number of applications per year, Social Security numbers of deceased people (numbers supplied by the U.S. government) and past fraudulent applications. When you apply to a bank for Visa or MasterCard, the bank is required to run your application through the ICS computer. In a few minutes, your bank knows whether to suspect you of fraud.

When the computer notices, for example, that more than five credit applications have come from your current address in the past year, a flag goes up. The ICS tells your bank, and any other banks that have issued you credit recently, to review their relationships with you. Have you been paying your bills? Are you the person you say you are? Or perhaps the computer notices that you've used the name and Social Security number of a deceased person. You'll have to explain why (and for that matter, *how*) you could still want a credit card when you're dead.

While computer records can catch schemes that follow patterns like these, the one-time fraud can also be caught with a few telephone calls. The thief who stole the wallet is a good example. A bank employee would check the phone book and call the applicant's previous-address phone number. If the person whose name is on the application still lives at the old address, then whoever lives at the "current address" is highly suspect.

Similarly, a call to the applicant's employer verifies that the person actually exists; talking with the applicant where he works can confirm that the application form was filled out by him. Some chiselers set up elaborate answering machine systems, or ask someone to verify their employment. But banks can sometimes get around that tactic by using their own phone books. They look up the main number of the company and call that number instead of the one given on the application.

Still, even massive computer records and intensive telephone inquiries can fail. It's nearly impossible to keep computer files completely up to date; obituaries run before death certificates are filed, for example, and a fraud can take advantage of the lag time. Perhaps the most difficult cheat to stop is one who uses any one of these schemes to apply for credit under a false name, and then maintains good payment patterns for a while before vanishing into thin air.

?

How do members of Congress make themselves sound articulate in the *Congressional Record*?

WHENEVER THE U.S. HOUSE OF REPRESENTATIVES and the U.S. Senate are in session, their public proceedings are published in the daily *Congressional Record*. The *Record* was first published in 1873, and it continues to be the official account of congressional debate.

Each house of the legislature maintains a staff of court reporters, who transcribe the speeches made from the floor by members of the House and Senate. These transcriptions make up the *Congressional Record*. Within half an hour of finishing a speech, a member of Congress is presented with a typescript of it. He then has an opportunity to make sure his words have been taken down accurately before they are included in the *Record*. Members are not supposed to make any revisions that change the meaning of their speeches. The rules of the Congress restrict them to correcting grammar, spelling, and so forth.

When a representative or senator delivers a speech prepared ahead of time, he simply presents a copy of it to the transcribers. Often he won't even bother to check the typescript, since he assumes the transcriber has copied the prepared document accurately. Most speeches, in fact, are prepared in advance, so the speaker will have had all the time in the world to make himself sound articulate.

Remarks made extemporaneously, on the other hand, do not always come off smoothly. When speaking off the cuff, most people, including most legislators, abandon precise, textbook English. They use run-on sentences, mix plural subjects with singular verbs, dangle participles, and commit many other linguistic transgressions. These errors don't necessarily prevent the listener from understanding the point of the speech, but they would seem pretty awful if put into print. When a speaker is ad-libbing, the court reporters record every grammatical foible, including all the "ums" and "ahs." Later, it is the job of *Congressional Record* copy editors to put it all into proper English. The copy editors delete pause words, add words to complete broken sentences, patch sloppy transitions, and introduce punctuation where necessary. Copy editors are not in any way allowed to change the meaning of a speech; they merely clean up the grammar to ensure that the remarks are coherent enough for the printed page.

Occasionally, a legislator will, in the heat of debate, say something universally offensive. When this happens, one of the unruly speaker's colleagues will usually raise an objection and the body will vote by unanimous consent to have the offending words "taken down," or expunged from the *Congressional Record*. Members can also petition to take down their own words. Sometimes, after expressing an opinion in a speech, a member will think better of the opinion and begin to rue his words. He can then request that those words be deleted from the official transcript. Barring any objections from his colleagues—and usually none is raised—the request will be granted. A good example of such after-the-fact tinkering occurred during the Clarence Thomas confirmation hearings. Senator Orrin Hatch, a Republican from Utah and a Thomas supporter, took the floor to defend the nominee. His defense took the form of a direct attack on his avowed friend, Senator Edward Kennedy, who opposed confirmation. Senator Hatch said something like, "And if you believe that, I've got a bridge to sell you in Massachusetts," referring none too subtly to the infamous bridge at Chappaquiddick Island. Hatch meant to imply that Kennedy's judgment was so impaired no one should listen to anything he had to say about Judge Thomas. Later, after he had cooled down a bit, Hatch asked to have "Massachusetts" changed to "Brooklyn," thus transforming his personal and malicious statement into the generic "And if you believe that, I've got a bridge to sell you in Brooklyn." No one objected.

After material has been printed in the daily *Congressional Record*, members of congressional staffs examine it to make sure the words of their bosses have been presented accurately. If a staff member discovers a mistake, he can ask that a correction be printed in the next day's *Record*. The permanent *Record*, the hardbound, comprehensive tome that is published at the end of each congressional session, will then reflect the correction. As is the case with the daily *Record*, senators, representatives, and their staffs are not allowed to revise meanings for the permanent *Record*, only to repair errors in transcription.

How do they "make" veal?

ACCORDING TO THE United States Department of Agriculture, a vealer is "an immature bovine animal not over three months of age: the same animal after three months, and after having subsisted for a period of time on feeds other than milk, is classified as [a] calf." Veal meat, then, comes from a younger animal than does beef. Unlike beef, which comes from a grain-fed cow or steer, veal comes from an animal raised for slaughter on a strict diet of milk, milk by-products, or milk substitutes.

Because of the young animal's severely restricted diet, the meat of a vealer is noticeably different from mature beef. While healthy beef is pink, veal, because of the absence of iron from the vealer's diet, has a pale, grayish appearance. Beef is marbled and trimmed with fat; veal comes from an animal that has not yet developed substantial fat, and the flesh retains an even, creamy texture. The soft, slender, and reddish bones of vealers also distinguish them from their older counterparts, whose bones are heavier, whiter, and harder.

The two types of meat are taken from significantly different breeds of cattle. Veal, which is sort of a dairy spin-off, comes from the young of dairy cows, predominantly Holsteins and Guernseys in this country, while beef comes from the larger, meatier breeds, such as Hereford and Angus. Only cows that have recently calved produce milk, a fact that necessitates a high birthrate among dairy cattle. The high birthrate leads to surplus calves, and surplus calves lead to veal cutlets, which, coming from animals not bred

61

for meat production, are more delicate than cuts from big, mature beef cattle.

In recent years, veal has become something of a political issue, with various animal rights activists attacking as inhumane its method of production. They find offensive the fact that veal breeders often pen the vealers in such a way as to prevent their muscles from developing, so that the meat of the animal remains soft and tender. The combination of enforced immobility, iron-free diet, and the young age at which the vealers are slaughtered, is more than enough to turn some people off Wiener schnitzel for life.

How do they determine the profit of a Hollywood movie?

IN THE MOVIE BUSINESS, as in every other industry, profit equals gross revenue minus costs. For movies, the biggest money maker is box office ticket sales. Additional income is derived from video sales and rentals. Other movie markets include cable and free TV, airlines, and shiplines, but in general these ancillary outlets provide only a fraction of the income generated at the box office.

The average Hollywood movie costs about $25 million to make, a figure which includes salaries for high-priced stars and directors as well as the blue-collar army of gaffers and bestboys and so forth who work behind the scenes. Add to that $25 million the amount spent on advertising and distributing the movie and you have its total cost. Deduct that cost from the revenue generated at the box office and through sales and licensing fees for video, television, and the ancillary markets, and what remains is profit.

Of the six bucks or so that moviegoers shell out for a ticket to the latest release, only about half goes back to the movie studio. The rest is kept by the cinema. Movie theaters contract with movie distributors for the rights to show a particular movie; generally the distributor collects between 42 and 52 percent of a movie's box office receipts, more or less as a rental fee. Therefore, when the entertainment media reports that some blockbuster made a whopping $40 million at the box office over the weekend, it means that the movie has earned roughly $20 million for its makers. Whether or not that amount is profit, depends on how much the movie cost to make and how long it has been running.

Officials at Entertainment Data, Inc., the independent company that contracts with many studios to compile and release box office figures, report that they get their information straight from the movie theaters. Every night, EDI's large reportorial staff calls the theaters to get figures for those movies that the company has contracted to track. At the end of the week EDI adds up all the numbers and announces them to the parent studios. Then it delivers the news to the press. Some studios bypass EDI and do their own tracking, a pretty big chore considering that at any one time a major movie will be showing on anywhere from 800 to 1,800 screens nationwide.

?

How do they decide who gets nominated for Oscars?

THE ACADEMY OF Motion Picture Arts and Sciences has 4,830 members, each with expertise in some branch of the film industry, who nominate their peers for the various Oscars. Cinematographers nominate cinematographers; directors nominate directors; actors nominate actors; and everyone nominates movies for the Best Picture Award.

The nomination process begins at the end of the Academy year, December 31, when ballots containing all the qualified candidates—basically any movie that came out during the year and played in Los Angeles for at least fifteen days—are sent out to each member of the Academy. Members pick the five people they think have done the best work in their branch that year, and also mark their choices for Best Picture. Polls close on February 1. After the nomination forms are collected, they are delivered to Price Waterhouse, an accounting firm, to be tabulated. The top five vote-getters in each category are placed on the final ballots, which are sent out to members at the beginning of March. During the next two weeks, every movie on the final ballot is screened twice so that voters will have a chance to see the work before the polling deadline. As with the nomination, each category in the final election is broken down by Academy branch: members of the actors branch vote only in the acting categories, and so forth. Price Waterhouse counts the votes and the winners are announced, with much hoopla and speechifying, at the made-for-TV ceremony near the end of March.

The peer-based nomination process sounds perfectly credible, but there are a couple of big problems. First, voter turnout is worse than in general political elections, averaging no better than 60 percent in good years, and often dipping as low as 40 percent. By default, control of the voting process is often left to studio flaks, who do everything to carve their employers a share of the Oscar pie. Second, the Academy is a backward-looking, Old Guard sort of institution, many of whose members are resistant, or oblivious, to innovations in the movie-making business. (A person becomes an Academy member after being nominated by two current board members and approved by a vote of the board of directors.) Of the directors, 70 percent are older than sixty, 45

64

percent have not made a movie in ten years, and 20 percent have not made a movie in twenty years. Cutting edge they're not. Also, this being Hollywood, backbiting is endemic. One of the most celebrated cases in recent years was the treatment received by Steven Spielberg in 1985, when his picture *The Color Purple* garnered eleven nominations but he was left off the Best Director ballot. If the movie was that good, indignant critics railed at the time, *someone* must have been responsible, and it was probably the director. Indeed, Spielberg had already won that year's Directors Guild Association award. According to widespread rumor, the Academy was turned off by Spielberg's cocky attitude and not a little jealous of his ever-growing fame and fortune.

The Academy's credibility problems are almost as old as the institution itself. Founded in 1927 to generate publicity for the huge studios, the Academy quickly grew from fewer than a dozen members to 1,200 in 1932. During the early thirties, omnipotent producer Louis B. Mayer, in an attempt to freeze legitimate labor unions out of Hollywood, tried to turn the organization into a studio-controlled union. Members began resigning in droves, and by the time Frank Capra became president, in 1935, the ranks had dwindled to forty. The Academy has expanded steadily since then, but it has never outgrown its penchant for bestowing its awards on safe movies. Among the dubious Best Picture winners are *How Green Was My Valley*, which beat *Citizen Kane* in 1941; *Patton*, which topped *M*A*S*H* in 1970; and *Rocky*, winner over *Network* in 1977.

How do they make nonalcoholic beer?

LEGALLY SPEAKING, in the United States there is no such thing as nonalcoholic beer. According to government definition a nonalcoholic drink is a beverage that contains no alcohol of any sort. The law also maintains that a beverage containing less than 0.5 percent ethanol cannot be called beer. The end result is a semantic issue, which brewers of alcohol-free drinks that look like beer, come in six-packs like beer, smell like beer, and taste more or less like beer, resolve by calling their products "nonalcoholic malt beverages."

Nonalcoholic beverages and low-alcohol beers have been around since Prohibition, but no one ever mistook them for the real thing and they remained largely shunned. In recent years, however, a surging national awareness of health and fitness has created a viable market for alcohol substitutes, and now brewers are applying new technologies to the quest for a really good, beery, nonintoxicating brew.

There are two ways to make nonalcoholic malt beverages. They can be specially brewed to avoid alcohol, or they can be brewed as normal beer, with the alcohol removed later. However it is done, something must be used to compensate for the missing alcohol, which adds to both the flavor of beer and its characteristic foaminess. Beer is made by steeping a mixture of barley and hops, called mash, in hot water to produce wort. The liquid wort, high in organic sugars and enzymes, is caused to ferment by adding yeast to it. The fermentation process turns sugar into alcohol and carbon dioxide, producing the foamy, slightly bitter drink enjoyed the world around.

There are a few basic ways a brewer can prevent alcohol from forming in the wort, and thereby brew a nonalcoholic beverage. He can use a weak, low-sugar wort, devoid of the ingredients yeast feeds on to produce alcohol. He can refrain from adding yeast. Or he can add yeast but do so under conditions, such as low temperature and excess CO_2, that make fermentation impossible. The last method works particularly well because it uses normal yeast and wort, and the yeast enhances flavor by reducing noxious by-products in the wort while leaving desirable ingredients—glucose, fructose, maltose and amino acids—intact. Flavor extracts and stabilizing agents are also used sometimes to duplicate the taste and feel of real beer.

Removing alcohol from fully brewed and fermented beers is becoming a popular alternative to preventing fermentation. The product, linguistic wrangling aside, is beer minus the alcohol, spiritually akin to decaffeinated coffee. The most effective way to remove alcohol from beer is by vacuum distillation. The fermented beer is warmed and then pumped into a vacuum chamber and condensed, a process that separates the alcohol from the body of the beer and reduces the beer to a thick concentrate. The concentrate is then cooled and water and CO_2 are added to produce a carbonated malt beverage. Vacuum distillation is advantageous because in removing the alcohol it avoids the extreme high temperatures that damage color and flavor.

Another way to remove alcohol from beer is by something called the "ultrashort time evaporation," or Centri-therm process. Beer is placed in a centrifuge and made to pass over a heated surface, which causes the alcohol to evaporate. The process damages yeast and removes some flavor compounds, but since the beer is in contact with the heating device for only about half a second, no significant harm is done.

Alcohol can also be filtered out of beer through a semipermeable membrane. The beer is placed under great pressure so that it breaks down into its component molecules. Ethanol and other small molecules are able to escape through a membrane that retains the larger, desirable molecules. In essence, filtration squeezes alcohol out of the beer, leaving behind a concentrated solution that is diluted with water before being bottled and sold as a "non-alcoholic malt beverage."

Most of the upscale pseudo-beers, the ones that masquerade as imported ales in the liquor store cooler, and taste pretty close, are made by a vacuum distillation alcohol removal technique.

How do they know there was an ice age?

THE MOST OBVIOUS CLUE to ice ages past is that in some parts of the world, things seem markedly out of place. This is how, in the late eighteenth century, Swiss peasants discovered that there had been ice ages past. Noting that glaciers in the Alps were slowly transporting and depositing rock masses down-valley, they correctly inferred that boulders strewn in their pastures had arrived in similar fashion centuries earlier. They also noticed that the polished and scratched or finely grooved and rounded bedrock knobs along the valley walls and floors resembled those surfacing from beneath the melting ice of existing glaciers. This similitude hinted that the knobs had been produced by moving glacial ice during a time when the glaciers extended farther down the mountain valleys.

Similar discoveries were made in Germany and Scandinavia. Eventually geologists concluded that huge sheets of moving ice had traveled from the far north to the plains of northern Germany. They deduced, furthermore, that the world had experienced a period of glaciations that had occurred and would recur in 10,000-year cycles, each glaciation lasting some 100,000 years. They called this vast period—in which we are still living—the Great Ice Age.

During the Pleistocene Epoch, which began about one and a half million years ago, mountain glaciers formed on every continent, and vast glaciers, as thick as several thousand feet, sprawled across northern North America and Eurasia. These far-reaching glaciers intermittently covered nearly a third of the earth's present land surface. Today, remnants of the great glaciers encase almost a tenth of the planet, demonstrating that conditions somewhat similar to those that spawned the Great Ice Age are still operating in polar and subpolar climates.

The first Ice Age studies in North America began in 1846, when Swiss geologist Louis Agassiz arrived in the United States. Early analysis of this country indicated that large parts of the north central and northeastern United States had once been blanketed by thick ice sheets. Traces of glacial erosion and deposition were ubiquitous: rock outcrops were smoothed and polished, scratched or striated; hills were rounded and wrapped with glacial debris; valleys were smothered by sand and gravel deposited by glacial melt waters. All these conditions were the result of the slowly advancing ice sheets, which had sucked up soil and loose rock, plucked and gouged boulders from outcrops, and hauled this clutter elsewhere, often great distances away. En route this hard material served as an abrasive—smoothing, polishing, and scratching all rock outcrops in its path, thus producing a more subdued landscape with rounded hills and higher valleys.

When glaciers melted, blends of clay, sand, gravel, and boulders were deposited as an unconsolidated mantle on the countryside. Thus, the once rolling hills of the Midwest are now level, and great river valleys such as the Mississippi and Ohio, overwhelmed by ice sheets, were forced into new channels. Ancient Lake Bonneville, the largest glacial lake in the western United

States, once covered more than 20,000 square miles and was more than 1,000 feet deep. The Great Salt Lake in Utah is but a puddle compared to its original size.

Although the first appearance of man remains unknown, scientists attribute our rapid physical and cultural development during the Great Ice Age to the necessity of adapting to the changing climates of that time. Our most primitive tools and skeletal remains from ancient deposits are concurrent with periods of glaciation in Africa, Asia, and Europe. The melting of the immense ice sheets sparked the evolution of the Bronze and Iron Age cultures. And animals suited to cooler climates became extinct, particularly larger mammals such as the woolly mammoth, mastodon, dire wolf and saber-toothed tiger.

?

How do they correct nearsightedness in ten minutes?

IN 1974, a Soviet ophthalmologist named Svyatoslav Fyodorov developed a surgical procedure that has proved a speedy and sometimes very effective method for correcting nearsightedness. The basic idea is to alter the curve of the cornea, which is the window into the eye, by means of tiny surgical scars. Performed under local anesthesia, the procedure, called "radial keratotomy," usually takes a half an hour, but some doctors claim to do it even faster. It costs about $2,000 for each eye, and the patient can go back, with a patch and some discomfort, to what he was doing that day. Here's how it works.

A person with nearsightedness sees blurry images because his cornea is too convex, causing light rays to focus in front of—rather

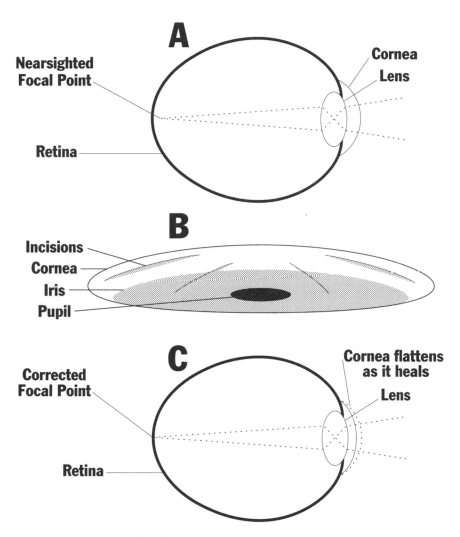

A

Nearsighted
Focal Point

Cornea
Lens

Retina

B

Incisions
Cornea
Iris
Pupil

C

Corrected
Focal Point

Cornea flattens
as it heals

Lens

Retina

In a nearsighted person, the uncorrected eye (A) focuses images in front of the retina. To correct the problem, an opthalmologist cuts a tiny starburst on the cornea of the eye (B). As the wounds heal, the cornea flattens. The flatter cornea (C) focuses images on the retina, where they should be for clear vision.

than *on*—the retina in the back of the eye. To correct that condition, an ophthalmologist uses a diamond-bladed knife and a microscope to make four to sixteen very small incisions that look like a perfect star burst on the cornea. As the tissue heals, the cornea flattens, so that without the aid of glasses or contact lenses it now brings light rays to a focus where they should be.

71

Doctors do worry about complications with this procedure, because it tampers with otherwise perfectly healthy eyes. The worst possible scenario is an infection in the scars called bacterial keratitis, which, if unchecked, could result in a complete loss of sight. More likely is the possibility of overcorrecting the curve of the cornea so that it focuses light behind the retina. In such instances, the patient actually becomes farsighted. Still another problem is that, while the results of the operation are evident soon after surgery, the cornea actually requires four or five years to heal completely. It is therefore hard to predict exactly how the cornea will finally be shaped.

One extensive study, funded by the National Eye Institute and begun in 1980, tested the eyesight of 435 patients, 99 percent of whom had 20/50 vision or worse. Highly skilled and well-trained ophthalmologists performed radial keratotomy on one eye of each of the patients. Three years after surgery, 51 percent of the eyes that had undergone the procedure could see with 20/20 vision or better, with the moderately nearsighted patients having the best results. But 16 percent were farsighted by more than a diopter (a unit of measurement of refractive power). And 26 percent of the eyes were "undercorrected": still nearsighted by more than a diopter. Some patients found they could no longer tolerate contact lenses, though they still needed them. Some experienced a halo-like glare at night from the scars, and some reported fluctuations in their eyesight from morning to night. Still, if you are nearsighted you can probably understand why many patients in this group were satisfied with even imperfect results; the surgery left them less dependent on corrective lenses than they had been before. About three quarters of the whole group opted for the same surgery on the second eye.

A new technique using a computer-controlled laser beam instead of a diamond knife is being explored. "Photorefractive keratectomy" may be a more precise method than its forerunner, but the jury is still out. In either case, some doctors are suggesting that people wait a few more years before ditching their glasses, until both techniques are better known.

?

How do lawyers research members of a jury before deciding whether to challenge them?

JURY SELECTION ISN'T just based on instinctive hunches. As the stakes of cases have increased, lawyers on both sides of a case are carefully weighing each potential juror and trying to eliminate those who may have predispositions against their client. It is a tricky task requiring rapid psychological analysis by lawyers, assistance from jury consultants, computer character profiles, and carefully crafted questions.

In all courts, judges have tremendous discretion about how the selection will proceed, and lawyers in the court need to familiarize themselves ahead of time with the particular judge's modus operandi. The selection in federal courts is generally quick, often under an hour. Each side is permitted only three peremptory challenges; that is, the counsel for the defense and the prosecution can each strike only three prospective jurors without providing a reason. (However, recent Supreme Court cases have limited this right somewhat.) Both sides are also allowed unlimited challenges for cause, but here the lawyer must provide a reason for eliminating someone, usually tangible evidence that that person cannot be unbiased. Federal judges tend not to dismiss candidates for cause, however, and that helps expedite the process. Every state court has different policies about the length and type of questioning permitted. The process can take days, especially if the case is to be a long one in which juror alternates will be needed.

What do lawyers look for and how? "The trial lawyer can't just glance or casually look at a member of the jury panel," explains William H. Sanders of Blackwell Sanders Matheny Weary and Lombardi. "The trial lawyer has to *eyeball* each and every member of the jury panel. Just as a portrait painter sees so much in his subject's face, the trial lawyer must scrutinize the body language, demeanor, expressions and dress of each individual." During the seconds before the candidate is seated, the lawyer watches his or her stride—is it forceful or lazy? How is the candidate dressed—high heels or running shoes? Is the candidate carrying any reading material, and if so, what kind? The lawyer is looking for clues about how this potential juror will view his client. Does he or she appear liberal or conservative, rigid or easygoing, sympathetic or not to the plight of his client?

After eyeballing the prospective jurors, the lawyer may pose a series of questions (or in some cases have the candidates fill out a questionnaire) about each candidate's occupation, marital status, age, and residence. Usually the lawyer is not allowed to inquire about religious affiliation or political leanings. Inevitably the lawyer will rely somewhat on occupational stereotypes. For example, in a case of wrongful death of a child, a young mother who will sympathize with bereft parents will be more desirable for the defense than a seventy-year-old widow. But the lawyer must also try to read between the lines. Is this young mother an angry, frustrated person? How does she feel about her work, her kids? He must reach rapid conclusions drawing on general demeanor and personality type.

If a trial lawyer is challenging for cause, he does so at the close of the questioning, or voir dire. To obtain a reason he can ask leading questions. Say the case involves a drunken-driving accident and a potential juror professes to be a teetotaler. The lawyer would highlight the candidate's preference for abstinence while inquiring whether he could indeed be fair to the defendant; wouldn't he be likely to award more damages against the driver because of his drinking? If the lawyer can demonstrate to the judge that the candidate is prejudiced, then that person will be disqualified.

In big cases lawyers often hire jury consultants who study social patterns and personality types for insight into what motivates an individual. Some jury experts try to read personality traits through somatotypes, or body types. The endomorph, for instance, who is obese, tends to be free and direct in answering questions. His generosity makes him a desirable juror for plaintiffs in civil cases. At the opposite end of the spectrum is the terribly thin ectomorph, who is considered anxious, rigid, tight with money, a juror for the civil defendant.

Some lawyers use personality typing by psychiatrists in the selection of a jury. Take the obsessive-compulsive—a motivated, meticulous achiever and go-getter. "That's the person I don't want for the plaintiff," writes lawyer Bill Colson in *Jury Selection: Strategy and Science*. "That person really thinks that you work your way to heaven—you should never get anything for nothing and that we can always overcome. So for me to stand up and say that I want him to give some money for intangibles, for pain and suffering or for future disability or for a scar on a body or a burn—that just wouldn't enter his mind."

Other experts classify prospective jurors in five social categories: leaders, followers, fillers, negotiators, and holdouts. Lawyers generally don't like leaders, whose independence makes them hard to sway. If, however, the lawyer is sure a leader is on the "right" side, then he or she would be a good pick. A lawyer who has found such a person would then try to put as many followers on the jury as possible. That's because followers, the passive ones more accustomed to receiving orders than giving them, are likely to fall in line with the leaders, or strongest members of the jury. What lawyers call filler types might also be desirable. Because fillers display indecision but not outright resistance, any lawyer worth his salt will think he can sway them to his client's cause. Of course, a prosecutor or plaintiff's lawyer would never want a holdout, a person unlikely to go along when the majority of the jurors want to convict or find for the plaintiff. The lawyer must carefully weigh, then, not only each individual but the dynamics of the group. And stereotyping, however useful, isn't foolproof.

To help make jury selection more scientific, Decision Research, a market research firm with a strong litigation service practice in Lexington, Massachusetts, stages mock trials in which a "jury panel" is presented with the facts of a "hypothetical" case. Observing through a one-way mirror, lawyers and Decision Research analysts study how people react to the arguments and lawyers. Says Robert Duboff of Decision Research, "You start to see fairly predictable patterns." In a euthanasia case, for example, he found that people under forty and over sixty were more likely to sympathize with the defense. Those in between, in the forty- to sixty-year-old range, were the least sympathetic. "Possibly they felt some trepidation that someone would do that to them when they're not ready to go," suggests Duboff. "But cases are usually not that clear-cut." When the data are more varied and complex, Decision Research does computer runs to establish patterns. In general, it seems inadvisable in a criminal case for the defense to select a jury too much like the defendant. (Recall the Scarsdale Diet Doctor case in which Jean Harris was convicted for murder by a strategically selected bunch of middle-aged, middle-class women.) "If you are similar to the defendant, you judge him or her by your own standards," says Duboff, "and you say to yourself 'I'd be tempted to do that, but I wouldn't,' so you want to punish him."

Despite all the computer analyses, surveys, and studies, every time a lawyer steps up to a panel of jurors he is, in the end, dealing with unpredictable individuals, and their responses may hinge on unperceived quirks and foibles. Even so, it can't hurt for lawyers to try to ensure the scales of justice aren't tipped against their client.

?

How does an electric eel generate electricity?

IN THE WARM, murky waters of the Amazon and Orinoco Rivers of South America lives a sluggish fish with a shocking capability. The electric eel can emit an electrical discharge of 550 volts. In the animal kingdom, fish alone can produce electricity, and of the 250 species that do so *Electrophorus electricus* is the most powerful. It can deliver a nasty shock to a man ten feet away or stun other fish, which it then consumes. According to ichthyologist C. W. Coates, "Any average electric eel of three feet or longer has a power pickup of about 150 horsepower per second, a fact which seems to belong in the 'Believe It or Not' class."

The electric eel usually reaches four to eight feet long. It moves stiffly by undulating its long anal fin, which runs from the throat to the tip of the tail. All essential organs are located in the front fifth of the body. The rest houses the tail musculature and the electrical works, consisting of two small "batteries" and a larger one. These organs, which derive from muscular tissue, are made up of specially coated units called electroplates. Seventy columns of electroplates run along the sides of the electric eel's body, and each column contains from six thousand to ten thousand plates. The electroplate surfaces face the head and tail, all positive poles lying one way, negative poles the other. Electricity flows from the tail to the head.

Cranial motor nerves power the electric organs. Impulses race through the eel's body twelve to fifteen times faster than the speed at which impulses travel from the human brain to the nerves. The electroplates each contribute 150 millivolts; connected in series, they combine to produce a remarkably high voltage.

The first small battery in the electric eel's tail is operating all the time. As the eel moves, this battery emits low-voltage waves that set up an electric field in the water. When an object enters this field, it causes a distortion, which is registered by pits in the eel's head. In this way the eel apparently perceives the size and nature of things around it; even with poor eyesight, the electric eel successfully finds food in the murkiest of water.

Scientists believe that the second small battery ignites the larger battery, which in turn discharges a series of quick, powerful pulses. Each pulse lasts three milliseconds and is delivered with incredible speed. So fast is the pulse that, even though its voltage is more than sufficient to light up many light bulbs, it would come and go before the inertia of an ordinary light bulb was overcome. The lamp would require one fifteenth of a second to go on, whereas the rapid-fire discharge of the electric eel pulses and passes in one tenth that time.

How does an invisible fence keep your dog from straying?

HOW DO YOU KEEP Fido faithful to the homefront in the face of overwhelming temptation—a female trotting by or the cat next door? Traditional fencing is pricey, and furthermore, some dogs dig under a fence or even scale the chain-link type. An alternative solution is invisible fencing.

The system consists of a thin antenna wire of whatever length you need to circumscribe your property, or the area in which you wish to contain your dog. The wire is buried one to three inches underground, and both ends are attached to a radio transmitter placed, say, in your garage or in your home. The transmitter emits a radio signal that is picked up by a receiver in a small rectangular box affixed to a special collar worn by the dog. The receiver, which is positioned under the dog's neck, has two posts (available in short or long) that extend from the box to the dog's skin. When Fido approaches the wire outlining his terrain, he hears a warning beep. The depth of the signal field, or area on either side of the wire that will activate the collar, is usually six to eight feet but can be varied to fit your particular property. If the dog ignores the sound, keeps going, and crosses the wire, it receives a mild shock, the strength of which can be adjusted to meet the level of your pet's doggedness. The receiver is powered by a 7.5-volt battery. No hazardous electricity is involved, so the system is safe for households with small children.

One wonders how the poor dog can guess where it's safe to wander without getting zapped. The training process is crucial. According to the Invisible Fence Company, Inc., based in Wayne, Pennsylvania, which began marketing the system in 1979, many dogs can learn their boundaries after receiving only a single, harmless shock. The system relies on a technique first discovered by the Russian physiologist I. P. Pavlov in the early 1920s—the dog's susceptibility to being conditioned. The dog can learn a particular response to a particular stimulus. In the case of Pavlov's dogs, a ringing bell first associated with food evoked a certain response, and continued to do so even later when no food was presented. In the case of the invisible fence, the dog becomes conditioned to step back the instant it hears the beeper on its collar.

When you first install an invisible fence, its parameters are marked by clearly visible flags placed six feet apart and about three feet inside the loop wire. The dog should be at least five months old and used to walking on a leash. Lead the dog to a flag, shake the flag and say "NO!" when the warning beep sounds.

79

Then let the dog walk on its own into the signal field and feel the correction. One hopes that once will suffice and that the dog will take note of the flags and the beep thereafter. When the dog returns to the safe area, praise it. You must work with the dog about fifteen minutes each day for a week. During the second week the flags are gradually removed and Fido can be trusted to play outdoors unattended.

Although invisible fences are popular and largely effective, some dogs persist in breaking through them if the call of the wild is strong enough. Another drawback is that even if your own dog is obedient, an invisible fence does nothing to prevent neighborhood pets from trespassing and disturbing dear Fido—and you.

?

How does a thief break into your car and drive off with it in less than a minute?

ALL TOO EASILY, according to the New York FBI Auto Theft Task Force. It should know. In the city with by far the largest number of vehicle thefts in the nation, the FBI grapples with the large-scale professional syndicates that enjoy most of the profits of this lucrative crime. Meanwhile, its task force vehicles are repeatedly stolen when parked in front of its headquarters.

The techniques of the professional thief are so slick that it takes him an average of only sixty seconds to break into a car, no matter how well locked and alarmed. As a result, a motor vehicle is stolen somewhere in the U.S.A. every twenty-two seconds, adding up to about a million stolen nationwide each year. About 133,000 were swiped in 1989 in New York City alone. And the rate continues to increase.

Just how does a thief get into your locked car? He may poke the lock or pry down the windowpane with a "slim jim," a long, very thin metal tool that can be slipped down between a car's windowpane and door frame to reach the door's lock mechanism. In a matter of seconds the thief is able to move a bar on the lock and open the door.

Once in, the thief can start the car without its key by using one of a number of devices readily available to him on the open market, through crooked suppliers, or through theft. For instance, he may have a supply of master keys, and if those are insufficient, a portable key cutter. Certain makes of car have their key code numbers engraved inside the glove compartment or passenger door lock. A thief can pull out a door lock with pliers, find the key code number, check in the manufacturer's manual to see what corresponding key to make, and cut it on the spot with the portable key cutter in a matter of moments. Failing that, there are a number of tools, such as dent pullers (also known as slide or slap hammers), that can start a car instead of a key.

Since the value of a luxury car such as a Mercedes-Benz decreases considerably if damaged—as it is quite likely to be if broken into by such techniques—car thieves often steal them *with* their keys by entering parking garages and bribing an attendant. They also may take a car at gunpoint when its driver is stopped at a red light, or bump into it with another car from behind and then flee with the expensive car when the owner gets out to examine his fender.

Car alarms are no deterrent, since thieves can readily get hold of directions explaining how all available alarm systems can be cut off. Experienced thieves can fool even the most elaborate alarm systems of expensive cars with a meter that can be bought for $150 from any electrical store. It analyzes the diodes in the electronic brain of the alarm system so the thief can then electronically simulate the right key with a resistance diode.

There is little you can do to protect your car against a thief who wants to make off with it. Concealed cutoff switches that have to be turned on to start the engine sometimes prevent thieves from making a rapid getaway but generally not from taking the car. Steering column locks can be broken, and marking your car's VIN (vehicle identification number) on all its major strippable parts does not deter chop shop operators, since they can conceal even deeply etched numbers.

According to police estimates, the "joy rider," or casual thief, accounts for only a small percentage of vehicle theft, although what this precise figure is is not known. A surprisingly larger proportion (25 to 30 percent) is made up of ostensibly solid citizens who want to get a new car out of their insurance company by arranging the "theft" of their present one, often in collaboration with corrupt auto repair or chop shops. Most vehicle thefts, though, are carried out with professional efficiency and speed by organized criminal groups whose hefty profits add up to big business and contribute largely to the over $4 billion annual loss sustained by the nation. Car theft is second only to drugs as organized crime's biggest money earner, and the two activities are closely linked.

?

How do they get the oat bran out of oats?

YOU DON'T GET THE OAT BRAN out of oats, but *off* of oats. The bran is the husk, or outer covering, which is removed during the milling of oats. First the oats are cleaned to remove foreign matter and inferior specimens. Then the grain goes through a drying and roasting process to reduce their moisture content. This process also develops flavor, helps prevent spoilage, and facilitates the subsequent separation of the hull from the groat, or internal grain. After the oats are cooled by circulation, they are ready for the hulling process.

The hulling machine separates the groat kernel from the surrounding hull and produces the following: hulls, groats, broken groats and meal, flour and unhulled oats. These materials are separated by air aspiration and sifting: they are placed in rotating, meshed, cylindrical frames and the hull (bran) is either sifted or flung out of the frame. It's a little like panning for gold. In this case, though, what used to be discarded or used primarily for animal feed is now regarded as valuable for humans.

In the early sixties scientists discovered that oat bran could significantly lower cholesterol levels in human beings. Other grains, such as wheat, contain only insoluble fiber, which passes right through the body. Only oat bran has both insoluble and soluble fiber. Soluble fiber gets absorbed into the bloodstream and helps remove cholesterol from inside the arteries and prevent it from being deposited on the artery walls. Moreover, the cholesterol that is decreased is the harmful LDL cholesterol. Oat bran does not affect levels of HDL cholesterol, which actually helps *prevent* clogging of the arteries.

With the increasing public awareness of these findings, oat bran has become the "miracle" ingredient in cereals, muffins, bread and even doughnuts. According to studies conducted at Northwestern University Medical School (funded by Quaker Oats Company), the average person needs to eat some thirty-five grams of oat bran or oatmeal every day to lower his cholesterol by about 3 percent. One ounce of pure hot oat bran cereal comes close to fulfilling that requirement. But you need to eat your oat bran pure and unadulterated to derive the maximum benefit. As it is, the benefit of the bran is lost in, say, an oat bran muffin whose unwholesome fat content may outweigh the healthy qualities of the bran. If you are buying oat bran specifically for its cholesterol-lowering capacity, you should always check the label to see what, besides the bran, you are buying.

How do they get the bubbles into seltzer?

AN ENGLISH CHEMSIT by the name of Joseph Priestley bears the distinction of having invented seltzer water, in itself a popular beverage and the precursor of the ubiquitous soft drink. One day in 1772, Priestley mixed up a solution of baking soda, vinegar, and water, a combination that produced carbon dioxide, which created a fizzing action as the gas escaped from the water. Priestley's experiment was regarded highly enough to win him the Copley Medal of the Royal Society in 1773, but a hundred years would pass before seltzer water caught on as a refreshment, when a beverage called Lemon's Superior Sparkling Ginger Ale became the first registered soft drink.

Carbon dioxide is still the agent of soda water's bubbles, but instead of relying on baking soda to get CO_2, modern seltzer bottlers inject CO_2 gas itself directly into the water.

Carbonation is a two-step process. During the first step, CO_2 is injected under pressure into water. From two different storage containers, pure water and CO_2 are pumped into a common refrigerated, pressurized tank, called the sparging unit. The water absorbs the CO_2, but only up to a certain point; after the water has reached its saturation point, the bubbly solution is pumped into a second pressurized tank, the carbonating unit, for the second stage of carbonation. A trough at the top of the second tank disperses the liquid into droplets, which will still absorb gas, and more CO_2 is introduced until the water is fully carbonated. The seltzer is pumped from the carbonating tank into a filling machine, which disgorges it into individual bottles and cans.

FACING PAGE: *Seltzer is made by combining water and CO_2 in a tank. After the water is saturated with gas, it is pumped into a second tank and broken up into droplets, which absorb additional CO_2.*

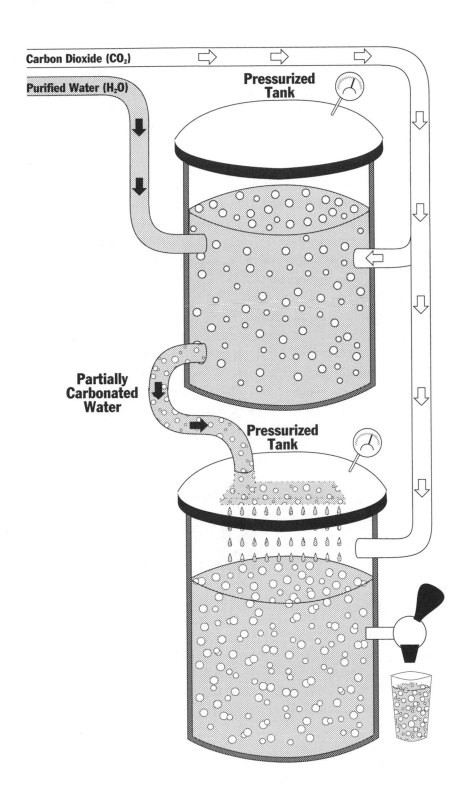

Carbon Dioxide (CO_2)

Purified Water (H_2O)

Pressurized
Tank

Partially
Carbonated
Water

Pressurized
Tank

About 80 percent of carbonation is achieved in the sparger, with the remaining 20 percent done in the carbonating unit. The whole process occurs without a break, water and gas flowing continuously through the system. A bottling plant can produce about fifty gallons of the bubbly stuff a minute, making three thousand gallons per hour.

To make flavored soft drinks, bottlers simply add syrup to the water as it is pumped through the system. Because a lighter liquid will absorb CO_2 more readily than a dense one, it is easier to carbonate pure water than a soda pop like root beer or ginger ale. It is also easier to carbonate a cool liquid than a warm one, so the various tanks are refrigerated: heat drives the CO_2 out of the solution. You've probably noticed that when you uncap a warm bottle of soda water, it gushes like Old Faithful. Seltzer made from water that has not been meticulously filtered also tends to bubble excessively. Bubbles do not float freely through water, but cling to naturally occurring microscopic particles. "Hard" water, which has a high alkali count, offers more bubble toeholds and consequently fizzes much more when carbonated than water that has been treated to remove alkali.

?

How do they teach guide dogs to cross at the green light?

SINCE DOGS ARE BELIEVED TO BE color blind, teaching a canine to cross at a green light sounds like a very difficult task. In fact, guide dogs don't look at the traffic light at all. They learn to stop at curbs so that their master may listen carefully for traffic before crossing.

Training a guide dog is a lengthy and serious process, one that can be undertaken only by professionals. It is done at any one of ten private, nonprofit schools, such as the Guide Dog Foundation in Smithtown, New York, that teach blind people and dogs to work together as teams. This type of dog is sometimes called a Seeing Eye dog. The term comes from another private school, Seeing Eye, Inc., in Morristown, New Jersey, which holds a trademark on the name.

Before the schooling starts, the dog is meant to enjoy a happy, well-rounded puppyhood. The Guide Dog Foundation breeds its own stock of Labradors and golden retrievers, which are farmed out to foster families, known as "puppy walkers." The family's primary responsibility is to care for the dog and expose it to as many different situations as possible. It is expected that the dog will be taught to walk nicely on a leash, sit, stay, lie down and come when called, but nothing more. When the puppy reaches a year old, it returns to the Foundation and begins its training, which will last from three to six months.

One of the first things the dogs learn is to walk straight down the center of the sidewalk without sniffing or being distracted by people or other dogs. Elane Siddall, an instructor at the Guide Dog Foundation, explains that this is done with positive and negative reinforcement: "You're constantly telling the dog, 'Straight, come on now, straight,' and when the dog's doing well you praise it—'Good dog.' When the dog does something inappropriate, you give a snap on the leash, 'No, now straight,' and give it something immediately to counterbalance its correction, something you can praise it for."

Once the dog has learned to walk straight down the center of the sidewalk, deviating only for obstacles, it is taught to stop at curbs. Siddall does this by approaching the curb while repeating to the dog, "Straight to the curb." When she is about six feet from the curb, she says, "Steady to the curb," slowing down the dog as she gives the command. If all goes well, the dog realizes that something is changing. About two steps from the curb, Siddall says, "Halt," and gives a slight jerk on the leash and a release. When she has stopped the dog, she pats the curb with her foot and says, "*Good* curb, *stay* at the curb, *good* curb." After many repetitions, the dog eventually begins to stop at the curb on its own.

Then it will be up to the owner to listen and determine when to cross. When he hears traffic start up at his side, he knows he can safely cross the street. If the traffic in front of him is moving, he knows he must wait.

If a blind person makes a mistake and winds up in an intersection with a car coming, the dog will either halt until the car passes, pull its master to the side and out of the way, or put itself between its master and the obstacle. When the car has passed, the dog will lead the blind person forward to the opposite curb.

?

How do they measure dream activity?

IN THE EARLY DECADES OF the twentieth century many scientists and philosophers speculated upon the nature of our dreams but could not study them scientifically. Researchers could wake up volunteers at different times in the night and ask them whether they had been dreaming and for how long. But the propensity of dreams to vanish into oblivion almost as soon as we wake made for such sparse and unreliable results that dream activity, however intriguing, was held unsuitable for scientific study.

In 1937 scientists began studying sleep with the help of an electroencephalograph (EEG). This equipment, invented in 1929, can record very small fluctuations in electrical activity, commonly known as "brain waves," constantly occurring in our brains. Five types of electrical activity were identified as taking place in recurrent sequences during a night's sleep. Then in 1953, a University of Chicago graduate student, Eugene Aserinsky, discovered distinct periods of rapid eye movement (REM) during babies' sleep. Scientific research into dreams took off in earnest.

Researchers found it quite easy to differentiate the periods of rapid eye movement (which can be detected under the closed eyelids of sleeping adults as well as those of children) from the eyes' immobility or slow rolling movements (non–rapid eye movement, or NREM) during the rest of sleep. Brain wave rhythm during REM sleep has been found to be more like that during the waking state than the other sleep states, and to recur regularly about every ninety minutes throughout the course of a night's sleep. So sleep was reclassified as NREM during stages 1 through 4 and REM in stage 5.

The possibility that the rapid eye movements might correspond with sleepers' watching their dreams prompted researchers to wake up their subjects during REM and NREM sleep and compare the results. They found that about 80 percent of the time that sleepers were awakened from REM sleep, they reported having been dreaming, whereas only 7 percent of the time did sleepers aroused from NREM sleep say they were in the midst of a dream. These findings led to the still continuing era of the sleep laboratory.

A research subject, often a psychology student earning experimental credits, goes to bed for a night's sleep in the lab with about eight electrodes applied to certain places on his head. The EEG amplifies the tiny shifts of electrical potential occurring within the brain and body that are detected by the electrodes. Continuous shifts from positive to negative charge within the subject's brain cells are transmitted to magnetic tape, which drives a row of pens, each of which reflects changes in a different part of the brain or body. When an electrical charge is negative, a pen will swing upwards to a corresponding magnitude; when positive, the pen will swing down. The height of the waves shows how much voltage is being generated by the area studied, and the distance between the waves indicates the rhythm and rapidity of electrical movement in progress.

In order to compensate for the distorting effects of sleeping in a laboratory, researchers commonly document their subjects' sleep patterns over five to ten consecutive nights in order to establish a normal pattern. Still, the possibility of a certain amount of "laboratory effect" inhibition is tolerated as unavoidable. Nightmares are rare, for instance, as are nocturnal sexual emissions in the lab. Some dreamers vigorously deny any violent or sexual content in their dreams, despite strong indications of agitation of this nature to clinical observers.

The experimenters monitor the sleeping subject as he progresses through stages 1 through 4 of (NREM) sleep, delineated by their different brain wave patterns. When, after about ninety minutes, the subject shifts into stage 5 (REM) sleep—presaged by a highly irregular, rapidly changing but low-voltage brain wave printout very similar to that of the waking brain—the dream researchers' attention focuses on the eye movement printouts (measured by two particular electrodes) on the polygraph paper. The script is now characterized by abrupt shifts, as the sleepers' eyes dart to and fro as though looking at a movie. If the subject is woken up at this point, the odds are ninety-nine in a hundred he will say he was dreaming. But the experimenters will probably let the subject dream for about five minutes, the approximate length of the first dream phase of the night, before they awaken him to discover details of the dream. Meanwhile, monitors recording data about the subject's physical state show an increase in oxygen consumption and internal brain temperature and irregularities—wild fluctuations even—in heartbeat and respiration, similar to those during violent emotion or exertion when awake. Although the dreamer may grind his teeth, the rest of his muscles are completely slack.

After being awakened briefly, the subject will be allowed to fall back to sleep. Again he will drift down through stages 1 through 4 of NREM sleep and, in ninety minutes to an hour, will again enter the dream phase, stage 5 (REM), which this time is likely to last around twenty minutes. During the course of the night, the sleeper will repeat this cycle four or five times, each time staying in the REM phase for a longer and more vivid dream period. In this way, thousands upon thousands of dreams have been meticulously and laboriously monitored, giving researchers increasingly comprehensive insight into this puzzling, and evanescent phenomenon.

?

How do they decide whose obituary gets published in *The New York Times?*

"ALL THE NEWS that's fit to print," boasts the motto of the venerable New York paper, and the editors there apply the sentiment not only to foreign and domestic bureau reports but also to death notices. An obituary in the *Times* is the ultimate tribute: it signifies that during his life the deceased made it big—big enough that *The New York Times* considers his death to be newsworthy.

According to the *Times*, journalistic value is the only criterion for determining who gets in. The subject of an obituary must have accomplished things that had some impact on the way the rest of us live. In general, these accomplishments arise from the fields of entertainment (famous actors), the arts (famous writers), sports (famous athletes), politics (famous former office holders), or business (famous captains of industry). Fame, of course, is a relative term: a concert pianist, for example, might be known by every classical musician in the country but not by the wider public. In the end it is the obituary editor who, like any other journalist, arbitrates between what is news and what isn't. Which is not to say that selection is a wholly arbitrary affair.

To prepare for a notable figure's death, the newspaper actually begins compiling information on the person's life while he is still among the quick. In many cases, the future obituary subject conducts interviews expressly for this reason, pragmatically tying up loose ends much in the way other people compose wills and buy cemetery plots.

The *Times* retains staff obituary writers whose job it is to keep abreast of deaths and write up the deeds of qualified recently deceased people. In the case of a particularly famous figure, the notice might be written by someone outside the obituary department, usually the reporter who covered the subject in life. When, say, a baseball great dies, the occasion is reported by a sports writer, who brings a special understanding to the subject.

Because not even *The New York Times* has the resources to track everyone's term on earth, the paper often accepts the help of outside sources, including the Associated Press wire service and families of dead persons, who send in announcements. Again, it is the job of the obituary editor to decide which of the many AP and private notification candidates are newsworthy.

How do they know there are more stars in the sky than grains of sand on an ocean beach?

IF BILLIONS OF PEOPLE devoted their lives solely to counting, they could actually count the numbers of stars and sand grains, because neither figure is infinite. The universe and its starry contents come to an end somewhere out there beyond our wildest imaginings. And although it may feel like the number of grains of sand on a beach is infinite, those too are limited. Using eyeball estimates, mathematical calculations, physical laws, and sophisticated photography, Dr. Neil D. Tyson, an astrophysicist at Princeton University, has come up with the numbers. Here's how he did it, and what they are.

Ever since Newton wrote the laws of gravity, astronomers have used the formula $M = \dfrac{av^2}{G\pi}$ (in which M is mass, v is velocity) to calculate the mass of planets, stars, and even whole galaxies based on how fast these bodies travel in orbit. Astronomers know, for example, that the sun's mass is 2×10^{30} kilograms and that our whole galaxy, the Milky Way, has a mass of about 100 billion times that of the sun. Most of this mass is composed of stars similar to the sun, so we can safely say that our galaxy has about 100 billion stars.

If we take our galaxy as average, then with the number of stars per galaxy in hand, Tyson now needs to know the number of galaxies in the whole universe. A sophisticated photographic technique that uses a very sensitive digital detector, called a charge-coupled device, enables astronomers to take a very deep photo of the sky. Correcting for the fact that some galaxies are too dim to see, and estimating the number of galaxies astronomers would find if they shot photographs of every piece of the sky, astronomers have determined that there are about 10 billion existing galaxies. Tyson multiplies the 10 billion galaxies by the average of 100 billion stars in each galaxy to arrive at an estimate of the total number of stars in the sky: one sextillion, or a one followed by twenty-one zeroes.

Now on to sand. Tyson took a day trip to New York's Jones Beach and counted the number of grains of sand along a length of one centimeter. He counted about twenty-five. Allowing for some beaches to have much finer grained sand, as on the American Gulf Coast, and others to have big grains, Tyson estimated that there are about fifteen thousand grains of sand in a volume of one cubic centimeter on any given beach. He then judged that the average beach is about five kilometers long, one kilometer wide (from the edge to the high-tide line) and 0.015 kilometer (fifteen meters) deep. The volume of the average beach is therefore 0.075 cubic kilometers, or 75 trillion cubic centimeters. With 75 trillion cubic centimeters of sand on a beach that size, and fifteen thousand grains of sand in each cubic centimeter, the total number of sand grains on a beach would be about one quintillion, or a one followed by eighteen zeroes.

A sextillion is a thousand times bigger than a quintillion, so there are quite a lot more stars in the sky than grains of sand on a beach. Now let's say there are a thousand big beaches on planet earth; that would mean a sextillion grains of sand, or about the same number as all the stars in the universe. But then keep going. You could also add the sand grains under the ocean, and the sand on the Sahara Desert. "And that's the ball game," says Tyson. Sand grains win. By how much? No one's counted yet.

How do they decide where to put a new book in the Library of Congress?

IN 1814 Thomas Jefferson, retired from government service and living at Monticello, donated his personal library to Congress, writing, "There is, in fact, no subject to which a Member of Congress may not have occasion to refer." The government took Jefferson at his word, and the Library of Congress has since become the world's most avid collector of books, manuscripts, documents, music and film. It holds about 100 million items, and adds some seven thousand more every day. No one, not even the Librarian of Congress himself, has ever really examined the entire collection. Library officials claim that "if you were to limit your examination to one minute per item, eight hours a day, five days a week, it would take 650 years to view everything in the Library of Congress, during which time another 650 million items would be added behind your back." The massive holdings are stored on shelves that stretch for 575 miles hither and thither through the Library's three Washington, D.C., buildings, a storage facility in Landover, Maryland, and a film archive in Dayton, Ohio.

With items pouring in at the rate of ten per minute, the Library has by necessity become a leading innovator in the distinctly bookish fields of classification and storage. The Library classifies books according to the Library of Congress System, which has a broader base and greater flexibility than the Dewey Decimal Classification System. The system uses twenty-three letters of the alphabet to represent twenty-one general categories; combinations of letters are used to indicate specific topics. A, for example, stands for General Works, and AE designates encyclopedias. Subjects are further delineated by the use of three-digit codes after the letter combinations. There are full-time employees whose job it is to place new acquisitions on the shelves according to their classification. New shelves are constantly being added. Occasionally, when old books begin to decay and are transferred to microfilm, or when books are found to contain gross inaccuracies and are removed from the collection, additional shelf space becomes available.

Some items are not placed in the stacks at all. Newspapers are recorded on microfilm within three months of being published and are stored in microfilm drawers. Telephone books are treated the same way. Manuscripts, of which the Library receives more than half a million a year, both published and unpublished, are indexed and stored in manuscript boxes. The eight hundred or so motion pictures that arrive annually are placed in film canisters, some of which are stored in Washington, some in Dayton. Maps, numbering close to four million, are kept in specially designed flat drawers in the Cartography Division, which also houses an extensive collection of globes.

The Library has by law received two free copies of every book, map, chart, print, woodcut, engraving, dramatic or musical composition, or photograph submitted for copyright in the United States since 1870. The Copyright Office currently registers about 600,000 claims a year, and about half of its holdings are delivered to the Library. Copyright items not selected for the permanent collection are kept in the Landover, Maryland, warehouse. Also stored in Landover are Thomas Jefferson's fragile, two-hundred-year-old library and bound newspapers dating back to the seventeenth century. To help preserve its collection of antiquities, the Library has developed a patented diethyl zinc process for removing acid from book paper, a treatment that can extend the life of a book five centuries.

Another way to preserve printed material is to transfer it onto optical laser disks, which last forever. A single twelve-inch disk can store ten thousand printed pages, making it a valuable space saver as well. The library is currently evaluating the practicality of switching to laser disks.

In addition to its general collection, the Library maintains special branches that oversee specific fields of interest. The Hispanic Division, for instance, deals solely with items relating to Spain and Latin America, while the Asian Division counts among its holdings passages from a Buddhist sutra printed in A.D 770, the oldest example of such printing in the world. Certain books and materials defy usual classification and become the property of the Rare Book and Special Collections Division. Among the titles maintained in the special collections is *Ant*, which at 1.4 millimeters square is the size of an ant's book and the Library's smallest volume.

How do they discover a new drug?

IN THE EARLY HISTORY of mankind, before the advent of micro-wave dinners and Food and Drug Administration product labeling requirements, hungry men and women had to work hard to find a nutritious meal. Conceivably, to learn which plants and animals were edible and which were to be avoided, food pioneers scoured the earth like teething babies, popping whatever they found into their mouths. Rocks are no good, bark is no good, carrots are okay. Modern pharmaceutical development proceeds in much the same manner.

One place the search for effective disease-combating mole-cules begins is in the world's sludge heaps, where drug manufac-turers, hoping to unearth microbes that contain new, medicinal molecules, go to collect dirt samples. Having amassed as many as fifty thousand compounds from various global dirt piles, drug company scientists begin randomly screening the compounds for useful attributes. The dirt compounds are cooked into a sort of laboratory witch's brew and tested against cells and viruses for activity. An "active" compound is one that modifies a healthy cell or kills a diseased cell or virus. After isolating an active com-pound, scientists must then identify the molecule behind its ac-tivity. If they are successful, and if the chemical agent is patentable, a new drug might show up on the shelves of the local pharmacy.

Drug screening's biggest drawback is its randomness. Unless the right compound is matched with the right disease, a hit-or-miss proposition, no new drug will be found. If an active compound is found, one that produces results against cancer, for instance, chances are pretty good that the effective molecule will contain superfluous, but inseparable, toxic elements. The molecule's toxic elements often cause side effects that seriously limit therapeutic potential. When scientists are able to isolate the active molecule within a randomly selected compound, and when the molecule's inherent toxicity is not self-defeating, they have the makings of a new drug.

Screening, as the scouring technique is called, has been the drug industry norm for fifty years, and given the odds, its success has been remarkable. One of the biggest achievements recently was the development of cyclosporine, a drug discovered in a dirt sample taken from just below the Arctic Circle in Norway. Cyclosporine prevents the immune system from rejecting transplanted organs. Belonging to the family of drugs called immunosuppressants, it has also shown promise in the fight against such diseases as multiple sclerosis, in which the immune system rebels against the body's native cells.

How do they get honey out of a honeycomb?

NO, NOT BY MACHINE ALONE. The beekeeper himself barehanded shoos away the swarming bees to carry off the honey-laden combs.

A man-made beehive—which will house a colony of fifteen thousand to sixty thousand bees—is constructed of stacks of wooden boxes, measuring twenty inches by sixteen and one quarter inches each. The uppermost boxes, called supers, will hold the surplus honey the hive produces—the harvest designated by the beekeeper for human consumption. Each box contains six or eight hanging frames, which hold sheets of pitted wax called comb foundation. During spring and early summer, worker bees in the hive construct wax honeycombs on the foundation using fat secreted from their glands. The comb cells are then filled with honey, which hive bees produce from flower nectar. By mid-July, after the clover and alfalfa have bloomed, the hives become so full of honey that a typical super weighs about sixty pounds. Then the bees start capping over the comb cells with wax.

How can the beekeeper get at the honey? First, he must get the bees to leave their combs. He wears a hat and veil to protect his face from stings during this procedure, but he usually doesn't wear gloves or other protective gear. The experienced beekeeper is accustomed to being stung, and in fact his body is resistant to swelling. Quite often he can avoid being stung at all. He knows which time of day to go about the business—sunny hours are better than chill and shadowy periods. On rainy, windy days, he can count on getting stung. Judging from the weather, then, and what the bees have had for forage, he can predict the mood of the swarms. Even if they're not irritable, he takes precautions to keep them calm. With a smoker, a bellows mounted on a little wood-burning stove the size of a large bean can, he settles down the hive with long puffs of smoke. Then he brushes the bees off the frames or allows them to pass through a one-way "bee escape" into the brood nest in the lower boxes of the hive. Some beekeepers use repellents to get the bees moving; some use forced air to blow them off the combs.

Now the beekeeper takes the supers to the extracting house, or another indoor spot away from potential robber bees. With a long, sharp, heated uncapping knife he shaves off the wax cappings. This is the best and lightest beeswax, which, after the honey drips off of it, can be sold for candle making. He suspends two to four frames inside a piece of equipment called a honey extractor: a centrifuge the size of a wide trash barrel. Large honey producers use bigger extractors that can accommodate several dozen frames. The extractor spins the frames inside it—it's rather like a washing machine on spin cycle. Centrifugal force sends the honey flying out from the combs and onto the sides of the tank; the liquid runs down and out a spout. The beekeeper collects it in a storage tank and strains it. Before being bottled, the honey is usually pasteurized by heating it.

How long does this whole process take? It depends on equipment and the size of the apiary, but usually a beekeeper allots about a day to pry the hives apart and get the supers inside. After that he can spread the extraction chores over a few days. How much honey can be harvested? A commercial beekeeper, with the best agricultural land and the best floral sources for his bees, needs to extract about a hundred pounds of honey from each colony per year. A hobbyist can usually be satisfied with sixty pounds.

After extracting the honey, the beekeeper stores the supers for next spring or, if he is hoping for a second harvest, he stacks the boxes on the hives again. When the bees are allowed back in, they begin repairing any damage the centrifuge did to their honeycombs.

?

How do they know what caste a resident of Bombay belongs to?

A CASTE, from the Portuguese word *casta*, meaning race, is a group of people sharing racial characteristics; in India the term is applied to the smallest endogamous groups existing within the general population. There are thousands and thousands of castes and subcastes in India, as many as thirty thousand by some estimates, which would make it very difficult for a resident of Bombay to identify, without asking, the specific caste of a fellow citizen. Traditionally, however, Indian castes have been grouped into four *varnas*, or classes, which is what most people mean when they talk about castes. In addition to the four varnas there is an outcaste group, whose members are at the bottom of the social hierarchy. The varna to which an individual belongs can be deduced from such things as that person's mode of dress, his trade, and his religious practices. The four classes are the Brahmans (priests), the Kshatriyas (warriors or barons), the Vaisyas (merchants), and the Sudras (laborers). The outcastes are called the Harijans, or "children of god," Mohandas Gandhi's name for the group once known as "untouchables."

According to ancient custom, the various jobs, dietary habits, and living conditions of each caste cause its members to become ritually unclean in varying degrees, with the highest caste, the Brahmans, remaining most pure, and the outcastes, the Harijans, being the most impure. For this reason, it was considered defiling to mix with people of lower social standing.

The caste system has been relaxed in modern times, and since 1947, when India gained independence, discrimination against "untouchables" has been illegal. These reforms are especially strong in great urban centers like Bombay, where it would be impossible for residents to completely avoid intercaste contact. Even so, the caste system continues to exert a strong social and political influence in India.

In modern, industrial Bombay, recognizing what caste another person belongs to is basically a matter of cultural literacy: each person advertises his social position by his name, the clothes he wears, the job he performs, and the food he eats. A Brahman, for example, will likely adhere to a strict vegetarian diet for religious reasons. A member of one of the lower classes will be less particular about what he eats. A Harijan will probably eat whatever food he can obtain, regardless of its ritual impurity. Some distinctions run along fairly universal class lines: a person who lives on the streets or in a slum is apt to belong to a lowly caste, while a person who resides in an elegant apartment in one of Bombay's exclusive neighborhoods probably belongs to a favored caste. Clothing tells a similar story. The quality, material, and style of a person's clothing, whether traditional or Westernized, says something about his social standing. There are hundreds of clues, and a native of Bombay would be proficient at reading them.

This situation is much the same in any culture. In the United States, for example, the name Rockefeller carries a certain cachet. If you were to meet a man by that name, and he happened to be getting out of a limousine wearing a very expensive-looking suit and top coat, you might assume a thing or two about his background.

The great difference between Indian castes and American classes is that the Indian system permits only very limited social mobility. In Bombay, members of different castes by necessity mingle during the course of a day, but they rarely become involved permanently. Marriage especially is governed by social taboos. While the sons and daughters of American Rockefellers might meet and marry daughters and sons of less socially prominent families, that is not likely to happen in India.

In India, a caste near the bottom of the social ladder might advance itself by adopting the customs of the caste above it. After a few generations, it would become almost indistinguishable from the higher caste, but there is no real upward movement of individuals.

?

How do they dry-clean clothes without getting them wet?

THE TRUTH IS DRY CLEANING is not entirely dry. Dry cleaners do apply liquids to silk dresses . . . it's just that the stuff contains no water and furthermore dries quite rapidly. It doesn't cause clothes to shrink or colors to run.

Routine dry cleaning is done in large, closed machines using a volatile chemical called perchloroethylene (C_2Cl_4), dubbed "perk" in the trade. Perk is a compound consisting mostly of chlorine, with a lesser part of carbon. As clothes are agitated in a machine, perk, along with a detergent, passes through the machine at a rate of two thousand gallons an hour. About every minute there's a new batch of perk running through the clothes, dissolving stains and leaving dirt stranded in a filter. After this process most clothes are ready to be pressed and bagged.

The meticulous dry cleaner may, however, spy a stain that withstood the perk and need to apply the finer skills of his trade. The first step—a crucial one—is to analyze and identify the stain. Many are unknown; a large proportion, called "sweet stains," contain sugar, salt or starch and come from spilled food. The spotter then selects from four standard methods of stain removal and goes to work at his spotting board. He may dissolve the stain with the appropriate solvent, such as volatile-type paint remover, hydrocarbons, or petroleum distillates. (Legend has it that the dry-cleaning industry originated with a Frenchman in the nineteenth century who accidentally doused his clothes with benzene and subsequently found grease stains easy to get out.) If the stain is

103

water soluble, the spotter can just blast it with his steam gun and blow it dry. Another approach is to apply a lubricant with a stiff brush or spatula and try to raise the stain to the surface of the fabric, where it can be removed more easily. If that tactic fails, the spotter may resort to chemical action: he applies an oxidizing bleach that removes the color from the stain and so camouflages it; or he converts the stain using acids or alkalis into a soluble substance that can be treated with solvents. The very last method is to digest the stain with enzymes, just as your gastrointestinal enzymes break down insoluble protein, albumin, and starches. The enzymes, which are from bacteria and yeast, convert insoluble substances into soluble ones that can be cleaned away quite easily.

The spotter, then, has an array of methods and chemicals at his fingertips, so you needn't despair when salad dressing drips down your tie. Just remember what you spilled, and half the battle is won.

?

How do they make glow-in-the-dark toys?

FROM DINOSAURS TO LEGO GHOSTS, from stickers to yo-yos, a battery of toys now add a cool greenish glow to their attraction.

The key ingredient that causes the glow is a phosphor (from the Greek for "light-bearer"), which has the ability to *phosphoresce:* it glows when exposed to visible light energy, and continues glowing for a period of minutes or hours after the exposure is stopped. This phenomenon occurs because the phosphor absorbs energy while exposed to light and later, in the dark, discharges the energy in the form of light. (A substance that *fluoresces*, on the other hand, stops emitting light once the source of energy is removed.)

In nature there is a chemical element called phosphorus, discovered about three hundred years ago by a German scientist, which has the remarkable ability to glow. Glow-in-the-dark yo-yos, however, contain a commercially made phosphor, often a compound of zinc or magnesium. The phosphor is made by heating to above 800 degrees Celsius pure, synthetic ingredients in the form of tiny crystals two ˊ ˎ fifteen microns in diameter, along with an "activator," or trace of heavy metal. After being heated, the atoms of the activator enter the crystal lattice of the phosphor and remain embedded there.

When light strikes the phosphor crystals, the electrons that orbit around the activator's atoms are thrown into a tizzy. They leap from their normal, relaxed orbits into an excited orbit farther away. It is a rule of nature that everything wants to be in its lowest energy state, so the atoms continually plummet back toward the nucleus. Because of the lattice structure of the crystal, some electrons get trapped, their descent is delayed, and they continue to release energy—in the form of light—over time. Oddly enough, the smaller the crystal the longer the glow.

"A good glow-in-the-dark bug will shine for as long as thirty minutes after you shut off your lights," says Robert Majka, project manager at Canrad-Hanovia, Inc., a company in New Jersey that manufactures phosphorescent pigments. "Eighty-five percent of its luminescence will be expelled by then. But even after that, the bug will continue to glow for as long as eight hours, with the 15 percent of its leftover luminescence. You can only see this low glow if you've been in the room with it, so that your eyes have adjusted to the dark and the fading bug."

Canrad-Hanovia makes a glow-in-the-dark pigment containing an inorganic zinc sulfide phosphor, which is nontoxic and nonradioactive. It comes in the form of a powder, which is sold to compounders who add it to any clear suspension, be it plastic, paint, vinyl, or ink. A carrier material that is not clear would absorb the phosphorescence. From these plastics and inks come glow-in-the-dark Frisbees and mobiles, reptiles and stickers. The brightest toys with a glow that lasts the longest have a higher concentration of pigments than those with a dimmer glow. Optimal luminosity occurs when the pigment constitutes 30 percent of the product, that is, the ratio of plastic resin to pigment is about 2 to 1. At that point, the carrier reaches a saturation point.

Most kids know how to make their Super Balls and alligators glow. "Simply hold the toy up to any light for about thirty seconds," says Majka. Kids may be interested to learn that you get the brightest glow if you use fluorescent lights.

How do they predict when a fine wine will be ready to drink?

"AGE," WROTE FRANCIS BACON, "appears to be best in four things: old wood best to burn, old wine to drink, old friends to trust, old authors to read." A fine enough sentiment, but it turns out that most wines, including virtually all rosés and white table wines, peak in taste within a year of being bottled and after that begin a steady decline. Predicting when these wines will be ready to drink is like betting on the outcome of a fixed fight: it's the proverbial sure thing. But there is a relatively small number of wines, representing the high end of the market, that actually improve with age, and predicting a maturation date for them is neither as easy nor as precise.

Wine is nothing more than fermented grape juice. Unlike hard liquor, which is preserved by its high alcohol content, wine is perishable and loses freshness when it is exposed to air. Al-

106

though some oxidation is good for some wines, increasing the wine's complexity of taste and aroma, too much oxygen will spoil it. Since wine continues to age in the bottle, where it is exposed to oxygen that either seeps through the cork or is present in the wine itself, the trick is letting it ripen to maturity but not beyond. A number of variables, including type of wine, variety of grape, vintage, and storage conditions, help experts guess when a wine's time has come.

Red wines, such as cabernet sauvignon, red Bordeaux, red Burgundy, and pinot noir, have a higher fixed acidity than white wines and tend to age better because of it. Based on their experience with these types of grapes, vintners are able to estimate when wines made from them will come to full maturity in the bottle. But the acidity of any one type of wine, cabernet sauvignon for instance, will vary from year to year and from vineyard to vineyard, depending on weather and soil conditions. In Europe, where the grape harvest is subject to quirky weather, winemakers apply the term vintage to years when conditions have been especially favorable to grape growing. Grapes from a vintage year, presumably, will have higher sugar and tannin contents than nonvintage grapes, and will therefore age better. In California, where the climate is very consistent, vintners are fond of saying that every year is a vintage year, but even there grapes and wines vary from year to year and the vintage label often signifies nothing more than a wine's age.

Experienced wine makers admit that there is no surefire way to predict when a wine will be ready to drink. Some vintages, heralded as masterpieces when they are bottled, rush headlong to maturity and become tired long before anyone expects. Others, like the 1794 Château Lafite, somehow survive their makers by more than a century.

Connoisseurs do know a few things that help them make well-informed guesses. Small bottles have a larger cross-section-of-neck to volume-of-bottle ratio than large bottles, and since exposure to air ages wine, and since air enters a bottle through its cork, a half-bottle of wine will mature before a full-size bottle of the same wine. Storage temperature is another important consideration. Wine is stored in cellars and not attics for the good reason that warmth accelerates the aging process. But too much cold will arrest the wine's development. A temperature of between 55 degrees and 60 degrees Fahrenheit is considered optimal. The single most important factor, though, in predicting wine maturity accurately is experience. Connoisseurs are able to predict when a wine will reach its peak of flavor by knowing its vineyard and the record of other wines from that vineyard. Based on a vineyard's past performances, wine experts have been able to draw up charts that show when a wine will in all likelihood mature. A chardonnay, for example, will improve for about three or four years, maintain its peak for a few more, and then decline. With a heavier, more tannic wine such as cabernet sauvignon, the general rule of thumb is six to fifteen years, depending, of course, on the growing and storage conditions.

Even the most astute student of wine will be caught off guard from time to time though, and some types of wine, such as claret, a deep red Bordeaux, simply defy precise forecasting. The best you can do with claret, experts advise, is wait ten to a hundred years before opening it, and maybe you will get lucky.

?

How do they know how much an aircraft carrier weighs?

HOISTING THE 100,000-TON *Nimitz* onto a scale is a formidable idea and not a very practical one. Fortunately, there are less cumbersome ways of determining the weight of such a massive ship.

If a new aircraft carrier is being built, technicians simply keep a running tab of all materials that are used in the construction. In some cases the weight of a particular piece may not be known but is estimated based on its size and material. The weight of electrical wiring and drainage piping, for instance, is difficult to calculate precisely and must be approximated. In addition to machinery and equipment, one must tabulate the ship's loads, consisting of fuel oil, water, ammunition, and a variety of stores. As older aircraft carriers are modernized they become heavier, owing to the installation of new equipment and support structure. Many of the airplanes carried become heavier, too. The *Enterprise*, for example, weighed a mere 86,800 tons in 1961 and now weighs closer to 92,800 tons. (The tons referred to here are long tons, each of which equals 2,240 pounds, as compared with a short ton, which is 2,000 pounds. The Navy uses long tons.)

Detailed weight records are maintained throughout the life of an aircraft carrier, but since some weights are estimated, the "paper ship" must be checked periodically against the real ship to determine its actual weight. To do this the Navy routinely reads the draft marks located on the sides of the carrier, at the bow and stern. The drafts are six-inch-high Roman numerals painted on the ship at one-foot intervals in a vertical line. These marks tell the Navy how much of the carrier's hull is underwater. By knowing the volume of the underwater hull, the Navy can figure the weight of the entire ship.

One can calculate the ship's weight because of Archimedes' principle, which states that a body immersed in fluid is buoyed by a force equal to the weight of the displaced fluid. This means that a body floating in water displaces a volume of water equal to its weight. To compute the weight, one multiplies the volume of water displaced by the density of water (weight = volume × density). To start, imagine a rectangular box twenty feet long, ten feet wide, and five feet deep. Let's say it rests in the water and sinks down two feet. The volume of the box that is submerged, which is also the volume of water displaced, is $20 \times 10 \times 2 = 400$ cubic feet. Now, the density of one cubic foot of sea water is 64.0 pounds, so the weight of the box may be calculated as follows: 400 cu. ft. × 64 lbs./cu. ft. = 25,600 lbs., or 11.43 long tons.

Typically, an aircraft carrier might have a draft reading of thirty-five feet, which means thirty-five feet of the hull is submerged. One multiplies thirty-five feet times the width and length of the ship to determine the volume that is submerged. Multiply this figure by the density of sea water and you have the weight.

Does it sound too simple? You're right. The tricky part is that the hull of the ship is not rectangular. "Although larger ships are somewhat boxy," says William Austin of the Naval Sea Systems Command, "all carriers are faired at the bow and the stern to allow them to move through the water more efficiently. From above, the outline of the hull would appear more like a tear shape than a box." Furthermore, as the hull rises from the keel, it slopes outward so that the volume is constantly increasing. In order to calculate the volume of this three-dimensional, nonlinear shape, an engineer must make a number of area calculations at various intervals above the keel. As an example, consider five horizontal planes slicing through the hull. One must compute the area of each plane and multiply it by the distance between it and the next plane. Each of these smaller volumes is then added to the next volume to obtain the total volume up to a specified draft. Converting the incremental volume to weight and plotting it against the height above the keel produces a curve which can be used by the ship's personnel to determine the ship's weight each time the drafts are read. The procedure is lengthy and is done only once—at the time the ship is built. As long as the shape of the hull is not changed during the life of the ship, the curve developed to determine the ship's weight will remain accurate.

?

How do they decide what or who gets honored on U.S. postage stamps?

MAKING STAMPS IS A FUNCTION of the federal government, and as is the case with most governmental projects, a committee has been appointed to get the job done. The fourteen members of the Citizens' Advisory Stamp Committee, representing expertise in American art, business, history, and technology, and sharing an interest in philately, are handpicked by the postmaster general to recommend subjects for commemorative stamps. The committee convenes every two months to sift through the thousands of suggestions that pour in continuously from the provinces. Of the twenty thousand or so subjects submitted by the general public each year, twenty-five to thirty-five eventually make it through the committee to the postmaster general; once he gives final approval, they can become stamps.

During the watershed postal reorganization in the early 1970s, one of those events that go largely unnoticed by the public but retain deep significance within the government, the postmaster general, with help from the CASC, established the elementary criteria by which stamp subject selections are made. Since then the list has been expanded to include twelve points:

1. U.S. postage stamps and stationery will primarily feature American or American-related subjects.
2. No living person shall be portrayed on U.S. postage.
3. Stamps honoring individuals will be issued in conjunction

111

with anniversaries of their birth, but not sooner than ten years after the individual's death. U.S. presidents are the only exception to the ten-year rule, and may be honored on the first birth anniversary following death.

4. Events of historical significance shall be considered for commemoration only on anniversaries in multiples of fifty years.

5. Only events and themes of widespread national appeal will be considered.

6. No commercial enterprise; specific product; or for-profit fraternal, sectarian, political, service or charitable organizations shall be recognized.

7. Towns, cities, counties, municipalities, schools, hospitals, libraries, or similar institutions shall not be considered.

8. Postage stamps commemorating statehood anniversaries will be considered only at intervals of fifty years from the state's entry into the Union. Other anniversaries pertaining to individual states or regions will be considered only for postal stationery and only at intervals of fifty years from the date of the significant event.

9. Stamps shall not be issued to honor religious institutions or individuals whose principal achievements are associated with religious undertakings or beliefs.

10. No "semipostals," stamps to be sold at a premium over their postal value to raise money for charitable organizations, shall be issued.

11. Significant anniversaries of universities and other institutions of higher learning shall be considered only in regard to Historic Preservation Series postal cards featuring an appropriate campus building.

12. No subject, except traditional themes such as Christmas, the U.S. flag, Express Mail, Love, and so forth, will be honored more than once every ten years.

Anyone can petition the Citizens' Advisory Stamp Committee with an idea, and if the proposed subject meets the guidelines, it will be considered and possibly recommended to the postmaster general. The rules, in addition to telling when and how something can be commemorated, dictate to some degree the subject matter itself. A stamp might be issued, for instance, to celebrate food in general, but rule number seven will prevent a specific product, like Spam, from ever gracing U.S. postage. Likewise, the government will not issue a stamp to honor one particular hospital, but health care in the abstract could be saluted.

How do emperor penguins stay warm in Antarctica?

THE EMPEROR PENGUIN, which happily swims and romps in killing temperatures of minus 40 degrees Fahrenheit, is the only bird that can, and often does, spend its entire life on coastal or shelf ice, without ever coming ashore. Basically, three mechanisms are at work in safeguarding the emperor penguin's body heat: its feather construction, its weight, and its behavior.

The emperor penguin's body is totally covered with feathers; it has no bare patches around the feet or head as are found on penguins of warmer climates. The tiny, overlapping feathers, numbering about seventy per square inch, are packed so closely they form an impermeable barrier to the wind. Coated with oil, they also resist water. The shafts of the feathers have tufts that, along with a layer of air next to the skin, provide insulation. Below the skin is a layer of blubber thicker and heavier than that of birds in milder climates.

Penguins in Antarctica are in general bigger and heavier than other penguins, and it serves them well. As George Gaylord Simpson explains in his book *Penguins*, heat loss is proportional

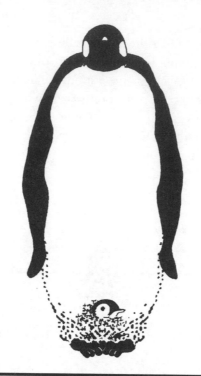

A.

Penguins move around edge from windward side toward leeward side...

TOP VIEW

...then enter warm middle of group, eventually going back to the windward side

Wind

B.

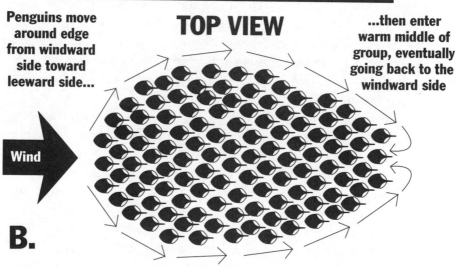

A: A baby emperor penguin gets off the ice by perching on its parent's feet. It nestles against the soft belly feathers for protection against the piercing wind.
B: Emperor penguins huddle in groups for warmth. Individuals systematically move from colder to warmer spots in the group, thereby taking turns in the warm center and ensuring the group's survival.

to the ratio of surface area to body volume. Larger animals have a lower ratio of surface to volume, and consequently proportionally less surface area from which heat escapes. The emperor's average weight is sixty-six pounds, as compared with the Galápagos penguin, which at five pounds enjoys balmy temperatures and seventy degree water.

Perhaps the most incredible survival feat of the emperor penguin is its ability to raise young in inhospitable Antarctic weather. The female lays one egg, usually in May, and then leaves the homefront, sometimes ranging as far as sixty miles in search of food. Papa is left to guard the egg. He holds the precious cargo on his feet, protected under a fold of skin, and does not leave his post for sixty-four days. He eats nothing during this period. At about the time the young hatch, the females return and the weary males can at last go in search of food. The chicks have only fluff at first, not a full suit of feathers, so they need a shield against the cold. Perched on the parent's feet, beneath layers of feathers, the baby snuggles against the grown-up's belly.

The adult emperor penguins, meanwhile, huddle against each other in a large circular mass to maintain body heat. They turn their backs to the piercing wind, and can raise the temperature within the group by as much as 20 degrees Fahrenheit. Those positioned farthest upwind, that is, those with their backs most exposed, periodically move around the outside of the huddle to the front of the group. As more penguins from the back move up, those at the front wind up in the middle—the warmest spot. The well-coordinated system continues so that each penguin in turn shifts from colder to warmer to colder spots in the huddle.

In these ways emperor penguins manage to keep quite warm in their Antarctic habitat. So warm, in fact, that penguin expert Bernard Stonehouse feels the real problem is: How can the emperor penguin ever cool down? Given its impervious feathers and blubber, how can it let off heat when intensely active? The emperor penguin's solution is to ruffle its feathers, allowing body heat to escape, and spread its wings, exposing more of its body to the icy Antarctic winds.

?

How do they make it easier for celebrities to attend concerts or Broadway shows?

IN SHOW BUSINESS, getting good seats at a performance is simply a matter of knowing the right people. And celebrities tend to know most of them.

Before tickets go on sale for any concert or Broadway show, a certain percentage are put aside as "comps," or complimentary tickets. Say, for example, Joe Rockstar plays a gig at the XYZ Theater and has signed a contract with a promoter to publicize the event. The contract includes a provision that sets aside a certain number of free tickets for the show. These tickets are divided among the performers, the promoter and the management of the building in which the show will take place. So if 1 percent of the seats in a ten-thousand-seat venue are designated comps, Joe Rockstar might get sixty, while the promoter and the XYZ Theater pocket twenty apiece. The breakdown varies according to the particular contract.

Now let's say Joe Rockstar wants to go to a Marilyn Operastar performance that is already sold out. If he knows Marilyn, then it's easy—he calls her and she gives him one of her comps. If he doesn't know her, it's still pretty easy. Chances are Joe or his manager knows Marilyn's manager, or her promoter, or the management of the theater in which she will perform. One of them supplies some comps. In the event that Joe doesn't know anyone who knows anyone, he could as a celebrity approach the performer, the promoter, or the theater, introduce himself and request a ticket. If Joe is indeed famous, he'll probably get a comp as a professional courtesy if one is available. The promoter or the theater might in fact have some professional interest in doing Joe Rockstar a favor . . . one or both of them might want to put on a Joe Rockstar concert one day. That's show business.

How do they treat drug addiction with acupuncture?

IN TREATING DRUG ADDICTION, acupuncture is used to suppress the addict's physical craving for narcotics and also to combat such debilitating side effects of withdrawal as nausea and extreme anxiety. By easing an addict's symptoms of addiction and withdrawal, acupuncture facilitates the patient's ability to receive other therapies, including counseling.

Acupuncture treatment is based on the presence in the body of certain pathways through which a vital energy, called *qi* in Chinese, flows like a bioelectric river. The pathways, or meridians, are each associated with a specific bodily function and interconnect with one another to form one continuous loop. Ancient Chinese physicians hypothesized that a blockage of *qi* along its meridian caused the base organ to malfunction, resulting in disease. They charted the meridians and discovered more than 365 points on the body at which *qi* could be reached and stimulated by inserting needles into the body. Because of the intricacy of the meridian system, the acupuncture points associated with an organ are often far removed from that organ. The stomach meridian, for instance, begins under the eye and descends all the way to the toes. The thirty-sixth point of the stomach meridian, located below the kneecap, is used to treat digestive disorders such as gastritis and dyspepsia. Modern tests show that the acupuncture points possess an electric current distinct from that of the rest of the body.

The acupuncture points commonly used in treating drug addiction are auricular, with five on each ear. Stimulation of these points with thin flexible needles causes the body to release organic opiate-like chemicals that defuse the craving mechanism, enhancing an addict's mental and physical stability. When properly administered, drug treatment acupuncture produces a sharp increase of metenkephalin in the subject's cerebrospinal fluid. Metenkephalin is a chemical with analgesic properties that occurs naturally in the human brain. A standard acupuncture detox program lasts for two weeks and consists of twelve forty-five-minute-long sessions. All ten of the patient's ear points are stimulated simultaneously, which means that during a session he will have ten needles protruding from his head. While this picture may seem unpleasant to most of us, urban clinicians note the fortunate circumstance that intravenous drug users seem to be undaunted by all the needles.

Detoxification is a relatively new application of the ancient medicine. The Chinese, looking for a way to curb opium abuse, first experimented with acupuncture as an antidote to addiction in the 1940s. In this country, acupuncture detox was developed in the 1970s, at Lincoln Hospital in the Bronx. The Lincoln program, which combines acupuncture and intensive A.A.-type counseling, treats 250 addicts a day and maintains a success rate of 50 percent. At about twenty-five dollars per person per visit, acupuncture costs far less than any inpatient rehab program, a factor that has led many cities around the country to adopt the Lincoln model.

In 1989, a group of doctors from Minnesota published the results of a study they had conducted on the efficacy of acupuncture treatment for chronic alcoholism. Eighty severe, long-term alcoholics participated in the study. Of these, half belonged to a treatment group that received acupuncture at points specific for

118

substance abuse. The rest, who made up the control group, received acupuncture at nonspecific points on their ears. The study was divided into three phases. During the first phase patients received five acupuncture treatments a week over a two-week period. Frequency of treatment was reduced to three times a week and twice a week in the second and third phases, respectively. The patients were then discharged and asked to return to the hospital after one, three, and six months had elapsed.

The doctors in charge of the study reported that 52.5 percent of the patients in the treatment group, as opposed to only 2.5 percent of the control-group patients, completed all three phases of the program. During the follow-up period twice as many control patients as treatment patients reported episodes of drinking. Also during that time, twice as many control patients as treatment patients were admitted to a detox center. Of the twenty-one patients who were admitted to detox at least five times over the six-month study period, fifteen came from the control group, five were treatment patients who had dropped out of treatment early, and only one was a treatment patient who had completed all three phases of the program.

Although acupuncture cannot "cure" drug addiction, studies like the one in Minnesota show that it can be a clinically effective treatment.

?

How do tightrope walkers stay on the wire?

THERE ARE NO REAL TRICKS to staying on a tightrope. One does it the same way one gets to Carnegie Hall: practice, practice, practice.

Angel Quiros, a high-wire artist for Ringling Brothers and Barnum & Bailey Circus has been walking the wire for sixteen years. One must be in good physical condition, he says, "but the main thing is to practice a lot." Acrophobes need not apply.

Quiros learned his trade in his grandfather's circus in Madrid at twelve years of age. First he and his siblings tried their natural abilities on a taut elevator cable held three feet in the air. They got up, tried to walk and often fell the short distance to the ground.

Within three years they were walking, running, dancing, jumping rope, doing gymnastics and sword fighting on the cable, still at an altitude of three feet. When they had mastered these skills, they gradually raised the cable in approximately seven-foot increments until the Quiros clan was doing its act some forty feet up in the air. This is the height at which Quiros performs for Ringling Brothers with no net below and no safety wire—a clear line attached to the artist's belt.

Using a pole gives the high-wire artist a better sense of balance—when Quiros uses one he is able to carry his brother on his shoulders—but the added weight of the pole slows down running and makes jumping more difficult. It's also easier to balance barefoot, but this is tough on the feet, so Quiros wears Capezio dance shoes with rubber soles.

Still, no matter how much an aspiring tightrope walker practices, there is no guarantee that he'll stay on the wire. Angel Quiros has had broken ribs to prove it.

How do they recycle newspapers?

FOR YEARS, mountains of old newsprint were blithely tossed out along with other household and commercial waste. Today, as we slowly realize our natural resources are less than infinite, we are recycling about a third of the country's newspapers. In order to reuse paper, one must first return it to the consistency of virgin wood pulp. After that, it can be cleaned and prepared for a second (or third or fourth) feeding through paper-making machines. Let's start at the beginning of a typical mill process.

First the newspapers are collected by towns or commercial trash haulers and separated from higher grades of paper (the latter, incidentally, can be turned into higher-grade final products). Then the newspapers are either bagged in brown paper or bundled with string, sold to mills and stored in warehouses until use. When a mill begins to fill an order for recycled paper, its conveyor belts dump measured amounts of the newspapers, with water, into a giant thirty-foot-diameter blender called a hydrapulper. Rotating blades loosen and roughen the cellulose wood fibers; reduced to a slushy, papier-mâché-like consistency, the newspapers are now called a "slurry."

To remove staples and paper clips, the slurry is now fed into rotating cylinders with coarse screens that trap the contaminants while letting the slurry escape through thousands of holes. Fine screens remove the smaller impurities, particularly the small pieces of binding glue called "stickies" that can make several sheets of paper tear in the presses later on. The mixture is now called "stock."

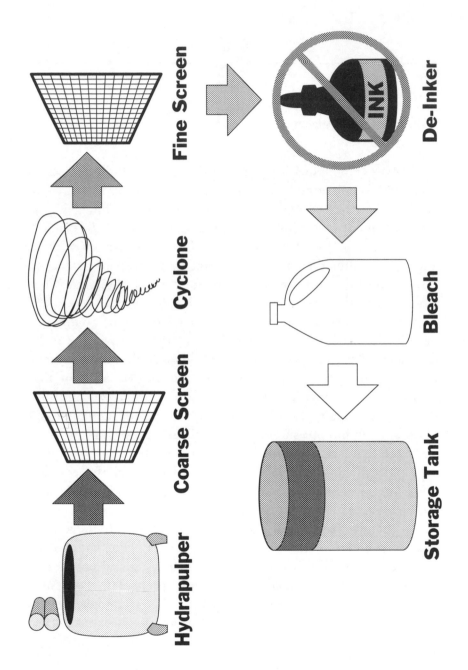

Hydrapulper   **Coarse Screen**   **Cyclone**   **Fine Screen**

De-Inker   **Bleach**   **Storage Tank**

In newspaper recycling, first the newsprint has to be reduced to a pulp, then it can be rebuilt into paper. Here you can see both halves of that process: In the steps from hydrapulper to storage tank, the newspaper becomes clean, deinked pulp.

BELOW: From header box to the finished roll, the pulp is shaped, dried, and smoothed into paper again.

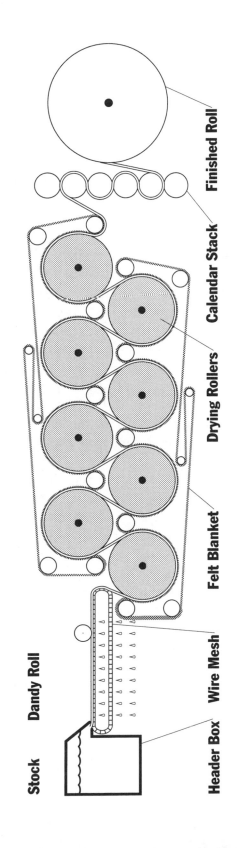

Finished Roll

Calendar Stack

Drying Rollers

Felt Blanket

Stock

Dandy Roll

Wire Mesh

Header Box

A wash system and/or a flotation system is used to strip the ink off the stock. In a typical wash system, the stock is shot with liquid through wire screens and slits at high speed; the wires grab the fibers while the liquid takes the ink with it. The flotation method calls for the stock to be submerged in a tank while air bubbles, clay and chemicals are run through it. Under high temperatures, the ink adheres to the clay and bubbles; it gets carried to the surface as a foam and is skimmed off. (Clay, incidentally, is often added to paper to improve opacity, make the paper surface smoother and increase the paper's ability to hold ink.) If an order calls for especially white paper, the mill washes the stock with chlorine bleach, sulfur dioxide or hydrogen peroxide.

At this point virgin wood pulp can be piped into the recycled stock to strengthen it. It's important to keep in mind that the slurrying, the forceful screening, and the de-inking will eventually damage the fibers in any paper, so that unlike aluminum and glass, the same paper can't be recycled indefinitely. Pure recycled paper can clog high-speed newspaper presses: adding virgin pulp reduces the chances of that happening. Barry Commoner, in his book *Making Peace with the Planet*, reports that *The Los Angeles Times* prints its news on paper that's about 80 percent recycled material.

The next step in newspaper recycling is building the fibers in the stock back into paper. In a massive piece of equipment called, rather predictably, a paper-making machine—some are as long as two football fields—more than 90 percent of the water is removed from the stock. First, the stock is fed at high speed in a continuous stream through a slit in a component called the head box and gently shaken on a thirty-foot-long fine-wire mesh. The mesh feeds the stock into several sets of rollers that squeeze out more water. Then a set of felt "blankets" carries the still-wet stock through more pressing and drying rollers and delivers it to the final sections of the paper-making machine. These can include vacuum suction driers, steam-heated drying drums and banks of infrared lamps—anything that will clear water from the paper.

Lastly, the paper stock is peeled out of the end of the machine and wound on rolls for delivery to the printer.

Recycled newspaper can't be made into fine stationery, but it can effectively be turned into such products as brown paper, toilet paper, cereal boxes, construction paper, egg cartons, insulation, animal bedding, cat litter, soil enhancer, telephone directories and, of course, newsprint.

?

How does a magician pull a rabbit out of a hat?

THE WHITE RABBIT and the black top hat have long been symbols of the magician's art—his uncanny ability to conjure objects and cause them to vanish again. Rabbits first appeared onstage, popping out of top hats, in the late 1830s. Though the originator of the trick is unknown, John Henry Anderson of Scotland, dubbed The Wizard of the North, was among the first to perform it, in 1840, at the New Strand Theater in London. Another nineteenth-century conjurer, Joseph Hartz, caused a skull to rise out of a top hat, while the French wizard Jean-Eugène Robert-Houdin produced nothing less than a cannonball.

Whatever the object, the technique remains virtually the same. The magician needs a table, draped with a tablecloth, which prevents the audience from seeing a small shelf, known as a servante, perched at the back of the table. Sometimes the tablecloth itself is simply pinned up, thereby creating a small pocket in which to house the rabbit or other object to be produced. The magician wraps a large silk handkerchief around the bunny and

In this classic trick, the magician first conceals the rabbit in a handkerchief on a small shelf behind the table. He then grasps the bundle along with the brim of the hat and, while flipping over the hat, swiftly moves the rabbit bundle inside. After a wave of the wand, the magician pulls out the rabbit.

ties the ends with a rubber band. At the outset of the trick, he removes his hat and displays the inside—empty. He may even pass it around the audience for all to inspect. When it has been returned he sets it down, right side up, near the back of the table. While waving his wand with his right hand, he grasps both the brim of the hat and the corners of the handkerchief with his left. (The ends of the handkerchief are sandwiched between his thumb and the brim and therefore well concealed.) With a swift, graceful move, he turns over the hat. The bundle drops into the hat, he removes the rubber band, and presto, with another wave of his wand he raises the live and wriggling rabbit into the air.

How do they make long-life milk?

MOST OF US WOULDN'T consider drinking milk that has sat on the supermarket shelf *unrefrigerated* for some three months. Then again, many people, especially those without small children, have never heard of ultrahigh-temperature (UHT) milk.

Farm Best milk, made by Dairymen in Savannah, Georgia, is one of a number of long-shelf-life milks now available. You'll find it not in the dairy section but probably along with boxes or cans of juice that are not refrigerated. How can it sit there so long without spoiling?

First, this milk is processed at 280 degrees Fahrenheit rather than at 170 degrees Fahrenheit, the normal temperature for pasteurizing milk. The high temperatures kill microorganisms that might escape unscathed by conventional processing. What you have, in fact, is sterile milk, totally free of any spores or bacteria that could multiply and cause the milk to spoil.

Secondly, the product is securely packaged to keep out air, light, and bacteria. After the milk has been purified by the UHT process, it is transferred to an aseptic packing machine which loads the milk into sterilized cartons. These sturdy containers are made up of five layers of materials—three polyethylene, one paper, and one aluminum foil—and hermetically sealed. You can keep the cartons for months. Once you open them, you should refrigerate the milk, but even then it won't turn sour for about three weeks.

How do they pick Pulitzer Prize winners?

PULITZER PRIZES ARE AWARDED annually for distinguished work in twenty-two categories of journalism, arts and letters, and music. The fourteen prizes in journalism are meritorious public service, spot news reporting, beat reporting, national reporting, international reporting, investigative reporting, explanatory journalism, editorials, editorial cartoons, spot news photography, feature photography, commentary, criticism, and feature writing. The six arts and letters categories are fiction, drama, general nonfiction, history, biography, and poetry. One prize is awarded in the music category, for a "distinguished musical composition . . . which had its debut in the United States during the year."

The meritorious public service prize is given to an outstanding newspaper; all other prizes go to individuals who have distinguished themselves in their various fields during the year. Unlike Nobel Prizes in literature, which are awarded to writers on the basis of their whole body of work, Pulitzers recognize specific works. John Steinbeck, for example, won the Pulitzer Prize for fiction in 1940, for *The Grapes of Wrath;* in 1962 he won a Nobel Prize in literature for his achievements over the course of a lifetime.

The prizes are administered by Columbia University, which relies on the Pulitzer Prize Board, an eighteen-member body composed of publishing executives and academicians, to select the prize recipients. Because of the huge volume of submissions, the board depends on prize juries to screen the entries. Members of the juries—there is one jury for each prize category—sift through all the entries in their category until they come up with three finalists. Each jury submits its list of finalists to special three-member subcommittees of the board—again, one subcommittee for each prize category. The subcommittees then recommend winners to the full board, which passes the recommendations on to the president of Columbia, who announces the winners. The board rarely rejects a recommendation from one of its subcommittees; the subcommittees rarely overturn the findings of the prize juries. Since 1975, when the trustees of Columbia University withdrew from the Pulitzer process, the president of the university has accepted all of the board's recommendations.

The Pulitzer Prize competition is open to anyone willing to fill out an entry form and remit the $20 entry fee. In journalism, the vast majority of entries are submitted by newspapers, which relish the prestige that comes with winning a Pulitzer. There is no limit to the number of entries a single newspaper can submit; in fact, most large dailies make multiple submissions: in 1990 New York *Newsday* led all comers with forty-one entries, followed by *The Washington Post* and the Associated Press, each with forty. *The New York Times* had thirty-five. A total of 1,770 entries were made that year. The same rules apply to the book awards. Not surprisingly, entries are dominated by large publishing houses. In 1990, 590 different books were submitted: 181 in general nonfiction, 123 in poetry, 115 in fiction, 92 in biography, and 79 in history.

The president of Columbia announces Pulitzer Prize winners at a press conference in early April; the actual judging begins long before that. For books, the process begins on December 31, the entry deadline. A copy of each entered book is sent by the Pulitzer Prize administrator, a Columbia University official, to each member of the five different book juries. Each book category has its own three-member jury, composed of college professors and

129

writers with expertise in the category they oversee. History professors, for example, serve on the history book jury, and novelists serve on the fiction jury.

Jurists for each category have until January to compare notes, usually over the phone, and come up with three finalists to submit to the Pulitzer board. That means a total of fifteen books, three in each of the five book categories, is nominated for judging by the Pulitzer board. Rather than having every board member read all fifteen finalists between January and April, the board breaks down into seven subcommittees of three, with some members serving on more than one panel. There is one subcommittee for each of the five book categories.

Members of the subcommittees have until April to read the books and formulate their opinions. That way, by the time the whole board convenes at Columbia for two days in early April to judge the finalists, the subcommittees will be ready to recommend winners in their respective bailiwicks.

The drama and music juries, each composed of three individuals with expertise in the field they are judging—theater critics in the drama category, composers and music critics in the music category—submit three finalists apiece to the board on March 1. Members of the board's drama subcommittee then have a month to see the plays performed, or, if that is not possible, to read them; the music subcommittee listens to tape recordings of the three nominated compositions to reach its decision. Final recommendations are made to the board as a whole when it assembles in April.

The journalism awards work slightly differently. Each of the thirteen journalism juries has five members rather than three. The thirteen juries (one jury covers both photography categories) gather at Columbia for two days in early March to sift through all of the 1,770 or so entries in fourteen categories and come up with three finalists in each category. The sixty-five jurists, primarily working journalists, editors, publishers, and former Pulitzer winners, are not paid anything for their labor. (Book jurists receive a $1,000 stipend.) At the end of the two-day judgment period each jury nominates three finalists, which will then be submitted to the Pulitzer board for final judgment. Juries list their nominations in alphabetical order and do not indicate any preference among the three finalists. A total of forty-two nominations in fourteen journalism categories are made to the Pulitzer board.

When deciding among the journalism finalists, the board does not divide into subcommittees. Each final entry is read by all eighteen board members during the two-day judgment period in April. Winners are picked by a vote of the board. Since the board is composed of editors and publishers, many of whose newspapers are involved in the competition, rules have been adopted to prevent a conflict of interest. A board member must leave the room when entries from his newspaper are being discussed. A board member is not allowed to vote in any category that includes an entry from his newspaper.

The Pulitzer Prizes have been called the Academy Awards of journalism, and like the Academy Awards they have suffered their share of controversy. Since 1917, when the prizes were first given from a trust established by newspaper magnate Joseph Pulitzer in his will, many dubious choices have been made. In 1941 for example, Hemingway's *For Whom the Bell Tolls* was rejected on the grounds that it was "offensive and lascivious." The board awarded no fiction prize that year. More recently, in 1981, Janet Cooke of *The Washington Post* received the prize for feature writing for "Jimmy's World," a story about an eight-year-old heroin addict living in Washington, D.C., which included eyewitness accounts of "Jimmy" shooting up. It turned out that the reporter had completely made up the story, and the *Post* had to give up the award.

Despite the Pulitzers' long history of controversy, only two winners have ever refused their prizes: Sinclair Lewis, who won for his novel *Arrowsmith*, in 1926, and William Saroyan, who won for his play *The Time of Your Life*, in 1940. "All prizes, like all titles, are dangerous," Lewis wrote in rejecting his Pulitzer. Even so, he had no problem accepting a Nobel four years later.

131

Pulitzer Prize For Fiction

2003, Middlesex
Jeffrey Eugenides

2002, Empire Falls
Richard Russo

2001, The Amazing
Adventures of Kavalier &
Clay
Michael Chabon

2000, Interpreter of Maladies
Jhumpa Lahiri

1999, The Hours
Michael Cunningham

1998, American Pastoral
Philip Roth

1997, Martin Dressler
Steven Millhauser

1996, Independence Day
Richard Ford

1995, The Stone Diaries
Carol Shields

1994, The Shipping News
E. Annie Proulx

1993, A Good Scent from a
Strange Mountain
Robert Olen Butler

1992, A Thousand Acres
Jane Smiley

1991, Rabbit at Rest
John Updike

1990, The Mambo Kings Play
Songs of Love
Oscar Hijuelos

1989, Breathing Lessons
Anne Tyler

1988, Beloved
Toni Morrison

1987, A Summons to
Memphis
Peter Taylor

1986, Lonesome Dove
Larry McMurtry

1985, Foreign Affairs
Alison Lurie

1984, Ironweed
William Kennedy

1983, The Color Purple
Alice Walker

1982, Rabbit Is Rich
John Updike

1981, A Confederacy of
Dunces
John Kennedy Toole

1980, The Executioner's
Song
Norman Mailer

1979, The Stories of John
Cheever
John Cheever

1978, Elbow Room
James Alan McPherson

1976, Humboldt's Gift
Saul Bellow

1975, The Killer Angels
Michael Shaara

1973, The Optimist's
Daughter
Eudora Welty

1972, Angle of Repose
Wallace Stegner

1970, Collected Stories
Jean Stafford

1969, House Made of Dawn
N. Scott Momaday

1968, The Confessions of
Nat Turner
William Styron

1967, The Fixer
Bernard Malamud

1966, Collected Stories of
Katherine Anne Porter
Katherine Anne Porter

1965, The Keepers of the
House
Shirley Ann Grau

1963, The Reivers
William Faulkner

1962, The Edge of Sadness
Edwin O'Connor

1961, To Kill a Mockingbird
Harper Lee

1960, Advise and Consent
Allen Drury

1959, The Travels of
Jaimie McPheeters
Robert Lewis Taylor

1958, A Death in the Family
James Agee

1956, Andersonville
MacKinlay Kantor

1955, A Fable
William Faulkner

1953, The Old Man and
the Sea
Ernest Hemingway

1952, The Caine Mutiny
Herman Wouk

1951, The Town
Conrad Richter

1950, The Way West
A. B. Guthrie Jr.

1949, Guard of Honor
James Gould Cozzens

1948, Tales of the South
Pacific
James A. Michener

1947, All the King's Men
Robert Penn Warren

1945, A Bell for Adano
John Hersey

1944, Journey in the Dark
Martin Flavin

1943, Dragon's Teeth
Upton Sinclair

1942, In This Our Life
Ellen Glasgow

1940, The Grapes of Wrath
John Steinbeck

1939, The Yearling
Marjorie Kinnan Rawlings

1938, The Late George Apley
John Phillips Marquand

1937, Gone with the Wind
Margaret Mitchell

1936, Honey in the Horn
Harold L. Davis

1935, Now in November
Josephine Winslow Johnson

1934, Lamb in His Bosom
Caroline Miller

1933, The Store
T. S. Stribling

1932, The Good Earth
Pearl S. Buck

1931, Years of Grace
Margaret Ayer Barnes

1930, Laughing Boy
Oliver La Farge

1929, Scarlet Sister Mary
Julia Peterkin

1928, The Bridge of San Luis Rey
Thornton Wilder

1927, Early Autumn
Louis Bromfield

1926, Arrowsmith
Sinclair Lewis

1925, So Big
Edna Ferber

1924, The Able McLaughlins
Margaret Wilson

1923, One of Ours
Willa Cather

1922, Alice Adams
Booth Tarkington

1921, The Age of Innocence
Edith Wharton

1919, The Magnificent Ambersons
Booth Tarkington

1918, His Family
Ernest Poole

?

How do they measure the unemployment rate?

EVERY MONTH, the Census Bureau surveys 59,500 American households, asking members about their current work habits. Once the data is in, the census takers ship it over to the Bureau of Labor Statistics, where analysts weigh the figures to project the national rate of unemployment.

To arrive at an unemployment figure, labor statisticians first determine the size of the work force, which equals all employed persons plus all unemployed persons. Children under sixteen years of age, prison inmates, and patients in mental institutions, sanitariums, and homes for the aged, infirm, and needy are excluded from the labor force. Not every jobless person qualifies as unemployed. Some are independently wealthy, some are retired, and others are just layabouts. Technically, by government definition, an unemployed person is "a civilian who had no work during the survey week, was available for work, and had made specific efforts to find employment during the prior four weeks." Laid-off workers who are waiting to be recalled to their jobs are automatically counted as unemployed, whether or not they are looking for alternative jobs. The unemployment rate is calculated by dividing the number of unemployed people by the number of people in the labor force. So, if survey figures show that the 59,500 sample households contain 80,000 workers and an additional 20,000 people who are of age and would like to work but have been thwarted in their attempts to find jobs, it means the work force stands at 100,000. By dividing the 20,000 would-be workers by the total labor force of 100,000, one arrives at the jobless rate, in this case 20 percent.

Strictly speaking, the jobless rate applies only to the 59,500 households that answered the government survey, but since the control group represents an accurate demographic cross section of the American public, the Bureau of Labor Statistics weighs the returns to arrive at a national number. Households from all fifty states and the District of Columbia are represented in the monthly sample, which covers 729 areas in more than 1,000 cities and counties. Any occupied living unit, excluding jails and long-term health-care facilities, is eligible for interview. A typical sample group might include single-family dwellings, apartment complexes, public housing units, and homeless shelters. People without any residential address, such as the unsheltered homeless, are not represented in the survey.

In order to keep the survey fresh, the sample households are constantly rotated. The total sample group of 59,500 households is broken down into eight subgroups, each of which is interviewed for a total of eight months. In any one month of the survey, one eighth of the respondents are new, one eighth are in their second month, one eighth are in their third month, and so on up to the final eighth who are in their final month of enumeration. The rotation system is designed to reduce statistical discontinuity by ensuring a 75 percent overlap of subgroups from month to month and a 50 percent overlap from year to year.

The survey is now a little over fifty years old. Begun in 1940, the business of counting the country's unemployed was originally a WPA project, conceived as a way to put people to work.

How do they interview and hire simultaneous interpreters at the United Nations?

THE UNITED NATIONS EMPLOYS 142 simultaneous interpreters, whose job it is to orally translate speeches at the very moment they are being delivered. A simultaneous interpreter listens to words spoken in one language and instantly relates in another language what is being said. Unlike translating a written document from one language to another, simultaneous interpretation is live—it is done almost instantaneously, without recourse to reference books or other aids. The work has been likened to "driving a car that has a steering wheel but no brakes and no reverse."

All UN speeches are simultaneously interpreted into each of the organization's six working languages: Arabic, Chinese, English, French, Russian, and Spanish. A UN diplomat who wants to use a language other than one of these six—Tamil, say, or Quechua—must provide his own interpreter.

The first step toward becoming a UN staff interpreter is to

135

take a comprehensive language test, which is open to anyone with a college degree in languages. The exam consists of oral and written sections that are designed to test speed, accuracy, clarity of accent, and familiarity with idiom. The UN administers tests when it decides it needs more interpreters. It may be given at any of the UN's sixty-seven information offices scattered around the world.

A job candidate who passes the test is granted a personal interview so that the UN may learn more about the candidate's character and background. Interpreters must be able to interpret all speakers accurately and dispassionately, regardless of their own political opinions. Since interpretation is more a scholarly exercise than a political one, candidates are not screened specifically for political biases. Such policing is not necessary: a staff interpreter who editorializes on the job will not last long at the UN. Although the interview is not, theoretically at least, a further test of language skills, the interviewer might well use more than one language during the session; once a person has passed the test, the superiority of his language skills is accepted without question.

A few things can happen to a candidate who successfully negotiates the interview. If there are staff openings, the candidate can be recruited for a job, sometimes just on a temporary basis to help out when the work load is especially heavy. If there are no immediate openings, he can be placed on a roster of qualified candidates from which future openings will be filled. UN officials have found, though, that many test takers are angling for an altogether different option: a letter of recommendation that says they have been positively screened for UN interpretation. That letter can be worth quite a bit more in the private sector than at the UN, where salaries for simultaneous interpreters start at just over $20,000 a year—scarcely a livable income in New York City.

?

How do they spread a computer virus?

A COMPUTER VIRUS IS a piece of written code that copies itself, spreads itself around, and tells a computer what to do. It might, for example, infect all the IBM-compatible computers it can, and on the next Friday the 13th, find all the decimal points in the data where it is and move them one digit to the right. Or it might simply destroy all the data and write "Gotcha!" on the screen.

Human viruses are spread by all sorts of contact. Anyone who works in an open office knows how fast a cold can spread, with everyone sneezing on each other, sharing telephones, shaking hands. Computers obviously don't sneeze. But they have plenty of chances to come in contact with each other, and every contact is a chance to transmit a computer virus.

Virus codes can be added to the lines of written code that make up computer programs, hidden among thousands of lines of commands that tell the computer what to do, and when. A computer hacker—one of those highly capable computer programmers who works day and night at his keyboard—could write a virus into a "bootleg" program before giving a copy of the disk to a colleague. Once the disk is inserted into a healthy computer, the virus copies itself onto other program files on the main computer and even into the computer's operating system, its brain.

The next time anyone inserts a disk into the infected computer to play a computer game, the new disk will be infected too. Or if the computer sends some program by modem, the virus goes along. And when the computer taps into a network, the virus

137

sends itself, too. Traveling by network, a virus can infect hundreds of thousands of computers in just a few hours. Most viruses are started by one person who's up to no good, but very few are *spread* intentionally.

In 1988, a Cornell University computer science graduate student created a virus and released it into two networks that scientists use for exchanging information. The student meant only to show off his skills by gaining access to hundreds of research facilities' computers. But the virus went wild, replicating itself faster than the student ever intended and crippling computers all over the United States. The Computer Virus Industry Association estimated that $98 million was spent to clean up the damages left in its path.

Expert hackers have proven themselves capable of finding access to corporate and federal government computers and leaving virus code behind. Sometimes this is done through "trapdoors," the secret ways into a system that avoid the usual security measures like passwords.

In 1988 the Chaos Computer Club of West Germany gained access to NASA's computer and maintained access for five months before being discovered. Its members claim to have left behind viruses that will activate in the future, although NASA's own computer experts deny this.

Virus guards—codes written by the good guys—have helped curb the spread of viruses. They can detect typical virus language (and some can detect particular, known viruses) before the infected program runs on a computer.

---?---

How do they get the caffeine out of coffee?

THE BITTER, WHITE SUBSTANCE caffeine makes up only about one percent of the composition of coffee beans. The U.S. Food and Drug Administration requires 97 percent of that tiny amount to be removed before the label may say "decaffeinated," and some manufacturers do even better than that.

The difficult part of the decaffeination process, as any coffee lover can attest, is to maintain the rich flavor and aroma of regular coffee. Coffee beans contain more than a hundred chemical compounds, and it is virtually impossible to replicate coffee's aroma in the lab. During decaffeination, many of those compounds leak out of the bean. Getting only the caffeine out, and leaving those compounds in is the trick. And it's not just the consumer who benefits from good extraction processes: pure caffeine drawn from the beans is sold to pharmaceutical and soda companies.

The method of caffeine extraction most commonly used by manufacturers removes the caffeine by means of an "agent," or solvent. The agent used is either methylene chloride, which is also used in degreasing fluids, and ethyl acetate, a substance found in fruits.

The agent method can employ either a direct or an indirect process. In direct processing, green coffee beans are steamed for at least a half hour to soften them, open their pores and loosen the caffeine molecules. Then they are rinsed in the agent over and over again for hours. The solution and the caffeine are drained off and the beans are steamed again for several hours to drive out all traces of the agent, and finally dried.

139

In the indirect process, the green coffee beans are soaked in hot water for several hours to extract the caffeine; the water draws off a slew of flavorings, too. The watery solution, then, rather than the beans, is treated with an agent to remove the caffeine, and heated so the agent and the caffcine evaporate together. The rest of the solution and flavorings are returned to the beans and the beans are dried.

It's generally believed that almost none of the agent is left in coffee beans after either process is completed. Furthermore, roasting evaporates most of the few traces that are left. Still, consumer concern over the use of these chemicals has led some manufacturers to favor yet another method of decaffeination: the Swiss Water Process. This method calls for soaking the beans in water for a day, then running the watery solution through charcoal or carbon filters that sponge off the caffeine. Afterwards, the water is recirculated with the beans and the beans are dried. This takes longer than other methods, and some people think it doesn't return as much of the flavor to the beans as other methods. Other people say it has improved over the years. Anyway, a lot of consumers are willing to pay the extra cents per pound for what seems a natural way to decaffeinate.

Yet another method uses oils from spent coffee grounds. The beans sit for several hours at high temperatures in a container filled with decaffeinated coffee oils. Triglycerides in the oils pick off the caffeine in the fresh beans, which are then drained and dried.

Coffee companies are trying out a new method, using "super-critical" carbon dioxide, a pressurized liquid-gas similar to the carbon dioxide that effervesces in your soda can. Pumped through a vat of beans, the stuff seems remarkably capable of picking off the caffeine and then vanishing completely.

?

How do they test golf balls before offering them for sale?

THE UNITED STATES GOLF ASSOCIATION enforces strict standards governing the characteristics of golf balls. An official ball must not weigh more than 1.620 ounces; it must have a diameter of at least 1.680 inches; it must be spherically symmetrical; the velocity of the ball must not exceed 250 feet per second when launched by a USGA-approved mechanical striker; the ball must not travel farther than 280 yards when struck by a standard testing apparatus at the USGA proving grounds.

When golf ball manufacturers want to introduce a new product, they set up a pilot run to produce a limited number of new balls. The balls are tested at the manufacturer's in-house research and development labs. The tests determine what production changes must be made for the balls to meet USGA specifications. After passing in-house testing, sample balls are sent to the USGA headquarters in Far Hills, New Jersey, for official USGA testing. If the balls make the grade, the manufacturer calibrates the factory machinery to duplicate the approved ball and proceeds with a full production run, making the balls that will finally be stamped, packaged, and sold. Select balls from this run are tested for deviation; if any flaws are detected, the machines are readjusted until the production-run balls meet USGA requirements.

The USGA testing facilities include three indoor laboratories. In the first lab, balls are tested for spherical symmetry and for behavior when struck. The USGA impact standard holds that a ball should remain in contact with the driver clubface for

0.000450 seconds. To test this, an air gun fires balls at a metal plate and a computer records the amount of time the ball spends in contact with the plate and the velocity at which it rebounds. Conformity to the symmetry standard, which maintains that a ball must fly the same height, the same distance, and remain in flight for the same length of time regardless of how it is placed on the tee, is tested with the help of Iron Byron, a robotic golfer. Iron Byron has the ultimate golf body: one club connected directly to a mechanical shoulder, with no knees, hips, back, head, or other mobile parts to interfere with his perfect swing. He always hits the standard ball 280 yards, with a 6 percent margin of error. Since Iron Byron is perfectly consistent, any deviation in the flight of the driven ball must stem from the ball.

The aerodynamics lab consists of a wind tunnel, slightly longer than six feet, where balls are tested for flight properties such as backspin and wind resistance. The flight trajectory of a golf ball is the product of its dimples, which create an air flow pattern that reduces wind resistance, and of the backspin that is the normal result of hitting a ball with a club. To measure "lift force," the air flow pattern created by a dimpled, back-spinning ball, testers mount a golf ball in a vise-like device in the wind tunnel and buffet it with high-speed air streams that simulate the wind currents experienced by a golf ball in flight. By recording the effect of wind on the mounted ball, technicians are able to measure lift force and predict how it would perform under ordinary conditions.

The third lab, where size testing is done, is kept at a constant temperature of 23 degrees Celsius to prevent the balls from shrinking or swelling because of temperature changes. The size test consists of dropping balls through a ring gauge equal in diameter to the legal ball minimum—1.680 inches. A test victory is declared if fewer than twenty-five out of one hundred randomly dropped balls pass through the ring. This lab is also where balls are measured for initial velocity, or the speed of the ball off the clubface. To test for initial velocity, balls are launched into the air by a mechanical striker that has been adjusted to send the balls flying at a speed of 250 feet per second, the legal limit. The flight of the ball is measured photoelectrically, and any ball that exceeds 250 feet per second, plus or minus 2 percent, is deemed too springy.

After passing the indoor lab tests, the new batch of balls is taken out to the test range to be checked for conformity to the overall distance standard. Iron Byron strokes bucket after bucket of balls 280 yards straight down the fairway. If too many of the test balls resist Byron, either by soaring too far or falling short, the batch is discarded as faulty.

Golf ball manufacturers produce thousands of test balls, none of which are ever labeled or sold, before making a single ball for retail. The balls carried by sporting goods stores have not themselves been tested, but represent instead exact duplications of successful test balls.

?

How do they see a black hole?

THEY DON'T, ACTUALLY. A black hole is created by the collapse of an aged and massive star, and its gravitational force is so strong that it draws in even the light around it that would make it visible. And even if black holes were visible, their small size would still make them hard to see from Earth; some are only two or three miles across.

However, the location of black holes can be deduced by their strong effect on what's around them. If an ordinary star is near a black hole, for example, hydrogen and helium gases from the star's outer layers will spiral into the hole. As they do, they become highly compressed and heat up, giving off high-frequency radiation including X rays. Astronomers record the otherwise inexplicable radiation between the star and its invisible companion with sensitive satellites outside the earth's atmosphere. As many as six X-ray sources that almost certainly involve black holes in our galaxy have been detected with satellites.

If a very massive black hole is at the center of a galaxy or a star cluster, astronomers will also note increases in the velocities and densities of stars as they approach the area where the hole probably is. This is because the black hole's force, although it will not always pull the stars directly into itself, affects the movement and even the weights of the bodies around it.

---?---

How do they get the music onto a CD?

IN MARCH 1983 a new technology appeared on the U.S. music scene that would make the traditional LP record a mere item of nostalgia, a curio to be picked up at yard sales by baby boomers. The digital compact disc (CD) marked a radical departure in quality and convenience from the twelve-inch long-playing record.

The LP is an analog recording, which means it is an analogy or model of the actual music. Sound is stored in continuous grooves, whose side-to-side squiggles and variations in depth correspond to the original audio signal. A stylus running along the groove converts the mechanical motion into an electrical signal, which is then amplified by your speakers. A nice system, but not without its flaws. Records can warp and develop mysterious crackles. Small children with sticky hands need only handle them once to leave lasting reminders. And the mere action of the stylus running over the surface hundreds of times can result in wear that causes hissing and static.

The musical information on a CD, on the other hand, is engraved on a disc that is safely sandwiched between two protective layers of plastic. A laser beam—not a stylus—scans the disc to reproduce the audio signal; thus there is no mechanical damage, be it the first or thousandth time you play the disc.

The CD is a digital recording, which means that the information is broken down into discrete values. In this case, each nuance of sound is assigned a numerical value in a binary code, that is, strings of ones and zeros. Each *second* of music is sliced into 4.3 million discrete units and then coded. The code is engraved on the CD in the form of microscopic pits—some fifteen thousand per inch or 3 billion per disc.

The making of a CD is a complex and *clean* affair. Workers wearing plastic jumpsuits and visored headgear operate in a "clean room," in which no more than one thousand particles of dust per cubic foot is permitted. A single speck of dust settling in one of those tiny pits could be disastrous. Production starts with a circle of ultraclean optical glass, which has been coated with an adhesive chrome layer and photographic film. The music to be stored on the CD is now in the form of a digital tape with binary data. A computer plays the tape and assigns precise pit measurements to each element in the code. The glass plate, meanwhile, rotates, and a laser beam marks the photographic film with millions of indentations corresponding to the pit sizes determined by the computer. Once completed, the disc is coated with nickel. Then technicians make a metal cast of the master, with microscopic peaks corresponding to the pits. From this cast come metal stampers, which are inserted into injection-molding machines where they impress load after load of melted polycarbon-

The first step in making a CD is to break the sound into discrete units, each of which is assigned a value in binary code and stored on digital tape. Next, a laser burns the binary code in the form of pits into photographic film on the CD master. A laser beam in your CD player scans the microscopic pits and reproduces the audio signal.

Recording

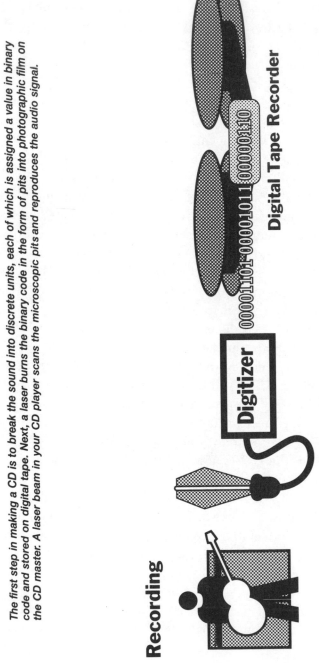

Digitizer

0000110100000101100000110

Digital Tape Recorder

Mastering and Copying

00001101 00001011 00001

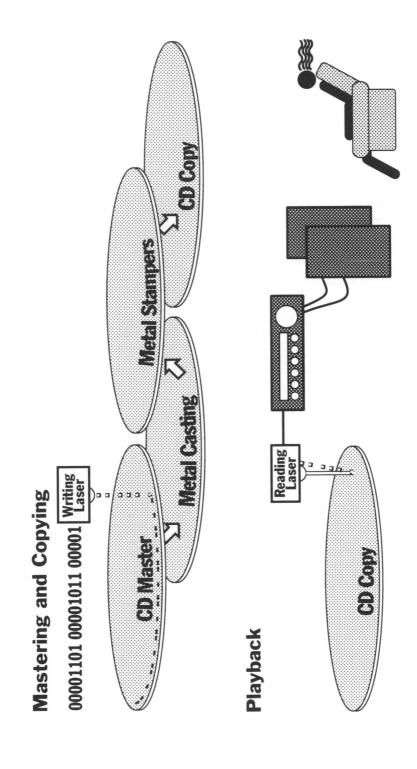

CD Master

Writing Laser

Metal Casting

Metal Stampers

CD Copy

Playback

Reading Laser

CD Copy

atc plastic to produce the actual CDs. Finally, the impeccably clean, precise disc is covered with aluminum and a protective resin, then dried by ultraviolet light. In your hand, safely stored in millions of pits, lies seventy-five minutes of ageless sound.

?

How do they make the Hudson River drinkable?

SURPRISINGLY, the first impurity to consider in the Hudson is salt, which is easier to avoid altogether than to remove. That's why the five communities in New York State that draw drinking water regularly from the river—Waterford, Highland Falls, Port Ewen, Rhinebeck, and Poughkeepsie—are all located north of the "salt front," which floats between West Point and Poughkeepsie. Here the Atlantic Ocean meets the Adirondack springs; the dense, heavy salt water forms a kind of wedge below the sweet water, which can be siphoned off for water treatment. New York City draws on the Hudson only in a drought emergency, but it pipes the water from upstate, and even then, river water may constitute no more than 10 percent of the supply.

Douglas Fairbanks, Jr., (no relation to the actor) is chief operator of the Poughkeepsie water treatment plant, which processes 11 to 12 million gallons of water a day. He claims, "People have a misconception of the river. Communities have really buckled down in the last ten or fifteen years and stopped dumping raw sewage into the river. And testing has shown that there are no dangerous chemicals there in any significant quantity. By all the criteria that are available to judge these things, the Hudson is an excellent source [of drinking water]."

148

But not everybody agrees with Fairbanks; the question lies in how you measure the water's purity. In the nineteenth century, civil engineers concerned themselves with bacteria and the spread of infectious diseases such as cholera and typhoid. Now scientists are studying the long-range effects of newer kinds of waste.

Says Cara Lee, environmental director of the civic organization Scenic Hudson, "The federal government doesn't have water quality standards for a lot of carcinogenic substances. Every year the Hudson receives 200,000 pounds of industrial toxins that are known or suspected to cause cancer in people: lead, cadmium, mercury, PCBs, pesticides, dioxins. The water-treatment plants test for bacteria and pathogenic organisms almost every day; they test for these toxins very infrequently, if at all." Lee cites studies showing that traces of these chemicals may cause cancer and disorders of the nervous system, and affect fetal development over the long term.

Susan Shaw, an environmental engineer with the Public Water Supply Section of the Environmental Protection Agency (EPA) in New York, doesn't deny Lee's claims. "The EPA can't regulate every substance in the river. We have standards for the most common ones," she explains. "There are always going to be some pollutants where there are industries discharging."

The same spirit of compromise underlies the EPA's stand on chlorination. When chlorine atoms bond with naturally occurring acids in the water, they form trihalomethanes (THMs) such as chloroform and bromoform, which are associated with cancer of the intestine, bladder and rectum. "We'd like to see a balance," states Shaw. "You need enough chlorine to provide adequate disinfection for waterborne diseases, which are an acute risk to health. A whole town could get gastroenteritis. But we have to weigh the long-term chronic exposure to disinfection by-products."

Apparently the EPA has been experimenting with filtering out natural acids before chlorination and with substituting ozone as a disinfection agent, but the agency aims to lower the levels of

THMs, not to eliminate them. Right now the EPA allows up to one hundred micrograms of THMs per liter; some activists are trying to reduce that figure to twenty. How many micrograms per liter in the Poughkeepsie plant? Fairbanks says sixty to sixty-five.

Here's how Poughkeepsie's traditional water filter system works:

The river water is pumped into floculators—enormous, rectangular concrete basins divided in two, each with a million-gallon capacity. The plant supervisor adds a mixture of chemicals that includes alum. The chemicals attract the sediment and particles in the water, which include such pollutants as bacteria, viruses, rocks, plant matter, and sewage. The pollutants and chemicals clump together and settle at the bottom of the floculators. Two to four hours later, the water is pumped into the second half of the basin as a pipe feeds in a precise flow of chlorine to kill any remaining microorganisms.

The water from the basins flows through a filter to remove the tiniest particles which have escaped coagulation. The filter is composed of blocks of perforated tile that hold two or three graduated layers of stone; the stone ranges in size from peas to golf balls, getting coarser toward the bottom. Next, the plant supervisors add fluoride and also treat the water for "corrosivity," by mixing in lime, a process that makes the water more alkaline so that it won't eat into pipes and release toxic metals like lead.

And then you have drinkable water. Or do you?

How do they pack Neapolitan ice cream?

DESPITE WHAT CERTAIN NOSTALGIA-HAPPY entrepreneurs would have you believe, ice cream production is a big, industrial business. The United States produces more than 900 million gallons of ice cream every year. During the first half of this century ice cream tycoons opened vast plants where noisy stainless steel machines replaced the old hand-cranked wooden ice cream freezer. In addition to increasing productivity, the new equipment allowed for the perfection of the Neapolitan brick's tri-flavored parallelism.

The three individual elements that together make a carton of Neapolitan—chocolate, vanilla, and strawberry—are frozen in separate ice cream freezers. When the ice cream attains a stiffness desirable for packing, the three freezers pump their flavors into distinct compartments of a rectangular device called a header. The header molds the ice cream into a manageable brick, and then the contents of all three compartments are simultaneously extruded into a waiting box. Because the flavors settle differently in the box, surface area is not divided equally among the three flavors.

The label Neapolitan was originally used to designate a layered ice cream that included Italian ice, preferably orange or lemon, among its constituent parts. The people of Naples, it seems, were pioneers in the field of ice cream development. Marco Polo brought the original recipes for water ices to Italy from China in the thirteenth century. Neapolitan, by the way, is

151

now the fourth most popular ice cream category, surpassed only by vanilla, candy confection mixes, and chocolate.

?

How do they make sure condoms won't break?

A ROMANTIC INTERLUDE isn't the only time people worry about condoms breaking. Manufacturers worry about it all the time. So they put the condoms through elaborate tests to make sure they're leakproof and strong.

The key ingredient in the success of the multimillion-dollar modern condom industry—Americans buy some 420 million of them a year—is latex. It's strong, light, and malleable. The manufacture of condoms begins with huge vats of liquid latex, containing anywhere from 250 to 1,000 gallons. The liquid is tested for consistency and filtered through cheesecloth to remove impurities. Once a batch of quick-drying liquid latex is ready, machines dip glass condom molds, called mandrels, into the opaque, viscous fluid. The liquid latex adheres in a thin film to the cylindrical mandrels; the film dries when exposed to air. After the film of latex has dried, the mandrels are dipped into the vat a second time to achieve a double thickness. The process is something like taking a plaster of Paris mold of an object, except in this case the molding material is thin and elastic.

After condoms have been shaped they're stretched by 15 percent onto large steel molds, and tension and strength tests are performed. The condom-encased steel molds are dipped into a vat of charged water. If the electric charge passes through the condom to the steel rod, the condom is discarded as faulty. In a

152

second test, pumps fill the condoms with water to make sure they don't leak. A number of condoms from each production batch are also randomly selected to undergo the inflation test: condoms are blown up like balloons to see how much pressure they can withstand. Industry guidelines specify that condoms have a breaking volume of an almost unbelievable twenty-five liters or more.

Condoms that pass the battery of tests are rolled off the mandrels and hermetically sealed in foil. Depending on the model, a water-based silicon lubrication might be applied to the product before it is packaged. The tensile strength of latex allows condoms to be rolled off the smooth rods as easily as a sock can be rolled down a leg. On the fully automated production line the rolling is done by cylindrical devices that slide down the mandrels, pushing and rolling the condoms free. Human workers monitor the system for glitches.

Latex, which is made by mixing synthetic chemical compounds with the sap of the rubber tree, was developed in the 1930s. Coupled with mechanized production, the new material made inexpensive, reliable condoms a practical reality for the first time ever. In the late nineteenth and early twentieth centuries, condoms were commonly made of vulcanized rubber. The old material was relatively bulky and, as they say in the business, unresponsive.

Vulcanized "rubbers" were, however, less expensive than natural-membrane condoms, which have been around since at least 1350 BC, when Egyptian men of the upper class wore them as decorative sheaths. A natural-membrane condom is made from a sheep's cecum, an intestinal appendage similar to the appendix. You can make only one condom per sheep, and the production process is laborious, both factors contributing to the expense of the item. Such devices were commonly used by men of means right through the eighteenth century. In fact, natural-membrane condoms are still available, at a cost of about four times that of latex models. Advocates claim they are more sensitive and conduct heat better.

Recent condom innovations include adhesive strips around

the open end and large-size condoms. The adhesive condom was developed by Carter-Wallace, whose Trojan brand is the U.S. best-seller. Company officials say the adhesive band will prevent slippage, thereby providing additional comfort and security. A number of companies are currently manufacturing bigger-than-average-sized condoms, the norm being seven and a half inches long and 2.08 inches in diameter. Although there apparently isn't any great physiological need for them, research done by the Kinsey Institute indicates some psychological need might exist: 70 percent of the men contacted in one poll said they would be happy if their condoms were larger.

?

How do they make stainproof carpets?

E. I. DU PONT DE NEMOURS AND COMPANY, headquartered in Wilmington, Delaware, was among the first companies to come up with a new technology for making stain-repellent carpets. In the early eighties one of du Pont's research chemists, Armand Zinnato, was developing a nylon fiber that could be dyed at room temperature. He worried that such a fiber would be very susceptible to stains and started applying to the nylon certain agents formerly used to help keep a product colorfast when washed. These agents proved effective in resisting all manner of stains from food.

In September 1986, du Pont launched Stainmaster carpets, guaranteed to resist food stains and even accidents by the dog. How does it work? Before the carpet is made, the nylon fiber is dyed. During the dying process, technicians heat the fiber to a high temperature and then apply a top-secret stain-resistant chemical, which seals the microscopic pores of the fiber. Just as a sealant on a molar prevents tooth-harming bacteria from getting at the tooth, so the chemical envelops each fiber in a protective sheath. Spills merely sit on the nylon's surface and so can be mopped up with a sponge, just as the commercials demonstrate.

Later in the manufacturing process, after the carpet has been made, the nylon is sprayed with fluorocarbons that provide surface protection against soil. After much wear and tear, this treatment rubs off, but the stain-resisting chemicals locked into the fiber continue to work.

How do they teach a bear to ride a bicycle?

BEAR CUBS AND HUMAN CUBS are built in kind of the same way: they're sturdy, fairly well balanced, and capable of walking upright. In addition, they both put their heels down first when they walk. So for trainers at the Ringling Brothers and Barnum & Bailey Circus, where bears have been performing since the turn of the century, teaching a cub to ride a bike is almost like taking a kid out with his first two-wheeler.

The bear is given a small bicycle with training wheels and a custom seat to fit its bearish behind. Stirrups hold its rear paws on the pedals; the bear leans forward with its front paws on the handlebars. The trainer pushes or gently pulls the bike to familiarize the bear with the pedals turning. Once the bear can pedal pretty well itself, the training wheels are lifted. The bear's first solo run with no side wheels is bound to include a few spills, but it has thick fur and decent balance, so it gets few bumps and practically no scraped knees.

A bear cub can be frustrating during these training sessions because it's so playful at this age and its attention span is short; it doesn't always feel quite like staying on the seat. But the cub can be coaxed into compliance with food and praise. Trainers say that bicycling isn't as foreign to bears as people may think. If the cub trusts its trainer and if it gets lots of positive reinforcement (i.e., more food and praise), then its riding a bicycle is no different from a dog darting after a Frisbee. Bears also can learn to juggle, jump rope, bounce on a trampoline, walk a tightwire and ride a motorcycle.

?

How do they measure the ozone layer?

CONCERN ABOUT THE DEPLETION of atmospheric ozone really took off in the mid-eighties when scientists of the British Antarctic Survey first detected an ozone "hole" over their research station on Halley Bay. They found that the springtime quantity of ozone over Antarctica had decreased by more than 40 percent between 1977 and 1984. The "hole," or area of extreme ozone depletion, was even wider than Antarctica and, extending from about seven and a half miles above earth to a little over fifteen miles above, spanned most of the lower stratosphere where atmospheric ozone is concentrated.

Ozone is simply a form of oxygen with a slightly different chemical composition: it comprises three atoms (O_3) rather than two (O_2). Ironically, this substance is toxic to human beings and other animals when it occurs at the lowest levels of the atmosphere. In the stratosphere, however, ozone is essential to maintain life of any kind on Earth. The ozone layer not only protects human beings from skin cancer by screening out harmful ultraviolet radiation, but it also protects the most elementary organisms in the food chain (bacteria, algae, protozoa) from lethal damage to their genes. The largest concentration of ozone is found in the lower stratosphere, from about nine and a half to nineteen miles above earth (fifteen to thirty kilometers), where it attains more than a thousand times the normal peak concentration in the air we breathe. Chemicals that dissociate ozone to oxygen by knocking off its extra molecule—namely nitrogen oxides and chlorine, each atom of which has the ability to destroy multitudes of ozone molecules—can remain in the stratosphere for years, devastating the ozone layer.

How have scientists learned so much about the ozone layer? Basically, through instruments on the ground, in balloons, in airplanes, and on orbiting satellites.

Ground-based equipment measures solar radiation at slightly different wavelengths, some of which are known to be readily absorbed by ozone, and some of which are known to pass through it. If, over time, scientists find there are more of the wavelengths that can be absorbed by ozone than the kind that cannot, they deduce that ozone is decreasing. Conversely, if absorbable-wavelength radiation decreases, ozone has increased. From such measurements the thickness of the ozone layer is calculated.

In 1987 a map of the ozone cover and hole over the Antarctic was created on the basis of data collected on board NASA's *Nimbus 7* satellite by the Total Ozone Mapping Spectrometer (TOMS). At the same time, 150 scientists drawn from around the world participated in the Airborne Antarctic Ozone Experiment in which specially outfitted, medium-altitude, long-range DC-8 and high-altitude NASA-ER2 airplanes measured the ozone-depleted region's size and chemistry. In addition to the renowned "hole," they found more widespread ozone loss over the Southern Hemisphere and markedly higher amounts of chlorine monoxide

157

(a constituent element of the chlorofluorocarbons—CFCs—that are believed to be major culprits in ozone destruction) than those at other latitudes. They also found severely depressed levels of nitrogen oxides that can protect ozone by hindering chlorine's ability to attack it. A polar-orbiting satellite continues to track the development of the ozone hole over time, relaying its information to the Goddard Space Flight Center in Greenbelt, Maryland.

Long-term records show that ozone levels over the Arctic ice-cap have dropped roughly 5 to 6 percent over the last seventeen years. Recently a hole has been observed over the most northern latitudes in the spring. A team of one hundred scientists, with over $10 million funding supplied by NASA and NOAA (National Oceanic and Atmospheric Administration), has just completed a study of this hole and the role of man-made CFCs in causing it. With the aid of airplane- and balloon-borne instruments, the research team found that patches of stratospheric air contained up to fifty times the normal amounts of CFCs' chemical constituents and a significant absence of the protective active nitrogen.

On the basis of the vast bodies of data that have been painstakingly accumulated by scientists, NASA experts now predict that the hole in the Antarctic ozone layer could repair itself by the year 2100. They stipulate, however, that for such repair to occur there would have to be a worldwide phaseout of practically all emissions of CFCs and halon gases by the year 2000. Although the European Community countries are fully behind this and the United States almost as much so, several large industrializing nations have yet to commit themselves.

?

How do they count calories in food?

ENERGY IS TRAPPED in the molecular bonds inside food, and used by the body for all sorts of physical activities: shopping, studying, jogging, reading this book. A calorie is a way to measure that energy—both as it is supplied, and as it is burned.

Energy is discussed in terms of heat. One calorie—the term *calorie* here actually referring to a *kilocalorie*—is the amount of

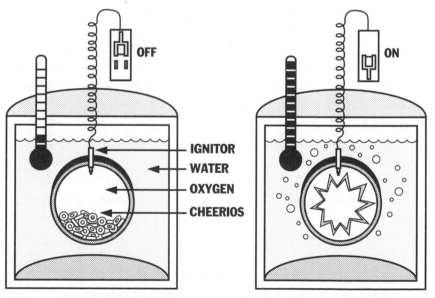

OFF

ON

- IGNITOR
- WATER
- OXYGEN
- CHEERIOS

This bomb calorimeter measures the calorie count in food. Here, some Cheerios are placed in the inner chamber, or "bomb," which is filled with oxygen. The cereal is ignited and burns, increasing the temperature of the water in the outer chamber. The amount of temperature increase is used to calculate the calorie count, or the amount of energy contained in the food.

heat it takes to raise the temperature of one kilogram of water (about a quart) by one degree Celsius. When you read that a bowl of Cheerios and milk has 150 calories, it means that this breakfast contains the energy to raise about 150 quarts of water one degree Celsius.

Obviously, if you added a bowl of Cheerios to a kilogram of water it wouldn't automatically raise the temperature. You have to break the chemical bonds to first release and then to measure the energy. Your body's cells break the bonds and store the energy, and so does a piece of equipment called a bomb calorimeter.

A bomb calorimeter is small enough to sit on a table. It has an inner chamber called a "bomb," and an outer chamber filled with water, and both are surrounded by insulation. The bomb contains only oxygen and an electrical igniter. A thermometer measures the temperature of the water in the outer chamber.

An item of food—for example, that bowl of Cheerios (*without* the bowl, unless you want to know the calorie content of that, too)—is placed inside the inner chamber, and ignited with the fuse. As the Cheerios and milk burn, the chemical bonds in the food are broken, and the water temperature rises in the outer chamber. The thermometer tells us that the cereal and milk have warmed the kilogram of water; we can calculate the calories by how much that amount of water was warmed.

You can probably guess that nutrition researchers hardly use the bomb calorimeter anymore. Using it years ago, they discovered that one gram of pure carbohydrate always supplies 4.10 calories; that one gram of pure protein supplies 5.65 calories (in the body, 4.35 calories), and that one gram of pure fat supplies 9.45 calories. After laboratory analysis of the fat, carbohydrate and protein content, researchers know the makeup of our bowl of Cheerios simply by doing the math. And the U.S. Department of Agriculture has done the math for almost every imaginable kind of food already, and has published the results.

Incidentally, one way to measure the energy used by a person (rather than eaten by a person) is in a device similar to the bomb

calorimeter, but bigger. A person working in the inner chamber burns off calories and the air gets warmer. (Have you ever been in an aerobics room after class? Same thing.) The energy raises the temperature of water in pipes located at the top of the chamber, and we can see how many calories have been burned.

?

How do they know how much money will come out of a cash machine?

WHEN YOU HUSTLE TO the bank for some quick cash, it's easy to wish that that anonymous machine would just once spit out a few extra bills, or accidentally hand out fifties instead of tens. But such fortuitous errors are rare.

Why? Inside an automatic teller machine, or ATM, are bricks of cash in various denominations, stacked in open-ended boxes with up to three thousand bills in each box. When you punch in your secret code and your withdrawal request—of, say, one hundred dollars—a computer in the machine sends signals to your bank's computer, telling it who you are and how much cash you want. If you're good for the money, the computers activate mechanical arms inside the teller machine, and they instruct the arms which bills to select and how many of each. In this case, the computer might designate five twenty-dollar bills.

At the end of the mechanical arm is a suction cup similar to that on a rubber dart toy. A vacuum hose within the cup strengthens its grip. Each arm picks a single bill off the top of the cash brick and passes it into a set of rollers. The arms' movement and suction make the noises you hear while you wait. A less-common

161

system contains rollers that use friction to peel bills off the cash brick. As the bills roll one by one through the conveyor system, they pass between a light beam and a sensor, which measures the typical opacity of a U.S. twenty-dollar bill. (Using the opacity test, ATMs sometimes throw dirty bills into the bin, so banks prefer to use new money if they can get it.) Some machines have a sensitive set of rollers that measures the thickness of single bills as they pass through it. Either way, the machine can calculate how many bills you are getting. If it's more than your allotted one hundred dollars, the conveyor dumps all the money into a bin and tries the transaction again.

If, on your turn, an ATM runs out of twenty-dollar bills, then it will probably tell you it is out of money altogether. However if the machine has other denominations—ten-dollar bills, for example—then the next person to request a withdrawal will be given his cash in tens. So if the teller claims to be dry at first, be sure to try your withdrawal one more time.

?

How does the Pennsylvania Department of Agriculture get mentioned on cereal boxes?

IF YOU'VE EVER FOUND yourself alone at the breakfast table without a newspaper, you've probably resorted to reading the cereal box for diversion. There, along the side of the box, buried deep within the fine print, lies the cryptic notation, "Reg. Penna. Dept. of Agri." What, you may have wondered, does the Pennsylvania Department of Agriculture have to do with your box of cornflakes, made in Michigan and bought at your corner store?

162

The answer dates back to 1933, when the state of Pennsylvania enacted the Pennsylvania Bakery Law. The law was a direct response to the technological revolution of the early twentieth century, which enabled large manufacturing concerns to flood local markets with their goods. Baking became a big business with resourceful state, national, and even international baking companies supplanting small neighborhood bakeries. Pennsylvania passed its law to ensure that baked goods arriving from out of state met the same high standards as those produced locally. It stipulated that in order to peddle baked goods—including everything from potato chips and pretzels to pasta—in the state of Pennsylvania, companies must hold a Pennsylvania bakery license. Then, as now, to obtain a license a bakery must pass an annual inspection for cleanliness and labeling accuracy, and its employees must undergo yearly medical examinations.

Rather than try to visit each out-of-state bakery personally, officials at the Pennsylvania Department of Agriculture rely on the agriculture departments of other states and countries to annually inspect bakeries under their jurisdiction and submit their findings to Pennsylvania. The notation on the box stands as proof that the product within has met required standards and is licensed to be sold in Pennsylvania. Most bakeries find it easier and less costly to include the notation on all packaging, rather than specially printing just those boxes destined to wind up on grocery store shelves in Pennsylvania.

Pennsylvania is not alone in requiring bakery inspection and licensing—in fact, all fifty states now do so. But only Pennsylvania requires an inspection notation. Since standards still vary from state to state, the mark continues to ensure the quality of baked goods sold in the Keystone State. Recently, however, there's been a move afoot at the U.S. Department of Agriculture to standardize bakery licensing. If approved, the new rules could spell the end for Pennsylvania's unique notation. Naturally, officials at the Pennsylvania Department of Agriculture would hate to see it go. It's good advertising, they say, for a state that since 1933 has been certified pure.

?

How do they detect wind shear?

UNLESS YOU SPEND A LOT of time flying airplanes, you probably haven't given a great deal of thought to the subject of wind shear. Wind shear is the phenomenon of radically differing wind velocity and direction at slightly different altitudes. The occurrence of an adjoining northerly twelve-knot wind, say, and a southerly twenty-knot wind would constitute wind shear. It is a phenomenon of grave concern to pilots. Wind shear causes the aircraft to feel turbulence and lose speed; if the differences between the adjoining winds are great enough, the effect can be extremely detrimental to sustained flight. Wind shear is especially dangerous when it occurs at a low altitude in the vicinity of an airport, where it can affect planes in the vulnerable takeoff and landing phases of flight. Wind shear can cause a low-flying, slow-moving plane to lose airspeed and lift, sometimes so suddenly that the pilot does not have enough time to adjust to the new conditions and the plane crashes. Although wind shear can occur at any altitude, a plane flying high and fast will usually have plenty of time to compensate for its negative effects. For this reason, low-level wind shear—wind shear below roughly 800 to 1,200 feet—is of greatest concern to flyers.

Many airports in the United States are equipped with the low-level wind-shear alerting system (LLWAS), which detects weather conditions likely to produce wind shear. The system consists of a network of anemometers—fancy weathervanes—arranged to monitor wind speed and direction at various points around the airport. Data received by each of five or six anemometers on the perimeter of the airport and one at its center are fed into a computer in the control tower. If the computer detects strong discrepancies, it sets off an alarm. Control tower officials are then able to send out a wind shear warning.

A variety of meteorological phenomena can cause wind shear. Any kind of frontal zone, the boundary between different air masses, can produce it. Fast-moving cold fronts create prime wind shear conditions as they overtake slower warm air masses.

Thunderstorms are another wind shear breeding ground. They contain strong downward currents of air, called downdrafts and microbursts, that strike the earth and fan out horizontally. An airplane flying into a downdraft produced by a thunderstorm will experience all sorts of unenviable events. First, as the craft enters the downdraft, it meets with headwinds created by the flow of air across the earth's surface, and its lift and airspeed are increased. Then, as the airplane continues across the downdraft, downward currents become more pronounced and the plane is pushed toward the ground—it loses lift. At the same time, a rapid change from headwind to tailwind conditions causes the plane to lose airspeed, a situation that further erodes lift. And all of this can transpire in a matter of seconds.

Since wind shear often accompanies specific types of weather, experienced pilots can usually be alerted to it by checking for fronts and thunderstorms along the flight route, even before taking off.

How do they make fake photos on magazine covers?

IF YOU HAVE EVER READ *Spy* magazine you are probably familiar with doctored magazine cover photos. The satiric New York monthly once ran, for instance, a cover that included a picture of Henry Kissinger wantonly dancing the hula. It was not really a picture of Dr. Kissinger. Rather, it was a picture of Dr. Kissinger's laughing head attached to a picture of the jiggling body of an overweight dancer. The fusing of the two pictures was done so seamlessly, however, producing such a strong photographic likeness, that it is almost impossible to believe that Henry Kissinger did not actually do the dance we see him performing. *Spy,* of course, is not the only magazine that runs doctored photos on its cover; it just uses them to funnier effect than most.

Any picture—from a Monet painting to a Polaroid snapshot— is just a collection of different colors, organized in such a way as to create a likeness of a three-dimensional object. With the aid of new computer technology the colors of a picture can be rearranged in such a way that a new picture is created from the colors of the original. Fake magazine covers are made in photo studios by feeding an original image (a photo of Henry Kissinger, say) into a computer scanner, the desktop version of which is roughly the size and shape of a laser printer. The scanner records the photograph's picture information (colors and color placement), translating it into a digital code. The digitally coded picture, an electronic document, is transmitted to a computer, where it can be called up on the monitor as an image of the original photograph.

166

Think, for example, of a jigsaw puzzle. When assembled properly, the five hundred individual pieces create a large, cohesive picture. What a scanner does is turn an ordinary picture into a jigsaw puzzle. It isolates pixels, which are like electronic jigsaw puzzle pieces, except that each one is only the size of a pinhead. This jigsaw puzzle can be reassembled in any fashion—the pieces can be made to fit anywhere. Once the scanner has broken down the picture into its composite elements, the elements are manipulated into new shapes, making it possible to create a new, electronic image by rearranging elements of the original picture.

Unsightly wrinkles can be removed from a model's face by replacing the pixels that contain wrinkle information with smooth-skin pixels. Shadows can be deleted, backgrounds altered, celebrities decapitated, their disembodied heads reattached to other bodies. A tiff, that is, a hard copy of the new image as it appears on the computer monitor, can be printed by a color offset device. The finessed picture can then be reproduced on the cover of a magazine.

While a picture may be worth a thousand words, in the new age of computer technology there is no guarantee that those words are not lies. Any person with the right equipment can create a convincing, fake picture.

?

How do they make shredded wheat?

A STAPLE ON THE American breakfast table for decades, good old wholesome shredded wheat dates back a century. The story goes that at a small-town hotel in Nebraska in 1892, lawyer and inventor Henry D. Perky was suffering from indigestion one morning when he noticed a fellow guest eating an oddity for breakfast: boiled wheat covered with milk. The stranger, a fellow indigestion sufferer, claimed his bland dish cured their common ailment. This inspired Perky to set out to produce the stuff and to make it more palatable.

With the help of his brother in Denver, Perky devised a machine to extrude boiled wheat paste in stringy filaments, which were then woven into pillows of "shredded wheat." After leaving them for a day to settle, the inventor then baked them to keep them from spoiling.

The first commercial shredded wheat biscuits were produced by a Denver cracker bakery in 1893. Their intrepid inventor then headed east to promote their healthful virtues to the mass market. In 1901 Perky opened a conspicuous red-brick Shredded Wheat bakery at Niagara Falls, New York, dispensing free samples of the "original Niagara Falls cereal" to its thousands of annual visitors.

Whether because of its curative qualities or simply its novelty, Perky's shredded wheat caught on in a big way. In 1928 a large-scale manufacturer, the National Biscuit Company (predecessor of RJR Nabisco), bought the company, opening two new plants and introducing modern processing and packaging methods.

Today each plant processes daily several thousand bushels of soft white winter wheat that has been stored in adjacent grain elevators until needed. After the wheat has been cleaned and moistened in hot water, it is cooked in immense kettles for over half an hour. This 100 percent wheat gruel is then run through driers and cured in steel storage tanks to equalize its moisture content so as to yield a cool, dry paste of uniform consistency that can be shredded mechanically. The shredded filaments are then stacked up in layers on a moving strip which passes under a cutter that separates the straw-like material into biscuits. These glide on to the oven to be puffed up and baked crisp and golden before being sealed in moisture-resistant packages and shipped to grocery stores.

In addition to the traditional "big biscuit," shredded wheat is now made by competing manufacturers in snackable and child-friendly spoon sizes. And to please health nut and child alike, the wholesome wheat can be found bolstered with the bran of oat or wheat—or doused in sugar frosting.

?

How do they write words across the sky in airplane exhaust?

WHEN WE THINK OF skywriting, most of us picture a small airplane looping-the-loop to scrawl advertising slogans or "I love you's" with a vanishing vapor trail. But such laborious acrobatics are almost a thing of the past. Since the wind can wipe out a letter even before the daring aviator finishes it, an imaginative skywriter has dreamed up a longer-lasting, if less romantic, method of "skytyping." Although you occasionally see the original form of skywriting in this country, now you are more likely to see messages rapidly "typed" out across the sky in dot matrix form by a close formation of five or six airplanes.

The inventor of traditional skywriting is thought to have been a British flying ace, Major John C. Savage, who got his inspiration from the use of airplanes during World War I to spread smoke around ships and troops to camouflage them from the enemy. In 1922 he wrote "HELLO" to the crowds at a British racetrack. Later that year, a plane traced "HELLO, U.S.A." over the Polo Grounds in New York during a World Series game and followed up with: "CALL VANDERBILT 7200." Those who did reached the first commercial skywriting company in America, headquartered at the Vanderbilt Hotel.

Advertisers took to skywriting in a big way, but the business took a nosedive in the late 1940s, when television became a competitor. Despite the ingenuity of some pilots in holding their audience's attention—like the one who spent hours misspelling the name of a local furniture company in ever more creative ways—advertisers perceived TV as more efficient in getting across their message.

U.S. Navy pilot Andy Stinis, celebrated as the most skilled American skywriter, saved his vocation by patenting "Skytyping" in 1949, an innovative method of writing in the sky designed to make the medium faster and more versatile. Skytypers can write twenty letters in the time an old-fashioned skywriter can manage one. For instance, to write the letter *M*, a solo skywriter has to put his aircraft through these time-consuming maneuvers:

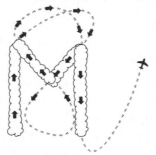

A "front-line" formation of five skytyping aircraft only needs to fly straight ahead, maintaining a distance of 225 to 250 feet between planes. When commanded by computer, they emit brief bursts of smoke according to this format:

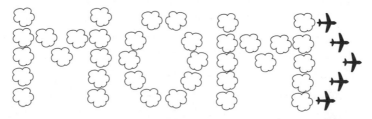

Messages to be skytyped are transposed onto a tape as a sequence of punch marks along the lines of the diagram above, indicating when each aircraft should emit smoke. When the planes are at ten thousand feet and over their prospective audience, the tape is fed into a specially designed computer housed in the lead plane of the squadron. The computer reads the tape and triggers the lead plane's radio transmitter to send out radio signals on different frequencies specific to the radio receivers of each other plane in the formation. The radio signals activate each receiver to command a valve to open and start the process that releases a burst of smoke. The entire system is rather like an antiquated nineteenth-century piano roll.

To keep the typed-out message hanging in the sky for as long as possible, a patented solution is added to the planes' exhaust that makes it more visible and holds it in place longer. On a windless day, a skytyped message can be read in its entirety for as long as twenty-five minutes, as opposed to the few minutes of a conventionally skywritten one.

The exact recipe for Stinis's patented solution is a secret, but essentially it is a highly distilled form of paraffin gas, 100 percent biodegradable, nonpolluting and EPA-approved. Each time a plane's receiver is activated by radio signal, a valve releases a small amount of the distilled mineral oil into the plane's extremely hot (2,000 to 2,300 degrees Fahrenheit) manifold. The oil is instantly vaporized and forced out through a ten-foot pipe running along the top of the starboard wing and extending six inches beyond it. When the very hot vapor hits the very cold air at ten thousand feet, it condenses as a little, intensely white, artificial cloud, its steam molecules held together by the paraffin.

Skytyped messages usually run a thousand feet tall and six to eight miles long. With six aircraft the letters can be made even taller. The writing is visible for four hundred square miles; over a crowded urban area a message can be seen by as many as three and a half million people, and a single plane formation can print out thirty messages a day. Commercial skytyping has included pictures of diapers and diamonds strung out across the sky, and the aerial writers have taken on all sorts of personal missives, too. Sometimes skywriting the old-fashioned way with a solo plane (for no extra charge) they have proclaimed "ALICE DIVORCE ME.

171

GOOD-BYE HOUSE. HELLO ALIMONY" and, in another case, "RE-
PENT. THE END IS NEAR." But the sky must be blue and the wind
below thirty-five knots (forty miles per hour) or no one will see
the message.

How do they determine who gets into Harvard?

MORE THAN 14,000 hopeful students apply for admission to Harvard each year, competing to fill out a freshman class of about
1,600. In an average year, roughly 15 percent of the applicants will
be accepted; about 75 percent of successful applicants matriculate.

The basic admissions requirements include graduation from
secondary school, and completion of the Scholastic Aptitude Test
(SAT) and three achievement tests (ACH) in subjects of the applicant's choice. An applicant's high school academic load should include four years of English, four years of mathematics, three
years of science (with labs), three years of foreign language, and
three years of history. Some training in music and art is also recommended. An applicant must have an interview, either on campus or with a local alumna or alumnus, and provide letters of
recommendation from three teachers.

Such are the perfunctory requirements. Most applicants meet
them easily. To actually get in, an applicant must have excellent
grades and test scores: 98 percent or so of successful candidates
rank in the top fifth of their high school class. Average SAT scores
of those admitted are around 660 verbal, 700 mathematics, for a
combined score of 1,360 out of a possible 1,600. (The national
SAT average is 896 combined—422 verbal, 474 mathematics).

Still, straight A's and near perfect SAT scores alone do not guarantee admission to Harvard. If they did, it would be very difficult to decide between the fourteen thousand applicants, most of whom distinguished themselves academically in high school. An applicant must also meet other important criteria. Harvard's thirty-five member admissions committee looks for special talents—virtuosity on the flügelhorn, say, or a unique knack for computer programming. Extracurricular activities are important, and ethnic origin and geographic location play a role.

It has been said that Harvard is less interested in well-rounded students than in a well-rounded class: the budding poet with no aptitude for physics might get in, and so might the brilliant amateur chemist who has never read a novel that wasn't assigned in English class. A well-rounded class also means a broad geographic and ethnic distribution of students. In a recent freshman class, all fifty states and dozens of foreign countries were represented. Almost as many students now come from out west as do from New England. In terms of ethnicity, better than one student in four is of a minority, and about 45 percent of entering freshmen are women. Roughly 70 percent of all students receive some kind of financial aid. These figures represent a dramatic departure from the stereotypical Harvard student of years gone by: an affluent white male graduate of a New England prep school.

Since Harvard wants a diverse class profile, a geographic edge can sometimes make the difference between acceptance and rejection: a kid from Montana who is class valedictorian, star quarterback of the football team, and scored 1,400 on his SATs might get the nod over a kid from Massachusetts with equal accomplishments. This is because, in essence, the student from Montana is competing with other students from Montana, where the applicant pool is relatively small, while the Massachusetts student is competing against all other applicants from Massachusetts, which leads the fifty states in number of Harvard applicants. Conventional wisdom has it that the best way for parents to get their kids into Harvard is not to send them to an exclusive prep school in

173

the East, but rather to move to some rural county in a state such as Montana.

The surest way of all would be for the parents to have graduated from Harvard themselves. About 40 percent of applications from children of Harvard alums are accepted; "legacies," as such students are called, are three times as likely to get into Harvard as unaffiliated applicants. Legacies constitute nearly 20 percent of Harvard's enrollment. Harvard admissions officials argue that the relatively high acceptance rate for sons and daughters of Harvard grads is only natural, since legacies have smart parents and usually come from privileged backgrounds where education is emphasized. The admissions people have also said that the legacy factor is only used to break a tie between equally qualified candidates.

Recently, however, the U.S. Department of Education's Office for Civil Rights decided to take a look at Harvard's classified admissions files. The OCR found that contrary to the university's claims, legacies were, on average, less qualified than their nonlegacy classmates. Based on an examination of admissions ratings of accepted students in a variety of categories, including academics, extracurriculars, personal qualities, and recommendations, the OCR concluded that "with the exception of the athletic rating, nonlegacies scored better than legacies in all categories of comparison."

The real reason so many legacies get into Harvard is financial: every year Harvard grads contribute millions of dollars to their alma mater. To shut the door on the children of wealthy alums might have a negative effect on their generosity. And that generosity, university administrators argue, feeds the scholarship fund that allows Harvard to admit eminently qualified students regardless of their ability to pay.

In the words of one Harvard official, "If you have a perfect SAT score, are first in your class and captain of an athletic team, you've got a good shot" at getting admitted. Add "child of Harvard-educated parents" to the equation, and you're a shoo-in.

?

How do chameleons change color?

THEIR LIPS CAN TURN YELLOW. Their strange little bodies fade from shoe-leather brown to grass green. The acclaimed herpetologist Angus Bellairs even reported in his 1970 two-volume work, *The Life of Reptiles,* that "if an object of distinctive shape is held against the flank of a [chameleon] for a couple of minutes, its outline will appear as a pale print on the darker skin."

Chameleon skin is full of cells called chromatophores, whose business is color. The bottom layer of skin is made of chromatophores filled with a dark brown pigment called melanin—the same pigment that colors human beings' skin. These particular cells are also called melanophores. The color cells above them vary, depending on the species of chameleon. Closer to the surface of the skin are cells that may contain yellow or red pigment; other cells have a substance called guanine, which is a reflector

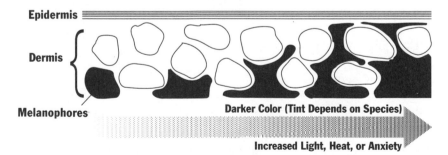

A chameleon can change color because of melanophore cells in its skin. When the chameleon is under stress, melanophores fill with pigment and surround all the other pigment cells.

175

and produces the effect of white color. When guanine is near melanin, it produces the color blue. Near yellow pigment, it produces green.

Color changes in chameleons seem to depend on the movement of melanin pigment into branches of the spider-shaped melanophore cells, which extend up toward the skin's surface. When the "legs" of the cells are full of melanin, the skin darkens. When they're empty, it lightens. The other pigment cells that the animal sports are either masked or exposed in the process, and wonderful colors result.

Although reports continue to say that chameleons change color to match their background, this doesn't always seem to be the case. Nervous system responses to light, heat, "emotions," danger and mating are highly correlated to color changes. Quite often a chameleon changes color and becomes *more* conspicuous. The melanophores of an anxious chameleon fill to the tips with melanin and the reptile washes dark brown. In a calm animal, on the other hand, melanin concentrates in the center of the melanophores and its color is pale.

?

How do they make high-definition television?

HIGH-DEFINITION TELEVISION, the experts tell us, will deliver pictures up to five times sharper than the current standard, with a larger field of vision and with sound comparable to that produced by a compact disk. The new system, which should be commercially available by the mid-1990s, will mark the first real change in television since color was introduced in 1954. The picture that appears on a standard television screen is transmitted as a series of images, each containing 525 horizontal lines of picture information, at a rate of thirty frames per second. All told, standard television pictures contain 212,520 dots of picture information, called pixels. High-definition television (HDTV) will achieve its revolutionary clarity by increasing to 1,125 the number of horizontal lines that compose each image and doubling the number of frames per second. HDTV pictures will contain five times as many pixels as current pictures, resulting in rich, seamless images. This is wonderful news for TV bugs, many of whom are probably ready to shell out the $2,500 necessary to buy a high-definition set.

But the change from traditional television to high definition involves more than tuning in a hypersensitive new television set: HDTV demands a brand-new way of broadcasting television signals, and the signals will be beyond the reach of ordinary television sets. HDTV carries too much information to fit into current broadcast channels. All those pixels can be squeezed into a standard channel about as readily as a camel can pass through the eye of a needle. Before the new sets begin appearing in stores, broadcasters must figure out how to broadcast high-definition signals without making obsolete the 160 million or so television sets now operating across the country.

To protect the consumer, the Federal Communications Commission (FCC) has ruled that HDTV will have to fit within current bands on the television spectrum. The sooner broadcasters figure out a way to comply with FCC requirements, the better, according to various electronics manufacturers who are dying to get their new high-definition sets on the market.

There are a variety of ways HDTV signals might be transmitted. One possibility would be for existing stations to send the extra signals necessary to complete a high-definition image through unoccupied channels on the television band. In local markets, to prevent interference, television stations are separated by vacant channel space. The FCC could assign each extant station an empty channel for the broadcast of HDTV signals. A station could broadcast one set of signals on ordinary VHF (channels 2 through 13) and send the additional picture information over a blank channel. Traditional TV sets would pick up the regular channel, while viewers with high-definition sets would pull in both sets of signals, which would be combined by their televisions into a single enhanced image.

Another possibility is direct-broadcast satellite. High-definition images could be beamed by satellite to homes equipped with satellite dishes. High-definition television sets would pick up both the new satellite transmissions and traditional broadcasts.

A third idea under discussion is to use the fiber-optic cables, currently being installed by telephone companies, to carry high-definition television signals. After buying new high-definition sets, viewers would subscribe to fiber-optic cable service, in much the same way as some traditional-TV-set viewers now buy cable TV packages.

When high-definition television eventually becomes available, the new hardware will have more in common with computers than with ordinary television sets. Traditional television works on an analog system: audio and visual elements are converted to undulating electric waves for transmission to television receivers (TV sets), which reconvert the waves into visible light rays (pictures) and audible sound. High-definition television will be digital. The new sets will convert analog waves into digital code, with strings of zeros and ones representing each bit of picture information—color, shade, placement. A microchip in the new sets will process the digital code, paying strict attention to each light element, to produce richly detailed pictures.

HDTV is not without its critics, some of whom contend that the enhanced pictures are barely discernible from those on old-fashioned TV. Even so, market analysts predict HDTV will be worth billions of dollars a year to the electronics industry; therein lies the real incentive. In the United States, where only one major company, Zenith, continues to make TVs, the financial motive is especially strong. The good news for American companies interested in regaining a toehold in the consumer electronics market is that current U.S. and Japanese HDTV standards are incompatible. The bad news is that Japan began HDTV broadcasts in 1989, giving it a big head start in perfecting the equipment.

How do they wrap Hershey's Kisses?

WHEN HERSHEY'S CHOCOLATE KISSES were introduced in 1907, just four years after Milton S. Hershey built his first chocolate factory, the bite-size candies were wrapped individually by hand. In 1921 the chocolate makers added the Kiss's identification plume, the little paper streamer printed "Hershey's Kisses" that sprouts from the top of the foil wrapping. The company made the name a registered trademark in 1923, and the candy's size, shape, wrap, and plume became registered trademarks the following year.

At about the same time that the Kiss was patented in the form that it has kept to this day, the company replaced its manual workers with a mechanized "single-channel wrapper." This handled the more elaborate wrapping and met increasing demand faster and more cheaply. The present-day "multichannel" Kiss wrapping machines are based on the concept and design of the original system, which was fed by one conveyor belt (single channel). Another five conveyor belts have been added per machine and other minor modifications made to speed up and otherwise improve performance. The current equipment now wraps approximately 33 million Kisses a day in the company's two factories in Hershey, Pennsylvania.

179

How, exactly, does it do this? First, the specially blended melted chocolate is squirted mechanically into uniform Kiss shapes on wide, continuously moving stainless steel belts that pass through a cooling tunnel for about eighteen minutes. The Kisses emerge in solid form, ready to be wrapped. The rows making up the broad array of Kisses are then separated. If a Kiss is properly aligned, standing upright on its base, it moves on with the others in single file onto narrow, steep-sided conveyor belts toward the wrapping machines. But if the Kiss has toppled over or is otherwise askew, a little mechanical finger pushes it off the line and it is set upright and mechanically recirculated onto the broad conveyor belt to wait its turn again.

A machine can simultaneously wrap the Kisses delivered to it by twelve such narrow conveyor belts, each of which passes over its own "wrapping chamber." Perforated squares of wrapping foil, still attached to one another on an unwinding roll but prepared like postage stamps to be torn off easily, are mechanically inserted through a side of a wrapping chamber and centered over its floor just in time to receive a Kiss brought onto it by the conveyor belt. When the Kiss is in position at the center of the piece of foil, a strip of tissue (the identification plume) is introduced mechanically from above, and at the same time a plunger pushes the Kiss down on the foil with sufficient pressure to tear off the section of foil without damaging foil or chocolate.

The wrapping chamber has a top and bottom section consisting of plastic-like bands of material that rotate in different directions and tighten against the Kiss, firmly twisting the foil around the chocolate. No sooner is the Kiss pressed down and the section of foil detached than the twisting mechanism is activated. This wraps the foil around the Kiss so that it captures and binds the printed streamer of tissue securely between foil and candy, allowing a jaunty plume to emerge at the top which is automatically cut to the proper length by a mechanical knife. Each step of the process is minutely calibrated to occur within a fraction of a second of those before and after it.

The instant the Kiss is wrapped, the conveyor belt moves it

out to be packaged with other Kisses for shipment, and brings along the next candidate. The entire wrapping process has taken about a second.

?

How do they teach a computer to recognize your voice?

IT WON'T BE LONG BEFORE you can carry on lengthy conversations with a computer, schedule business appointments by negotiating with a machine rather than a secretary, even instruct your VCR by voice when to record a certain show. IBM already has a computer in the works that can recognize twenty thousand words. How does it do it?

Basically, the computer "recognizes" your voice by converting its sound waves into digital signals. When you speak into a microphone, the computer compares your voice signals with a set of patterns it has stored in its system. The computer will show you what it thinks you're saying by instantly flashing up your words on a computer screen. You can then edit (by voice or keyboard), store, print, or transmit. In the labs at AT&T, for instance, researchers play video games, guiding a mouse through a maze simply by saying "left" or "right."

But before a computer can perform for you, it has to get used to your voice. (This type of computer will respond to only one voice and is dubbed "speaker dependent." Others, referred to as "speaker independent," will respond to any voice.) A speaker-dependent computer first listens for twenty minutes as you read a special document into a microphone. When you've finished, it will have stored two hundred sound patterns that characterize

181

your voice, and when you use the system it will match them against your speech. A selection of words that roughly match those sound patterns is drawn from a twenty-thousand-word vocabulary. These words are then matched against a second model that has a vast data base of words commonly used in the office. The computer can reduce the number of possible candidates by determining which words are most likely to follow the two previous words. For example, the computer knows that *bows*—and not *boughs*—would follow the word *actor*. The system makes its final selection of the best word after it has determined that analysis of subsequent words (*to the audience*) won't affect its choice. Within a second or so, the word appears on the system's display screen.

This contextual ability enables the system to distinguish between words that sound alike but are different, such as *know* and *no, air* and *heir,* and *to, too,* and *two.* Punctuation can be added verbally by simply saying "period," "comma," and so on.

When IBM first started working on this system in 1986, the system occupied an entire room. Now it has been reduced to desk size and IBM feels it won't be long before it is used routinely in business offices. AT&T is experimenting with an automated directory system for the employees at Bell Labs. The caller simply picks up the phone, spells out the last name and first initial of the person he or she is trying to reach, and the call automatically goes through. Who knows? Before long you may be able to pick up the phone and just say, "Get me Mom, please."

How do they know who has won an election before the polls close?

IN 1980, the television networks caused a bit of a ruckus when they declared, before polls had closed in the West, that Ronald Reagan had won the presidential election. Soon after that announcement was made, with still more than an hour of voting time left on the West Coast, Jimmy Carter conceded defeat on national television. The scenario was repeated in 1984, when the networks correctly named Ronald Reagan the victor at eight-thirty Eastern Standard Time—voting rush hour in the West. In Congress, legislators from some western states raised the hue and cry, complaining that the practice of reporting results from the East before the polls had closed in the West disrupted voter turn-out in the Pacific Time region. The truth is that the networks did not even have to wait for the polls to close in the East before knowing the results.

Journalists depend on exit polls, accurate to within a few percentage points, for their election numbers. Each network employs thousands of exit-pollsters to sample a fraction of the eighty million or so people who cast votes. The information collected by the pollsters, including party affiliation, candidate voted for, and reason for the vote, is fed into network computers, which prorate the data to arrive at state-by-state figures.

The exit poll was first used in 1967 by CBS in three separate state elections. During the 1972 presidential election, CBS conducted the first-ever national exit polls. And by the 1980 election

ABC, NBC, *The New York Times*, the *Los Angeles Times*, and the Associated Press had all joined CBS in carrying out exit polls. The big difference between an exit poll and pre-election tracking polls is that the exit poll measures a *fait accompli*, a cast vote, which is obviously more accurate than measuring *potential* votes before an election.

By 1985, the controversy surrounding exit polls—not whether they were accurate, but whether early forecasts deterred voters from turning out by creating in their minds the impression of a foregone conclusion—prompted the networks to sign a pledge to forswear "projections, characterizations, or any use of exit polling data that would indicate the winner of the election in a given state before the polls were closed." Some Western states had already taken matters into their own hands: Washington and Wyoming passed legislation prohibiting pollsters from interviewing voters within three hundred feet of a voting place.

None of the opposition to exit polls has prevented the media from conducting them; it merely stanched the flow of information. Whereas the networks once would have begun releasing figures the minute they became available, usually with the disclaimer, "Remember, this is not a result, just a trend," before going on to say, "but if the trend continues Hart looks all but unbeatable," the networks now wait until the polls close before stating what they have known for hours.

?

How do they train structural steelworkers to walk on unprotected beams five hundred feet in the air?

FIRST, WHAT GETS THEM UP there at all? "Youth is number one," says John Kelly, coordinator of the Joint Apprenticeship and Trainee Committee of Ironworkers Locals 40 and 361 in New York. "Adventure is number two. And it used to be a hand-me-down, father-to-son business. Or you'd be hanging around on the street like a bum and someone would say, 'Why don't you do this?' And when you were young you'd say, 'Gee, this is great work.' It's lovely up there. You're by yourself, or with your partner—it's like being up in a balloon. It's an interesting way to make a good buck. . . . And later you could look at the skyscrapers around town and say, 'I worked on that' or 'I helped build that.'"

It might be breeding, youth, good paychecks or pure guts that gets steelworkers and bridge painters comfortable at such great heights, but it isn't training. Apprentice school teaches safety and ironworking skills; the walking is up to the novice. An apprentice steelworker (more commonly called an ironworker) in New York City starts low—as low as twelve feet off the ground—working on the first floor of a building. Usually he's eighteen or twenty years old and cocky as they come. He looks forward to $27.50 an hour if he can advance to journeyman. If he's sure of his footing, he'll walk the five- or ten-inch-wide beams right off the bat. If he's shaky, he'll sit down, straddle the beam and monkey his way across. He sees experienced journeymen moving with ease around and above him. He notices that they watch the beam ahead of them and don't look farther (that is, lower) than their feet. Although most are extremely careful, some of the old pros will take unnecessary chances, actually jumping from beam to beam rather than taking the longer way around. When the apprentice thinks he's ready, he moves up and begins to work where high winds and dangling steel beams are a constant hazard.

Up until ten years ago, the unions lost up to six men a year on the job, some falling twenty or thirty stories to their deaths. Today, government standards and collective-bargaining agreements in New York City have considerably improved the working conditions, and fatalities have decreased. For example, every two floors of a building under construction must be solidly planked or decked over. If an ironworker happens to fall into, rather than out of the structure, he has only two-dozen feet to drop. Carelessness on the ground is more often the cause of accidents now: men have been hit by cars while setting up cones, and have fallen off ladders. For the painters, nets are hung under the bridges to stop a fall. You can imagine how grateful certain men have been for the union efforts to get the nets—plenty have experienced a fall that at one time would have meant sure death.

Despite such safety measures the work remains perilous. When you see a steelworker hammering a bolt into the outside skeleton beams at five hundred feet or more—standing there as if he were working on the bathroom closet—he *could* just as easily fall outside the building as inside. The bottom line is he's being careful.

How do they find heart or liver donors?

THE OBVIOUS OBSTACLE TO finding heart and liver donors is the singularity of these organs: a person has only one of each and cannot afford to part with either. A transplanted kidney, by comparison, can come from a live donor, who has two of them but needs only one to survive. The pool of heart and liver donors is necessarily small, consisting primarily of healthy people who die suddenly in accidents.

To simplify the search for transplantable organs, the National Organ Transplant Act of 1984 established the United Network for Organ Sharing (UNOS). UNOS maintains a data bank of available organs and matches donors and recipients according to location, compatibility and urgency of need. By law, all transplant centers must be tapped into the network. The law also makes provisions for acquiring organs: all hospitals receiving Medicare funds are required to ask the next of kin of brain-dead patients whether they want the dead relative's organs donated. Forty-two states provide organ-donor check-off boxes on their driver's licenses, but such identification is construed merely as a willingness to donate, and the final decision falls to the deceased person's relatives.

UNOS maintains local, regional, and national computerized lists of patients awaiting transplants; each patient is ranked according to need and the length of time he has been waiting. People waiting for new livers, for instance, are rated from 0 to 4: status 0 patients are considered temporarily unsuitable for trans-

187

plants; status 1 patients are at home and functioning; status 2 patients require continuous medical care; status 3 denotes required hospitalization; and status 4 signifies acute and chronic liver failure. When a liver becomes available for transplantation, the computer scans its lists for compatible recipients. Final allocation is made based on compatibility, urgency and geography: local status 4 receives top priority, followed by all other local patients; next come regional status 4 patients, then all other regional patients; finally national status 4, and then all other national patients. Local and regional patients have priority over national patients because the transplant must occur as quickly as possible after the organ is removed from the donor.

Ideally, the UNOS system works like this: a person dies, needed organs healthy and intact. The hospital transplant coordinator is called in to talk to the family about organ donation. The family acquiesces. The organs are examined and the vital information—blood type, tissue type, size—is plugged into the UNOS data bank. The computer, beginning with the local list, scans the patients awaiting transplants. If no match is made locally, the computer jumps to the regional list, and finally to the national list. In 1989, organs were found for slightly better than half of the almost 23,000 people awaiting transplants.

It was in 1989 that surgeons performed the first liver transplant involving a living donor. The procedure allows doctors to replace a child's ailing liver with a piece of a liver cut from a healthy adult—for compatibility reasons, usually a parent. So far, surgeons have performed the operation only on children, because they are small and can survive without a full-sized liver. The technique is possible because the liver, alone among human organs, is capable of regenerating: what remains of the donor's organ will return to normal size after a few months, while the recipient's organ will grow as the child does. The operation could make it much easier for children to receive life-saving transplants—more than seven hundred require them each year—but the procedure is potentially very dangerous for the donor, leading some doctors to speculate that cadaver donations will always remain preferable.

Once an organ has been found and transplanted, the recipient faces the hurdle of organ rejection, which occurs when the recipient's body attacks the new organ as a foreign object. Rejection is very common—it occurs in all cases of heart transplantation—even when the donor and recipient have been closely matched by blood and tissue types. The only way to treat rejection is by suppressing the recipient's immune system with steroids, a strategy that can make even a common cold fatal.

?

How do they get the cork into a bottle of champagne?

TWO SECRETS APPLY: first, the cork was soaked and thereby softened before being driven into the bottle, and second, the cork was originally a bit slimmer than the one you see fly across the room on a festive occasion—it has expanded over time because of the pressure of carbon dioxide within the bottle.

True champagne is a sparkling wine from the Champagne region of France. In contrast to still wines, which are fermented once, champagne is fermented twice, once in a cask or tank, a second time right in the bottle. Fermentation occurs when yeasts act upon sugar in the wine, converting it to alcohol and carbon dioxide. One of the first to make a study of this double fermentation was a monk by the name of Dom Pierre Pérignon, who became cellar master of the abbey of Hautvillers in 1670. He toyed with the sugar content of the wine and so began to learn how to control the bubbliness of the stuff. He also garnered wines from different fields and blended them in order to produce the same taste year after year, a practice continued to this day. While at

Hautvillers Dom Pierre encountered some Spanish pilgrims whose gourds were sealed with cork. Until that time he had been stopping his bottles with wooden plugs wrapped in oiled hemp. He quickly saw the advantages of the more elastic substance, which expanded in the bottle, sealed it better, and reduced leakage and explosions.

Cork trees grow in the Iberian peninsula, southern France and southern Italy, Corsica, Sardinia, and North Africa. The best corks—those suitable for capping a fine champagne—come from Spain and Portugal, from cork trees at least fifty years old. After a lengthy process of drying, boiling, and cutting, the corks are milled with emery to produce a smooth finish and sometimes treated with paraffin to help them slide more easily into the bottle. Champagne corks are forty-seven millimeters long and thirty to forty-eight millimeters in diameter, substantially larger than corks for still wines. The substance is ideal for its purpose, being durable and impervious to liquid. And when it is cut, some of the cells that are divided develop the characteristic of adhering well to a slippery surface.

After a bottle of champagne has fermented the second time and been left to ripen in a cool cellar for a number of years, it is skillfully turned each day and eventually left standing on its head. Any sediment in the wine falls down to the cork. Then the bottle is ready for *degorgement,* in which a highly trained worker pries off the first cork, allowing sediment and as little wine as possible to fly out of the bottle. Today the neck of the bottle is often frozen first to facilitate the procedure and reduce waste. When the bottle is opened, a frozen lump of sediment and a little wine is shot out by the buildup of pressure within. More wine is then added to replace what was lost, usually along with a liqueur of aged champagne and sugar. At last the bottle is ready for the final cork. Corking machines have clamps that compress the cork, making it smaller than the neck of the bottle, and a vertical piston that drives the cork into place. It will expand in the bottle where pressure is five to six times that of the outside atmosphere. Finally, other machines add metal caps secured with twisted wire.

?

How do they make Hostess Twinkies stay fresh for years and years?

PERHAPS YOU'VE HEARD health nuts remark that Twinkies, the ultimate junk food, are so loaded with chemicals they can sit on the shelf for twenty years and the consumer wouldn't know the difference. Not so. "That's a popular misconception we're not too happy about," says Patrick Farrell of Continental Baking Company, producers of the familiar creme-filled snack. "The shelf life is actually seven days," says Farrell. "Then they go to thrift stores. After fourteen days, you wouldn't want to buy them. They taste like cardboard." Are any preservatives used? "Just flour extenders," claims Farrell, "and the kind of preservatives used in any commercially baked bread."

Despite the protests of health fans who would choose a more nutritious snack, Americans apparently don't leave Twinkies on the shelf for long. They consume some 500 million of them a year. It takes forty thousand miles of cellophane to wrap those Twinkies—enough plastic to encircle the globe one and a half times at the equator.

?

How does the SEC know when someone's doing inside stock trading?

INSIDE TRADING, the illicit profiteering by brokers on stock sales based on advance information about companies, is illegal because it gives the guilty trader an unfair advantage over his competitors; it can also lead to a fiscally damaging betrayal of trust. A lawyer, for instance, retained by Huge Company to assist in its secret buyout of Lucre, Inc., could stand to make a quick buck by investing heavily in Lucre before the buyout goes public, at which time the price of Lucre stock would inevitably rise. Through his work for Huge Company the lawyer would have gained an advantage on the stock-trading public. By capitalizing on his inside information, the lawyer would also hurt his client, Huge Company, by driving up the price of Lucre Inc. stock, thus making the buyout more expensive. The shifty attorney could further increase his windfall by selling his scoop to an amoral broker, who would profit by investing heavily in Lucre Inc., just before news of the buyout was released to the public.

The main way in which the Securities and Exchange Commission (SEC) learns of possible inside trading is by monitoring stock sales. By watching Wall Street trading, the agency might notice a jump in the stock of a target company just before a takeover bid is announced. If, over the course of months, it becomes apparent that a certain broker has repeatedly capitalized on corporate takeovers by the early purchase of target company stock, the successful broker might become an inside trading suspect. Prov-

192

ing the illegality of a trade is not so easy: the broker could always argue that his trades were guided by market research and accompanied by luck.

The SEC only really knows that someone is engaging in inside trading when an informant tips it off. Until then, the agency may possess suspicions, but not definite knowledge. Once tipped off, the SEC examines the record; if it finds a disturbing pattern of trading, it serves subpoenas to every person remotely connected with the fishy trades. Usually a case can be pieced together from the testimony of the subpoenaed dealers; then the agency can present its evidence to the alleged inside trader in hopes of squeezing out a confession.

The biggest inside trading scandal in the history of Wall Street began to unravel in 1985, when the SEC received an anonymous tip about the fantastically acute transactions of Dennis Levine, a thirty-two-year-old mergers and acquisitions specialist with Drexel Burnham Lambert. The agency decided to examine the young investment banker's record. With the help of the New York Stock Exchange, which maintains a computer system to monitor stock trades, the SEC found fifty-four incidents of prescient trading by Levine. Apparently his $3 million in salary and bonuses was not enough. The investigators began contacting Levine's more devoted clients, companies that had made a lot of money through their dealings with him. By May of 1986 the SEC had unearthed enough frightened investors to corroborate the case against Levine. Levine, realizing he had been caught with his hand in the cookie jar, made a bid for leniency by cooperating with the investigation. Then the dominoes began to fall.

Based on testimony from Levine, the SEC fingered Ivan Boesky, the biggest arbitrageur in town. Boesky was eventually sentenced to three years in jail and ordered to pay penalties totaling $100 million, but not before he agreed to cooperate with the SEC by wearing a secret wiretap during his illicit dealings. His conversations proved damning; after weeks of taping the SEC began preparing cases against Martin Siegel, a Wall Street mergers expert, and Michael Milken, Drexel's infamous junk bond king.

193

Because it would be very difficult to convict an inside trader solely on the basis of suspicious trading patterns, the SEC relies a great deal on the kindness of strangers. As Gary Lynch, the SEC's enforcement director put it, "There's nothing more important than a phone call from someone with helpful information."

?

How do they decide what goes on the cover of *People* magazine?

THERE'S AN OLD FORMULA at *People* called the Law of Covers: "Young is better than old," it goes. "Pretty is better than ugly. Rich is better than poor. TV is better than music. Music is better than movies. Movies is better than sports. And anything is better than politics."

The Law was conceived by *People*'s founding editor, Dick Stolley, back in 1974 when the pop-culture magazine was launched, and today it's still a pretty good formula for predicting newsstand sales. The people on *People*'s covers are largely responsible for the weekly's phenomenal success on the newsstands, where slightly more than half the readers buy their issues. It's as simple as this: if you see someone on the cover you want to read about, you'll buy the magazine. But it's also as complex as this: Why didn't you buy the issue with Roseanne Arnold on the cover? And why *did* you buy the one (that seemed riskier) featuring New Kids on the Block? Anyway, it all evens out. In 1991, *People*'s weekly newsstand sales averaged 1.7 million copies; the only weekly boasting higher numbers was *TV Guide*.

Stolley's Law needs two amendments to bring it completely up to date. Tributes to stars who've died suddenly or catastrophically sell more magazines than any covers in the history of *People*. And royalty, particularly of the British persuasion, came into vogue with *People* readers in the 1980s with the wedding of Prince Charles and Lady Diana. In fact, Diana is *People*'s favorite "cover girl," having appeared on the cover forty-four times as of 1991. These are the other top favorites: Liz Taylor, John Travolta, Sarah "Fergie" Ferguson, Jackie Onassis, Farrah Fawcett, Cher, Madonna, Princess Caroline, Bruce Springsteen, Michael Jackson, Olivia Newton-John, Jane Fonda and Brooke Shields. And here's the list of *People* covers that ranked highest in newsstand sales as of this writing:

John Lennon: A Tribute (December 22, 1980)

Princess Grace: A Tribute (September 27, 1982)

Royal Wedding of Prince Andrew and Sarah Ferguson (August 4, 1986)

Princess Diana: "Oh Boy!" (the birth of Prince William; July 5, 1982)

Royal Wedding of Prince Charles and Lady Diana (August 3, 1981)

Karen Carpenter's Struggle with Anorexia Nervosa: A Tribute (February 21, 1983)

Olivia Newton-John (July 31, 1978)

Brooke Shields and Chris Atkins: *The Blue Lagoon* (August 11, 1980)

Priscilla Presley Talks about Elvis (December 4, 1978)

Farrah Fawcett—Why She Left Lee Majors (August 20, 1979)

While Stolley's Law is a nutshell formula for success, *People*'s cover subjects can't always be pretty, rich TV stars; in fact, the cover occasionally features such political personalities as Ted Kennedy and the Reagans. A more general rule of thumb calls for cover stories that grab you because they're "what you and your friends are talking about on Saturday night," says Assistant Managing Editor Susan Toepfer. To find out just what that is, *People* sometimes invites readers at random from the streets of New York City for a "cover lab," says Toepfer. These readers are asked to vote for potential covers that appeal to them most and to answer specific questions about which headlines and photographs they like. "But you can't take that as gospel," Toepfer remarks. "What they say and what they do are not necessarily the same." So most of the time, the cover decision is made in a weekly meeting of *People*'s top editors, a group of about fifteen. They plan enough cover stories for two months ahead and pick two or three cover subjects for the next week. By the following Tuesday, or Wednesday at the latest, the cover choice is narrowed to one, and that one is sent to press.

Unless, that is, something happens between the meeting and press day: war breaks out in the Persian Gulf, for example, or a princess's husband dies in a tragic boating accident. Toepfer points out that *People* is news-oriented, with the kind of staff that can research, write, edit, photograph and fact-check a story in a few hours. For example, when Lucille Ball died on Wednesday, April 26, 1989, the editors decided to hold the cover they had planned for the next issue (which would be dated May 8 but was due at the newsstands on May 1). Then at least one senior editor, two writers, five correspondents, and a crew of photo and editorial researchers put together an eleven-page tribute to Lucy, in what was probably record time even for *People:* about two and a half hours. "Lucille Ball: 1911–1989" was that year's best-selling cover.

What about covers that don't sell? "We're often stunned by a cover that doesn't sell," Toepfer says. Here, in order of bad to all-time worst, are the all-time lowest newsstand sells:

Harry Hamlin: Sexiest Man Alive (March 30, 1987)
How to Make Your Kid a Star (November 12, 1984)
Ted Danson (May 11, 1987)
Dustin Hoffman and Warren Beatty (May 25, 1987)
Broadcast News (February 1, 1988)

Jacqueline Bisset and Alexander Godunov (April 1, 1985)
Avenging Sergeant Kenneth Ford (April 28, 1986)
Jay Leno (November 30, 1987)
Michael Caine (May 4, 1987)
American Hostages in Lebanon (July 18, 1988)

?

How do they put the smell into scratch-and-sniff advertising?

IN YET ANOTHER clever ploy to attract customers, Madison Avenue invented the scratch-and-sniff ad. Used mostly by the cosmetics industry to sell perfumes and colognes, the ads are inserted into magazines, so you can get an idea of what the product smells like before buying it. Scratch-and-sniff strips are composed of globules of oil-based scent coated with gum arabic, which are suspended in glue for printing. When you scratch the strip, you burst the gum that hold the globules and the smell escapes.

To create the globules, the laboratory takes an oily essence of any odor desired and adds it to gum arabic in a "jacketed vessel," a steel container of water in which a glass vessel floats. (The double layers keep the mixture from getting too hot so the fragrance won't break down and escape into the air.) Attached to the side of the vessel is a projecting arm with an electric motor on top and a hanging paddle below for stirring. When the paddle moves, it beats the mixture into an emulsion: the scent breaks up into droplets and the gum arabic surrounds them and coats them. The speed of the stirring and the size of the vessel determine the size of the capsules created. "When you go a little slower than an

197

eggbeater you get capsules about fifty microns in size—each micron being one millionth of a meter," explains Jim Conklin, a chemist at Lawson Mardon, Inc., one of the packaging and printing firms associated with the popularization of scratch-and-sniff advertising in the early seventies.

After about two hours of stirring, the lab technicians place the mixture on mesh screen, allowing the unbonded materials to drain away, and wind up with a moist cake of scent about the consistency of coarse sand. The technicians then transfer the cake to a new vessel, gently break it up with a spatula, and add water and an ink-paste with an alcohol base. Then the globule mixture is ready to print.

Just like ink, it lies in a pan underneath the press and a roller passes over it, dipping in a little rubber pad which prints a specified amount on each sheet of paper that goes by. Ordinarily, the mixture is applied after all the rest of the printing has been done; then the paper is ready to be whisked through a dry oven on a mechanical belt at about fifteen miles per hour—often the last step in ordinary four-color printing. Finally the scratch-and-sniff strip is ready: the rich globules lie waiting for a finger to release their cache of scent to the air.

?

How does sunscreen screen out the sun?

AS THE OZONE LAYER wears thinner (see "How do they measure the ozone layer?"), the risks of skin cancer from sun exposure increase. About 90 percent of all skin cancers arise from exposure to the deceptively kind, warm rays of the sun—hence the advisability of sunscreen on a sizzling day at the beach.

Sunscreens are classified as drugs and as such are regulated by the Food and Drug Administration (FDA). Manufacturers use FDA-approved chemicals—oxybenzone, padimate-O, octylp-methoxy-cinnamate, and others—in different amounts and combinations, each arriving at its own unique and well-guarded formula. What these chemicals do is absorb or reflect radiation in the ultraviolet spectrum; older products like zinc oxide, on the other hand, are opaque and mechanically block radiation, including visible light. When the sun's rays strike the chemical molecules in sunscreen a transformation occurs: energy in the form of light is converted into a different kind of energy—heat, which is given off into the air. This phenomenon, in photochemical terms, is *absorbance*.

Ultraviolet radiation is characterized by the length of its waves, which are measured in nanometers, one nanometer being one millionth of a millimeter. At one end of the range of wavelengths called ultraviolet are the shorter wavelengths of 280 to 320 nanometers. These high-energy rays are called ultraviolet B (UVB), and they are responsible for causing visible sunburn. Longer ultraviolet rays, at 320 to 400 nanometers, are known as ultraviolet A (UVA). Scientists have recently found that they penetrate the skin more deeply than UVB and, though leaving no evidence of sunburn, do cause skin damage. Most sunscreens are designed to block UVB, and the sun protection factor (SPF) listed on the product refers to its effectiveness against UVB. However, according to Patricia Agin of Schering Plough HealthCare Products, any sunscreen with an SPF of over 10 will also provide some protection against UVA.

?

How does bleach get clothes white?

MOST LAUNDRY BLEACHES, including the household wizard Clorox bleach, are oxidizing agents. In the washing machine they release free-roving molecules of sodium hypochlorite or peroxide. The color of a stain or spot is made up of a group of atoms and molecules linked together by a pattern of double and single bonds. The oxidizing agent tears into those bonds, destroying the bond pattern and fading the color or changing it completely to white. The stain is still there, albeit invisible, until detergent and the agitation of the machine lift most of it off.

Fabric colors are also made up of bonds, so that if you add bleach to the wrong kinds of wash loads—clothes that aren't colorfast—you'll notice that the colors you liked might also become invisible.

?

How do they get rid of radioactive nuclear waste?

THE ANSWER IS . . . not very well. Ridding the earth of nuclear waste that continues to emit radioactivity is a formidable, if not impossible, task, and experts disagree over how it should be packaged and where it should be put.

There are two general types of nuclear waste—low-level and high-level. Low-level waste is composed mainly of the by-products of nuclear reactors, such as contaminated work gloves, tools, and irradiated reactor components. Such waste need not be shielded from personnel and does not require heat-removing equipment. Often it is filtered (much like coffee), reduced to sludge and burned in incinerators. The resultant gases contain very little radioactivity, but the ashes must be treated as low-level waste and buried.

Some low-level waste is compacted in order to reduce its volume and produce a more stable structure for disposal; some is solidified by mixing it with concrete or asphalt to resist attack by water and make the waste less subject to leaching or seeping out.

Next, the low-level waste is packed in reinforced plastic-and-concrete or steel containers and buried twenty-five feet or more beneath the surface. Much of this burial (called shallow land burial) is currently done on-site, but efforts are under way to find permanent burial places that are not subject to volcanoes, earthquakes, landslides or excessive weather and are far from commercial and housing sites. Moreover, such areas must have a water table deep enough to prevent immersion of wastes, and contain no springs to bring contamination to the surface. Of course, these areas must never be mined.

Alternative methods of disposal being considered for low-level waste include below-ground vaults with a drainage channel (to prevent water gathering) and a clay-topped concrete roof. Above-ground concrete vaults, another option, would be more accessible and the waste more readily retrievable for monitoring purposes, but might be eroded by the weather, particularly by acid rain. Some experts favor sinking deep into the ground a shaft with radiating corridors at the bottom for storage.

High-level waste consists mostly of liquid from defense production and of used fuel rods (produced from uranium) that have powered nuclear reactors for three to four years and continue to be radioactive long after their fuel is spent. These materials must be immobilized before being placed underground. Spent fuel rods, which are hot and highly radioactive, are stored underwater in large pools or stacked in racks at the reactor site until they cool down sufficiently to be packed into containers and buried. Liquid waste must be mixed with some material that will resist water or any other solution that may be underground. This material must also be immune to heat and radiation from fission decay. Most liquid waste is combined with borosilicate glass containing glass-forming chemicals. The mixture is then heated to 1,150 degrees Celsius, which not only destroys organic matter but also dissolves inorganics into the glass.

Interment is a problem because high-level waste remains radioactive for centuries (eighty thousand years for plutonium). So far, burial in salt has been the preferred choice because it is abundant, far from earthquake zones and inexpensive to excavate. If a hole could be made sufficiently deep—say six to ten miles below the level of moving groundwater—other types of terrain could be considered, but little is known of geologic activity at that depth. Scientists are considering dropping high-level waste onto rocks a mile beneath the earth; the rocks would melt from radioactive decay, mix with the waste, solidify and finally, cool down after a thousand years. Another remarkable solution still in the testing stages is hydrofracturing: first, water is forced into rocks such as shale, causing the layers to separate, then the waste mixed with cement or clay is pumped into them and left to harden.

Scientists have dismissed the idea of shooting waste into the sun or space and letting it orbit, because of the likelihood of accidents. Allowing decay heat to melt through either polar ice cap, which would then form a freeze seal above it, has also been rejected because of difficult weather conditions and the problem of coordinating different countries involved in such a project.

Solutions for the safe disposal of nuclear waste should be found before we permit more of it to accumulate. We have not yet disposed of waste produced from World War II. Although the Nuclear Regulatory Commission claims that the hazard from nuclear waste which seeped out of single-walled steel containers buried in shallow trenches was not a widespread threat, it nevertheless contaminated the surrounding earth and air and has caused certain areas, in Washington State and New Mexico for example, to be designated "sacrifice" zones.

The sad fact is that although billions have been spent in the last forty years on producing nuclear defense weapons, only $300 million has gone toward researching and testing what to do with the deadly waste that is left behind.

?

How do they keep Coca-Cola drinkable in polar regions?

IN VERY COLD CLIMATES, the easiest way to keep Coca-Cola from freezing is to store it inside, in a heated shop or home. Exposed to the elements for an extended time, Coke would freeze, causing an indefinite postponement of the pause that refreshes. Actually, before the soda could freeze, the can itself would burst. The aluminum cans are structurally incapable of handling the change in pressure brought on when the liquid within them freezes. So, even though Coke is best when served cold (Coke officials say 40.1 degrees Fahrenheit or below is ideal), it won't keep well in a snowbank. It can, however, be stored in an outdoor vending machine, even in subfreezing temperatures.

The trick to outdoor vending machines is to keep them warm enough to prevent the beverage from freezing, but cool enough that the Coke isn't heated. Warm Coke is even less appealing than frozen Coke. Large heating units, therefore, are not desirable. Instead, cold-climate Coke machines are equipped with a sixty-watt light bulb and a fan. The light bulb, situated at the top

203

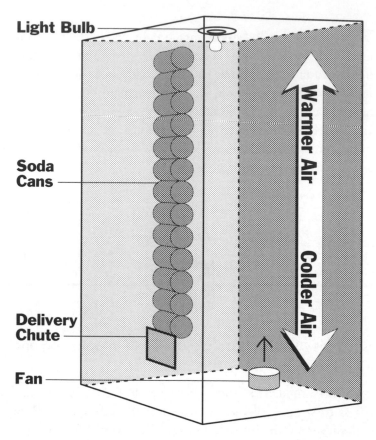

Light Bulb

Soda Cans

Delivery Chute

Fan

Warmer Air

Colder Air

of the machine, generates heat; the fan, situated at the bottom of the machine, circulates cold air from the bottom of the machine to the warm area at the top.

Cans of Coke are stacked lengthwise in a chute inside the machine. The circulation of air within the machine ensures that all the cans are exposed to warm air; because hot air naturally rises, and because the source of heat—the light bulb—is at the top of the machine, the cans at the top of the chute stay warmest. When a person deposits money in the machine, the bottommost can in the chute is dispensed and all the other cans drop down one position. With each drop in position, the cans experience a corresponding drop in temperature, so that by the time a can reaches the bottom of the chute and is dispensed, it has achieved perfect drinking temperature.

?

How do they know if a runner false-starts in an Olympic sprint?

A ONE-HUNDRED-METER RACE lasts about ten seconds, so the difference between first and last place may be mere tenths of a second. The incentive is high to get out of the starting blocks as fast as possible, but if a sprinter false-starts more than once in a race, he is automatically disqualified. False starts just make the other runners skittish.

The starters are responsible for judging whether a runner moved before the gun was fired, and for the most part they do that with the naked eye. Like an offsides referee in a football game, or an umpire in baseball, they've watched so many races they can detect a runner's slightest motion in the blocks. The best of them can keep the runners calm and release them smoothly out of the tense "set" position and into the race. Basically, starters are not "trying to fool the runners," says Olympic sprinting coach Mel Rosen.

Starters for the Olympics and a few other high-level track meets do employ a clock and computer as a backup to their well-trained eyes. The clock and computer are wired to pressure-sensitive pads in the starting blocks and to the starter's pistol. If a runner pushes off the pads before the gun is fired (or too soon afterwards to be within possible human reaction time), the starter hears a tone and calls a false start. Usually the starter uses the information only to double-check the lane number in which a false start occurred.

Human reaction time is a bit tricky to define categorically, especially when Olympic athletes are the humans reacting. The electric starting blocks at the second World Championships in Athletics in Rome in 1987 were set for a reaction time of 0.120 of a second, or 120 milliseconds. Canadian sprinter Ben Johnson left the blocks 109 milliseconds after the gun was fired but before the set human-reaction time. The starter did not call a false start, and film footage from the race confirmed the starter's judgment. Johnson just happens to react fast, *and* run fast. He placed first in the race. Coach Rosen noted, however, that Johnson uses an unorthodox start: he throws forward his hands, under which, of course, there are no pressure-sensitive starting blocks.

?

How do crocodiles clean their teeth?

THE EGYPTIAN PLOVER (*Pluvianus aegyptius*) has long been called the crocodile bird for its symbiotic relationship to this most ferocious of reptiles. Sitting coolly in the gaping mouth of a basking crocodile, the bird picks leeches, flukes and tsetse flies from the animal's gums to eat.

In nearly all other circumstances the crocodile is an extremely dangerous creature, singularly responsible for dozens of human lives lost every year in Africa. But it seems to have an instinctive tolerance for the plover.

Although the bird is a definite asset to the crocodile, its value as a hygienist is a little overrated. Crocodiles have widely spaced teeth, and rarely chew their prey but just bolt it down—so there isn't much call for flossing. Also, the crocodile sheds worn, decayed and broken teeth regularly throughout its fifty- to one-hundred-year life and replaces them with fresh ones. Humans, of course, "shed" their teeth only once.

?

How do lawyers get paid when a company files for bankruptcy?

UNDER THE FEDERAL BANKRUPTCY CODE, administrative costs of running a bankruptcy are given priority over debt owed to creditors. Therefore, both the counsel for the debtors and the official committees representing the creditors are ensured payment because technically they constitute an administrative expense of running the case.

A lawyer cannot represent a bankrupt entity. So, when a company voluntarily files for bankruptcy, attorneys are paid for all fees and expenses up until the time that court proceedings begin. Thus it is not unusual for attorneys to be compensated in large sums on the eve of the commencement of the case. When a company is in distress and may be forced into involuntary bankruptcy, lawyers make sure that they are paid routinely and promptly in the event such action occurs. In other words, they don't want to be stuck with a huge unpaid bill if the company's assets cannot cover its liabilities.

When the judicial procedure for filing for bankruptcy begins, so does a whole new tab on the behalf of the legal counsel. Lawyers for the bankrupt entity and the official committee of creditors then make applications to the court to be retained. At this point, the counsel for the official committee of creditors may object to fees and expenses proposed by the debtor's attorneys. Once rates and expenses are settled, counsel proceeds with the work and submits quarterly bills for review by the court. Once again this application is subject to objection from a creditor or other party of interest. If the court so decides, a hearing is held between lawyers for the debtor and those for the official committee of creditors. Often, creditors are very precise in their protestations; they will question, for instance, why three lawyers participated in a conference call rather than two, or why the debtor is being charged twelve cents for each photocopy rather than ten cents. If the court agrees, rates and fees are adjusted accordingly. Local judges in some parts of the country will not allow New York lawyers to be paid their hometown rates. For this reason many high-paid attorneys reduce their fees by as much as one third to ensure court and creditor approval.

After the court approves these interim payments, a percentage is usually withheld until the case is finished. In New York's Southern District, for instance, that percentage is typically 25 percent, to be paid from the debtor's estate when the case closes.

How do they decide how much to pay the queen of England?

CALCULATING HOW MUCH TO PAY the richest woman (and fourth richest person) in the world is a job which may seem akin to deciding how much sand to take to the beach, but HRH Elizabeth II, and the whole Windsor clan, take the matter quite seriously. In fact, despite complaints and resistance from Labour party MPs, Her Majesty has asked for a raise on more than one occasion—and her requests have been met.

While the queen's cash flow comes from various sources—rents, stocks, foreign investment—her actual *salary*, which in 1989 was $7.9 million, is drawn from the public treasury called the Civil List. In addition to that salary, she is reimbursed from the Civil List for her expenses incurred during her duties and for the cost of running Buckingham Palace, Windsor Castle and Holyrood House. A few expenses that year included, among other things, $350,000 for garden parties, $200,000 for care of her ceremonial horses, $98,000 for flowers and about $6.2 million in staff salaries. However, no one is getting rich working for the queen: a footman will only make $12,000 in a year. She also subsidizes relatives like the duke of Kent and Princess Alexandra, first cousins not provided for by Parliament.

Increases in the Civil List are decided by the House of Commons, based on information regarding her expenses assessed and provided by a select parliamentary committee headed by the chancellor of the Exchequer. Her first raise was not granted until 1971, nineteen years after she ascended the throne. (Her starting salary and expenses were $1,187,500. Her first raise brought the Civil List up to $2,450,000.)

In 1989 the Civil List totaled $10.5 million. In July of the following year a vote in Commons increased it to $20.3 million, a figure which will hold for ten years. In arguing for her raise, sympathetic MPs will often point out that the queen performs her state duties with skill and dignity. In 1989 those duties included 147 official visits and opening ceremonies, 73 banquets and receptions, 18 working days abroad and 268 other audiences.

Expenses not covered by the Civil List are often provided for by the government in other ways. For example, the Ministry of Defence paid $33.2 million to refit the royal yacht *Britannia;* physical upkeep of the royal palaces is paid for by the Department of the Environment; and royal postage, stationery and telephone service is free. Costs of maintaining the royal trains and aircraft are also deferred directly to Parliament.

The Civil List was created in 1760 when George III agreed to turn over all of England's crown properties to the state, with the exception of the 55,000-acre Duchy of Lancaster, and the 128,047-acre Duchy of Cornwall. Rent collected on the former property is reserved for the reigning monarch. (The latter property is the domain of the heir apparent—in this case, the queen's eldest son, Charles, prince of Wales.) That money, the "privy purse," is intended to pay for the queen's personal expenditures, such as clothing and the upkeep of Sandringham and Balmoral castles, which she owns outright. Occasionally, when the costs of running her residences and public entertaining exceed her official grant from the Civil List, the queen will dip into these funds to make up the deficit. It is at that point that she'll put in for a raise.

The best part of all this? In Britain, where the top tax rate is 40 percent, all of the queen's income is tax-free. Of course, this may change in the future. She does, however, voluntarily hand back to the state some of her salary. Even with that concession, her total worth in 1991 was estimated by *Harpers and Queen* to be $13 billion.

?

How do they raise a sunken ship?

IT ALL DEPENDS ON the ship and its location in the water. If the main deck of a stranded vessel is above water, salvagers patch the holes that caused the ship to sink and pump out the water. The lightened ship will then refloat. If the main deck is submerged, but not deeply, it is possible to build a waterproof wall, called a cofferdam, that extends around the deck and above the surface. Once the cofferdam is in place, the water in the cofferdam is pumped out and the vessel is patched and refloated. Another

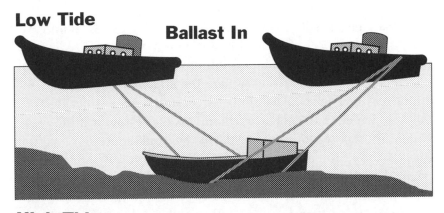

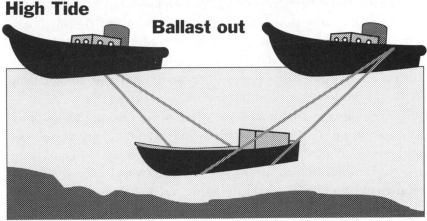

Cables holding a sunken ship to the rescue craft are tightened at low tide, when the distance between the rescuers and the wreck is smallest. All three vessels are lifted on the rising tide. The ships are raised further when the rescue craft discharge ballast, increasing their height in the water.

method, known as foam-in-salvage, works by displacing water with urethane foam. A diver armed with a massive hose fills the ship with a mixture of liquid polyol, fluorocarbon gas, and liquid isocyanate, which combine to form a quick-hardening, lightweight foam. The foam forces water out of the ship, and the buoyancy of the foam raises the ship to the surface. Two similar methods call for expanded plastic beads and hollow polystyrene balls about the size of pumpkins instead of foam.

Ships weighing less than a thousand tons can be hauled to the surface by floating cranes and then pumped out. Barges and other comparatively small vessels are often raised with pontoons, which, having been filled with water and chained to the distressed craft, are then pumped full of compressed air. The giant balloons float to the surface, pulling the attached ship with them.

Divers recover heavier ships by passing thick wire cables under the wreck and anchoring them on two attending lift craft, which are moored on either side of the sunken ship. First, the lift craft take on ballast water to increase their draft. At low tide, when the laden craft are riding very low in the water, the rescue crew pulls the cables taut. The lift craft release their ballast with the rising tide, thereby raising the sunken ship the combined height of the new tide and the decreased draft of the lift boats. The downed ship, dangling as if in an underwater hammock, is then regrounded in shallower water, where the whole process is begun anew, and subsequently repeated until the sunken ship rests above water and can be drained.

By employing one or a combination of ship-raising techniques, salvagers have the technology to recover virtually any vessel. Often, however, physical and financial risks conspire to make a raising unfeasible, which is why even the world's most famous shipwreck, the *Titanic*, will probably never be raised.

?

How do they know how long a second is?

THE OLD WAY (AND the way most of us still use) is derived from the time it takes for a complete day to pass. For centuries we have split a day into twenty-four hours, an hour into sixty minutes and a minute into sixty seconds. But though the Earth's movements from day to day are constant enough to schedule business lunches by, they do vary minutely. Military defense systems, communications satellites and space travel require literally split-second timing. Without it, for example, a few instants of the Academy Awards would be lost in space instead of beaming from Hollywood to the network satellite, to the network affiliate, and to you. The ramifications in defense and space travel are significantly more sobering.

In the late 1940s, Isidor Rabi, a physicist at Columbia University, found that certain atoms vibrate consistently at exactly the same rates. He suggested that atoms could make good clocks. Electronically counting the tiny vibrations of millions of atoms in fourteen-foot vacuum tubes, U.S. and British scientists found that the atom ^{133}cesium (the isotope of cesium with the atomic weight 133) was one of the most consistent and easy to measure. After hundreds of tests carried out over several years, they determined that it vibrates exactly 9,192,631,770 times in what they considered an average second.

The General Conference of Weights and Measures, an international treaty organization, met in Paris in 1967 and officially changed its definition of a second. No longer measured by the Earth's movements, the second became the exact length of time occupied by 9,192,631,770 vibrations of a ^{133}cesium atom. The beam of vibrating cesium atoms was essentially the pendulum of an incredibly accurate clock.

How accurate? The best atomic clocks in the world will be off by one second after 300,000 years of steady running, compared with a quartz wristwatch, which will (theoretically, of course) miss the mark by at least a million seconds, or 278 hours, over the same time period.

How do they decide what to charge for a minute of advertising during the broadcast of the Super Bowl?

IN ANY GIVEN YEAR, advertising rates for the Super Bowl are set by the network that owns the broadcast rights for that year's game. There are no strict equations for setting a price. Instead, the network will decide what price it thinks the market can bear and charge accordingly. In 1991, ABC figured $800,000 was about right for a thirty-second spot, the standard commercial time unit. ABC sold all fifty-six of its thirty-second advertising slots that year, for a grand total of twenty-eight minutes of network commercials. At $1.6 million per minute, that translated into $44.8 million in advertising revenues for the network. Not bad for an hour of football.

Although the networks have no absolute formula for determining the price of commercial time, they do follow one rough guideline: the price never goes down. The only time the cost of Super Bowl advertising declined was in 1977, during a recession, when the price fell by $25,000 from the previous year, from about $150,000 for thirty seconds to roughly $125,000. In the next two years the price jumped up to just over $200,000. Rates have risen every year since. The increase might be as much as 15 percent or as little as 5 percent from one year to the next, but there is always an increase.

Inflation accounts only partially for the skyrocketing price of Super Bowl ad time. The real reason commercial slots have become so costly is that the Super Bowl has developed into a showcase event for corporations. The big manufacturers in every industry, from computers to beer to athletic footwear, have seized upon it as the time to unveil new products and launch new ad campaigns. Some companies now spend as much as 30 percent of their annual advertising budget on the Super Bowl. The single most compelling reason for this corporate strategy is the game's huge television viewership. It almost always draws the largest audience of any show broadcast during the year. In 1991, more than 100 million people in the United States, and hundreds of millions more abroad, tuned in. According to Nielsen Media Research, Super Bowls account for five of the ten all-time most popular programs in American television history. Advertisers know there will be a large audience for their spots. As one executive whose company has spent a bundle in recent years explained it, "The game is not a typical football event that caters to male viewers. It really is the convening of American men, women, and children, who gather around the sets to participate in an annual ritual."

Despite all the hoopla surrounding the game, the size of the viewing audience has actually been shrinking in recent years. The highest-rated Super Bowl of all time was the 1982 game, which pulled down a 49.1 rating. (Each rating point represents 1 percent of all U.S. households with televisions.) By 1990, the rating had slipped to 39. But that still represented 35.9 million households and more than 100 million individuals. Considering the size of the audience, Super Bowl advertising is not really so expensive. During the height of its popularity, for instance, *The Cosby Show* commanded $300,000 for a thirty-second ad spot, and the audience was less than half that of the Super Bowl. On the other hand, while the peak *Cosby* episodes were usually pretty good television shows, the Super Bowl often turns out to be a dud of a football game.

?

How do they know what a particular dinosaur ate?

WE GROW UP ABSORBING explicit illustrations from picture books of sauropods nibbling leaves and tyrannosaurs ripping flesh, and yet some paleontologists maintain that these images are largely conjecture. We can speculate about what the dinosaurs ate, but in fact no one knows for sure, just as we can only imagine what color the dinosaurs were and what sounds they made. Our guess-work about what dinosaurs consumed is based on parallels with mammals we know today, yet dinosaurs were of course extremely different from any creature we have ever known. Bearing this in mind, we can look at some different species and simply theorize about their diet, largely by peering into their mouths at the size and shape of their teeth.

Take *Diplodocus*, for instance, which had stubby, pencil-like teeth jutting slightly forward from the jaw and located mostly at the front of the mouth. It would seem impossible for this slim-limbed creature to have chomped down on an armored dinosaur or even gnawed down a tree. Instead, it probably used its teeth like a sieve to obtain tiny organisms from fresh water and, since excavated teeth of this species show signs of wear, it may also have combed or cropped twigs and leaves.

Tracks show that the huge, peaceful, herbivorous sauropods ("lizard feet") like *Diplodocus, Apatosaurus,* and *Brachiosaurus* may have traveled in herds. With their long necks they could have grazed easily among the treetops, some forty feet high. They would have spent most of their waking hours munching, because

216

an eighty-ton brachiosaur, if cold-blooded, would have required some three hundred pounds of vegetation a day to sustain itself, if warm-blooded it would have had to consume a ton of greens each day. Since its teeth were little help in breaking down food-stuff, one theory goes that the sauropods swallowed rocks, which ground food to a pulp inside a gizzard. Thousands of such stones, known as gastroliths, have been found along with the bones of these reptiles.

While the sauropods may have held sway over the forest can-opy, other dinosaurs were equipped to feed on the lower tiers of woods and in swamps. *Iguanodon* had numerous sharp cheek teeth for consuming twigs and leaves. It roamed warm swampy areas and probably ate tough marsh plants such as horsetails. Horned dinosaurs such as *Triceratops* had a strong beak for tear-ing down and stripping tough, woody vegetation. Its many sharp teeth meshed like scissors to masticate spiky palm fronds, magno-lias, and fibrous plants. A long, thick muscle that stretched from the lower jaw to the frill at the back of the neck added strength to its jaws.

A very different creature, whose teeth are a notable indicator of life-style, is the well-known *Tyrannosaurus rex*. This animal's stupendous teeth measured seven and a quarter inches in length and, like steak knives, were perfectly designed to slice flesh. They were narrow and serrated, curving slightly inward to clench hold of prey. Some scientists believe that this enormous dinosaur, which weighed about seven tons, was one of the most ferocious hunters that ever lived, bringing down even tough horned and armored dinosaurs. Others maintain that *Tyrannosaurus* was too large and clumsy to tackle live prey and that it merely lumbered about in search of carrion.

Other carnosaurs, or "flesh lizards," such as the allosaurids and megalosaurids, also had saw-edged fangs, powerful jaws, and two- or three-fingered hands which could have been used for grasping prey. Probably the earlier species, which were smaller and more active than the later ones, were nimble enough to run down a browsing plant-eater.

There has been just one instance in which paleontologists uncovered the actual stomach contents of a dinosaur. In 1922 an *Anatosaurus* was found with a belly full of twigs and pine needles. At the time the finding was ignored because the scientific community believed that anatosaurs and other duck-billed dinosaurs ate like ducks, that is, aquatic plants. Over four decades later John H. Ostrom of Yale University reintroduced the find and demonstrated that the anatosaur, and other hadrosaurs, were not aquatic. It so happens that the teeth of the anatosaur would have been well suited for chewing its dinner. Behind the bill of a hadrosaur lay rows of packed teeth, and beneath them, new teeth growing up to replace those that wore out. Hadrosaurs munched on hard dry-land fare, such as branches and seeds, and over the course of a lifetime would have grown and put to work some two thousand teeth.

One hopes that paleontologists will be fortunate enough to find other species of dinosaurs mummified with a full stomach, but until they do, much of what we suppose about these unique creatures must hark from the land of make-believe.

?

How do they measure the heat of distant stars?

WHEN YOU LOOK at the grill on an electric stove as it heats up, you see it turn from black to bright red, and you know by the color that it's hot enough to blister your fingers. Astronomers determine stars' temperatures in much the same way—by studying their colors. Of course, stars are a lot hotter than a stove: the coolest are red. Progressively hotter ones are orange, yellow, green, blue and, finally, violet. Blue and violet stars are rare; red stars are common because, for one thing, they burn out more slowly.

The next time you are out on a clear night (a dry winter sky far from city lights is best) take a look at Orion, a large constellation suggesting the shape of a hunter brandishing a club and a lion skin. The bright red star at Orion's shoulder is Betelgeuse (pronounced "beetle juice"); the foot star of Orion is Rigel, a clear blue star. These colors are visible with the naked eye.

Astronomers determine the color of light emitted by a star with equipment called a spectrophotometer. The light waves are then characterized by wavelength. Astronomers use a mathematical formula that involves the speed of light and some other universal constants to convert wavelengths to temperature: the longer the wavelength, the lower the energy, the cooler the star. With that formula, they have calculated that Betelgeuse is about five thousand degrees Fahrenheit, and Rigel is about four times as hot. Knowing how hot a star is, astronomers can begin to understand its mass, its distance from Earth and how much it has aged.

?

How do they know there's going to be another ice age in two thousand years?

NO ONE KNOWS for certain when the next ice age will begin, but geological evidence indicates that it could start within two thousand years. During the past 2 million years, ice ages have been coming and going according to a fairly regular schedule. They seem to last about 100,000 years or so, and are usually separated by short interglacial periods lasting about eight thousand to twelve thousand years. We are living in an interglacial period that began when the last ice age ended, roughly ten thousand years ago. The historical model would therefore suggest that the next ice age is probably already on its way, and should arrive in a couple thousand years.

The term *ice age* has come to refer to the peaking of the ice sheets during the Pleistocene Epoch. The Pleistocene epoch began about 1.5 million years ago; it was a time of regularly reappearing ice ages. The end of the most recent ice age, about ten thousand years ago, marked the close of the Pleistocene and the start of the modern, Holocene Epoch, the interglacial epoch during which the human race has flourished. At the height of the last ice age the average global temperature was about five degrees Celsius cooler than it is today. One third of the Earth's surface, including northern Europe, Canada, Greenland, Antarctica, parts of the United States, and areas of Australia, New Zealand, and South America, was blanketed in ice sheets up to ten thousand feet thick. The huge glaciers contained 5 percent of the world's water, which caused sea levels to be lowered by as much as four hundred feet.

The rising and falling of sea levels that comes with global glaciation has helped scientists chart the succession of ice ages. Coral grows only in warm waters close to the surface of the ocean. When the sea level dropped with the last ice age, coral dropped with it. As the glaciers melted and the sea began to rise again, new coral grew on top of the old. Each level of coral growth marks what was once the surface of the sea. By dating coral growth scientists have been able to put together a fairly detailed chronology of the last ice age.

Another way scientists have been able to date ice ages is by examining the fossil record. The presence of leafy plants, for example, indicates a warm climate. By studying and dating vegetable fossils, scientists can tell what the global climate was like during a certain time. One thing they have learned is that during the interglacial period prior to the last ice age, the Earth was warmer than it is today. The strongest evidence for this belief comes from rock sediments from the ocean floor. The levels of carbon dioxide in such sediments indicate that there was more carbon dioxide in the atmosphere during the previous interglacial period than there currently is. High atmospheric carbon dioxide levels create a greenhouse effect, whereby radiation from the sun is trapped inside the Earth's atmosphere, causing the global temperature to rise. During the last century, the greenhouse effect has caused global warming at an annual rate of 0.3 to 0.4 degrees Celsius. Sometime during the next century the global temperature should reach as high as it was during the last interglacial.

When global temperature rises, the polar ice caps melt. If the ice caps were to thaw, they would surge toward the ocean. As a result, massive icebergs would be discharged into the sea. The flow of ice into the sea would raise sea levels around the globe, which would cause total inundation of coastal areas, which in turn would cause more ice to spill into the water. As all this ice entered the ocean, ocean temperatures would drop, causing more sea ice to form. Since ice reflects rather than absorbs heat, the extra sea ice would radiate heat back out of the atmosphere, causing temperatures to drop further. More ice would then form. And so on. Once the ice gets going it pretty much takes care of itself. In this way, some scientists speculate, one unlikely and unwholesome effect of global warming will be to bring about the next ice age.

Sources

How do they detect counterfeit bills?

Bureau of Engraving and Printing, (202) 447-0193.
Crane and Company, (413) 684-2600.
"Know Your Money," distributed by the Department of the Treasury and the United States Secret Service.

How do they keep you from registering to vote in more than one jurisdiction?

Kimberly, Bill. National Clearinghouse, Federation Election Commission, (202) 376-3155.

How do they get ships through the Panama Canal?

Encyclopedia Americana. Danbury, Conn.: Grolier Inc., 1988.
McCullough, David, author of *The Path Between the Seas: The Creation of the Panama Canal, 1870–1914*. New York: Simon and Schuster, 1977.

1987 Information Please Almanac®, Atlas and Yearbook, The,
   40th ed. Boston: Houghton Mifflin.
World Book Encyclopedia. Chicago: World Book, Inc., 1985.

How do they make a breed of dog "official" at the American Kennel Club?

Derr, Mark. "The Politics of Dogs." *The Atlantic*, March 1990.

How do they write headlines at the *New York Post*?

Colasuonno, Lou. *New York Post*, 210 South Street, New York,
   N.Y. 10002; (212) 815-8500.

How do they find arbitrators for baseball contract arbitrations?

Brown, Laura. American Arbitration Association, (212) 484-4129.
Players Association, (212) 826-0808.
Schack, Arthur, attorney. Office of the Commissioner, (212) 339-
   7800.

How do they make margarine taste like butter (almost, anyway)?

Bradley, Dr. Robert L., Jr., professor of food science. University
   of Wisconsin, Madison.
Freund, Dr. Peter, manager of product applications, and Pamela
   J. Kokot, product manager. Both at Chr. Hansen's Laboratory,
   Inc., Milwaukee, Wis.

How do so many Japanese play golf in a country with so few golf courses?

"Personal Affairs." *Forbes*, July 11, 1988.
Reilly, Rick. "Japanese Golf." *Sport Illustrated*, August 21, 1989.

How do they set the price on a new public stock offering?

Downes, John, and Jordan Goodman. *Dictionary of Finance and Investment Terms*. Hauppauge, N.Y.: Barron, 1985.
"The Billionaires." *Fortune*, September 9, 1991.

How do they know Jimmy Hoffa is dead?

"Hoffa Outgunned." *Time*, July 5, 1982.
"Jimmy Hoffa Is Legally Dead." *Newsweek*, August 9, 1982.
New Encyclopaedia Britannica. Chicago: Encyclopaedia Britannica, 1986.
Sifakis, Carl. *The Encyclopedia of American Crime*. New York: Facts on File, 1982.
Treaster, Joseph B. "Hoffa Ruled 'Presumed' Dead." *The New York Times*, December 10, 1982.
Witkin, Gordon. "Jimmy Hoffa's Deadly Lunch." *U.S. News and World Report*, July 11, 1988.

How do they get rid of gallstones without operating?

Good Housekeeping, September 1989.
National Center for Health Statistics, (301) 436-8500.
Saturday Evening Post, The, May-June 1981, October 1988, May-June 1989.
Yin, Dr. Lillian. Food and Drug Administration, (301) 427-1180.

How do they make telephones for the deaf?

Dreyfus, Barbara. Ultratec, Madison, Wis.; (800) 233-9130.
National Association for the Deaf, (301) 587-1788.
National Information Center on Deafness, (202) 651-5051.

How do banks make money off of credit card purchases even when you don't pay interest?

Anglin, David. Visa U.S.A., Research Department, P.O. Box 8999, San Francisco, Calif. 94128; (415) 513-1103.

"Heart from Hart." *United States Banker*. Kalo Communications, Inc., August 1991, national edition.

Wasserman, Gail, director public affairs. American Express Travel Related Services Company, Inc., American Express Tower, World Financial Center, New York, N.Y. 10285-3130; (212) 640-2675.

How do they choose cartoons for *The New Yorker*?

Lorenz, Lee, art editor. *The New Yorker*, New York, N.Y.

Menand, Louis. "A Friend Writes." *The New Republic*, February 26, 1990.

How do they make rechargeable batteries?

Kluzik, John D. Lighting Information Center, General Electric Company, Cleveland, Ohio 44112; (216) 266-8346.

Mantell, Charles L. *Batteries and Energy Systems*. New York: McGraw-Hill, 1983.

How do they set the minimum bid on a painting that is up for auction?

Hughes, Robert. "Sold." *Time*, November 27, 1989.

Sotheby's, Old Master Paintings and Drawings Department, New York, N.Y. (212) 606-7230.

How do antilock brakes work?

Dinan, Jack. General Motors, Dearborn, Mich.; (313) 986-5717.

How do they know television viewers don't cheat during the Nielsen ratings?

Buono, Diane. Nielsen Media Research, 1290 Avenue of the Americas, New York, N.Y. 10019; (212) 708-7500.

How do they manufacture genes?

"Amazing Gene Machine, The," *U.S. News and World Report*, July 16, 1990.
Benson, Don, senior sales specialist. Ependorf North America, (908) 526-1389.
"Gene Therapy." *Mirabella*, December 1991.
"Genetic Age, The," *Business Week*, May 28, 1990.
"Genetic Engineering." *Encyclopedia of Chemical Technology*, 3rd ed. New York: Interscience Publishers.
New Encyclopaedia Britannica. Chicago: Encyclopaedia Britannica, 1986.

How do they stop you from getting a credit card under a false name?

Crone, Kenneth R., vice president. Visa U.S.A., San Francisco, Calif.
Ferrell, Jack, sales manager. Fraud Management Division, First Data Resources, Omaha, Neb.
Mandell, Lew, author of *The Credit Card Industry: A History*. Boston: Twayne Publishers, a division of G. K. Hall, 1990.
"Visa Risk Management and Security," a booklet from Visa U.S.A.

How do members of Congress make themselves sound articulate in the *Congressional Record*?

Nicestrom, Dwayne, editor. *Congressional Record*, Washington, D.C.; (202) 224-6810.

How do they "make" veal?

Ellis, Merle. *Cutting Up in the Kitchen*. San Francisco: Chronicle Books, 1976.

Evans, Travers Moncure, and David Greene. *The Meat Book*. New York: Charles Scribner's Sons, 1973.

National Livestock and Meat Board, Chicago, Ill.; (312) 467-5520.

How do they determine the profit of a Hollywood movie?

Cohn, Lawrence. *Variety*, New York, N.Y.; (212) 779-1100.

Creer, John. Exhibitor Relations, Los Angeles, Calif.; (213) 657-2006.

Hanover, Debbie. Entertainment Data, Inc., Los Angeles, Calif.; (213) 658-8300.

National Amusements, Inc., Dedham, Mass., (617) 461-1600.

How do they decide who gets nominated for Oscars?

Brown, Peter N., and Jim Pinkerton. *Oscar Dearest*. New York: Harper and Row, 1987.

Whirton, Bob. Academy of Motion Picture Arts and Sciences, (213) 385-5271.

How do they make nonalcoholic beer?

Brewer's Guardian, March 1987.

Modern Brewery Age, May 16, 1988.

Sharalambas, George. Brewing Technical Services, Anheuser-Busch, Inc., (314) 577-3222.

How do they know there was an ice age?

"Learning the Language of Climate Change." *Mosaic* 19, Fall/Winter 1988.

Ray, Louis L. *The Great Ice Age*. Washington, D.C.: U.S. Department of the Interior/U.S. Geological Survey.

How do they correct nearsightedness in ten minutes?

"Goodby Glasses?" *Consumer Reports*, January 1988.

Hacinli, Cynthia. "Eyes Can See Clearly Now: Surgery for the Nearsighted." *Mademoiselle*, June 1990.

Krantz, Paul. "Don't Toss Your Glasses—Yet." *Better Homes and Gardens*, June 1990.

Lynn, Michael, director. The Statistical Coordinating Center for the Prospective Evaluation of Radial Keratotomy, Emory University School of Public Health, Atlanta, Ga.

How do lawyers research members of a jury before deciding whether to challenge them?

Colson, Bill, Lisa Blue, and Jane N. Saginaw. *Jury Selection: Strategy and Science*. Callaghan Trial Practice Series. Deerfield, Ill.: Callaghan, 1986.

Duboff, Robert. Decision Research Corporation, 33 Hayden Avenue, Lexington, Mass. 02173; (617) 861-7350.

Owen, Robert. Owen and Davis, 605 Third Avenue, New York, N.Y. 10158; (212) 983-6900.

Sanders, William H. "The Voir Dire in a Civil Case." *University of Missouri Kansas City Law Review*, Vol. 57, No. 4. Kansas City: University of Missouri Kansas City School of Law, 1989.

How does an electric eel generate electricity?

Bridges, William. *The New York Aquarium Book of the Water World*. New York: American Heritage Press, New York Zoological Society, 1970.

Burton, Maurice, and Robert Burton. *Encyclopedia of Fish*. New York: American Museum of Natural History, BPC Publishing Ltd., 1968.

Dozier, Thomas A. *Dangerous Sea Creatures*. Based on the television series *Wild, Wild World of Animals*. Time-Life Films, Inc., 1974.

Ferraris, Dr. Carl. Department of Ichthyology, American Museum of Natural History, 79th Street and Central Park West, New York, N.Y. 10024.

Gray, Peter, ed. *Encyclopedia of Biological Sciences*. New York: Reinhold Publishing Corp., 1961.

Marshall, N. B. *The Life of Fishes*. New York: Universe Books.

Schultz, Leonard P. *The Ways of Fishes*. New York: D. Van Nostrand Co., Inc.

How does an invisible fence keep your dog from straying?

Invisible Fencing, 724 West Lancaster Avenue, Wayne, Pa. 19087; (215) 732-4100.

How does a thief break into your car and drive off with it in less than a minute?

FBI Auto Theft Task Force, 26 Federal Plaza, New York, N.Y. 10278; (212) 335-2700.

How do they get the oat bran out of oats?

Cornell Medical College, 1300 York Avenue, New York, N.Y. 10021; (212) 746-5454.

Encyclopaedia Britannica. Chicago: Encyclopaedia Britannica, 1991.

General Mills, 1 General Mills Blvd., Minneapolis, Minn. 55426; (612) 540-2311.

Institute of Human Nutrition, Columbia University, 701 West 168th Street, New York, N.Y. 10032; (212) 305-6991.

How do they get the bubbles into seltzer?

Encyclopaedia Britannica. Chicago: Encyclopaedia Britannica, 1991.

Mid-Atlantic Cans Association, (413) 586-8450.

Ostendarp, Beth, communications and public affairs specialist. Cadbury-Schweppes, (203) 329-0911.

How do they teach guide dogs to cross at the green light?

Siddall, Elane. The Guide Dog Foundation, Smithtown, N.Y.; (516) 265-2121.

How do they measure dream activity?

Cartwright, Rosalind Dymond. *A Primer on Sleep and Dreaming.* New York: Addison-Wesley, 1978.

Feldman, Professor Sam. Department of Neurophysiology, New York University, (212) 998-7852.

Hobson, Professor Allan. Harvard University, (617) 734-1300.

LaBerge, Stephen. *Lucid Dreaming.* New York: St. Martin's Press, 1985.

Luce, Gay Caer, and Julius Segal. *Sleep and Dreams.* New York: Coward-McCann, 1966.

Rappaport, Dr. Joyce. Sleep Research Laboratory, New York University Medical School, (212) 340-6407.

How do they decide whose obituary gets published in *The New York Times*?

The New York Times, (212) 556-1234.

Thompson, Marty, managing editor. Associated Press, (212) 621-1610.

How do they know there are more stars in the sky than grains of sand on an ocean beach?

"Sand and Stars." *The New York Times*, Science Times section, March 19, 1991.

Tyson, Dr. Neil D. Department of Astrophysical Sciences, Princeton University, Princeton, N.J. 08544; (609) 258-2303.

Tyson, Neil D. "A Sentimental Journey to the Googolplex." *Star-Date*, February 1982.

How do they decide where to put a new book in the Library of Congress?

Library of Congress, Public Affairs Office, (202) 707-2905.

How do they discover a new drug?

Werth, Barry. "Quest for the Perfect Drug." *New England Monthly*, February 1990.

How do they get honey out of a honeycomb?

Encyclopedia Americana. Danbury, Conn.: Grolier Inc., 1988.

Mace, Herbert. *The Complete Handbook of Bee-Keeping*. New York: Van Nostrand Reinhold, 1976.

Morse, Roger A., and his book *The Complete Guide to Beekeeping*, rev. ed. New York: E. P. Dutton, 1974.

How do they know what caste a resident of Bombay belongs to?

Jacob, Louis. Asian Division, South Asian Section, Library of Congress, (202) 707-5600.

Kolenda, Pauline. *Caste in Contemporary India*. Prospect Heights, Ill.: Waveland Press, 1985.

Olson, Mancur. *The Rise and Decline of Nations*. New Haven, Conn.: Yale University Press, 1982.

How do they dry-clean clothes without getting them wet?

Grimes, William. "Every Day, a Magic Show at the Dry Cleaners." *The New York Times*, November 14, 1991.

Ray, C. Claiborne. "Dry Cleaning." *The New York Times*, November 5, 1991.

Spotting: The Art of Stain Removal. Neighborhood Cleaners Association, New York School of Drycleaning, 116 East 27th Street, New York, N.Y. 10016-8998; (212) 684-0945.

How do they make glow-in-the-dark toys?

Brown, Harvey E. *Zinc Oxide: Properties and Applications.* New York: International Lead Zinc Research Organization, 1976.

Encyclopedia Americana. Danbury, Conn.: Grolier Inc., 1988.

Majka, Robert. Canrad-Hanovia, Inc., 100 Chestnut Street, Newark, N.J. 07105; (201) 589-4300.

Ruddick, Douglas H. Zinc Corporation of America, 300 Frankfort Road, Monaca, Penn. 15061-2295; (412) 774-1020.

Wagner, Dr. Peter J. Michigan State University, (517) 355-1855.

How do they predict when a fine wine will be ready to drink?

Adams, Leon D. *The Commonsense Book of Wine.* New York: McGraw-Hill, 1986.

Johnson, Hugh. *Hugh Johnson's Encyclopedia of Wine.* New York: Simon and Schuster, 1983.

Kressman, Edward. *The Wonders of Wine.* New York: Hastings House, 1968.

Tchelistcheff, André, vintner, (707) 224-5502.

How do they know how much an aircraft carrier weighs?

Austin, William H., III. Department of the Navy, Naval Sea Systems Command, Washington, D.C. 20362-5101; (703) 602-9083.

How do they decide what or who gets honored on U.S. postage stamps?

Arroyo, Norma. U.S. Postal Service, (202) 268-2323.

How do emperor penguins stay warm in Antarctica?

Burton, Robert. *Bird Behavior*. New York: Alfred A. Knopf, 1985.

Pearce, Q. L. *Tidal Waves and Other Ocean Wonders*. Englewood Cliffs, N.J.: Julian Messner, 1989.

Simpson, George Gaylord. *Penguins: Past and Present, Here and There*. New Haven, Conn.: Yale University Press, 1976.

Stonehouse, Bernard. *Penguins*. New York: Golden Press, 1968.

How do they treat drug addiction with acupuncture?

Bullock, Milton L., Patricia D. Culliton, and Robert T. Ollander. "Controlled Trial of Acupuncture for Severe Recidivist Alcoholism." *The Lancet*, June 24, 1989.

"How Does Acupuncture Work?" *British Medical Journal*, Vol. 283, September 19, 1981.

O'Rourke, Ellen, licensed acupuncturist, (413) 256-8320.

Requena, Yves. "Acupuncture's Challenge to Western Medicine." *Advances*, Vol. 3, No. 2, Spring 1986.

How do tightrope walkers stay on the wire?

Quiros, Angel, high-wire artist for Ringling Brothers; c/o Beth Painter, Public Relations for Ringling Brothers, (703) 448-4118.

How do they recycle newspapers?

Cogoli, John. *Photo Offset Fundamentals*. Bloomington, Ill.: McKnight, 1973.

Commoner, Barry. *Making Peace with the Planet*. New York: Pantheon Books, 1990.

"Recycled Paper Facts and Figures," a fact sheet of the National Recycling Coalition, Inc., Washington, D.C.

Steger, Will, and Jon Bowermaster. *Saving the Earth: A Citizen's Guide to Environmental Action*. New York: Alfred A. Knopf, 1990.

"Tough Business of Recycling Newsprint, The," *The New York Times*, January 6, 1991.

How does a magician pull a rabbit out of a hat?

Christopher, Milbourne. *The Illustrated History of Magic*. New York: Thomas Y. Crowell, 1973.

Dawes, Edwin A., and Arthur Setterington. *The Encyclopedia of Magic*. New York: W. H. Smith Publishers, 1986.

How do they make long-life milk?

Dairymen/Farm Best Division, 11 Artley Road, Savannah, Ga. 31408; (912) 748-6185.

How do they pick Pulitzer Prize winners?

Bates, J. Douglas. *The Pulitzer Prize*. New York: Birch Lane Press, 1991.

Hohenbert, John. *The Pulitzer Prizes*. New York: Columbia University Press, 1974.

The New York Times, May 12, 1991, and January 24, 1988.

How do they measure the unemployment rate?

Cohany, Sharon R., economist. U.S. Department of Labor, Bureau of Labor Statistics, (202) 523-1944.

How the Government Measures Unemployment, Report 742, U.S. Department of Labor, 1987.

How do they interview and hire simultaneous interpreters at the United Nations?

Aimé, Monique Corvington, chief of Interpretation Service, United Nations, (212) 963-8233.

UN Chronicle, September 1991.

Visson, Lynn. *From Russian into English: An Introduction to Simultaneous Interpretation*. Ann Arbor, Mich.: Ardis Publishers, 1991.

How do they spread a computer virus?

Fites, Philip, Peter Johnston, and Martin Kratz. *The Computer Virus Crisis*. New York: Van Nostrand Reinhold, 1989.

McAfee, John, chairman of the Computer Virus Industry Association, and Colin Haynes. *Computer Viruses, Worms, Data Diddlers, Killer Programs, and Other Threats to Your System: What They Are, How They Work, and How to Defend Your PC, Mac, or Mainframe*. New York: St. Martin's Press, 1989.

Schram, Martha. McAfee Associates in Santa Clara, Calif.

How do they get the caffeine out of coffee?

Heiss, Bob, co-owner of the Coffee Gallery in Northampton, Mass.

"Key Facts About Decaffeination," a brochure from the Coffee Development Group in Washington, D.C.

Kummer, Corby. "Is Coffee Harmful?" *Atlantic*, July 1990.

Lewis, Charles, a coffee trader for Cofinco, New York, N.Y.

National Coffee Association, New York, N.Y.

How do they test golf balls before offering them for sale?

Forbes, William T., communications manager. United States Golf Association, (908) 234-2300.

Spaulding Corporation, Chicopee, Mass., (413) 536-1200.

How do they see a black hole?

Wald, Robert M., professor at the University of Chicago and author of *Space, Time and Gravity*. Chicago: University of Chicago Press, 1977.

How do they get the music onto a CD?

Birchall, Steve. "The Magic of CD Manufacturing." *Stereo Review*, October 1986.

Booth, Stephen A. "The Digital Revolution." *Rolling Stone*, January 20, 1983.

Dumaine, Brian. "The Compact Disk's Drive to Become the King of Audio." *Fortune*, July 8, 1985.

Greenleaf, Christopher. "CD Boom! Compact Disc Pressing Plants Are Spreading Across North America." *Stereo Review*, June 1987.

Seligman, Gerald. "Saved! How Classic Rock Tracks Are Kept Forever Young on CD." *Rolling Stone*, September 11, 1986.

Strawn, John, series editor. *The Computer Music and Digital Audio Series*. Vol. 5: *The Compact Disc: A Handbook of Theory and Use*. Madison, Wis.: A-R Editions, Inc., 1989.

How do they make the Hudson River drinkable?

Fairbanks, Douglas, chief operator. Poughkeepsie Water Treatment Plant, (914) 451-4173.

Lee, Cara. Scenic Hudson, (914) 473-4440.

Shaw, Susan, environmental engineer. Public Water Supply Section, Environmental Protection Agency, (212) 264-4448.

How do they pack Neapolitan ice cream?

Belanger, Michael. Merriam-Webster, Inc., Springfield, Mass., (413) 734-3134.

Encyclopedia Americana. Danbury, Conn., Grolier Inc., 1989.

Erickson, Don. Public Affairs, H. P. Hood Company, Boston, Mass.; (617) 242-0600.

How do they make sure condoms won't break?

Beheler, Linda. Bloom Public Relations, Inc., New York, N.Y.; (212) 370-1363, ext. 403.

Men's Fitness, May 1991.

How do they make stainproof carpets?

E. I. du Pont de Nemours and Company, Wilmington, Del.; (800) 438-7668.

How do they teach a bear to ride a bicycle?

Ringling Brothers and Barnum & Bailey Circus.

How do they measure the ozone layer?

Lindley, D. "Ozone Hole Heading South Prematurely." *Nature*, November 9, 1989.

McGraw-Hill Encyclopedia of Science and Technology. New York: McGraw-Hill, 1992.

Monastersky, R. "Depleted Ring Around Ozone Hole." *Science News*, November 18, 1989.

Prather, M. J., and R. T. Watson. "Stratospheric Ozone Depletion and Future Levels of Atmospheric Chlorine and Bromine." *Nature*, April 19, 1990.

Schoeber, Mark R. "Arctic Ozone Succumbs to Chemical Assault." *Science News*, March 24, 1990.

How do they count calories in food?

Katch, Frank I., and William D. McArdle. *Nutrition, Weight Control, and Exercise*, 2d ed. Philadelphia: Lea and Febiger, 1983.

How do they know how much money will come out of a cash machine?

Jensen, Roger, senior product manager. NCR Corporation, Dayton, Ohio.

How does the Pennsylvania Department of Agriculture get mentioned on cereal boxes?

Readel, Dick, and Dyan Yingst. Pennsylvania Department of Agriculture, Commonwealth of Pennsylvania, (717) 787-5085.
United States Department of Agriculture, (202) 447-2791.

How do they detect wind shear?

Aircraft Owners and Pilots Association, Frederick, Md.; (301) 695-2000.
Federal Aviation Administration, Washington, D.C.; (202) 267-8521.
McCarthy, John. National Center for Atmospheric Research, Boulder, Colo.; (303) 497-8822.

How do they make fake photos on magazine covers?

Guiseffi, Ralph. AGT Printing, Washington, D.C.; (202) 955-2491.
Murphy, Eric. Tru-Color, Greenfield, Mass.; (413) 774-7901.

How do they make shredded wheat?

Nabisco Brands, Inc., East Hanover, N.J. 07936-1928.

How do they write words across the sky in airplane exhaust?

Arkin, Mort. Skytyping Inc., Marine Air Terminal, Flushing, N.Y.

How do they determine who gets into Harvard?

Colodny, Mark M. "Building Observatories Helps: Writing Backwards Doesn't." *U.S. News and World Report*, August 25, 1986.

Fischgrund, Tom, ed. *Barron's Top 50*. Hauppauge, N.Y.: Barron, 1991.

Greene, Howard. *Scaling the Ivy Wall*. Boston: Little, Brown, 1987.

Larew, John. "Why Are Droves of Unqualified, Unprepared Kids Getting into Our Top Colleges?" *The Washington Monthly*, June 1991.

How do chameleons change color?

Bellairs, Angus. *The Life of Reptiles*. New York: Universe Books, 1970.

Martin, James. "The Engaging Habits of Chameleons Suggest Mirth More Than Menace." *Smithsonian*, June 1990.

How do they make high-definition television?

Boston Globe, The, March 18, 1991.
Business Week, December 21, 1987.
HDTV 1125/60 Group, The, 1615 L Street, Washington, D.C. 20036; (202) 659-1992.
Newsweek, April 4, 1988.
Popular Mechanics, July 1986.
Popular Science, January 1987.
Time, December 21, 1987.
U.S. News and World Report, January 23, 1989.

How do they wrap Hershey's Kisses?

Fortna, Bob, Hershey plant manager. Hershey Foods, Hershey, Penn.

Great Chocolate Story, The, Hershey Foods promotional videotape.

Hershey Foods, Office of Public Information, Hershey, Penn.

How do they teach a computer to recognize your voice?

IBM, 1 Old Orchard Road, Armonk, N.Y. 10504; (914) 765-1900.

How do they know who has won an election before the polls close?

Harper's, July 1984.

New Republic, The, March 28, 1988, and November 28, 1988.

Newsweek, March 19, 1984.

U.S. News and World Report, November 12, 1984.

How do they train structural steelworkers to walk on unprotected beams five hundred feet in the air?

Kelly, John, coordinator of the Joint Apprenticeship and Trainee Committee of Ironworkers Locals 40 and 361, New York, N.Y.

Kittle, Martin, business manager, Local 806, Structural Steel and Bridge Painters, New York, N.Y.

How do they find heart or liver donors?

Benenson, Esther L., publications director. United Network for Organ Sharing, Richmond, Va., (804) 330-8500.

Business Week, August 28, 1989.

Newsweek, December 11, 1989.

241

How do they get the cork into a bottle of champagne?

Kaufman, William. *Champagne*. New York: Viking Press, 1973.

Larousse Wines and Vineyards of France. New York: Arcade Publishing, Inc., 1990.

Lichine, Alexis. *New Encyclopedia of Wines and Spirits*. New York: Alfred A. Knopf, 1982.

How do they make Hostess Twinkies stay fresh for years and years?

Farrell, Patrick. Continental Baking Company, St. Louis, Mo.; (314) 982-2261.

How does the SEC know when someone's doing inside stock trading?

Business Week, May 26 and December 1, 1986.

Newsweek, September 19, 1988.

Securities and Exchange Commission, Public Affairs, (202) 272-2650.

Time, July 14 and December 1, 1986.

U.S. News and World Report, December 22, 1986, and September 26, 1988.

How do they decide what goes on the cover of *People* mgazine?

Toepfer, Susan, assistant managing editor. *People*, New York, N.Y.

How do they put the smell into scratch-and-sniff advertising?

Conklin, Jim. Lawson Mardon, Inc.

How does sunscreen screen out the sun?

Agin, Patricia. Schering Plough HealthCare Products, Memphis, Tenn. 38151; (901) 320-5111.

"Sunscreen." *Consumer Reports*, Vol. 56, No. 6, June 1991.

How does bleach get clothes white?

Sullivan, Sandy, manager of consumer information and education, and Dave Deleeuw, project leader. The Clorox Company, Oakland, Calif.

How do they get rid of radioactive nuclear waste?

League of Women Voters Educational Fund Staff. *Nuclear Waste Primer*. New York: Nicklyon's Books, 1987.

Murray, Raymond L., and Judith A. Powell. *Understanding Radioactive Waste*. Columbus, Ohio: Battelle Press, 1988.

Office of Civilian Radioactive Waste Management, Department of Energy, 1000 Independence Avenue, Washington, D.C. 20585.

How do they keep Coca-Cola drinkable in polar regions?

Adams, Robert. Consumer Affairs Office, Coca-Cola USA, Atlanta, Ga.; (404) 676-2603.

How do they know if a runner false-starts in an Olympic sprint?

International Amateur Athletic Federation 1990–91 Handbook, 2nd ed. London: International Amateur Athletic Federation.

Mahoney, Peter "Duffy," assistant to the executive director for teams, technical services and training. The Athletics Congress, Indianapolis, Ind.

1987 International Athletic Foundation/IAAF Scientific Project Report on the II World Championships in Athletics.

Rosen, Mel, sprint coach for the U.S. Olympic team in 1984, head coach for the 1992 Olympic track team, head coach at Auburn University, Auburn, Ala.

How do crocodiles clean their teeth?

Mayer, Greg, Postdoctoral Fellow, National Museum of Natural History, Smithsonian Institution, Washington, D.C.

Neill, Wilfred T. *Last of the Ruling Reptiles.* New York: Columbia University Press, 1971.

Taylor, Peter, reptile keeper, and John Behler, Reptile Department curator, New York Zoological Society, Bronx, N.Y.

Whitfield, Dr. Philip, ed. *Macmillan Illustrated Animal Encyclopedia.* New York: Macmillan, 1984.

How do lawyers get paid when a company files for bankruptcy?

Harwood, Mitchel. Gibson, Dunn and Crutcher, (212) 351-4000.

How do they decide how much to pay the queen of England?

People, Royals Special Issue, 1990.

Time, April 27 and December 27, 1971, May 15, 1978, April 6, 1990.

The Washington Post, February 7, 1991.

How do they raise a sunken ship?

Baptist, C. N. *Salvage Operations.* London: Stanford Maritime Press, 1979.

Barranca, Peter S. "Ship Salvaging." *McGraw-Hill Encyclopedia of Science and Technology.* New York: McGraw-Hill, 1987.

Mowat, Farley. *The Grey Seas Under.* Boston: Little, Brown, 1958.

Peterson, Mendel L. *History Under the Sea: A Handbook for*

Underwater Exploration. Washington, D.C.: Smithsonian In-stitution, 1969.

How do they know how long a second is?

Beehler, Roger, manager. Time and Frequency Broadcast Ser-vices, National Institute of Standards and Technology, Boulder, Colo. (NIST is a division of the U.S. Commerce Department.)

How do they decide what to charge for a minute of advertising during the broadcast of the Super Bowl?

Furie, Val, sports planner. CBS, (212) 975-1029.
New York Times, The, January 6, 1991.
Sella, Bill, vice-president. Sports Sales, ABC, (212) 456-7777.

How do they know what a particular dinosaur ate?

Gaffney, Dr. Gene. Department of Paleontology, American Mu-seum of Natural History, New York, N.Y.
Lambert, David. *A Field Guide to Dinosaurs: The First Complete Guide to Every Dinosaur Now Known*. New York: Avon Books, 1983.
Lauber, Patricia. *The News About Dinosaurs*. New York: Brad-bury Press, 1989.
Wilford, John Noble. *The Riddle of the Dinosaur*. New York: Al-fred A. Knopf, 1985.

How do they measure the heat of distant stars?

Arny, Tom, associate professor of astronomy. University of Massa-chusetts in Amherst.
Encyclopedia Americana. Danbury, Conn.: Grolier Inc., 1988.
Spitzak, John, Ph.D. student. Department of Physics and Astron-omy, University of Massachusetts.

How do they know there's going to be another ice age in two thousand years?

Burten, Bjorn. *The Ice Age.* New York: G. P. Putnam and Sons, 1969.

Chorlton, Windsor. *Ice Ages.* Alexandria, Va.: Time-Life Books, 1983.

Erickson, Jon. *Ice Ages: Past and Future.* Blue Ridge Summit, Penn.: TAB Books, 1990.

Major, Virginia L. Geologic Inquiries Office, U.S. Geologic Survey, Reston, Va., (703) 648-4383.

Radok, Uwe. "The Antarctic Ice." *Scientific American*, August 1985.

Index

dream activity, measurement of, 88–91
Drexel Burnham Lambert, 193
drug addiction, acupuncture treatment
    for, 117–119

drugs:
  new, discovery of, 97–98
dry cleaning, 103–104
Duboff, Robert, 76
Dunlop Tire Company, 50

ectomorphs, 75
Education Department, U.S., 174
EEGs (electroencephalographs), 88, 89
eels, electricity generation of, 77–78
Egypt, ancient, condoms in, 153
Egyptian plover, 206–207
E. I. du Pont de Nemours and
    Company, 154
elections, exit polls during, 183–184
electroencephalographs (EEGs), 88, 89
Electrophorus electricus, 77
electroplates, 77–78
Elizabeth II, salary of, 208–210
emperor penguins, warmth of, 113–115
endomorphs, 75
Enterprise, U.S.S., 109
Entertainment Data, Inc., 63
Environmental Protection Agency,
    U.S., 149–150
ether, gallstones dissolved by, 35–36
Europe, grape harvest in, 107
exit polls, 183–184

Fairbanks, Douglas, Jr., 148–149,
    150
false starts, judgment of, 205–206
Farm Best milk, 127
Farrell, Patrick, 191
fat, pure, 160
Fawcett, Farrah, 195
FBI (Federal Bureau of Investigation),
    33–34, 80
FCC (Federal Communications
    Commission), 177, 178
FDA (Food and Drug
    Administration), 97, 199
Federal Bankruptcy Code, 207
Federal Bureau of Investigation
    (FBI), 33–34, 80

Federal Communications Commission
    (FCC), 177, 178
Federal Election Commission, 17, 18
Federal Reserve, U.S., 15
Ferguson, Sarah (Duchess of York),195
fermentation:
  champagne, 189
  of grape juice, 106–108
  of wort, 66–67
fiber, dietary, 83
fiber-optic cables, 178
Fitzsimmons, Frank, 34
floculators, 150
fluorescence, 104–106
Fonda, Jane, 195
Food and Drug Administration (FDA),
    97, 199
Ford, Kenneth, 197
For Whom the Bell Tolls (Hemingway),
    131
Freund, Dr. Peter, 28
Fyodorov, Svyatoslav, 70

Galápagos penguin, 115
gallbladder, 35–36
gallstones, removal of, 35–36
Gandhi, Mohandas K., 101
gastroenteritis, 149
gastroliths, 217
Gates, Bill, III, 31
Gates, Robert, 24
Gatun Locks, 20
General Conference of Weights and
    Measures, 213
General Motors, 49
genes, 52–55
gene therapy, 54–55
  utero, 55
George III, king of England, 209–210
Giants Stadium, East Rutherford, N.J.,
    34
glaciation, 69, 70
global warming, 221
glow-in-the-dark toys, 104
Goddard Space Flight Center, 158
Godunov, Alexander, 197
golf:
  in Japan, 29–31
  video, 30–31
golf balls, testing of, 141–143